Principles of
INTERNATIONAL
POLITICS

Principles of
INTERNATIONAL
POLITICS

Charles O. Lerche, Jr.

ASSOCIATE PROFESSOR OF POLITICAL SCIENCE
EMORY UNIVERSITY

TO MY MOTHER

Preface

THIS book is designed to serve as an introductory guide to a subject whose complexity is matched by its significance: international politics. Its object is to discover and point out the basic principles that determine the course of the political relations among sovereign states, and to seek to demonstrate their applicability to at least some of our contemporary dilemmas. It is neither a history of recent diplomacy nor an apology for the foreign policy of any government; the author has made a real effort to preserve some of the 'scholarly objectivity' that is so frequently a casualty in discussions of contemporary international relations. Being intended primarily for American readers, however, the role of the United States in world affairs serves as a frequent point of reference. The book is designed as a college text, but it is hoped that the general reader will discover some value in it.

This study has grown out of the author's experience in teaching the general course in international politics at several universities and colleges in the United States. It has become clear to him that if such a course is to be anything more than a discussion of current events with only limited educational value to the student, the factual data must be given perspective, form and meaning. Such insights in the student are forthcoming only if it is possible to provide him with a framework of systematic theory. This book, emphasizing principles and fundamentals, is the author's attempt to provide such a theoretical foundation.

C. O. L., Jr.

Emory University, Georgia
January 1956

Acknowledgments

N̲O author can properly thank everyone for the assistance, much of it unwitting, extended to him while he is preparing a book. The individuals listed below, however, must be singled out:

> Several generations of students at Knox College, and others more recently at Emory University, from whose inspiring and persistent minds came the initial inspiration for this study and the necessity of organizing and clarifying its content.
>
> William Ives, '55, George Latturner, '56, and Edward Myers, '54, of the student body at Knox College. Reading the entire manuscript with great care, they gave it the benefit of the trenchant criticism that only undergraduates are in a position to provide.
>
> Professor Richard W. Van Wagenen, Princeton University, and Professor John H. Herz, of the College of the City of New York, who read the manuscript at the request of the publisher. Their comments were uniformly just, appropriate, and helpful.
>
> Professor John Lars Johnson, of Knox College, who read much of the manuscript and who immeasurably improved its literary style.
>
> The administrators of the Faculty Research Fund of Knox College, who provided financial assistance in completing the manuscript.
>
> Mr. Richard W. Ellison, Mr. Don M. Redfoot, and Mr. Charles Dunlap, of the Service Pipe Line Company, Tulsa, Oklahoma. Their interest was manifested in many tangible and intangible ways.
>
> Finally, the author's wife, Margaret Evans Lerche. Her scholarly interests and training, her unflagging zeal, and her unfailing companionship have made this book in a real sense a collaboration.

For whatever merit this volume possesses, the above must receive much of the credit. For its inaccuracies and shortcomings, the author is solely responsible.

Contents

Contents

I

Fundamental Concepts

1

The International Scene

A generation ago, authors of books on international relations written for American readers often felt obliged to begin their analysis with a statement stressing the importance of their subject and explaining why it merited serious study. Today, however, the necessity for this sort of apology has disappeared. The second half of the twentieth century is not a time for illusions; all literate Americans are aware of the impact that world politics has had and is continuing to have upon our personal lives. The process which we call international politics will determine the major outlines of the future of every one of us. War or peace, atomic destruction or atomic plenty, frustration or security: these are only a few of the personal problems that arise out of the clash of nation-states. International politics is immediately pertinent to all of us.

It is the purpose of this book to lay down some of the fundamental principles that govern international politics and to discover a way to apply these principles to actual international situations. If such a set of principles and the technique for their application can be mastered by the student, he should have a better understanding of international events and should be able to act more effectively and responsibly in his role as democratic citizen.

Before beginning our detailed consideration of the processes of international politics, it is desirable to take an over-all look at the international scene to view our subject 'in the round.' In this way it will be possible to gain some perspective and to be better able to maintain a sense of proportion as we examine the various facets of international politics in detail.

THE STATES OF THE WORLD

International politics, as the term is used in this book, consists of the political relationships of states. The 'nation-state' is discussed in detail in Chapter 2, so at this point it is sufficient to consider the state merely as the participant in international political life. In other words, the state is the international person.

Although almost all of the land surface of the earth is divided among the

3

states of the world (there are still some bits of territory on the Antarctic continent that are unclaimed by anyone), there are only approximately seventy states in the world. Peculiarities in the legal status of some political organizations cloud their claim to statehood to such an extent that it is impossible to stipulate an exact figure. In the case of at least sixty-five states, however, there is no doubt; they are full-fledged members of international society. It is the relationships among these relatively few entities, therefore, that constitute international politics.

When does a state become a state? Although international lawyers have made many attempts to lay down positive legal criteria by means of which to determine the precise moment when statehood is acquired, none of them is controlling in the conduct of interstate relations. The actual practice of states indicates that statehood is obtained for international purposes when the other participants in world affairs accept the new member into their group. Professor Edwin Borchard once summed up this situation succinctly: 'A state is, and becomes, an International Person through recognition only and exclusively.'

DIVERSITY OF STATES

When the student looks at the states of the world, the initial impression he receives is one of great diversity. No two states are alike in their physical characteristics; each state is unique and differs from all its fellows in almost every measureable way.

Area. One of the most immediate and obvious differences to be discovered among states is in their geographic area. The division of the earth's territory among them is very unequal. Some few states encompass enormous areas; most of the rest are relatively small. The differences in area, of course, exert profound influence upon the course of international politics.

The largest state in the world, covering over one-sixth of the land area of the world, is the Soviet Union; it includes over eight and one-half million square miles. The other large states are Canada, with over three and three-quarter million square miles; China, almost as large as Canada; Brazil, three and one-quarter million; the United States, three million; Australia, just under three million; and India, with one and one-quarter million.

At the other end of the scale are a number of tiny bits of territory which have survived from an earlier day and which, although insignificant for international politics, maintain a precarious independence. These include the Principality of Monaco (0.59 square miles), the Republic of San Marino (38 square miles), the Principality of Liechtenstein (65 square miles), and the Republic of Andorra (191 square miles). The smallest actual participants in international politics are the Vatican City (108 acres—powerful because of the unique international role of the Pope), the Grand Duchy of Luxembourg (999 square miles), the Republic of Lebanon (four thousand), the Republic of Israel (under eight thousand), and the Republic of Haiti (ten thousand).

The remainder of the states of the world fall somewhere between these extremes. Taking the seventy-one political units with the most valid claims to statehood, we find that their mean area is 647,382.8 square miles. This would make Iran (628,000 square miles) the most 'typical' state as far as area is concerned. Remembering the huge size of some few states, however, we can easily see that most states are much smaller than this theoretical average.

Location. Another factor of great diversity among states is their location with respect to the land and water areas of the world. Certain natural categories of location suggest themselves immediately. Some states—notably Great Britain and Japan—are composed entirely of islands and this fact automatically creates conditions of international existence which govern much of their foreign policy. Other states are primarily coastal, such as Italy and Chile; this again materially influences their international role. Bolivia, Switzerland, and Czechoslovakia illustrate another type: the landlocked state without access to the sea. Other states have what is termed a 'balanced' location, with a favorable relationship between seacoast and interior; France and Argentina are examples. Finally, we must mention the continental state with great area and balanced land-water relationship; the United States is an ideal example of this group.

Shape. A glance at a world map reveals much variety in the shape of states. International boundaries are sometimes drawn in harmony with natural terrain features, and sometimes are the result of political conflict and bargaining; the result frequently is to make particular states resemble pieces in a jigsaw puzzle. Among the oddities in shape are Chile, the 'shoestring republic,' over two thousand miles long and less than one hundred miles wide; Pakistan, broken into two portions separated by a thousand miles of Indian territory and with communication possible only by sea or roundabout air route; Japan, Indonesia, and the Philippines, each of which is an archipelago of over a thousand islands; and Italy, whose boot-shaped peninsula is familiar to us all.

Population. The human population of states is another factor of great diversity. The most populous state in the world is China, although no one is certain exactly how many Chinese there are. The 1948 census, largely a matter of more-or-less informed guesswork, produced a figure of 463 million; in 1954 the Communist government of China made public an estimate of over 600 million. Other leading states in population include, in descending order, India (roughly 350 million), the USSR (just under 200 million), the United States (over 160 million), Japan (nearly 90 million), Indonesia (80 million), and Pakistan (75 million).

Several states have very small populations. In some cases, the total is under one million, less than such American states as Maine, Colorado, or Oregon. The smallest of these are Iceland (137 thousand), Luxembourg (293

thousand), and Costa Rica (837 thousand). Some of these smaller populations are scattered over great areas; perhaps the most graphic illustration is
the case of the new state of Libya (which attained its independence in 1952),
whose population, estimated in 1952 as one and one-quarter million, is
spread out over a territory of over a million square miles. Organizing such a
population for national existence and foreign relations is obviously a very
difficult task.

Society and Culture. Anyone who visits a foreign country soon becomes
aware of the differences in social organization and cultural pattern which distinguish states from one another. Some states are industrial, others agrarian;
some incorporate modern technology, while others are yet in a primitive
stage of development. Some have a rigid class structure of society, while
others have great social fluidity. Some are built upon a religious base, while
others minimize or ignore religious influences. Some seek to embody and
perpetuate a peculiar tradition, while other cultures are eclectic and synthe-
sizing. By almost any standard of measurement, social and cultural diversity
among states is normal.

PATTERNS OF INTERNATIONAL POLITICS

The diversity among states inevitably lends an appearance of confusion
and disorganization to interstate relationships. This impression of anarchy is
heightened by the concept of 'sovereignty,' a legal characteristic of states
which we shall analyze in the next chapter. The effect of sovereignty is to
make states refuse to accept any common superior in international life, and
thus to make each one the judge of its own actions. The differences among
states and the notion of sovereignty combine to give the international scene
an apparently shifting and almost formless character.

International political life, however, is much more organized than would
appear. Closer study reveals that the necessities of national existence compel
states to organize themselves in many ways so that each may better serve its
purposes. The resulting patterns of international politics provide a great deal
of the framework upon which states base their foreign policies and exert
much effect upon international life.

FORMAL PATTERNS

The 'formal' patterns of international politics are the multistate organizations that states create to accomplish common purposes. There is a surprising
number of them; Chapters 9 and 10 deal with them in detail. In the aggregate
their influence upon interstate life is of real importance, although many of
them deal with only small segments of the total of international relations.

The United Nations. The best-known and the most inclusive (in scope only
—other organizations have larger memberships) of the formal patterns of

international politics is of course the United Nations. It grows out of a long history of attempts to organize the political relationships of states and is the most ambitious of all of them.

Seventy-six states are members of the United Nations, including all the major powers (Communist China and Germany, however, were unrepresented in late 1955). Its organization is rather elaborate, matching its correspondingly broad range of functions. Its structure is considered in detail in Chapter 10, so at this time we need only mention what the Charter terms its 'principal organs.' These include the Security Council, a small body of five permanent and six non-permanent members, designed to deal with immediate threats to the peace; the General Assembly, in which all members are represented, with a broad scope of political, economic, and social competence; the Economic and Social Council, a smaller body which deals with and seeks to improve economic and social conditions throughout the world; the Trusteeship Council, another small body with a general responsibility for the 'non-self-governing territories' of the world; the International Court of Justice, designed to provide facilities for the judicial settlement of controversies between states; and the Secretariat, consisting of technical and clerical personnel to assist the other five organs.

The great goal of the organization is the preservation of peace. It attacks the problem of war and its prevention on two levels. The Security Council seeks to cope with immediate threats to the peace; the General Assembly and its sub-agencies works to eliminate war by destroying the social and economic conditions out of which it grows.

No one claims today that the United Nations has fully accomplished this dual mission. The present disturbed state of international affairs is eloquent testimony of its inability to restore and guarantee peace and security in an atmosphere of cold war. Yet it is significant that no present member of the United Nations seeks to withdraw, and that those few states that are not yet members are seeking admission. Obviously, the realistic and practical men who direct the foreign policies of the states of the world have found something valuable in the United Nations and are all hoping to perpetuate it.

Other Formal Organizations. There are over seventy formal international organizations in addition to the United Nations. These are generally organized about a single function representing a shared need, and each constitutes a more-or-less effective vehicle of international co-operation. From among the many examples of this type we may cite the Universal Postal Union, a 'specialized agency' of the United Nations, which makes possible the international delivery of mail, and the International Bureau of Weights and Measures, a relatively small and inconspicuous body that performs the vital task of maintaining internationally recognized standards of weights and measures. These specialized organizations operate within narrow limits and with very

simple administrative structures, yet so numerous are they and so fundamental their functions that they encompass a large part of international relations.

INFORMAL PATTERNS

The formal organizational structures of international politics do not exhaust the observable patterns of interstate behavior. States often move along
predictable channels without formalizing their position by the creation of organizations. These non-structured patterns we call 'informal.'

Alliances. For special purposes and for limited times, states frequently
form alliances. An alliance is an understanding between two or more states to
co-ordinate their policies in the pursuit of a common objective of security.
Common defense is the keynote of an alliance; therefore it is usually aimed at
a common enemy of each of the allies. So long as the security threat continues,
the conduct of the members of the alliance toward it is predictable and constitutes a particular type of recognizable pattern.

Other Forms of Co-operation. Security arrangements are not the only form
of co-operation between states. Agreements for joint action are numerous,
covering almost every phase of international life. Economic agreements on
international trade and finance are very frequent; other areas of agreement
include social, cultural, and political matters.

Power Blocs. The power bloc is perhaps the most pertinent to present-day
world politics of all the informal patterns. This is a grouping of states so
closely tied together as to make it possible for them to act as a unit in foreign
relations, employing highly co-ordinated policies. Usually a power bloc is
under the effective direction of its most powerful member; at least, this is true
of those which function in the contemporary world. So important have they
become that it is not too much to say that the opposition and conflict between
the massive groups provide the dominant characteristics of international
politics today.

There are two solidified power blocs in the world, with a third in the
process of formation. The appearance of the newest bloc is a relative innovation; in 1947 it seemed that the whole world was divided up between the
initial groups, and there was much talk of 'bipolarity.' The grip which the
United States and the Soviet Union (leaders of the two older blocs) held has
been loosened and some states have escaped to a perilous neutrality while
others have joined the evolving 'Afro-Asian' group. This latter bloc is composed of North African and South Asian states, with India as potential leader
and frequent spokesman. Although it is dangerously easy to overestimate the
extent to which these groups are actually unified and single-minded, there is
little doubt that the major questions of international politics are fought out
between them and that they affect the conduct of foreign policy by every state
in the world.

The Interdependence of Peoples

The interdependence of all the peoples of the world is a fundamental condition of international politics of which our introductory survey must take account. Despite the marked divisions among men produced by the existence of states and the depth and seriousness of the differences of policy which arise among them, it is an undeniable fact that under conditions of modern life men everywhere depend upon one another for most of the good things of life.

The Influence of Technology

Mutual dependence has always been a characteristic of social life; it has been brought to its height, however, by the development of modern technology. Before the beginning of the Industrial Revolution in the eighteenth century, most men were able to live out their lives within a sharply delimited provincial culture and to satisfy their relatively simple needs from its own resources. In the nineteenth and twentieth centuries, however, industrial technology has expanded at a constantly accelerating pace. Its effect has been to bring people into ever more close contact with each other and to create new needs which could be satisfied only by an increasing degree of co-operative effort. Today, the world is truly a technological unit; the political relations of states must be conducted within the requirements of a unifying technology.

Transportation and Communication. The improvements in transportation and communication have played a leading part in making the world smaller. No region of the earth is beyond reach of rapid contact with any other part. When Americans can reach Europe in twelve hours by air, and when instantaneous communication is possible by radio, telephone, or cable, it is no longer possible for us to remain ignorant or uncaring about what happens there. The effects of political, economic, and social events in remote portions of the world are felt in the United States within a very short time of their occurrence. Domestic events here are similarly immediately significant abroad.

The Need for Raw Materials. Modern industry is largely a process of the fabrication of raw materials, and the raw materials of modern industry are scattered throughout the world with no concern for political boundaries. So great is the demand for raw materials that individuals and governments are constantly searching for new sources of supply, and the discovery of a new deposit (frequently in an out-of-the-way place) immediately makes that area of the world of great importance. The United States, for example, has only become seriously concerned with the Middle East since 1945; not the least of the reasons for this interest is the discovery of enormous deposits of petroleum in the area. Central Africa is important to us because of its great uranium reserves; a primitive area of Labrador is the scene of a new discovery of high-grade iron ore. Many similar examples could be cited of the manner in which concern with the raw materials of our technology has brought formerly remote areas of the world into intimate contact.

Patterns of Consumption. As technology has continued to pour out its great flow of new products, new patterns of consumption have evolved. The impact of the technological way of life has spread throughout the world and thus, at the other end of the industrial process from the search for raw materials, interdependence has increased as men have sought to obtain more of these new commodities for themselves. Problems of trade, of development, and of finance have grown up out of the hunger of men for the products of technology; the category of economic problems has come to be of increasing importance to international politics.

AREAS OF INTERNATIONAL CONTACT

The lives of people of different states touch each other at many points. Although the increasing rigidity of modern nationalism has made crossing frontiers much more difficult in the twentieth century than it was in the nineteenth, individuals continue to display persistence and ingenuity in carrying on international contacts of increasing complexity and frequency.

Political Contacts. In later chapters we shall see how all the states of the world are tied together in a network of relationships through the medium of diplomacy. Very few indeed are the states that dare to allow themselves to go unrepresented at the capital of any other state; all of them are so closely bound together that the maintenance of communication by means of diplomatic agents is vital.

It is sometimes said that diplomacy has declined in importance in the modern world. Negotiation now takes place directly between governments (thanks to the devices of modern communication) and the diplomat has been reduced to the status of a 'messenger boy.' It is undeniable that the nature of diplomacy has changed; much of the old glamour has disappeared. The volume and the necessity of interstate political communication are both much greater than they were in a more leisurely day, however, and in the process of expediting communication the diplomat performs a function no less significant than his earlier one.

A special form of political contact between states arises through the existence of international organization, notably the United Nations. Under ordinary circumstances a diplomat operates in a bilateral relationship: he assists in the conduct of relations between his own government and that of the country to which he is accredited. In the United Nations, however, any diplomat is thrown into intimate contact with representatives of all the other seventy-five members; the result is multilateral 'conference' diplomacy, as many states consult simultaneously. Most of the notable successes of the United Nations have come about as a result of this type of diplomatic contact.

Economic Contacts. We have already referred to some of the economic consequences of our evolving technology. The search for raw materials and the urge to consume have created a complex of economic relationships among people which cannot help but materially affect the course of international politics. The United States, for example, maintains trade relationships with over seventy distinct political organizations all over the world; most of the major free world states trade upon as broad a basis.

Social Contacts. Perhaps fundamental to the future of the world, however, is the category of international contacts which can be called 'social.' These include all the personal relationships between individuals of different states which are neither political nor economic. The increasing interdependence of peoples has vastly increased the number of such relations in the world outside the Iron Curtain, and there are some signs that even Communists are not immune to the effect of this kind of contact.

Virtually all aspects of private life have acquired an international flavor today. Americans particularly have become subject to this tendency as our fate has pushed us into a position of world leadership. All of us feel the result. We have come to appreciate Japanese art, Scandinavian architecture, Italian and French motion pictures. Our taste in foods, in clothing, in industrial design has been significantly altered by influences from other lands (for example, we have all noted the trend toward European 'sports car' styling in our automobile design). What is more, the trend shows no sign of abating. More of us are going abroad, more of us are becoming acquainted with visiting foreigners from all walks of life, more of us are having our provincial horizons pushed out by the effects of internationalization.

The same is true, to varying extents, in other states. Much of the free world has become familiar with the products of Paramount Pictures and Coca-Cola, Incorporated. American machinery, American technicians, and American visitors are found throughout the world. This has had its political connotations, also; between 1953 and 1955 there were few quarters of the globe that had not received a personal visit from either Vice-President Nixon or Secretary of State Dulles. What has gone on between the United States and the remainder of the free world has been duplicated to some extent between almost any two states we could name. Individual contacts across state lines constitute a major reflection of the current interdependence of peoples.

UNITY AND DIVERSITY IN THE MODERN WORLD

Our rapid survey of the international scene has indicated that there are two forces at work in international politics: unity and diversity. On the one hand we have the institution of the state, conducting policy and forming alliances; its effect is to divide men into competitive and potentially hostile groups. At the other extreme we have the influence of technology, which obliges men to become increasingly interdependent. Which force will become dominant?

All the governments of the world are struggling with this dilemma, and each works out a solution in terms of its own concerns. The outcome of the conflict between unity and diversity is the central issue of international politics today, and it is to this point that much of this book is addressed.

2

The Nation-State

IT was pointed out in Chapter 1 that the state is the participant in inter-
tional politics. Before undertaking any detailed study of the relationships
among states, therefore, some consideration must be given initially to the institution of the state as it fits into the international political process. This is
the first in a series of three chapters devoted to this purpose; they deal respec-
tively with the nation-state in theory and fact, with national policy, and with
national power.

What Is the State? We begin with a definition. The state is a politically organized body of people, occupying a definite territory, living under a government, and incorporating sovereignty. This definition is sufficiently broad to
encompass all the states involved in international politics despite the almost
infinite variety in details which exists among them. In the language of international politics, however, the word 'state' should usually be read 'government.' The government is the portion of the state that actually conducts foreign affairs, exercising the collective power and making decisions in the name
of the whole. 'International' and 'interstate' relations are thus actually 'intergovernmental' relations.

The state is central to international politics. Individuals, of course, play a
critical role; the state can function in the real world only by means of the action of human beings. Individuals gain significance in international affairs,
however, only when they become clothed with corporate authority arising
from an official connection with a state. This applies whether the person involved is Prime Minister Anthony Eden or John Doe, a conscript in his national army. Neither is important as a person, but rather because of official
role.

COMMON CHARACTERISTICS OF STATEHOOD

Chapter 1 noted many instances of great diversity among states, yet a definition of the state has been formulated that includes all existing examples of
the state form. All states, regardless of their differences in terms of other criteria, have four characteristics in common: people, territory, government,

13

and sovereignty. Certain aspects of each of these should be considered in some detail.

PEOPLE

Obviously, the number of people necessary to statehood may vary widely from one state to another. Are there any limits upon the size of a population? More specifically, is there any maximum or minimum figure beyond which the size of a population impairs statehood?

Minimum Population. In a purely theoretical sense, the absolute minimum population of a state for international purposes would appear to be one, provided that that one person were accepted and recognized by other states and that he were capable of discharging the responsibilities of statehood. As a practical matter, however, all that can be said is that a state must have sufficient population to enable it to accomplish its international mission. Although this resembles the ancient saw to the effect that a man's legs should be long enough to reach the ground, it does reflect the actual situation. The minimum size of a population is a relative factor rather than an absolute number. Luxembourg, for example, has been able to maintain its international identity despite a tiny population, while large concentrations of people throughout Asia and Africa proved unable to avoid alien rule.

Maximum Population. The eighteenth-century French philosopher, Charles de Secondat, Baron de Montesquieu, maintained that it was possible for a state to grow too populous. His argument, which gained widespread acceptance for a time, was that after a certain point was passed in population growth, efficient government would prove impossible and the state would split. The point had considerable validity for the time; history affords many examples of states, such as the Roman Empire, that suffered dissolution as a partial result of over-expansion.

Today, however, the problem of maintaining control over large concentrations of people has been largely solved. It would be technically feasible to organize the entire world under a single government if modern devices of transportation and communication were given their maximum geographic effect. While it remains true that in certain 'backward' areas of the world (such as China) an overly large population impairs efficient government, no general rule can be deduced from these instances; indeed, there seems to be no logical upper limit to the possible population of a state. Maximum population, like minimum population, is relative to circumstances.

TERRITORY

Minimum Territory. We cannot lay down a generalization about the minimum territory necessary for statehood except to point out that it must be extensive enough to provide a base for mounting power sufficient to achieve its objectives. Obviously, questions of territory interact upon those of population; a great but sparsely populated territory can acquire statehood only with much more difficulty than a smaller but more thickly settled area.

Maximum Territory. It is no longer contended that a state, if it takes in too much territory, will break apart. Maximums of territory (like those of population) are not arrived at by establishing any raw figure, but instead are considered as functions of the level of technological development of the particular state. Today states of continental expanse are leaders in world affairs, and their great size—far from being a source of weakness—contributes to their strength. On the other hand, smaller but less well-organized states, such as Burma and Indonesia, have great difficulty in exercising effective control over their outlying regions.

Can a State Exist Without Territory? The question of the continued existence of a state after it has lost all its territory has arisen during both great wars of this century. It has been most pressing in the case of the various governments-in-exile forced to flee from hostile armies, such as the governments of Poland and Czechoslovakia during World War II. Their dominion over territory was suspended by conquest, but they retained their identity and were able to exercise control over *émigré* populations and financial resources. The official view of the western allies in both wars was that the governments continued to represent actual states.

This position agrees with the legal theory of statehood as well as with the practical requirements of world politics. It would seem, however, that although state existence may continue temporarily without any territory during a period when state authority is in suspension, it cannot be argued that it can thus continue permanently or indefinitely.

GOVERNMENT

Government consists of the public institutions for the accomplishment of state purposes. Every state must have a government, although within broad limits each state may erect such particular structures as it desires.

International Requirements. International life imposes a few requirements which must be met by any government. Effective arrangements must exist for the conduct of international relations. This pattern of offices must be competent to conduct diplomacy, to commit the state to action, and to take such action.

The techniques of international intercourse were stabilized in the days of absolute monarchs. It was therefore long ago established that there must be a determinate human head of government in every state. This person alone may officially speak for the state, and he is legally responsible for all policy steps taken by his government. This principle is in full effect today. The President of the United States, the Prime Minister of Great Britain, the Premier (*président du conseil*) of France, and the Chairman of the Presidium of the Supreme Soviet in the USSR all occupy such positions. Foreign states have official contacts only with this official, his principal deputy for foreign affairs (ordinarily the foreign minister or corresponding official), and with other designated subordinates. With the remainder of the governmental organization they have little concern.

A further requirement of a government is that it be capable of accepting responsibility for its decisions and actions. Treaties, once made, must be observed; policy decisions must be executed. It would serve little purpose for a government to make solemn promises and then to be too weak or too divided to carry them out. The maintenance of international responsibility ordinarily means, therefore, that the government which speaks for the state must actually be exercising effective control over its population and territory. Inability to do this usually deprives the state of its full international role.

Domestic Freedom of Action. After satisfying these few requirements, states may organize their governments very differently. Some have elaborate mechanisms for registering and executing popular will, while others confine the decision-making power to a small elite. The government may be strong or it may be weak; it may be stable or unstable; the people may be happy, quiescent, or restive and potentially revolutionary. All this is in the strictest sense irrelevant to international relations. With any questions of 'good' and 'bad' government no other state has any legal right to deal; if the state is organized to fulfill its international responsibilities the arrangement of its internal political functions is its own affair.

The Recognition of International Incompetence. The functioning of the government of a state becomes a matter of international concern only in exceptional circumstances. If internal political convulsions impair or destroy the capacity of the state to play its international part, other states may legitimately take note of this fact. If the state is unable to exercise its sovereignty in international relations, other states may suspend intercourse with the incompetent state, and resume official relations when stability has been restored and the international personality of the state is again complete.

This was the course followed by most states at the time of the Bolshevik revolution in Russia in 1917. The collapse of the Czarist government eventuated in the rupture of normal international contacts with the new Russian government. Full relations were entered into again after several years, as, one at a time, the other states of the world satisfied themselves that the Soviet government was capable of accepting international responsibility, at least upon a minimum basis. In the same way for the same alleged reasons, the United States has persisted in its refusal to extend recognition to the Communist government of China since 1949.

SOVEREIGNTY

Internal Sovereignty. Sovereignty has sometimes been referred to as 'the supreme political characteristic.' Although definitions abound, the general import of the term is clear. There must be, in order for a society to become and remain a state, a law-making authority in the state beyond which there is no legal appeal. When thought of as the source of domestic law—usually termed 'internal' sovereignty—the concept is comprehensible. It would be difficult to preserve even minimum order and peace within a society without there being some final source of law; the conduct of more elaborate governmental functions would be impossible. As long as voluntary co-operation cannot be counted upon to produce the social results men demand of government today, the state must continue to be the possessor of final legal authority.

External Sovereignty. International politics, however, is especially concerned with a different aspect of sovereignty. If it is true that in each state there is a legal authority that recognizes no superior, what will be the basis of the relationships between any two such states? Sovereignty has an international as well as a domestic implication; internationally, sovereignty means the legal freedom of the state from external control. Unless a state is free to determine its own national interest, lay down its own policy objectives, and to devise techniques for their attainment completely in terms of its own desires and without dictation from any foreign state, it cannot be considered as sovereign.

'Semi-sovereignties.' International law recognizes many 'semi-sovereign' political organizations. Some governments possess internal sovereignty but have lost (or never acquired) the power and the right to conduct independent foreign policies. An example of a small unit of this type is the Principality of Monaco; larger ones include the governments of Nepal and Bhutan in central Asia. A second classification of 'semi-sovereignties' includes such international oddities as the 'Free City' of Danzig between 1919 and 1939 and the 'Free Territory' of Trieste between 1945 and 1954. The former was created under the sponsorship of the League of Nations; the latter, by the United Nations. Both enjoyed only a short period of existence, ultimately being absorbed into their larger neighbors.

Another borderline group is formed by the many small states today that are so completely under the domination of a larger and more powerful ally as to raise serious doubts about their sovereign status. Is Bulgaria or Poland sovereign in any real international sense, or is Panama? Although the legal niceties are observed and these 'satellites' possess all the visible signs of sovereign statehood, no one for a moment believes that the major elements of their foreign policies are independently determined.

Sovereignty and the United Nations. Are all the members of the United Nations sovereign states? Article II of the Charter of the United Nations stipulates that the organization is founded upon the principle of the 'sovereign equality' of all its members, and practice and interpretation of the Charter agree that membership is available only to sovereign states. This principle,

18FUNDAMENTAL CONCEPTS

when applied to concrete cases, produces some puzzling results. The Byelorussian Socialist Soviet Republic and the Ukrainian Socialist Republic are both members of the United Nations and, according to the rule of Article II, they are therefore sovereignties. How they can at the same time be sovereign and independent and also constitute component parts of another sovereignty, the Soviet Union (itself a member of the United Nations) is a riddle beyond easy solution.

THE LEGAL NATURE OF THE STATE

International law considers the state to be the 'international person.' The only entities recognized in international practice as full participants are the states themselves; individual human beings have no international status except as we noted above. International politics, therefore, goes on among states as corporate beings; this legal assumption invests the state with certain juristic characteristics.

THE STATE AS CORPORATION

We can understand the legal nature of the state most easily by making a comparison with an institution with which most Americans have some familiarity, the private corporation. This approach throws much light upon some of the peculiarities of state existence.

The Analogy with the Corporation. The state, like the corporation, is held to be a person before the law in its external sense; both state and corporation, however, are abstract beings whose only existence is a legal one. A corporation may own property; a state may acquire territory (real property) and wealth (personal property). A corporation makes contracts; a state enters into treaties (many of the provisions of ordinary contract law apply to the law of treaties as well). A corporation may sue and be sued; a state may also become subject to formal jurisprudence, before an international court.

In the case of both state and corporation, the collective being has an existence apart from the individual human beings that make it up. The treasurer of a corporation is not personally liable for the debts of the organization; neither is the foreign minister of a state legally liable for an unsuccessful foreign policy.

The obligations of a state, like those of a corporation, continue independently of whatever particular persons are holding office within the government. Transformation of regimes has no legal effect. The revolutionary government of France in 1791, for example, succeeded to all the legal advantages and disabilities of the monarchical government it had replaced. In the same way, the Bolshevik government of Russia was unable to gain international consent to its proposal to repudiate the international debts contracted by the Czars. No principle of international law is more firmly grounded in practice than this rule of 'state succession'; in its essentials it is the identical doctrine that governs the practice of corporations.

The Internal Independence of the State. We have already noted that states have no legal right to concern themselves with the internal affairs of their fellows. This principle grows out of the idea of the corporate personality of the state. The legal façade of 'statehood' is a barrier beyond which no external agency may rightfully go. Whether or not the people of a state are efficiently governed, happy, or free is an 'internal' question, and the monolithic 'unity' of the state does not permit any legitimate grounds for questioning from the outside. Just as the motives of an individual are usually not open to legal question so long as his behavior is within the law, so also are the purely internal affairs of a state free from international scrutiny.

Several attempts have been made in recent years to force certain ruling groups to accept international responsibility for internal policies, but no marked change in the general rule has resulted. Nazi treatment of the Jews in Germany was condemned by civilized people everywhere, but it required the catastrophe of World War II to bring that policy to an end. The United Nations has sought to force the government of the Union of South Africa to modify its restrictive policy toward its non-white population, but the doctrine of internal sovereignty has stood firm against pressure, even from a world organization. Too many states are jealous of their own independence to be interested in setting a precedent that might some day be turned against them.

The Legal Immunity of Officials. As in the case of the corporation, government officials enjoy personal immunity from responsibility for official acts. Although the state, as an abstract being, is powerless to act by itself and all its functions are carried out by human agents, these individuals are not legally liable to any external agency. Whatever responsibility they bear is internal; international law is powerless to touch them. Penalties may be imposed upon the state, but its officials are protected by a cloak of legal anonymity. An analogous rule is found in corporation law; the principal in a transaction is responsible for the acts of his agent.

The 'war crimes' trials after World War II were hailed as modifications in this principle and as establishing a rule of private responsibility under international law. Many 'war criminals' in Germany and Japan were tried for their parts in the unsuccessful aggressions undertaken by their governments. Although penalties ranging from death to imprisonment were imposed upon many of the accused by special international tribunals, the broader implications of the verdicts have not been widely accepted as expressing a settled legal rule. The idea of personal responsibility, many critics argue, would be destructive of governmental efficiency and provocative of disobedience and evasion among government personnel. As a result many governments, including that of the United States, have found the principle unpalatable. Today the war crimes verdicts are generally thought of as examples of 'victor's justice' and the notion of the immunity of government officials is not seriously challenged in world affairs.

THE LEGAL CONSEQUENCES OF STATEHOOD

We have seen that legally the state is a personality and that the international order is composed of such self-contained entities engaged in relations with one another. Certain consequences arise logically from this general concept.

Equality. The first of these is the equality of states. If all states are complete legal sovereigns and none recognizes a common superior, perfect equality among them is the only possible basis of interstate relations. This legal principle obviously does violence to the political facts. States, in any rational political sense, are not at all equal; we have seen that inequality is normal by almost any criterion. Nevertheless, equality before the law is the theoretical basis of much of the day-by-day conduct of international affairs.

Formal international intercourse—diplomacy—proceeds upon the assumption of the equal status of all states. Treaties—even punitive treaties dictated by a victorious state to a vanquished enemy—are deemed to be agreements between legal equals. Much protocol is devoted to the demonstration and attempted proof of this idea. One of the continuing tasks of a diplomat is to arrange affairs so that the political factors that actually determine the course of events do not do irreparable injury to the fiction of state equality. It is important to preserve the illusion of equal status because, like so many other legal fictions, it has considerable practical utility; for example, it provides the only possible base for international legal action.

Independence. Closely allied with the idea of equality is the principle of the independence of states. As sovereignties, they may be bound only by their own consent and then only for so long as they wish to remain so. This is obviously another legal fiction; politically, states have only as much real independence of action as they have power to enforce or that they are permitted to exercise by the tacit consent of stronger states. Yet so appealing is the idea of freedom that many statesmen go to great lengths to make clear that their course of action is their own choice and not dictated from outside. Occasionally a state will reject an otherwise desirable policy for no more rational reason than its insistence upon avoiding the appearance of external dictation.

What the legal doctrine of independence tends to mean in practice is state irresponsibility. If a state is legally free to select any policy objectives it wishes and to implement them by whatever means are expedient, and if it can do this without reference to any set of fixed principles or to any international body, it is obviously behaving irresponsibly. It is true that a state may ultimately suffer the legal consequences of its action, but this is uncertain at best; furthermore, no legal means exists to prevent it from anti-social action. No form of international 'preventive jurisprudence' exists, for states are legally free agents.

Jurisdiction. A legal consequence of statehood with more real content than the preceding two is its jurisdiction over territory and people. A state exercises authority and power over all the territory within its boundaries and over all people (nationals and aliens) residing therein. There are some relatively minor exceptions to this rule, but it is applicable in most instances. The state also retains jurisdiction over its nationals when they are outside its territory. This legal power gives a broader sanction to political authority than mere physical force and is generally regarded as absolute.

Conflicts of jurisdiction between states are not uncommon. Sometimes they arise out of overlapping claims to territory, sometimes out of dual authority over particular individuals or pieces of property. National citizenship laws, for example, overlap to such an extent that it is not unusual for a person to have citizenship in two states simultaneously. Under current statutes, an American woman who marries a Norwegian citizen retains her American citizenship by United States law, but gains Norwegian citizenship as the wife of a citizen under the laws of Norway. Although such jurisdictional conflicts are usually sustained without great difficulty, it is not a happy condition in which to be found if the lawful commands of the two governments conflict.

Responsibility. As an outgrowth of the power of jurisdiction, states must also assume legal responsibility for events which occur on their territory or as a result of actions by their nationals while abroad. The responsibility is corporate, not individual; remedial action is taken by the government in the name of the state. From among many examples found in the history of diplomatic practice, two illustrations of this rule may be selected. The government of the United States paid an indemnity to Italy following a riot in New Orleans in 1891 during the course of which Italian citizens were attacked and lynched. In 1935, Secretary of State Cordell Hull apologized officially to the government of Germany after a riot in New York in which the Nazi flag was treated disrespectfully.

In both these examples, the problem was complicated by the federal form of government in the United States. The national government had no jurisdiction over the individuals committing the acts since the offenses were within :he reserved competence of the state governments; international practice, however, cannot take account of the peculiar governmental arrangements of a state and the government of the United States was obliged to assume full responsibility.

The principle of state responsibility works in reverse also. Not only does a state accept liability when one of its citizens errs; it also protects and assists him when his rights are invaded when he is abroad. In the example of the New Orleans mob, the government of Italy protested to the United States on behalf of its murdered citizens, even though they had been permanently residing in the United States for some time when the incident occurred. In 1954, the United States government urged action by the United Nations on behalf of some American military personnel who had been unjustly imprisoned as 'spies' by the Communist government of China after the close of the Korean war.

THE STATE IN INTERNATIONAL POLITICS

We gain an entirely different view of the state if we shift our emphasis from its legal characteristics and consider it as a 'political' organization—as a participant in international politics. From this point of view the state and its government may be thought of as the structure of public institutions through which a social group works in order to achieve its political objectives. In other words, the state is a group of people organized for the accomplishment of common political purposes. The government is the active arm of the state. Human beings and government, therefore, are the political components of the state.

FUNCTIONS OF THE STATE

Community Mission of the State. In all modern states, the people look to government to aid them in reaching certain goals, both private and public. This is true both in internal affairs and in international relations. Individuals, organized under government into a state, are able to mobilize political power that the government may use in the common interest. The objectives of the state are largely imposed upon it by popular demand. In a political sense, international politics is the struggle between organized social groups, with governments serving as the media of contact, for the accomplishment of those objectives which each group feels to be necessary or desirable.

Internal Functions of the State. For convenience of expression, the functions that people demand of the state are usually divided into the categories of 'internal' and 'external' (or 'domestic' and 'foreign'), although it is not possible to draw a clear line between them.

Internally, the state is initially charged with the task of protection. In every society, government has the duty of protecting the individual against other individuals, against society, and against himself; in other words, the government must maintain public order and redress individual grievances.

The state everywhere also has a welfare function. Although each political group works out to its own satisfaction the field of its welfare activity and the extent to which the government is to go in improving the lot of the individual, it is pretty well agreed throughout the civilized world that the state has a responsibility to guarantee and to improve in some way the happiness and well-being of its citizens. In recent years the trend has been toward the radical expansion of this welfare activity; today, at least in the western world, the older protective and regulatory activity of the state is largely overshadowed.

External Functions of the State. The external functions of the state do not permit of being so neatly catalogued. We shall see later that the state mechanism serves the national interest in international politics and that each people's version of national interest is determined by factors peculiar to themselves. It is not inaccurate to say, however, that the foreign policies of most states have two aspects, not dissimilar to the dual internal function of government. Protection and welfare appear in external state activity as well as in internal. Most foreign policies therefore have negative, protective features and positive, promotional ones.

THE ISSUE OF SOVEREIGNTY

Theoretical Attacks upon Sovereignty. The legal and political doctrine of sovereignty has so many practical and logical inconsistencies (we have already considered a few of them) that it has long been the object of frontal attack by scholars of many points of view. 'Political behaviorists,' armed with the findings of modern sociology and psychology, question the validity of the idea of sovereignty by denying the existence of any institutional power and explaining obedience to law as arising from a combination of consent, coercion, and habit. 'Political pluralists' demonstrate that the state does not in fact monopolize law-making power, but that instead it shares it with other groups. Indeed, so general have become the attacks that the whole juristic theory of the state (founded upon the doctrine of sovereignty) is in general disrepute in academic circles today.

At the international level, these critics claim that sovereignty, if it means anything at all, must include the ideas of the independence and the equality of all states. This condition, they claim, does not exist and never has existed; even if it were possible to realize, it would be undesirable. Certainly, the pure doctrine of sovereignty must be constantly modified by the realistic conditions of international political life; perhaps the modifications are necessarily so great as to impair the validity and utility of the whole idea.

Persistence of the Doctrine. Opposing this position, however, is another objective fact of international politics. States, although they may not in fact be really sovereign and independent, persist in acting and thinking as if they were. Effective institutional control over their actions is generally lacking, and they yield only to the superior power of other states. National policies incorporate the assumption that a state is ultimately answerable only to itself. This is most unsettling when large states exercise their free choice to plunge the world into war for their own private reasons, but throughout the entire international scene the idea of sovereignty acts to make world politics dynamic and unpredictable.

Sovereignty in terms of national independence is intimately associated with the urges of nationalism, and popular demand often forces statesmen today to insist upon the literal letter of the privileges of sovereignty even though such action might result in injury to the state's true interest. India's termination of dominion status in 1949, France's reluctance to permit the rearmament of Germany between 1949 and 1954, and American insistence after 1949 upon an inflexible policy toward Communist China, are all recent examples of this tendency. The doctrine of national sovereignty may be what it is sometimes called—an unrealistic and pernicious fallacy—but it is a political fact of which statesmen and students alike must take account.

NATIONALISM

The politically significant states of the world today are nation-states; that is, they possess the common characteristics of statehood and in addition the people of each feel themselves united into a nation. The transformation of the state proper into the nation-state has had a profound influence upon international politics; nationalism is today one of the dominant forces in world affairs.

THE NATURE OF NATIONALISM

The Nation. Although the literature of political science provides many attempted definitions of 'nation,' there does not exist complete agreement on its essential components. There is general understanding, however, that a nation is a people sharing a spirit of unity that makes them want to live together under the same government and to see their state prosper. Beyond this generalization, many suggestions have been made as to the specific unifying factors that weld a people into a nation. A common language, a common religion, a common racial background, or a common cultural heritage are among the most frequently cited of these.

Although most of the nations of the world do possess all or some of these characteristics, it is not possible to claim that they are of universal applicability. There are nations that do not have a common language, such as Switzerland; nations of great religious diversity, such as the United States; nations without racial 'purity,' such as India; nations without cultural homogeneity, such as Canada. The most that we can conclude is that nationhood is the product of a mass emotion and that it can arise from any of a great variety of stimuli. Those mentioned above are only the most common bases of this emotion.

Nationalism as a Mass Emotion. Nationalism is the emotion of nationhood. A nationalistic people feels itself an entity different from the total of its individual members. It recognizes certain goals identified with the nation-state which each citizen is supposed to accept as personally desirable. The nation's friends and enemies become the friends and enemies of each individual; the nation's successes and failures become individual victories and individual defeats. Often these reactions arise independently of any personal involvement; Frenchmen, for example, traditionally hate and fear Germany, even though many particular Frenchmen have never suffered pain or disability at the hands of any German.

The immediate effect of the spirit of unity of modern nations is to influence the individual to merge his identity with the greater whole of the nation. As a part of the mass, he reacts with it, responds to the same stimuli, performs the same semi-ritualistic acts. A population sufficiently nationalistic will behave as a unit, crushing dissent and making conformity to the patriotic code a matter of high civic duty.

NATIONALISM IN INTERNATIONAL POLITICS

Nationalism has a long history, but as a preponderant force in international affairs it dates generally from the era of the French Revolution, at the end of the eighteenth century. The rulers of revolutionary France, beset by enemies on all sides, succeeded in convincing the masses of the French people that each Frenchman had a personal stake in the government's policy. From that day forward, the spirit of nationalism has played an increasingly significant role in the framing of foreign policies.

The Democratization of Foreign Policy. The greatest result of the rise of modern nationalism has been the 'democratization' of foreign policy. A population, since its members are to be called upon to execute government policy by military service (the rise of nationalism made possible the mass conscript army) and perhaps to die for it, today demands and receives a voice in its formulation. This is true in every nation-state. No matter how authoritarian the government may be, every statesman keeps in constant touch with the nationalist feelings of his people. The major elements of all foreign policies are in reality determined by the nationalist attitudes of the respective peoples.

As new areas of the world have come under the influence of nationalism, rulers in those states have discovered that the direction of foreign affairs is to a large extent taken out of their hands and transferred to popular mass control. The old governmental elite still makes the detailed decisions and operates the government machinery, but their actions must be confined within the limits laid down by popular opinion. Leaders in a number of states in the Middle East and southeast Asia have on a number of recent occasions underestimated the power of a newborn nationalism, only to find themselves in serious difficulty as a result. Governments in Egypt, Iran, Burma, and Indonesia (among others) have been required since 1949 to make hasty alterations in their policy to make allowance for the new demands of nationalism.

Nationalism as a Tool of Policy. Policy makers often find nationalism a convenient tool of policy. Let a policy maker decide that a given step is wise and expedient; all he need do in order to gain the necessary popular support is to identify the policy in question with the nationalist credo. Nationalism makes public duty (including support of the government) a sacred trust of the individual. In the public interest he is expected to be willing to sacrifice his personal liberty, his property, and even his life. With this kind of mass support, any statesman finds his lot much easier.

To a leader engaged in a risky or reckless course it is usually a matter of sheer necessity to be backed by an inflamed and uncompromising public opinion. To the more conservative statesman, nationalist support provides a basis upon which to proceed and a protection in the event of unexpected adversity. Failure to identify policy with nationalist goals by either type of policy maker opens the government to the danger of popular repudiation.

The Rigidity of Nationalism. Statesmen have also discovered, however, that a sensitive nationalism may on occasion prove to be a serious hindrance to the execution of a realistic foreign policy. A strong nationalist spirit tends to be very firm in its likes and dislikes, thus robbing the policy maker of much of his necessary flexibility and freedom of maneuver.

Certain states may be objects of nationalist hatred, as in the case of Turkish attitudes toward Russia; certain policy objectives may become sanctified by tradition far beyond their true worth, such as British insistence upon the historic 'lifeline' of the Empire which passes through Gibraltar and Suez. Strong attachments may be formed for certain states or regimes; one pertinent illustration of this attitude is provided by American admiration for Chiang Kai-shek and the Kuomintang government of China. Less obvious than the foregoing is nationalist identification with certain techniques and procedures of policy. American nationalism, for example, distrusts propaganda as a device; British nationalism still yearns for the strategy of the balance of power despite present circumstances that make it unfeasible.

Changing any of these attitudes is most difficult and always at least potentially dangerous. It is easier for statesmen to be guided by them. Nationalism thus creates rigid channels along which the policy maker must move in designing strategies; all major policy decisions must obtain formal or informal popular ratification before success, or even maximum effort, can be achieved.

Making Unpopular Policy Decisions. In today's rapidly moving world, over-rigid nationalist viewpoints frequently conflict with changing conditions. Governments often find themselves in a position to gain great advantage—or at least to avoid suffering a setback—if they take rapid action in a crisis situation. Frequently, however, this action would conflict with the nationalist desires of the people. In such a case, the policy maker has a variety of alternatives open to him, all of them more or less unhappy.

He may choose to flout public opinion, trusting either that success of his policy will ultimately win popular approval or else, in case of failure, that the resulting popular outcry will die down without causing the repudiation of his policy. He may conduct a hurried program of 'educating' his people to the necessity of the new step—a move of uncertain value at best. He may temporize, hoping for a turn of events that will make the unpopular decision unnecessary. He may, finally, drift with the currents of opinion, even though he might feel that their direction is wrong and will result either in a lost opportunity for constructive action or else a positive defeat. In any case his lot is made harder by the inflexibility of nationalist stereotypes and the emotional orientation of much public opinion on foreign policy.

The Difficulty of Controlling Nationalism. An acute instance of the pervasive influence of nationalism is afforded by the course of international politics since 1945. Statesmen, working in an atmosphere of constant crisis and keenly aware of the possibility of global war, have found it dangerously easy to gain popular support for key policy steps by exciting nationalist passions to a high pitch. Playing upon fears of alien ideologies and the deeply rooted attachments men feel for familiar and sacred beliefs, governments everywhere have stirred their peoples to demand the dangerous moves which the leadership has already decided to be necessary and desirable.

To their sorrow, many statesmen have learned that nationalist emotions are easy to call into existence and to intensify, but difficult to control and sometimes impossible to dispel when the reason for their original appearance has disappeared. Governments have often been pushed beyond the point at which they were aiming by the pressures of public opinion. Egypt and Iran, among many others, have had cause since 1951 to regret the unleashing of mass nationalism upon a delicate political situation. The governments of the USSR and of the United States have been on occasion brought perilously close to the danger point by popular outbursts, but both have been able thus far to divert or to calm down the nationalist storm without having to take any unretraceable step.

The Manipulation of Nationalist Symbols. Nationalism, being emotional rather than rational, gains specific content for most people through symbols. These may assume many forms. National flags are among the most common; so are national uniforms and ceremonies such as the changing of the guard at Buckingham Palace and the dress parade of the West Point cadets. If a cartoon character gains favorable recognition and popular acceptance as a symbol of the national spirit it can exert great influence: 'Uncle Sam' and 'John Bull' are among the most prominent examples. Great men and national heroes are powerful stimuli to mass emotions: George Washington, Abraham Lincoln, the Duke of Wellington, Napoleon Bonaparte, Prince Bismarck, and Alexander Nevsky are illustrations drawn from five different nations. Great historical events—usually battles—also have symbolic value. Lexington, Gettysburg, Waterloo, Tours, and Poltava are all terms that evoke strong nationalist responses in the appropriate peoples.

The manipulation of nationalist symbols in order to produce the desired popular reaction is a major task of governments today. In this activity they are greatly assisted by the modern techniques of mass communication. Indeed, so necessary to the development of a strong nationalism are the technological means of communicating the patriotic message that it is probable that a people cannot become a nation today unless adequate means of communication exist within a state. Radio, television, motion pictures, pictorial art, and the printed word all can be used to subject the citizen of a modern technological state to a concentrated barrage of nationalist stimuli.

The lesson principally taught by this flow of propaganda is that the individual is part of something greater than himself, that his highest mission in life is to perform his public duty, and that all his fellow citizens share this opinion and are expecting him to assume his responsibilities. This sort of program has two objectives: active support for government policy is coupled with the minimizing of dissent.

THE CYCLE OF NATIONALISM

Before setting aside the phenomenon of nationalism at this point, we should reflect a little upon the apparently cyclical course it has run throughout history. The record of the rise and decline of nationalism in each people and the course it has followed in its expansion throughout the world both display a certain rhythmic pattern which suggests a possible natural trend.

Liberating Nationalism and Democracy. Originally, as nationalism grew to full stature in revolutionary France and spread outward from its point of origin, it was linked to political democracy and appeared as a liberating force. Its aim was to free national groups from foreign domination and individuals from oppressive social, economic, and governmental conditions. The great nationalist revolutions of the nineteenth century were democratic revolutions as well, or at least were allied to democratic aspirations. By 1914 this movement had reached its peak in Europe. The peace settlements at the end of World War I were based upon the assumption that the revolutionary and upsetting factors in nationalism would be eliminated by satisfying national demands for 'self-determination' and granting democratic government to all such liberated peoples.

The Failure of Liberating Nationalism. This judgment was speedily proved wrong. After 1919, the formerly intimate relationship between nationalism on the one hand and democracy and freedom on the other was destroyed. The western world entered the period some have called that of the 'degradation of the democratic dogma,' while nationalism came to be an even more potent force, plaguing the world with revolution, crisis, and war. The peacemakers of 1919 had overlooked the lesson taught by the successful nineteenth-century movements for the unification of Germany and Italy: nationalism does not need to be allied with democracy to achieve its ends. Indeed, an authoritarian government might prove to be a more efficient instrument for the accomplishment of national goals, if for no other reasons than its greater unity of organization and concentration of power. The peoples of Europe after 1919, when confronted with a choice between democratic ideals and nationalist goals, tended to choose the latter.

Totalitarian Nationalism. Totalitarian patriotism, involving the complete subjugation of the individual to the will of the state, replaced the 'joyful communion' of individuals with each other which had characterized the nationalism of another period. No longer did nationalism carry democratic connotations; instead it became the ally of authoritarianism. The nationalist leaders of the 1920's and 1930's—Mussolini, Hitler, Franco, and their lesser imitators—sneered at the democracies as being 'internationalist' and 'cosmopolitan' and drove home their message that only by rigid hierarchical dictatorship could nationalist aims be realized.

In the meantime, the older variety—liberating nationalism—had continued to spread beyond Europe. India, Turkey, China, and many other states outside western civilization came under its influence, setting in motion chains of circumstance with which the West is contending today. World War II was the logical outgrowth of the development of totalitarian nationalism in Europe (and in Japan) as it came into final collision with the democracies with their less militant national feeling.

The Cycle after World War II. After 1945, the evolution of nationalism continued along the same general lines. New areas of the world became subject to the pressures of liberating nationalism, most significantly southeast Asia and the Middle East. Other states passed through the liberating phase and entered the period of totalitarian nationalism: China, India, and the USSR are examples of this trend.

Under wartime and postwar conditions, American nationalism came to exhibit some of the 'pathological' characteristics the world came to recognize in Fascist Italy and Nazi Germany: the 'myth of the mass,' the cult of the state, the glorification of conformity, the suppression of dissent, and the vigorous manipulation of symbols to remind Americans of their duty. It is too much to claim, however, that the United States has passed into the extreme phase of nationalist orientation; such evidence as exists points rather to a condition in which such a shift could take place, rather than that it has already occurred.

The Decline of European Nationalism. During the period since 1945, however, a third phase of the cycle has begun in western Europe. The shattering impact of two world wars in thirty years has cooled the ardor of many of the most militant nationalists there. The former enthusiasm for nationalist expansion and the indulging of traditional animosities have largely disappeared; in their place has appeared a broadly based popular movement for international co-operation upon a formal institutionalized basis. Despite frequent anachronistic outbursts of the old attitudes, European nationalism today is

a far different matter than it was twenty years ago. Something new in nationalism has come into being.

It is too early to say that the prewar variety is forever dead in Europe, but
certainly there are strong indications that general disillusionment is widespread with much of the nationalist apparatus. The Germans, traditionally
the most 'warlike' people in Europe, have been reluctant to take up the
burdens of rearmament; the French, the most patriotic people in Europe,
have brought the Schuman Plan into existence and finally, early in 1955,
agreed to join a rearmed Germany in the defense of Europe; the Italians have
abandoned their search for a new Roman Empire in favor of a united Europe. Even the Scandinavian states have indicated some willingness to recon-
sider their cherished neutrality in the interest of continent-wide programs of
co-operation.

The Future of the Cycle. Does the European experience mean that nationalism is a self-limiting condition? Are there three distinct phases through
which nationalism passes naturally: liberating, totalitarian, and declining?
If so, does this mean that ultimately, through the growth of wisdom and the
accumulation of experience, men will realize the hollowness and futility of
the claims of one national group to supremacy and domination over the
other? We cannot be certain yet. The decline in European nationalism may
prove to be only temporary; furthermore, the giants of contemporary world
politics are largely in the grip of extremist attitudes. Inflamed nationalism is
a more serious threat to peace today than ever before in history, because the
states that are the most belligerent represent a great portion of the power-
in-being in the world.

If the pathological nationalism of the contemporary world is to cool in its
turn, will it require another world war to do it? Will the new nationalisms of
southeast Asia and the Middle East (and the yet-to-be-born nationalisms of
Africa) pass from the first stage to the third without ever menacing world
peace by expansionist and totalitarian tendencies? These critical questions
can be answered only at some time in the future when the validity of the
cyclical theory has been determined by the processes of history. For the
moment we can only point out that at least three distinct forms of nationalism
exist in the world at the present time and that their interaction provides
much of the subject matter of international politics.

STATE PERSONALITY

We have already seen that the state can be discussed in two different ways.
It may be approached either as a legal personality or as a political organization. Legally, the state enjoys a form of fictitious corporate personality;
politically, it consists of human beings organized in a particular fashion and
serving purposes related to the wants of those individuals. When, under the
pressure of modern state life and the demands of world politics, the idea of

corporate personality is blended with the organic reality of human beings, a new concept is created: the state as a living reality. This idea is of major significance in contemporary international affairs.

THE THEORY OF THE LIVING STATE

Nature of the Concept. The theory that the state has organic life is an old one. For centuries men have sought for the 'extra-substantial' elements of statehood as they found themselves unsatisfied that the external manifestations of the state—people, territory, and government—captured its innermost essence. Many schools of philosophy have invested the state with some type of metaphysical significance. The most important of these for the world today is that which finds the state to be a living organism.

Until recently, this dogma remained a matter generally confined to academic discussion. It was not until it allied itself with totalitarian nationalism and became a rallying point for the mass movements of the twentieth century that it came to occupy its present important place as an influence upon world politics. Today, the nationalist hypothesis of most major states and the point of view assumed by many individuals involve to some extent an implicit (sometimes explicit) acceptance of the idea that a state is a living organism with its own life cycle and its own destiny.

State Personality and Nationalism. To claim that the state is a living organism is an affront to the common sense of most western peoples. Their senses and their reason tell them that the state is not alive; the state is made up of human beings and the institutions they create, and nothing more. Yet so compelling is modern nationalism that the idea of state personality has already gained acceptance, although sometimes subtly, even among democratic peoples.

The very idea of 'national' interest—as apart from popular or individual interest—is the foundation of international politics, yet it is unintelligible without some idea of the reality of the state. This does not deter democracies from pursuing national interest as avidly as do dictatorships. All nationalistic peoples, free and unfree alike, accept as axiomatic that it is the duty of all individuals to sacrifice their own comfort and security so that the state might prosper.

In their thinking and speaking about world politics, individuals unconsciously reveal the extent to which the idea has taken effect. To Americans, for example, their great enemy is 'Russia'; very few draw any distinction between the Soviet Union as a legal entity, the Russian peoples, and the ruling clique in the government. It is easier to conceive of international politics as being carried on by organisms called Russia, France, China, and the United States than it is to make careful differentiations among the corporate entities, the living peoples, and the governments. Popular stereotypes furnish corroboration of this idea; we hear on all sides such statements as 'the United

States is peace-loving,' 'Russia is aggressive,' 'France is decadent,' and 'Germany is militaristic.' Most Americans would deny that they accept the organic hypothesis, but certainly many of its assumptions are incorporated into the American point of view on international politics.

IMPLICATIONS FOR INTERNATIONAL POLITICS

There are certain implications that arise naturally from the concept of the organic reality of the state. These bear immediately upon its conduct of foreign policy and the nature of the interstate relationship. We shall consider three: the separate existence of the state, the superior worth of the state, and the role of the individual in the state.

Separate Existence of the State. According to this theory the state has an existence apart from the lives of any or all of its citizens. While humans are mortal, the state is immortal—or at least the life cycle of the state is far longer than that of its people. The independent existence of the state makes it a force over which men have no control; the state moves in response to compulsions—the 'laws' of history, of biology, of logic, and so on—which are cosmic in their influence and thus are immune to the machinations of mere humans. The existence of the state transcends the here and now.

Superior Worth of the State. Since state existence is independent of individuals, it is an easy step to reason that the state organism is the highest and most perfect of all organisms, and specifically to claim that individuals must subordinate all their own wishes to those of the state. It would appear by this logic that the whole (the state) is greater than the sum of its parts (the people), but defenders of the theory insist that this is not true. The state is more than the sum of the individual citizens, but this does not exhaust its parts; the additional ingredient that makes the state greater than its people is its living personality and reality.

The Role of the Individual. Although it is clear that the state has an existence apart from individuals, individuals are by no means thought to be independent of the state. They are not permitted freely to choose their own role within the society. Using the ready analogy with the human organism, in the state organism individuals are deemed to be cells within the body politic.

Just as individual cells in a body do not question their mission but merely perform their function, so individual human beings have no right to dissent from any state decision. The body cells have specialized functions to perform and each is created for that purpose; in the same way certain men are born to rule, others to fight, and still others to labor. Muscle cells do not attempt to serve as brain cells, and neither should men whose fate it is to serve aspire to be masters in the state.

Cells cannot live by themselves, but survive only as part of a larger organism, and individual men can have no real existence or fulfillment outside the state. The whole organism moves and has its being only on command of the brain, the state by command of its government. Many other examples could be cited of the ingenious way in which the organic theory is used to emphasize the subordination of the individual to the living state.

The organic theory thus conceives of the state as a self-contained entity which moves as a unit to accomplish its ends in international politics. The state organism functions through its brain, the government; it executes its decisions through its body, the people. In this way foreign policy becomes the province of the ruling few, while the many have no mission except to follow where they are led. The adventurous foreign policies of Nazi Germany, Fascist Italy, and imperial Japan provide instructive illustrations of the probable result of this idea upon world politics.

3

National Policy

EVERY state has a policy. National (sometimes called foreign) policy may be defined as the over-all course of action taken by a state in seeking to attain its national objectives. The essential ingredient in policy is thus action directed toward a discernible goal. Within the concept of policy as treated in this chapter are included also the factors that enter into the making of a policy decision, the objectives to the accomplishment of which a policy may be directed, and the techniques followed by states in executing their decisions. International politics thus arises out of the contacts that states have with each other as each of them pursues its policy.

Relatively little in interstate relations is entirely fortuitous; international intercourse, conflict, and agreement grow out of purposeful behavior by governments. The adjustment of policy to meet the requirements of a constantly changing situation is the continuing task of a statesman. In attempting to attain his policy objectives he must apply both his insight into the nature of world politics and his skill in manipulating men and circumstances.

NATIONAL INTEREST

A state's policy objectives in international relations arise in the first instance out of what it deems to be its national interest. The concept of interest is basic to international politics. Because of its identity with deeply felt and often inarticulate national aspirations of a people it is difficult to isolate and to define with precision. In general, it may be thought of us as that which a state and its people feel to be permanently essential to continued national existence and development. It gains its specific detail in terms of the ego-image which a people have of themselves. It embodies either those aspects of national existence which the group possesses and insists upon retaining or those it lacks and wishes to acquire.

Sources and Nature of National Interest. National interest arises out of the interaction of a number of factors whose precise effect varies from state to state: geographic and strategic position; the level of political, economic, and social development; national history, tradition, and culture; the over-all *Weltanschauung* of the people. It is supremely egoistic in orientation. It

34

springs from sources that are entirely indigenous, and therefore the value system it incorporates makes no allowance for the existence or objectives of other states. It is thus a logical derivation from the idea of the anthropomorphic, 'personalized' state which we examined in Chapter 2.

If states are thought of as living entities possessed of distinct personalities, it follows that they have reasons for existence and specific goals to reach; in other words, they possess interests. The hopes and objectives of individuals become sublimated into a common pattern within the state. National interest is the state's interest and is thus divorced from any necessary connection with the interests of any particular individual or group. Furthermore, since today 'state morality'—the ethical code in terms of which state action is judged—is independent of private morality, the service of the national interest is for private citizens an act of great virtue.

There arises at this point a real possibility of conflict. Individuals are often required, while serving in a public role, to commit acts which their private code condemns as immoral. Yet today the concept of national interest and the requirements of citizenship have pretty well accustomed people everywhere to reconciling the disparity between what is moral behavior as a private person and what is moral behavior when the national interest is involved. Such conflicts in individual motivation are therefore relatively uncommon. Statesmen today are able to count upon the idea of national interest as an effective device to gain popular support for their policy decisions.

Permanence of National Interest. The national interest of a state remains operative despite change in any or all of the circumstances of its foreign policy. It is independent of the internal political struggle within a government and is not affected by the policies of other states. The idea of national interest and its impact upon the course of events thus furnishes a regularizing and continuing factor in international affairs.

Many dramatic examples of this continuity can be provided. The government of the Soviet Union, for example, has lately reverted to the Czarist idea of Russian national interest despite many attempts to strike out upon a new path. The Labour government of Great Britain which was elected in 1945, although pledged to thoroughgoing social revolution at home, nevertheless picked up the threads of British national interest abroad and carried on in much the same way as had its Conservative predecessor.

In like fashion the electoral reverse of 1952 which returned the Conservatives under Sir Winston Churchill produced no significant change in British interest. A change in party control in the United States, such as that which occurred in 1952, sometimes has greater repercussion in foreign policy than is the case in Britain; the one point of national interest which is generally agreed upon is the security of the Western hemisphere, with which Republican concern is as great as that of the Democrats.

Despite the relative permanence of the idea of national interest, it must not be assumed that it remains forever immune to change. Since the prevailing version of national interest at any time is really a product of the cultural and political outlook of a people, one would expect cultural, economic, political, and psychological evolution to produce corresponding development in the idea of national interest, and this is actually the case.

The modification of the prevailing American notion of security as an element in the national interest is illustrative. Half a century ago, security to the American people involved only United States hegemony over the Western hemisphere. Today, as Americans view their world role in a different perspective, security has connotations that lead our policy into Europe, Asia, and the Middle East. Perhaps it is more accurate to say that although the interest remains constant (i.e. the United States had just as much interest in security fifty years ago as it does now), its formulation and verbalization vary as the situation develops and the awareness of the people and their government grows. Certainly history offers many examples of interests that have broadened in their expression over a long period, and not a few of interests that have contracted.

Importance of National Interest. An understanding of what a people feel to be their national interest at any time will go far toward providing a basis for forecasting the future policy of the state.

Obviously this would be of great value to statesmen of other states but it is extremely difficult to determine with any degree of accuracy. Many aspects of national interest are irrational and are rooted in the mass psyche of a people. Often the people themselves are unaware of the particular version of national interest which they share, or else several different interpretations are competing for group acceptance.

Yet the elusiveness of the concept of interest in no way minimizes its key role in national policy. A statesman must be sensitive to the state of mind of his people and seek to base his decisions upon what they regard as national interest. This is a formidable task—to know a people sometimes better than they know themselves—but it is one of the primary requirements of political leadership.

Policy makers can do very little about altering the prevailing concept of interest; the best they can do is to have always a clear picture of what it is and to see to it that they do not depart from it in making decisions. Fortunately for most statesmen, national interest is usually conceived in general terms and they thus have considerable leeway in formulating specific steps in its service.

POLICY: THE MANIFESTATION OF INTEREST

THE POLICY PROCESS

Since national interest is the foundation upon which a statesman must build in seeking the achievement of his objectives, he must follow a fairly standard procedure. He must first translate the general idea of national interest into concrete terms and formulate a series of policy objectives; then he selects techniques appropriate to the attainment of these goals. This is the policy process pure and simple.

In framing policy, the statesman begins with two constants and many variables. The constants are the existence of the national interest he is expected to serve, and the existence of other states, each likewise pursuing its own policy. The variables include all the possible policy objectives deriving from his state's national interest, all the techniques available to him for reaching these objectives, and the many forms that the policies of other states might take.

Reaching a Policy Decision. The process by which a policy decision is made has been fairly well standardized in most states. Statesmen, as we have seen, are faced with a constantly evolving situation with which they must attempt to cope. The impact of developing circumstances upon national interest is always being evaluated; whenever action in its behalf becomes appropriate, policy decisions must be made.

When the responsible officials of a government become convinced that measures must be taken to guard or promote the national interest, their first step is to make as thorough and objective an analysis of the situation as is possible. Each separate issue that necessitates action is studied in the light of available information. For each of these issues, all the possible alternative courses which might possibly be followed by the state are outlined and canvassed. An estimate is then made of the probable outcome of each alternative if it were adopted. When this process is completed and all the alternatives and their likely results are examined, a choice is made among them. That policy is selected which promises the most gain (or the least loss) to the national interest, and steps appropriate to its accomplishment are then undertaken.

This summary of the policy process is somewhat oversimplified, but it is accurate in its essentials. So long as statesmen feel themselves obliged to serve the national interest exclusively and as long as the nation-state system imposes its peculiar requirements upon the foreign policies of states, the policy process will continue to be approached as a problem in determining that course of action which will redound to the greatest benefit to the state itself. The enumeration of the alternatives of action is not everywhere completely formalized, but in some form it is an essential step which precedes almost every policy decision taken by any state. Since policy decisions must be made every time a situational change occurs, and since the circumstances upon which decisions are based are in a state of constant flux, it follows that any state which seeks to play an active international role must be always overhauling its policy. Failure to do so would indicate either a remoteness from the main currents of world affairs or a remarkably inept leadership.

LIMITATIONS ON POLICY DECISIONS

Interest and Commitments. It should be pointed out at this point, how-ever, that the policy-making process does not in practice go forward with as much freedom of choice as might be inferred from the foregoing analysis. The statesman usually finds the realistic alternatives open to him in any situa-tion to be extremely limited. It is to his advantage of course to preserve the maximum freedom of maneuver, but he is always faced with many factors over which he has little or no control.

He is in the first place restrained by the prevailing concept of the national interest, which he must respect. Second, he is to a great extent bound by earlier commitments, the revocation of which is almost always difficult and is often impossible. Any policy maker must move with great caution in at-tempting to alter policies which his government has had under way for a long time and which it supports with considerable power. International disturb-ances of unsuspected proportions might develop from any such new de-parture. Any policy shift might produce a chain reaction of adjustment to it on the part of other states. We shall examine this condition in more detail in Chapter 5; for the moment it is sufficient to remark merely that once such a reaction begins in world politics, the final outcome is often unpredictable.

Other States. A third limiting factor upon policy choice arises from the nature of international relations. A statesman is more than a framer and executor of policy aimed at satisfying the national interest of his state; he is also the subject of pressure from other governments seeking to accomplish the same purpose on their own part. Policy makers therefore often spend as much effort in reacting to moves aimed at themselves by other states as they do in seeking to achieve their own objectives. This situation—the necessity of countering the policy steps of other states—often serves to reduce the al-ternatives open at any given time.

OPERATIONAL CRITERIA OF POLICY

Concreteness. Certain operational criteria affect all policy decisions. The primary fact that any objective selected must be intelligible in terms of the national interest has already been established. The objective and the program for its attainment must also be stipulated in concrete terms. Nothing is so self-defeating, for an individual as well as for a state, as to pursue an objec-tive couched in hazy and imprecise phraseology. Much effort, better spent elsewhere, is thus committed to the search after a will-o'-the-wisp that con-stantly recedes as it is approached. Such objectives as 'peace under the law' or 'an end to imperialism' tend to involve the state in a maze of inconclusive policies which can never be rationalized or completed.

What we are actually saying is that objectives and policies formulated in concrete terms and based upon actual situations are almost always relative in character and take into account the existence of other states and other competing policies. In those terms it becomes clear that a state must always content itself with something less than complete victory. Unclear and abstract objectives tend to the absolute and thus can never be attained short of complete hegemony. Policy, if its ends are to be accomplished, must enumerate specific goals in relation to real states and situations, and then follow courses of action which arise from those realities.

Attainability. Policy objectives must also be attainable. A state must seek to avoid biting off more than it can chew. No matter how insistent the promptings of national interest, it would be unwise for the government of a small state, such as Nicaragua or Burma, to undertake a policy looking toward the attainment of world domination. A rational statesman always keeps in mind the maximum effort he would be willing or able to make in support of any of his policies, and seeks to keep his selection of objectives within those limits.

Great states have collapsed as a result of seeking an objective that demanded more effort for its attainment than they were capable of mustering. One reason for the insistence on concrete and specific objectives is because only in that way can accurate analyses be made of the prospects for gaining them.

Flexibility. A policy must also be flexible. No area of human activity is more subject to sudden change than is international affairs, owing to the basically irresponsible nature of the state. The arena in which any state moves is one of great confusion of motivation, and a process of constant adjustment to the rapidly changing situation is going on.

A policy decision, as we have seen, is reached as a result of the application of a concept of national interest to a particular situation, the choice of appropriate objectives, and the selection of expedient means. The decision is affected by such factors as the relations the state is maintaining with all other states, the attitude of all other states toward the problem under consideration, and the general pattern of world politics. Any one of these may and probably will change momentarily. A policy that assumes the indefinite continuation of the *status quo* is doomed to futility and failure. No more common fault can be found of political leadership in the contemporary world.

Many of the international crises and wars that beset mankind could have been avoided if policy makers had recognized the possibility that conditions might arise that would make their assumptions invalid and their policy inappropriate. To assume that because a state has done thus-and-so in the past it will continue to do so is to assume that all the complex factors that produced the policy in the first place will continue to exert their influence in exactly the same fashion. It might so transpire; however, prudent statesmanship which recognizes the possibility of change will attempt to devise a policy sufficiently flexible to cope with a drastically altered situation if the need should arise.

Flexibility in policy is best attained by directing the state's course of action toward the accomplishment of a series of alternative objectives, with the final selection among them being determined by the changing situation. Whenever possible, statesmen embark upon a new departure in policy somewhat tentatively, hoping to verify the accuracy of their preliminary judgments before irrevocably committing themselves. The inevitable situation of pressure opposed by counter pressure which every state faces in international politics is such that only rarely will a policy result in exactly the outcome envisaged at the time of its inception. The dynamic quality of interstate relations requires that every state be constantly busy adjusting its policy. Good statesmanship foresees this and takes account of it, striving to arrange that the national interest will be served irrespective of the outcome of any particular policy move.

CLASSIFICATION OF NATIONAL POLICIES

Status Quo vs. Revisionist. Although many elaborate schemes have been drawn up to develop a system by which to classify the foreign policies of various states, the pattern of international politics is so variable that it resists simplification. It has also proved difficult to avoid an excess of moral judgment in establishing criteria. Policies have been classified as 'peaceloving' or as 'aggressive'; as 'liberating' or as 'imperialist.' These, and all others like them which clearly imply that one course of action is morally preferable to another, serve many useful purposes but accurate and objective measurement is not one of them.

Actually, there is only one criterion that can be successfully applied to the foreign policies of all states with any real result, and the classification is therefore a dual one. The standard of measurement is the state's attitude and policy toward the over-all *status quo* which it faces.

Although many fine distinctions can be drawn within each group, a state's policy either reflects a general satisfaction with things as they are or else a fundamental discontent. If the former be the case, most of the state's actions will be directed toward a preservation of the *status quo*. If the state is dissatisfied with present arrangements its policies will aim at major alterations in them.

States of the first group are termed 'satiated' or 'have' powers; states of the second are dubbed 'revisionist' or 'have-not' powers. It must be noticed that the 'have' or 'have-not' situation of a state depends not upon the attainment or non-attainment of any absolute level of security or standard of living, but rather upon its attitude toward that level which it has attained. In the postwar world the Soviet Union, despite its relatively favorable position in relation to most of the other states of the world, nevertheless remained dissatisfied with what it had. In its policy it was therefore a 'have-not' power.

The Formulation of Policy

Up to this point in our discussion we have used the terms 'statesman' or 'policy maker' to refer to the specific individuals who have the power to commit their states to action by making policy decisions. It is appropriate at this point to examine in more detail the process of decision making in order to make clear who these individuals actually are and the role each plays.

Officials Directly Concerned

By and large international politics tends to be a function of executive officers and heads of states. International law today retains the anachronistic fiction that interstate relations are personally carried on by the various heads of state. This is literally true only in special cases in the modern world, but the executive branch retains its dominant role.

In addition to the pervasive force of custom, two factors help explain the predominance of executive over legislative departments in the field of foreign policy. First, in the process of conducting foreign affairs these officials gain the detailed and technical information upon which alone intelligent policy decisions can be based. Second, foreign policy calls for the exercise of strong political leadership for which only executive officers are qualified. Legislatures (in those states in which an independent legislature exists under a theory of separation of powers) are also handicapped by the lack of machinery under their direct control which might be employed to implement any decisions they might reach on their own.

The Chief Executive. Within the executive branch of the government most states have a roughly similar arrangement for foreign affairs. The operating head of the state—the chief executive—still retains the key role in decision making, whether he be president, prime minister, or dictator. Although in practice he usually confines himself to broad policy considerations, leaving the detailed implementation of decisions to technically trained subordinates, the nature of his position is usually such as to give him as much personal power in matters of foreign policy as he cares to exercise.

Direct negotiation between heads of governments has been a relatively uncommon occurrence, although several centuries ago it was a normal channel of international intercourse. However, the practice is again on the increase. World War II saw a major revival of the custom through the agency of the 'Big Three' (later 'Big Four') conferences, wherein Churchill, Roosevelt, and Stalin dealt directly with each other. Although not taking place under such dramatic circumstances since the war until Geneva in 1955, face-to-face relations between chief executives is no longer regarded as unusual in interstate negotiation.

During the more acute stages of the cold war, between 1948 and 1952, there were many suggestions heard on both sides of the Iron Curtain that only by another round of top-level conferences between the opposing leaders could major progress toward the easing of the tension be accomplished. This demand for face-to-face diplomacy was intensified following the death of Stalin early in 1953. In 1955 the United States agreed to a renewal of top-level talks with the USSR. As a routine matter, however, the chief executive today permits the determination of day-to-day policy to rest in the hands of his subordinates, reserving his own activity to crisis situations or the establishment of broad policy principles. The critical role of the chief executive was dramatically demonstrated at the time of President Eisenhower's sudden illness in September 1955. His inability to perform his function, even for a short time, placed a great strain upon the foreign affairs machinery of the United States government, both as regards to the formulation of policy and the conduct of negotiations.

The Foreign Office: The Foreign Minister. Directly concerned with foreign policy in every state is the executive department of foriegn affairs. The foreign minister, the administrative chief of this department (his formal title varies, of course, from government to government), usually bears the greatest burden of decision making on foreign affairs in the entire governmental structure. His relation to his chief (the chief executive) is an elastic one, depending upon the personalities involved and the constitutional arrangements of the particular government.

In any case, the decisions that fall to him to make are peculiarly difficult. He works within the broad policy framework of his government (in the shaping of which he may have had only a small part, or none at all) and deals with the questions that transcend routine, either because of their scope or because of their inherent difficulty. He is required to combine insight and judgment with great administrative ability, because in addition to his policy-making function he normally oversees the execution of all the diplomatic procedures of his government.

The Foreign Office: Home Personnel. Within the cabinet department of foreign affairs are two groups, each of which plays a major role in policy making. The first is the home personnel of the department who direct the detailed activities of the overseas diplomatic corps and receive their reports. Here is a repository of specialized knowledge of particular areas and problems which does not exist at higher levels.

In the course of the performance of their fairly routine task, many policy decisions are made by this group. These decisions are not sufficiently important in themselves to merit being referred to higher-ranking personnel but in the aggregate they constitute a major portion of a state's policy. The influence of these near-anonymous bureaucrats is almost ignored by the public, but statesmen are acutely aware of it. The larger the organization a state has for the conduct of foreign affairs, the greater the part these people play in its determination.

In some ways this is unfortunate; in the execution of their functions, these lower-echelon officials develop precedents and commitments that are difficult to modify if the need to do so should arise. In this way, the decisions made by the home personnel of the foreign office constitute one of the more stable elements in the policy of a state, although it must be admitted that this is often to its detriment.

The Foreign Office: The Diplomatic Corps. The other significant group in the department of foreign affairs is of course the diplomatic corps of a state.

The improvements in transportation and communication of recent times have made it possible for governments today to remain in intimate contact with their diplomats abroad and to direct their activities much more closely than was formerly the case. This has resulted in a great diminution in the range of discretionary action and consequently in the immediate importance of the diplomat in decision making. Most governments carry on fairly close 'back-seat driving' of their representatives abroad. Not only has the day-by-day role of the diplomat been reduced; in time of crisis, it is likely that affairs will be taken completely out of his hands by a meeting of foreign ministers, special emissaries, or chief executives. Nevertheless, diplomats are in a uniquely advantageous position to influence the course of policy and often to make binding decisions themselves.

The current duties of a diplomat are three: representation, negotiation, and the gathering and reporting of information. Particularly in the last function is his role critical. By the selection and evaluation of the data he forwards to his home government he can so influence the thinking of the high-level decision makers as practically to stack the cards in favor of the policy he personally prefers. In addition, his on-the-spot recommendations carry with them an aura of authenticity that gives them much weight at home.

OFFICIALS LESS DIRECTLY CONCERNED

The Cabinet. Outside the foreign-affairs department itself in almost all states are several agencies that share in the policy process. Of these the most influential is often the cabinet or the corresponding body of general advisers to the chief executive. Normally the foreign minister is himself a member of the cabinet and plays a leading part in its discussion of foreign affairs, but to varying degrees the entire body enters into the making of policy.

Its usual mission is that of recommending broad policies to the chief executive, often approving or modifying projects that arise in the first instance with the foreign minister. The cabinet members bring to this task the point of view of non-specialists on foreign affairs. As such, they possess both advantages and disadvantages as policy makers. Cabinet recommendations often ignore situational aspects of a problem which might make their proposed policy inexpedient or impossible, but they sometimes (particularly in a democracy) display greater insight into the domestic implications of foreign policy than do the more specialized recommendations of the foreign minister.

Military Personnel. We have already established that the policy of a state is always limited by its ability to accomplish its purposes. It is obviously vital that military considerations be given much weight in arriving at a policy decision. The exact importance assumed by military personnel in the hierarchy of policy makers within a government is a question answerable only in terms of the political dynamics of the state concerned. A distinction may be drawn, however, between those states that view the military establishment as a servant of national interest and those that consider military power its determinant. The latter tend to make military considerations paramount in their calculations; the former restrain it to a role more auxiliary in character. Military men in general make their decisions and recommendations in terms of two variables: the impact of the proposed policy upon the military security of their state, and the military feasibility of the proposed steps.

Non-Foreign Affairs Bureaucracy. The non-foreign affairs bureaucracy of a state also participates in the policy process. To understand the role of this group one must keep in mind the peculiar processes of the bureaucratic mind. Each agency of a government is staffed by individuals who feel quite sincerely that the destiny of their government is bound up with the success of their particular mission. In this way bureaucracies tend toward a constant internecine conflict for prestige, power, and appropriations.

It is a common occurrence for bureaucrats in agencies concerned with domestic affairs to view international relations as a regrettable waste of effort and time, and to exert their not inconsiderable influence to direct foreign policy in directions which they feel to be desirable from their own point of view. The operations of this group, although quite apparent in effect, are almost always concealed from public view because their activity goes on within the governmental framework.

INFORMAL AND UNOFFICIAL DECISION MAKERS

Many other individuals participate in the dynamic process of reaching a foreign-policy decision. All of them in some way influence the responsible officials whose actions alone will give content to policy conclusions.

It is difficult in even the most favorable circumstances to determine beyond question the factors that influenced any individual statesman to choose one course of action over another. This much can be said, however. Matters of international politics are so important to so many people in all states that there are always many private individuals and organized groups which do not enjoy official status who seek to affect the considerations of the official policy makers. The exact importance any of them assumes and the combined effect of their efforts depend of course upon a variety of circumstances peculiar to each situation. Let us examine some of the most important of these factors.

Political Parties. Political parties, however organized and directed, obviously embody forces that play a great part in foreign policy. A distinction must be drawn between the parties of a democratic state and those monolithic mass movements which are such a familiar appurtenance of dictatorial governments today.

Democratic parties represent the most politically active segments of a population and therefore are thought of as peculiarly reliable barometers of public opinion. Furthermore, in a democracy executive officers, including those charged with foreign affairs, are also party members and the opinions of the party leadership cannot help but be given great weight by office holders. In such states as France and the United States, party politics aften serves as one of the real determinants of foreign policy.

Totalitarian parties are organized upon a different theory from democratic ones, being instruments of popular control rather than channels by which public opinion may be translated into governmental action. Conseqently, the opinion on foreign matters of the rank-and-file party member in a dictatorship is completely valueless. However, the totalitarian party in a dictatorship is in many ways even more important to foreign policy than is its democratic counterpart. Since government is a party monopoly in such a state as the USSR, this means that all government decisions are in the first instances taken within party leadership circles. The policy of the Soviet government is first and foremost the policy of the Russian Communist party; the same was true in Nazi Germany.

Pressure Groups. Pressure groups constitute another important segment of the unofficial decision-making elements in a population. Their effect is confined for the most part to states within the orbit of Western culture, since outside it conditions are not propitious for the formation of private groups that attempt to influence government action in the direction they advocate. But in the United States and in western Europe, organized groups of private persons—using the apparatus of modern propaganda—are able to mobilize campaigns of pressure in behalf of the particular foreign-policy move each advocates, and this pressure is very difficult for a statesman to withstand. Each new crisis in world affairs seems to be the signal for the creation of a number of organizations that seek to produce governmental action favoring their particular side of the case.

One famous example drawn from relatively recent history will illustrate this point. During the critical period of 1940–41, when the American people were slowly learning the magnitude of the choice that was being forced upon them involving entry into the war, a great debate raged across the United States. The principal antagonists in this controversy were two massive pressure groups, the 'Committee to Defend America by Aiding the Allies,' which advocated maximum United States commitment to the cause of the Allies, and 'America First, Inc.,' which preached neutrality, withdrawal, and isolation. As the debate continued, American public opinion slowly crystallized and government policy developed in harmony with it.

Private Individuals. Of all the unofficial elements in the policy process, perhaps the most difficult upon which to be specific is the shadowy role played by private individuals. No statesman confines his friendships to members of his official family, and whenever any individual stands in such a relation to a policy maker as to be privy to his thoughts and capable of influencing his decisions, such a relationship cannot help but determine policy. In some cases private citizens have played major parts in this way; President Wilson's friendship with Colonel Edward House is perhaps the most famous instance, while Harry Hopkins undoubtedly served as the unofficial architect of many of the policies of President Franklin D. Roosevelt. Often the general public is unaware of the extent to which private citizens such as these are influencing the determination and conduct of foreign policy, and no one except the men concerned can ever be certain of the importance of such a relationship.

Public Opinion. The final ponderable in the policy process is public opinion. Since popular sentiment embodies the prevailing concept of the national interest, and since any war today must command popular support to be successful, every statesman makes a constant effort to keep his policy in line with public opinion.

This is as true of dictatorships as of democratic states; often a totalitarian ruler stands in greater fear of popular disaffection than does a popularly elected chief executive. If the latter flouts public opinion in his foreign policy, the worst that can normally happen as a result is the loss of his position and personal power; if a dictator violates the wishes of his people he runs the danger of destroying his regime and possibly losing his life. However, to base one's policy upon national interest as expressed in public opinion is one thing; to do nothing but pander to popular prejudice is another, and a very much worse, thing. The rational statesman is aware of the attitudes of his people and is responsive to them, but at the same time he is constantly leading and educating them to an awareness of the responsibilities of foreign policy.

It is often possible for a statesman to create a public demand for a step which he knows to be desirable. Nevertheless, when on occasions public opinion runs away and insists that particular unwise policies be followed, it is an unusual statesman who is able to restrain his people and to avoid yielding to the pressure. Instead many leaders are more apt to allow decisions to be made for them by popular clamor, even though they might be aware that these policies are unrealistic and potentially dangerous.

The Internal Struggle over Policy. The foregoing enumeration of the several participants in the policy process naturally raises the question of how decisions are actually arrived at among the many conflicting recommendations advanced.

It seems to be true in all states that a struggle generally takes place among the would-be architects of policy, both official and unofficial, before most final decisions are reached. The controversy may be of long duration or it may be brief; it may involve the general public or it may be waged behind the closed doors of government. It may be rooted in domestic political considerations, or it may grow out of foreign relations pure and simple. Its ultimate outcome is determined by the relative strengths of the participants and the political arrangements of the state involved.

Further generalization about the nature of this recurrent phenomenon is not possible, except to repeat that few, if any, states are able to reach important policy decisions without first becoming involved in, and resolving, such an internecine quarrel. Two examples will perhaps emphasize the point. The struggle in Nazi Germany between the party hierarchy on the one hand and the military and bureaucratic elites on the other exerted a paralyzing influence upon Nazi foreign policy and hastened the ultimate disaster. Since 1950, the quarrel within the United States over Asian policy has made the execution of a clear course of action impossible until a consensus was reached.

Objectives of Policy

It is of course impossible to establish a single catalogue of the policy objectives sought by all states. The course of action followed by any state arises from circumstances peculiar to itself, and no two national policies are alike. For purposes of analysis and discussion, however, it is possible to reduce the common elements of most national policies into a series of categories which serve to illustrate the sort of objectives that states seek to achieve. No state necessarily seeks all of these simultaneously, and each state gives each category specific content and arranges them in priority as determined by circumstances. The listing that follows serves only to point out the frequently recurring broad objectives that regularly appear in the policies of all states.

Self-Preservation

In international relations as in private life, self-preservation is 'the first law of nature.' All states have at the heart of their foreign policies the necessity of their self-preservation and they make this their implicit and underlying objective in everything they attempt.

Self-preservation as an objective connotes, of course, much more than the mere continuation of national existence, although on occasion it may be reduced to nothing more than that. States seek to avoid being placed in a position that might endanger or reduce their capacity to exist. Two major sub-categories of self-preservation might be mentioned separately: territorial integrity and political independence.

Territorial Integrity. States accept as axiomatic the idea that the national territory is inviolate and no part of it is to be alienated except under extreme duress, most frequently encountered following military defeat. Once territory has been lost, or when the state feels that it does not possess certain territory that rightfully belongs to it, the acquisition of that territory becomes a major objecive of foreign policy. This is sometimes known as 'irredentism.' The name derives from the persistent demand by Italy between 1870 and 1914 that the provinces in northeast Italy which were yet 'unredeemed' from Austria—*Italia irrendenta*—be united with the homeland. Territorial integrity is a universal and frequently obsessive objective of the foreign policies of contemporary states.

Political Independence. Political independence is frequently insisted upon as well. Since the legal concept of sovereignty is so vigorously buttressed today by the energizing force of nationalism, it is to be expected that a state would make every effort to avoid being brought under another state's political control, and would make an ever greater effort once again to escape from it if such should occur. States conduct their policies so as to retain the maximum freedom of choice under all circumstances and no state willingly accepts subordination to another except in return for concrete advantages in another area of national interest.

Particularly are states jealous of their internal sovereignty. The jurisdiction of a state within its boundaries is claimed to be absolute, and what takes place within its borders is felt to be the business of no other government. Independence in this sphere is felt to be the *sine qua non* of national existence.

The slowness of the growth of effective international organization can be attributed for the most part to the reluctance of states to give up any real power to a central authority, since this would (as they see it) result in a loss of their political independence. An exception might be made in the case of some of the states of western Europe which, since World War II, have made the creation of regional authorities with sovereign power a major objective of their policy.

SECURITY

The international society is one in which states must constantly be on the alert against the possibility of attack by another state. This situation gives rise to another virtually universal category of policy objective, that of security. All states make a real effort to achieve it. So pervasive is its influence that modern international politics has often been summed up as 'the search for security.'

The Unattainability of Absolute Security. The concept of security is another of the elusive realities of international politics. It originates in the group attitudes of the people of a state and can best be comprehended in psychological terms. Security is a condition in which a people need not and do not fear a successful attack upon them by any combination of forces.

Viewed in this light, absolute security can be attained by a state only when it has under its direct control a great preponderance of the total power of the world. The attainment of security upon such a basis is theoretically possible for some states but the effort required to achieve it would be so great as to make the search scarcely worthwhile. Practically, any state that attempted to become secure by means of world hegemony would probably meet such resistance almost from the very inception of such a policy as to dissipate the security it was already enjoying.

As a rule, states today recognize the unattainability of absolute security. Instead of following the futile course of guarding against all possible enemies, they attempt to organize their policies so as to reduce the danger of a successful attack to the practical minimum. Given the irrational element in international politics, no state can completely eliminate the danger of attack by another state; the most it can do is to seek to guarantee that any foreseeable attack will be opposed by its own superior force.

Practical Security. This approach to security necessitates initially an evaluation of the situation in terms of the more probable sources of attack. In making this judgment, a statesman estimates the international conflicts engendered by his policy, the states with which he is in dispute, and the probable severity of their reactions. He then arranges the threats of his state's security in order of their importance and imminence and devises means to cope with each of them. If his contemplated policy provokes dangers beyond his capacity to handle he either adjusts his policy so as to reduce the threats to a level within the capacity of his government, or else takes a 'calculated risk' and proceeds anyway.

In this manner, the search for security is resolved into two parts: first, the protection of the minimum requirements of national existence (a continuing problem which is independent of other aspects of policy); second, the taking of measures to cope with expected dangers arising out of the implementation of deliberate policy steps.

Security Techniques. What sort of measures do states resort to in the search for security? When it is possible, a state guarantees its security unilaterally. This normally takes the form of maintaining as high a level of military preparedness as is expedient, keeping in mind always the probable circumstances in which the armed forces of the state would be employed.

A state playing a lone hand in this regard must also utilize its diplomacy in such fashion as to prevent there being ranged against it a bloc of states with greater aggregate power. States prefer to do as much of this as they can by themselves, because in return for the increase of strength which arises from the conclusion of an alliance they must forego a certain amount of their freedom of choice and action.

It is only the exceptional state, however, that is able to dispense with international arrangements to guarantee its own security, and various forms of alliances, ententes, and 'understandings' for a common security purpose are common. These take two forms: either they are non-agression treaties, whereby each party removes itself as a security threat to the other(s) by promising not to attack it in return for a similar guarantee from the other signatories; or else they are mutual-defense agreements, in which several states that feel themselves menaced by the same security threat agree to pool their strength against the common enemy.

In the modern world the Locarno pact of 1925, in which France and Germany agreed not to go to war over the issue of the western boundary of Germany, provides one of the most famous examples of a non-aggression treaty; the North Atlantic Security Pact of 1949 which tied the United States, Canada, and the states of western Europe into a common alliance against possible Soviet aggression is perhaps the most famous contemporary mutual-security arrangement.

It is a common characteristic of both sorts of agreement that they are short-lived. When the particular crisis that inspired the creation of any of them has passed, the common security objective which alone prompted the arrangement in the first place is replaced by the more familiar diversity of objectives, and each member once again sets about solving the common problem in terms peculiar to itself.

Collective Security. To provide a more stable basis for international relations, the twentieth century has seen a continuous effort to make vital the concept of 'collective security.' The idea is simplicity itself. If every state in the world, or at least a great majority of them, realized the universal urgency of the question of security, the whole problem could be neatly resolved by each state's guaranteeing every other state's security.

Thus, if any state's policy led it to the point of menacing world peace and the security of any other individual state, the remainder of the states of the world would range themselves against the disturber of the peace with such a preponderance of power that no sane statesman would risk a war. At one stroke the age-old problem of security would be solved. The idea, with its rallying cry, 'peace is indivisible,' underlay the League of Nations and is implicit in the peace-enforcing activities of the United Nations.

Thus far, collective security upon a world scale has proved ineffective in practice because there have always been a sizable number of great powers to whom other objectives have been more important than the preservation of peace or universal security. As a result, the arrival of a crisis produced mixed reactions among the states of the world: instead of the great bulk of world power being aligned against the disturber of the peace, part of it was supporting the aggressor, part was following the policy of 'hands off,' and only a portion was defending the principle.

Korea and Collective Security. This was clearly the situation that followed the most ambitious attempt to implement the principle, the United Nations intervention into the Korean crisis in 1950. One sizable power bloc, the Soviet world, pointedly ignored the United Nations and extended covert assistance to the aggressors. Another, the so-called 'neutrals,' led by India, expressed guarded approval of the action by the organization, but refrained from assisting in any way to carry it out. The third, and numerically the largest, group was led by the United States. It gave active military support to the attempt to apply collective force to restrain he aggressors.

Regional Collective Security Agreements. The various regional collective-security arrangements have been somewhat more successful. Both in the Western Hemisphere (the Organization of American States) and in other areas (the North Atlantic Treaty Organization and ANZUS—the United States-Australia-New Zealand alliance), such geographically limited alliances guarantee the security of the membership as regards aggression both from outside and from each other.

ECONOMIC WELL-BEING

Collective Economic Advantage. States commonly have economic objectives included as part of their foreign policies. These economic goals are usually related to the economic advantage of the state and of the people collectively and therefore they bear no necessary relationship to the gain or loss to any or all individuals.

For example, stockpiling rare raw materials may free the national economy from dependence upon foreign sources of supply and thus be advantageous to the state, but stockpiling is an expensive business and the result to individuals would be an increase in taxes and in the cost of the commodities produced with the stockpiled materials. Thus an added inconvenience would be placed upon citizens without any corresponding personal gain in return. Of course, some individuals will probably profit from any economic policy designed to improve the international economic position of the state, but the question of who these individuals are and of what percentage of the total population they constitute is of no pertinence in deciding upon the wisdom of governmental policy. If the program under consideration is desirable from the point of view of the national interest, it is undertaken. Perhaps in no other area is the conflict between national (state) interest and private interest so frequent and so obvious as in economic policy.

Relative Importance of Economic Objectives. It was formerly quite common to assign economic objectives first place in the priority of the policy objectives of states. To this point of view international relations, like all other forms of politics, was a manifestation of economic determinism, and world affairs was deemed to be a struggle for raw materials, markets, and productive capacity. The evidence of the past twenty years has served to reduce the validity and acceptability of this easy generalization. Far too many states have conceived and carried out foreign policies that not only were not economically motivated but were instead economically stupid and self-defeating. Today we can admit that economic factors play a significant role in the determination of the policy objectives of states, and that at a given time and for a particular state they may be primary, without proceeding then to argue that all international contacts reflect nothing but the clash of economic interests. Only Marxist analysts retain their rigidly determinist position, and their point of view is seriously compromised by the attendant paraphernalia of communist dialectic. Events simply have not worked out according to the determinist blueprint and today very few people defend it.

Protection and Promotion of Economic Interest. The pursuit of economic objectives by a state normally assumes an ambivalent form. The state is interested in the protection of its economy against pressure from without, and at the same time it seeks to move affirmatively to improve its economic position relative to other states.

The first, or protective, aspect of economic policy takes many forms in the contemporary world. Some of the more common ways include the protection of the domestic price level by means of a protective tariff, the protection of the wage level by restrictive and selective immigration policies, the retention within the country of critical materials and products by export controls, and the protection of the national monetary system by exchange limitations. Protection can be carried to the extreme by the policy objective known as 'autarky,' which establishes as a goal the complete freedom of the state from any economic dependence upon the outside world.

Examples of economic promotion, the second phase of economic policy, are equally numerous. They include the subsidization of exports, the making of international loans and grants, and the negotiation of favorable commercial treaties. Economic objectives of the latter sort are often particularly emphasized in the policy of a 'revisionist' or 'have-not' state. The *status quo* it seeks to change usually works out to its economic disadvantage and it aspires to a more favorable set of relationships.

Raw Materials. Some further attention must be paid to one great economic objective mentioned above. In a world grown industrialized, certain critical raw materials have become essential to the maintenance of a technology adequate to support great national power. Since these key raw materials are not distributed evenly throughout the globe but are concentrated in a relatively small number of locations, the search for guaranteed access to sources of their supply is an unending process for most states. As each major change in technology has taken place since early in the eighteenth century, different raw materials have, each in its turn, become critical. As each one of them became a matter of importance, it served to touch off anew the scramble among the states for a guaranteed supply.

Originally, the battle centered about coal and iron; then came the race for the non-ferrous metals; later the struggle for the ferro-alloy metals became significant as the world entered the age of steel. Today the great prize is petroleum, accompanied since World War II by the global search for sources of nuclear fuels. Any further technological revolution would produce still another battle for control of any new critical material.

A state involved in this struggle—as almost all of them are—seeks initially to discover adequate resources located within its borders, either by discovery within its historic frontiers or by the annexation of new territory containing sufficient resource endowment. Failing in this objective, it attempts to control a source of supply by some other means. If that does not succeed, it makes such policy arrangements as will guarantee a supply.

This was substantially the procedure adopted by the government of the United States as it sought to guarantee itself sufficient raw materials for atomic bombs. Ultimately, the United States was forced to come to an almost pre-emptive purchase agreement with Belgium with regard to the uranium deposits in the Belgian Congo.

POWER

Viewed rationally, power is a means rather than an end in international politics; it is a method of achieving policy objectives rather than an objective in itself. As such, its detailed analysis belongs in a later chapter. Nevertheless, the record of international relations indicates that states, particularly large and powerful ones, do actually view the augmentation of their power as a legitimate power objective.

It may be a derived objective; that is, the increased power may be desired in order to make possible the attainment of other goals impossible without such an increase. When the search for power takes this form, it is relatively easy to control and more apt to be brought to an end when the original objective has been reached. On the other hand, the irrational elements in such factors as nationalism may and often do provoke a state to view power as a pure objective, an end in itself.

When a state sets out seriously to make a permanent improvement in its power position, it must do so at the direct or indirect expense of other states. This is a profoundly unsettling influence in world politics and tends to provoke reprisals and countermeasures. In that event, the search for power is likely to break loose from control and to become the only element in the policy of the state. The pursuit of power for its own sake may lead a state into extremely reckless adventures and is a major menace to peace. Statesmen whose only or principal concern is a continual search for more power should be aware of the dangerous course they are following. They may themselves be convinced of the validity of their policy, or they may be merely yielding to public pressure; in any case, they should realize that their course will meet growing resistance and, if continued to its logical conclusion, will inevitably lead to major war.

PRESTIGE AND IDEOLOGY

The preceding categories of policy objectives have all had some degree of precision and concreteness about them; at least, all were capable of being given specific content in terms of actual situations. The twin objectives of prestige and ideology, however, do not permit of such translation into realistic terms, but remain abstract, absolute, and imprecise no matter how vigorously they are pursued. Their consideration in this connection must therefore be in somewhat different terms.

Prestige. Prestige as an objective of national policy is a manifestation of extreme nationalism, and is a significant contribution to the dilemma in which the world finds itself today. A state seeks to augment its prestige and avoids action that might result in a lowering of it. In general terms there can be little to quarrel with in such an objective; most of us have some such goal in our private lives. It is in its application to specific international situations that the trouble comes about.

At times of crisis, when popular attitudes are the most inflamed, states find it increasingly difficult to adopt acceptable compromise solutions to particular disputes because of the fear that anything less than complete victory might result in a loss of 'face.' Exactly what real loss to national interest would arise from a diminished prestige is seldom made clear even if it were certain that a lessened prestige would actually result from the settlement of a dispute upon a basis of give-and-take. The insistence upon considerations of prestige is such that statesmen often find themselves unable and unwilling to take the risk.

A further difficulty is the tendency of national groups to view prestige in terms of certain traditional symbolic attitudes. Some of these that are familiar to us are 'no appeasement,' 'millions for defense but not one cent for tribute,' 'blood and sweat, tears and toil.' These are often inappropriate to the particular situation, but statesmen today are offered very little choice when confronted with these formulas. They must guard the national prestige jealously and continue to do so until popular passions become less sensitive and the opportunity again arises to follow more realistic policies.

Ideology. Ideology as an objective of policy also plagues the contemporary world as it has several earlier ages. An ideology may be viewed as the summary version of the fundamental truths which a people believe, or believe they believe, about themselves and the world. As such, ideologies serve a very useful purpose by providing norms of social behavior and by helping to bring about social stability within the state.

Ideologies have certain characteristics, however, that make their function as objectives of national policy extremely troublesome. Any ideology, as it becomes widely accepted, comes to be phrased in terms of moral absolutes, as a series of self-evident propositions eternally true and immutable. These beliefs are not viewed objectively, but instead are matters of passionate conviction. Thus any dissenter from an official ideology is not only in error, but is evil as well.

When a state, in promoting its ideology as an objective of policy, comes into conflict with another state doing the same thing (or with a state merely attempting to protect its own belief system) the conflict is bound to be sharp and one permitting no compromise. Ideological conflict is exceptionally bitter because it is fought in moral terms and in periods during which popular emotions are aroused. When ideological differences have led to war, as in the religious wars of the sixteenth century, the wars of the French Revolution, or the nineteenth-century struggle against the Ottoman Empire, the conflicts have usually been particularly bloody and devastating.

Were all the harsh words that arise out of a clash of ideologies translated into deeds, war would be perpetual. Statesmen, although realizing the unifying and propagandizing value of the ideology accepted by their people, are ever on the alert to avoid being swept away by it. A major task of a policy maker during period of crisis is to keep the temperature of his people safely below the boiling point so that their moral fervor will not express itself in ill-considered action.

In the modern world ideological war (war for ideological objectives) is most unlikely. The hazards of major conflict are such as to make it unwise or inexpedient for any state to take the risk for such an intangible and almost unattainable objective. Even if the war were to be won on the battlefield, the aftermath of recent wars has demonstrated that military defeat does not automatically carry with it a sense of moral turpitude in the defeated people. A war settles which of the disputing parties was military master of the other; it does not prove which of the combatants was 'right' in the moral sense. No nation can convince another of the correctness of its ideological position by defeating it in combat.

The Execution of Policy

In executing policy decisions, the statesman has a wide choice among techniques. The impact of international relations today extends into virtually all aspects of state life, and in appropriate circumstances almost any feature of state activity can become an effective instrument of policy.

The selection of techniques that are suited to the situation and that will achieve the desired objective is one of the most important and frequently recurring tasks of the statesman. His choice among methods is governed by many factors, including considerations of time, available resources of power, and other obligations he must sustain.

Although his choice among alternatives is wide, it is possible to reduce the means of execution of policy to a series of general categories. There is no specific pattern of techniques that all states follow; indeed, most governments use all of the following general techniques simultaneously, but not in the pursuit of all objectives. The choice of which one or combination of them is to be utilized is dependent upon particular conditions.

POLITICAL TECHNIQUES

The political technique for the execution of policy is diplomacy. Diplomacy is the medium through which official contact occurs between governments, and includes the exchange of views, the communication of decisions, the discovery of disagreement, and the reaching of agreement.

Through effective diplomacy it is possible for a state to bring influence to bear directly upon the decision-making personnel of other governments so as to have them act in the way the state's policy dictates. The diplomatic technique comprehends a broad variety of measures designed to convince statesmen of the expediency of submission and agreement, ranging from persuasion and offers of a *quid pro quo* to coercive and semi-coercive procedures. This latter classification includes such steps as the rupture of diplomatic relations, the withholding of recognition, the exclusion of the state from (or the inclusion of other states in) international bodies, or the abrupt breaking off of negotiations.

It is through the diplomatic medium that adjustments of policy are made known and the delicate arrangements necessary to keep the state system in operation are made. Diplomatic communication is the normal channel of interstate intercourse and is in constant use by all states. Its principal target is other statesmen, however, and its effectiveness is greatly reduced when it is confronted with a hostile public opinion.

PSYCHOLOGICAL TECHNIQUES

Psychological techniques involving the new science of mass communication are extremely effective in coping with this last situation. This is a more indirect method of attack upon policy, having as its object the creation of a public opinion in the other state which will force its government to act in the desired way. It operates in a variety of ways.

It is often effective for a government to stir up its own people against the policy of another state and then to confront the leaders of the latter state with the phenomenon of an outraged public opinion, accompanied by a hint that unless it complies, popular emotion will transcend restraint. This often rebounds, however, when both disputing governments have done the same thing and inflamed public feelings oppose each other. The governments involved are thus in danger of being forced by mass attitudes to take inexpedient action.

Pressure may also be brought directly upon the people of the other state by a variety of propaganda devices, with the general objective of alienating them from the policy of their government. It is not necessary that the people of the other state be brought into complete agreement with the propagandizing state, although this is usually the propagandist's dream. The technique is effective if it causes the people to lose faith in their government and its leadership, and if they fall to quarreling among themselves. A government losing the confidence of its people must devote its major energy to the recapture of their trust and in this way it is weakened in the degree of resistance it can offer to outside pressure. Hitler used this device with great effectiveness before World War II.

Communist propaganda since the war, although convincing very few Americans of the validity of the Soviet position, has succeeded to some extent in sowing distrust and in dividing Americans into mutually suspicious and hostile groups. The American government, aware of the lack of unanimous confidence in its integrity and in the wisdom of its policy, has been required to confine itself to steps which it knew would receive popular approval, even though great doubt might exist about their effectiveness. It also has felt obliged to omit from its policy some measures which, although possibly worth-while in themselves, public opinion was in no condition to accept.

ECONOMIC TECHNIQUES

Economic techniques of policy exist in bewildering variety. This approach is also indirect, aiming to influence policy makers in other states by the application, or by the threat, of measures to weaken the national economy and to destroy the standard of living of the people.

An almost limitless number of possible ways are available to bring this kind of pressure to bear. The economic interdependence of the world is such that any major interruption or diversion of the flow of international trade carries with it serious consequences. Yet, statesmen do not today have the same blithe confidence in economic instruments of policy that they had twenty or thirty years ago during the heyday of economic determinism. During the era of the League of Nations it was widely felt that economic measures—boycott, freezing of credits, deprivation of commercial facilities—would suffice to convince any potential aggressor of the folly of its course. The example of the dictators of the 1930's, who braved the possible application of economic sanctions and demonstrated that states can endure the effect of economic pressure, has seriously weakened the confidence with which economic techniques are viewed.

It seems accurate today to say that in special situations, such as existed in western Europe after V-E day, when the economy of the continent lay prostrate, the economic instrument is not only supreme but it may be the only effective one (it proved to be so for the United States). But this is true only occasionally. The economic technique is normally most successful when it is used in conjunction with the others and with judicious discretion. Perhaps no other means of executing policy so causes resentment on the part of the state that is its target, and no other so invites reprisal. The current world scene of embattled economic nationalisms offers proof of the facility with which economic weapons are turned back upon their users.

The forms which the economic instrument can take are myriad. Import and export restrictions, the granting or withholding of international loans and grants, the manipulation of transportation and communication facilities, the freezing of credits, and even such naked pressure as the offering or withholding of food supplies are only a few examples of the economic devices statesmen are using today. The variety of policy steps in this field is limited only by the economic strength of the state invoking them and the ingenuity of its leaders.

MILITARY TECHNIQUES

Finally, states have available to them what might be termed the physical instrumentality, that of military force. It has already become clear in our discussion that force lies at the root of any international relationship as it does in all political situations.

The socially sanctioned alternatives to force which dominate private life simply do not exist on the international plane and self-help involving violence is a much more normal event in international life than it is among private persons. From the point of view of making policy, statesmen must always allow for the fact that they might at any time be faced with the alternatives of abandoning a policy or of implementing it by violence. So long as each state remains the sole judge of the propriety of its actions, force is, and will remain, the ultimate determinant in international politics.

The Role of Force. It is therefore incumbent upon a policy maker constantly to be aware of the relative expediency of the use of the military instrument in any particular situation. It is not always necessary to engage in open combat on the battlefield in order to win an objective by military power; often it is sufficient to be willing to do so and to make that willingness known to the possible enemy. The threat of attack by superior force, whether conveyed bluntly or subtly, will often produce the desired agreement from an opponent without the necessity of shedding blood.

In this sense it is clear that the military establishment of a state exists not so much to defeat the enemy in the field as to assist in the gaining of political objectives by the state. It may be that this interest can best be served by earning a victory over the armed forces of the enemy, but in other circumstances battlefield success might impede or even prevent the accomplishment of the state's political purpose.

The potential effectiveness of the military power of a state also has an obvious influence upon the way any government uses the other three forms of policy techniques, as well as placing upper limits upon their effectiveness. It would be somewhat difficult for a militarily weak state to carry on a 'strong' diplomacy against a powerful state, since the pressure it exerted would be conditioned by its limited capacity to support it. So also with the psychological and economic instruments. No powerful state will permit propaganda harassment or economic warfare against it by a minor neighbor to continue for long if either were to become a serious annoyance.

Limiting the Use of Force. One large part of the history of international relations is formed by the story of man's attempts to find a method of eliminating or limiting the use of the military instrument. States have solemnly renounced war in general terms as 'an instrument of national policy,' and particular pairs or groups of states have agreed to the pacific settlement of disputes arising among them.

Nevertheless, today the right of each state to go to war with its neighbor for any reason at all (or for none) is as perfect as ever. The United Nations has attempted to deprive states of some of their freedom in this respect, but the effectiveness of the prohibitions of the Charter depends not upon universal principles but upon the interacting interests of the members of the organization. The question of war or peace in any situation is answered by the same agency that has answered it for centuries—the national states themselves.

Some success has accompanied the effort to mitigate the severity of the application of the military weapon. Rules governing various aspects of warfare —the treatment of prisoners of war, the prohibition of certain weapons, the security from bombardment of 'open' and undefended cities, and the like— have been agreed upon by governments and in practice have been fairly well observed.

Less successful have been proposals for the reduction of armaments, since each state tends to view disarmament by another as an opportunity to gain a relative advantage over that state. Consequently it has been impossible to reach significant agreement.

The Growing Inexpediency of Force. Although states remain able to employ the physical instrumentality as freely as any other, the increasing destructiveness of even a victorious war has made statesmen quite reluctant to call it into operation. The upshot of this development has been that the effectiveness of the military technique of foreign policy has been strangely reduced in recent years.

It would be difficult, for example, to point to any victories gained by the United States during the period in which it enjoyed a 'monopoly' over the atomic bomb which are due only to that military advantage. Since no dispute arose during that time which made the use of such extreme measures appropriate, the opponents of the United States had no reasons to fear the bomb. So it has been with other states and other weapons. It is difficult today for a policy maker to use only a little force; the technology of modern warfare is so complex that there is a powerful tendency toward pushing violence to the ultimate once it has been called into play.

Consequently, since no violence is practical except total violence, and since states are not easily persuaded to risk so much for any objectives except those that are truly vital, physical force is not a really ponderable factor in great power relationships today, in most circumstances. Without the willingness to resort to the only final determining factor, it is no wonder that so much of international politics today is in a state of uneasy stalemate.

4

National Power

REFERENCE was made in Chapter 3 to the fact that force remains the ultimate determinant in world politics. A state is therefore seriously limited in its choice of objectives by the maximum effort it can put forth in their achievement. There are no automatic mechanisms in international politics which guarantee to a state possession of what it ought to have or what it has a right to. States are able to gain and keep only those things which they are strong enough to acquire and retain. States differ in their capability to attain objectives; some have adequate means to work major changes in the international scene by their own efforts, while others have so little power as to be unable by themselves to bring about any alterations in the course of world affairs.

The closer we look at international politics the more we are impressed by the extent to which the power of states influences the objectives and policies selected by them. Since power varies so much from state to state and since it plays such a critical role in determining the course of events, an appreciation of what national power is, what exactly is its role in world politics, what it is composed of, and how it is measured is indispensable.

THE CONCEPT OF POWER

National power is the capacity of a state to exert coercive influence upon other states and to resist such influence exerted by other states upon it.

The critical notion in the concept of power is obviously the element of coercion. When a state is able to achieve its purposes by argument, persuasion, or other means of securing free agreement from other states, such success frequently bears little relationship to the power it possesses. To qualify as a purely power relationship, one of the parties involved must be forced by superior strength to act contrary to his free choice. Therefore not all international situations are governed by power considerations. When there is indentity of interest between states their relations go forward relatively free of any coercive content.

We already know, however, that identity of interest between states is an unusual condition, and when it occurs it is usually of short duration. Most international relationships, including all crisis situations, are motivated by the criteria of power. Normally one can expect that the state with the greatest power at its disposal will enjoy the greatest freedom of action, with the policies of the others determined by their relative rank as power entities.

POWER IN POLITICS

Of course international politics is not unique in its reliance upon power as a motivating force. All political relationships are power relationships to varying extents. Political behavior at whatever level involves the dual functions of commanding and obeying, and political science divides the members of a political community into two groups, the governors and the governed. The problem of government at any time is that of determining appropriate commands to give to the mass of the people and then securing obedience to them. The element of physical coercion distinguishes political life from all other forms of organized social behavior. Men are constantly being forced to subordinate their personal wishes to those who speak in the name of the state and have the power to compel obedience. Political coercion takes place with the approval of society as being in the public interest.

Although most of the decisions of government are taken in full expectation of general compliance, public officers must always recognize the certainty that some disobedience will take place. In dealing with disobedience the state is free to use all forms of power, including the ultimate sanction of physical violence. The right to take such action has been conferred upon the government by the governed in recognition of the fact that it is socially desirable that order be preserved and that disorderly people be restrained.

A further concern of government is the ever-present possibility of mass disobedience—that is, revolution. Knowing that the people retain the power to bring down any government simply by refusing to obey it tempers the extremes of even the most authoritarian regime. Violence, the ultimate form of political power, is thus potentially a factor present in every political situation.

Differences between Domestic and International Power. There are certain major differences in the role of power in domestic affairs and in international politics. In civil societies there exist a number of alternatives to violence. Men have discovered that one of the outcomes of living together in groups is that they can no longer afford to govern their relations with each other purely by the verdicts of physical strength. Accordingly a system of general rules and procedures (which we call laws) has been adopted by each society to establish not only the rights and freedoms of individuals but also the non-violent procedures they are to follow in securing redress of their wrongs. Individuals no longer have the right in most civilizations to be their own law-enforcement agencies—'taking the law into one's own hands' is usually thought to be an antisocial act. Stipulated procedures prevent individuals from engaging in indiscriminate acts of violence; the justified application of naked coercion is largely monopolized by the state acting in the name of the community. Thus violence as a means of reconciling differences of opinion is reasonably far in the background in civilized societies and alternative methods are more commonly relied upon for the settlement of differences.

In international relations, owing to the lack of generally agreed-upon rules and devices to serve as substitutes, the only ultimately efficacious means a state possesses to protect its rights and to rectify injuries is violence. The non-violent methods that exist lack both sufficient group sanction and the operating mechanisms of enforcement necessary to make them work.

International politics does not go on within a superstructure of institutions so elaborate as that of domestic politics. The international community is a primitive and incomplete one with only rudimentary institutions to provide some stability. During periods of relative calm the imperfect structure provides widely accepted non-violent procedures based upon custom; in a time of crisis there is a constant danger that it will all break down. When this happens, techniques are extemporized to cope with a rapidly changing situation and often these prove ineffective. A state is thus afforded institutional protection in non-crisis situations, but it has no certain recourse except unilateral action when serious danger impends. Lacking the 'cushion' of institutions, international politics must thus operate with a more fundamental trust in naked coercion than is necessary in domestic affairs.

THE CHANNELS OF POWER

Political power at any level can be viewed as the capacity to force individuals to behave in a prescribed manner. There are several clear channels through which power is applied to its objects. In both international and domestic politics, power may be physical, economic, or psychological, depending upon which form of pressure is utilized to secure obedience.

Physical Power. The physical channel of power involves the application or the threat of application of personal violence to individuals, either to force compliance with directives or to punish non-compliance. It may be applied to particular individuals, to groups of people, or to an entire population. It is clear that the physical is the ultimate form of coercion.

We have seen that in international politics the primacy of physical power is even clearer than in domestic affairs. In civil society one often is in a situation where he cannot escape the application of economic or psychological power; in international affairs a state need never accept as final a decision reached by economic or psychological means if it wishes to put the issue to the test of physical strength—that is, to go to war. The lack of institutions and

accepted alternatives to violence in international politics—alluded to earlier
—illustrates the lesser role played by non-physical power in the relations of
states.

Economic Power. Economic power in politics has a dual effect. It secures
obedience either by granting economic rewards or by imposing economic
hardships upon its objects.

In private life economic pressures are often devastatingly effective, particularly so in modern, tightly knit, industrialized societies. They cover a wide
range of techniques, including all forms of man's multifarious economic ac-
tivites. In international affairs they are much relied upon but are applicable
most generally as supplementary to other forms of power except in the special cases when they are peculiarly suited to the conditions.

Usually economic power in international relations draws much of its
strength from the physical power of the state invoking the economic weapon.
States, in other words, yield to economic power of other states because it is
less unpleasant to do so than to undergo the application of physical coercion.
This is not to underestimate the impact of economic power, but rather once
again to stress the key role of violence and force in world affairs. Conversely,
the less likely the international situation is to break down into war, the more
effective economic power becomes.

Psychological Power. Psychological power in politics is fundamental in
many ways. No government can long survive if every person obeys each command only because of his fear of the consequences of disobedience. Government, in order to endure, requires an affirmative character; the people must
obey most of the time because they want to, or in any case without even
considering the possibility of disobedience. Particular attention is paid by
political leaders to the problem of securing consensus from the people; usually a government is more concerned with this than it is with the application
of coercive violence to disobedient individuals. This involves a liberal use of
a variety of forms of psychological pressure upon the people, which can be
thought of as education and propaganda. Plato pointed out that if this task
were performed to perfection no government would ever need to use violence,
and laws would be useless and unnecessary.

Even in as aboriginal a society as the international community, psychological power is of great importance. The object of warfare is to 'destroy the
enemy's will to resist' and to have him agree with you; obviously it is just as effective and much less inconvenient to secure agreement by psychological
rather than physical means.

As a result governments today use the psychological form of power in a
broad range of ways. Propaganda has won some important and spectacular
victories in modern times and the cold war today is marked by great propaganda efforts on both sides. The application of psychological power has certain limitations, however, in international politics. The problem of making

propaganda intelligible to another people of a differing culture and value system is a very difficult one, particularly when that people are probably subject to a constant barrage of 'information' from their own government.

There seem to have been two major effects derived from the recent increase in the intensity of international propaganda. Public opinion in most states has closed ranks behind the respective governments and people turn a deaf ear to all appeals from abroad; on the other hand, in some special instances propaganda techniques have served to separate a population from its government by undermining popular confidence, making the government concerned less able to resist the physical power of the propagandizing state. A good deal of the Nazi success in crushing France in 1940 stemmed from the successful German propaganda.

The Role of Power in International Politics

It has already been indicated that national power and the interrelations of states that have varying amounts of power at their disposal gives international politics its dominant coloration. In one form or another all international disputes tend to become power struggles and the only final settlements possible arise from the interaction of the factors of national power. Since states agree with each other only when their interests coincide or when forced to do so by superior power, it follows that any particular dispute will be resolved generally in terms of the commitments of power made by the disputing parties.

All states have some power with which they back their policy, and unless one state completely crushes its opponent in a war, most disputes end in some form of compromise based upon the investment of power made by each side. Although occasional exceptions may be found, this last point is a general principle which serves to explain much in international politics that would otherwise be confusing.

Power Calculations Made by Statesmen. Statesmen in planning and executing a foreign policy are eternally preoccupied with questions of power. It is of the utmost importance that a policy maker always have a realistic picture of the capabilities of his state to execute any decisions he might make. He must know his state's strength, weakness, and vulnerabilities and be aware of its military, economic, and psychological position with regard to other states. He must be aware of the extent to which the power of his state is already committed and of how much he has in reserve to meet unexpected crises. Equally as critical, he must have the same sort of information about all the other states with which he maintains relations, despite the great difficulty of obtaining such data. Statesmen measure the impact of each change in the international situation upon the power position of their own and of all other states. Objectives desirable in themselves are modified or abandoned entirely because of inadequate power to attain them, while others are often pursued simply because under existing conditions they are easily reached.

If a system of world law governed interstate relations there would be much less need for such a preoccupation. In civil life the rights individuals enjoy are usually independent of their capacity personally to defend them, but in international politics a state is absolutely secure in its freedom only to the extent that it is capable of unilaterally guaranteeing it. Statesmen must thus always be aware of the impact of power upon their own policy and that of all other states, and fit their program into the peculiar pattern imposed by it.

CRITICAL ASPECTS OF POWER

Certain aspects of the concept of power are always kept in mind by statesmen engaged in its analysis and evaluation. Three of these will be considered in some detail: the relative character of power, the changing nature of power, and the variable relationship between actual power and potential power. All of them illustrate the fact that national power in international affairs is not a simple and automatic regulatory mechanism, but is instead a complex and imprecise motion requiring much intense and constant application to make it useful.

THE RELATIVITY OF POWER

Power Relative to Other States. Power is not an absolute; there is no such thing as a 'powerful' state in a vacuum. Power is the means by which a state accomplishes its objectives in dealing with other states. Therefore, a state is more or less powerful than other states, when compared with them, or it is powerful or not in terms of its ability or inability to reach its objectives.

It is a common enough error to conceive of 'power' as a condition which a state seeks to achieve, but by itself the term is meaningless. Is a state such as Italy powerful? Obviously one cannot give an unqualified answer. Italy is a powerful state as far as Egypt or Peru or Thailand or Iceland is concerned, but it is a weak state from the point of view of the United States or the Soviet Union. Consequently a state's power is meaningful only in terms of the state or states by which it is measured.

This simple fact has a profound influence upon the calculations of policy makers. They maintain a close watch upon the power situation as it affects all states, but pay particular attention to the states with which they maintain close relations and those with which they are in dispute or are likely to become so. They make a constant attempt to keep the power balance tipped in their favor as regards those particular states even though this might necessitate weakening themselves as regards other states with which their relations are less intimate. Whether Ecuador is more powerful than Thailand is largely academic, but whether Ecuador is more powerful than Colombia is of the utmost importance to both the latter states. Power as a concept gains real content only when the power relationships of two or more states are compared.

Power Relative to the Objective Sought. In like manner power is also relative to the objectives a state is seeking. A state possessing adequate power to achieve its policy objectives is a powerful state, regardless of how much total power it has available or how its power compares with that of other states. Such a state is termed 'satiated'; it has achieved its objectives and now aims only to maintain its favorable position. Switzerland, for example, is regarded as a powerful state. It has a policy based upon its interest in maintaining the *status quo* as it sees it, and has adequate power to sustain its consequent policy of neutrality and trade. In so far as the concept of power has any intelligibility, Switzerland is a powerful state.

In the same way a state that is seeking objectives beyond its capabilities is weak and cannot be classed as powerful. Nazi Germany in late 1940, for example, dominated the European continent and controlled an aggregate power that dwarfed that of any other individual state in the world. Yet the Nazi policy demanded more than even Germany's enviable position in 1940 could furnish, and the effort destroyed the state.

Undercommitment and Overcommitment of Power. A further point must be made about the relativity of power. A state should apportion its power according to its objective. If a state undercommits itself and fails to support its pursuit of an objective with adequate power it will fail in its policy and all the power it did invest will be wasted.

This is well understood; much less widely comprehended is the converse of the proposition. Overcommitment of power is just as wasteful and often as disastrous as undercommitment. Any excess of power beyond what is necessary is useless and accomplishes no purpose. On the contrary, overcommitment often involves a state in policy steps beyond what its interest dictates and it gets entangled in the pursuit of worthless objectives or, what is worse, none at all. In addition, overcommitment of power usually requires the taking away of power from the support of another policy in order to use it unnecessarily.

In modern international politics, where most states are committed to the practical limit, any such overcommitment means that some other policy must of necessity suffer. Not very many states today can afford to allow one policy to fail while using the power that might save it to accomplish no useful purpose in another quarter. A statesman makes a constant effort to balance as accurately as possible the power requirements of any policy decision with his actual power commitments. True, a state always seeks to overcommit itself slightly in order to leave a margin for unexpected developments; however, this margin must necessarily be small and is calculated with great care.

THE CHANGING QUALITY OF POWER

Power is not a permanent and unchanging entity but is instead in a process of constant change. Some of the greatest policy blunders in history have come about as a result of a statesman's assumption that a given power relationship would endure indefinitely, or that factors that produced a power advantage in one situation would produce the same advantage in different circumstances.

The United States, enjoying a power superiority over the USSR at the end of World War II because of the 'monopoly' of atomic weapons, implicitly assumed in its policy that this advantage would continue permanently and had no alternative procedures available to cope with a changed relationship. Soviet mastery of atomic techniques forced the American government to improvise new policies reflecting the altered power situation. Another example of such a miscalculation of the permanence of power is furnished by the Nazi belief that the *blitzkreig* tactics that were so effective against the West in 1940 would be equally as devastating against the Russian armies in 1941.

Rapidity of Change. Actually, change in power relationships is only a special instance of the relativity of the whole concept. Each state's power is in a constant process of alteration, either developing or declining. No state can stand still in terms of power.

When we analyze the factors of power it becomes clear how many aspects of national existence affect the power position of a state. No two states are developing in power in the same way or at the same rate. As a result of this highly dynamic situation, the relations of any one state to any other are being perpetually modified. To push the point to an extreme, the power situation of Japan and China, for example, is not the same at this moment as it was five minutes ago. In one state or the other more babies were born, more technology mastered, more guns manufactured, more resources discovered; all of these and many other factors have a direct bearing upon the relative power relations.

Even more subject to rapid change are the intangible elements in national power. Such evanescent and immeasurable things as popular morale or political stability are vulnerable to a variety of pressures and may change in their effect with great speed from sources of strength to sources of weakness.

Policy Safeguards against Change in Power. It is not an exaggeration to say that any power calculation in international affairs is out of date as soon as it is made. No human judgment can keep up with all the factors that affect national power, and all the information that comes to the attention of statesmen and upon which they base their judgments is outdated by the rapid march of events. Nevertheless, decisions must be made.

The most any policy maker can do is not only to estimate the power situation at any given moment but also to attempt a projection into the future of the power status of all states involved, taking into account the trends of development as they exist. Of course this technique ignores sudden changes in conditions which might create new situations, but an attempt is made to cope with this factor also. In so far as possible a statesman seeks to leave open what might be called escape routes: alternative policies with adequate power support are held in reserve to be used in case sudden shifts in the situation make different tactics necessary.

Irrevocable power commitments are avoided whenever possible, being entered into only under extreme compulsion or when significant change in the over-all situation is unlikely. Finally, it may be repeated that policy decisions by a state are usually based upon providing a little more power than it is hoped will be needed, either actually committed or held in reserve. In all these ways statesmen seek to allow for the changing quality of power.

ACTUAL AND POTENTIAL POWER

Varying Bases for Power Judgments. Another special aspect of the relativity of power is the varying relationship among the total potential of a state, its actual available power, and the proportion of its available power it is willing and able to commit in support of any particular policy. Power comparisons of states may be and often are made in terms of each of these criteria.

Each method of comparison is valuable for a different purpose, and statesmen employ the technique appropriate to the nature of the comparison or analysis in which they may be involved. The measurement of power in terms of the total theoretical potential of a state is of particular value in making projections for the long-range future course of world politics and of considerable significance in estimating the possible outcome of a long and total war in which a state would be expected to muster as much of the theoretical total of its power as would be practical. The comparison of states in terms of their actual available power provides some guidance in predicting the short- and middle-range developments of world affairs. It also has relevance in isolating major power disparities among various states and thus in providing a means to determine probable future crisis areas.

An analysis of the power that states have available for commitment in a particular situation is the most frequent and useful form of power judgment. Regardless of theoretical potential or the available totality of power, only rarely is a state able to throw more than a portion of its power behind the support of any single policy. It is this portion of a state's power that is involved in any particular dispute and usually controversies between states are settled in terms of partial commitments of power. Only in wars of survival do states seek to put everything they have at the service of a single policy.

To say that disputes are settled generally in terms of the relative power commitments of the states involved is not to say that the more powerful state always gains its objective. Indeed, the opposite is often true, provided the lesser state is able to apply more pressure than the larger one in the given situation. Such, for example, was the outcome of the quarrel between Egypt and Great Britain in 1953 and 1954 over the presence of British troops in the Suez Canal Zone. Although Britain's total power far surpassed that of Egypt, the immediate power advantage lay with Egypt and Britain ultimately withdrew its armed forces.

The Time Factor. There is obviously a time factor at work in this connection. A state may increase the power it has available for commitment in any particular dispute, or it may translate a larger proportion of its potential into power-in-being. To do either of these things, however, requires time.

To add to the power supporting any particular policy without increasing the total available power usually involves withdrawing some elements of power presently engaged in executing another policy. This normally requires many policy adjustments in several areas before it can be consummated, often a slow and painful process. Likewise, to mobilize more potential power is not an undertaking that can be carried through to completion by any state without much planning and preparation, and the actual implementation of the decision is better carried out in stages rather than all at once.

Statesmen, making power calculations in the midst of a dispute, are sensitive to the time factor as it affects their own and other states. If a state has a sufficient immediate power advantage to press a dispute to a decision before its opponent can mobilize its potential superiority, it may be inclined to risk the change in the face of adverse odds in terms of total potential.

Germany took such a gamble twice in the twentieth century, but both in 1917 and in 1941 the German leaders miscalculated the rapidity of United States mobilization. In each instance they hoped to force a decision before American power could be brought into being in sufficient quantity to be decisive. Inability accurately to assess the time factor brought them defeat.

Variation from State to State. The relationship between potential power and actual power varies widely from state to state. One state may have vast potential but may be unable or unwilling to gain, or uninterested in maintaining, a high level of actual power. Such was the condition of the United States from 1920 to 1939. Others may have a much smaller potential but will keep a greater proportion of it in readiness at all times and thus cut a larger figure in world politics than a state of the first group. Pre-war Italy and Japan were both only meagerly endowed with the resources of power, but so much of what they had was in a state of permanent mobilization that they were among the giants of their day.

It is in time of war that states will attempt to narrow the gap between potential and actual power. The experience of World War II provided much data upon how effectively this task can be accomplished. It is clear that there is at best a great discrepancy between the theoretical potential of a state and the practical maximum of power it can bring into being.

No state can hope to realize its entire potential or even approach it; the requirements of the civilian population cannot be ignored. Even such totalitarian states as Nazi Germany and the Soviet Union discovered that a substantial portion of industrial production, transportation facilities, and human effort had to go into civilian and 'non-political' activity in order to maintain a sufficiently high level of morale. In the United States, although major changes were made in the civilian way of life, the greatest total power mobilization of all time went on alongside a civilian standard of living which surpassed that of peacetime levels in most of the other parts of the world. Theoretical potential is an unreliable guide to the actual power a state will make available, since so many factors peculiar to the particular society will govern the ratio it maintains between potential and realized power.

FACTORS OF NATIONAL POWER

Tangible and Intangible Factors. When we attempt to enumerate the many and various factors that enter into the power of a state it is soon apparent that 'power' is not a fixed quantity or a concrete commodity. The factors of power are both tangible and intangible, and each contributes to the over-all power of a state in a manner unique for that state. Furthermore, the factors are of unequal weight when applied to different states, and each interacts upon all the others. Power defies exact analysis; the most that policy makers can do is to make their judgments reflect as completely as possible reliable information and objective analysis.

The factors of power involve many aspects of state life, and power comparisons are therefore very difficult. One state may have great resource endowment but little military strength; another may have poor resources but great industry; a third, poor industry but a highly mobilized military machine. Which is the most powerful and which the least powerful? No general answer can be given, for power relationships among them would in practice vary depending upon the nature of any dispute and the over-all policies each state was following. Yet, making power comparisons, often as frustrating as comparing apples with typewriters or portraits with ball bearings, is an essential task of the practicing statesman. Without it international politics could not proceed.

The discussion of the factors of power that follows is best understood if it is considered as an enumeration of the various ways in which a state is viewed when an over-all power verdict is sought. The state's situation is analyzed with regard to the impact of each of the factors, and a judgment is reached regarding the extent to which each contributes strength or weakness. The extent to which each of them modifies the others is estimated, positive and negative results are balanced, and a general and final power judgment is reached.

Of course the process is seldom carried out in its entirety for any single state; each government in the world has made such an estimate long ago of the power of every other state, and it keeps all of them in a state of constant revision as new information keeps coming to light. Within this framework of power judgments a statesman moves, accepting objectives, devising policies to achieve them, and committing power to their support.

No Single All-important Power Factor. Although each of the factors of power obviously conditions the total power of the state, there have been many attempts made to argue that one or another was the single significant determinant of power relationships and the course of world affairs. Thus some geopoliticians argue that the geographic conditions of international politics are controlling; certain demographers see world politics as a struggle between peoples and find certain 'races' bound to dominate; there is a 'raw material' school of international affairs which claims that resources endowments govern power and all of world politics is merely a struggle for additional reserves; most common is the assumption that national power is synonymous with military power and thus power relationships are determined entirely by military strength-in-being. Similar contentions have been advanced in behalf of several other power factors.

Despite the great ingenuity with which the arguments are presented and the impressive accumulation of historical and logical evidence buttressing all such theories, we are safe in rejecting any simple single-factor formula for determining the power position of a state. Some components of power may be more critical than others in special situations and for particular states, but each of the nine factors discussed below has a direct bearing upon the vigor which a state prosecutes its policy. Statesmen rely upon them all as tools of analysis.

TANGIBLE FACTORS OF POWER

The tangible factors of national power are five: geographic situation, population and manpower, natural resources, industrial and agricultural production, and military organization. Because of their more obvious and immediate relation to the concept of national power it is appropriate that we begin our analysis with the visible and concrete factors that enter into it.

GEOGRAPHY

Power Aspects of Geography: Size and Shape. The state occupies a determinate portion of the earth's surface, and naturally geographic situation and configuration directly influence national power. No two states have the same geographic conditions of national life and consequently the impact of the geographic factor is different in every case. Certain geographic conditions are basic.

The size of the state is of great pertinence in its power situation. In the past states of small area have become great powers, but modern requirements of defense, dispersal, and organization place the small state at a real disadvantage. Today the major powers of the world are of continental (or sub-continential) expanse, as are most states likely to attain major status in the foreseeable future.

The shape of the state also has power significance. Ideally the perfect state is compact, with the minimum frontier commensurate with maximum area. Irregularly shaped or discontinuous states have problems of defense and internal communication that weaken their total power. France is a good example of compactness; Chile is the archtype of the poorly shaped state, being 2600 miles long and averaging approximately 100 miles in width.

Location. Location is a geographic criterion of obvious significance. Whether a state is insular, penninsular, coastal, landlocked, or continental automatically creates conditions of advantage or disadvantage which are fundamental to all subsequent power judgments. The insular and peninsular states naturally must give great concern to their sea defenses; the landlocked state can concentrate upon land armaments. The coastal state must operate in both areas. The histories of both Great Britain and Japan have definitely been affected by their insular location; the virtually landlocked situation of Russia has governed much of the policy and limited the effective power of successive Russian governments.

Topography. Topography is another geographic fact of immediate relevance to national power. The nature of a state's frontiers, whether 'natural' (rivers, mountain ranges, or oceans) and therefore easy to defend, or 'artificial' and presumably very much less defensible, tends to control much of the power planning of any state. The internal formation of the land again affects total power. If the interior of a state is of relatively easy access, efficient and economic means of transportation can be utilized with a consequent advantage. If the topography is broken so that a great amount of energy is required to move people and materials from place to place, to that extent the state is handicapped.

The topography of the United States is generally thought to be favorable in this regard, while that of China, where mountains, deserts, valleys, and rivers cut the country up into many smaller parts, is detrimental. Sometimes a broken terrain is a source of power advantage if the state is small and under constant threat of invasion. Switzerland and Norway each has made its rugged landscape an element of strength.

Climate and Neighbors. Climate is somewhat less obvious in its effect, although all the great powers of modern times have enjoyed temperate climate, and much interesting speculation has gone on in regard to the controling effect of climate upon national development. Certainly extremes of weather have a debilitating effect upon national power; it is quite a good deal more trouble to mobilize great amounts of power in conditions of extreme heat or extreme cold, of aridity or tropic rainfall, than in more moderate and varied climates.

A final factor, only partly geographic, might be included in this list. A state's neighbors affect its power position directly. If a state is surrounded by large and more dynamic states, it is in a much less favorable position in terms of power than it would be with weak and passive neighbors.

Permanence of Geographic Factors. Generally speaking, geographic factors are the most permanent of all of those entering into a state's power position. They can change; canals and bridges can be constructed, rivers diverted, mountain barriers pierced, deserts irrigated; but change in the physical conditions of a state's existence can be at most only relatively minor. What does undergo great modification, however, is the significance of any geographic fact in relation to the entire power picture. Developments in technology have altered many of the geographic bases of world politics. Water frontiers were formerly viewed as extremely strong; today many consider them a weakness. The sea is now more of a highway of aggression than it is a bastion. Modern transportation—land, sea, and air—makes light of once formidable obstacles. As a result geographic factors in power must be constantly revised so as to take account of the changing technological picture.

Geopolitics. Mention must be made of the attempt at the scientific study of the relationship of geography to world politics. Geopolitics, as this field is known, is a discipline somewhat in disrepute today because of its abuse by the Nazis preceding and during World War II. Nevertheless its contributions to the understanding of international affairs have been numerous and its point of view has had a real impact upon the foreign policies of contemporary states.

There are two broad schools of geopolitical thought: the sea-power point of view, which places emphasis upon the control of the waterways of the world; and the land-power or 'Heartland' theory, which asserts the dominant role of certain critical land masses.

Mahan and Sea Power. The sea-power approach is usually identified with the name of Admiral Alfred Thayer Mahan of the United States, who, about 1890, brilliantly expounded the thesis. He argued that owing to the greater mobility and economy of sea transportation, states that were tied to the land were forever doomed to inferiority to states enjoying naval supremacy. Under the technological conditions of his day the land depended upon seaborne commerce for its very existence and the states that possessed the ability to conduct, permit, or prohibit this trade were by that fact the masters of the landsmen. He drew upon military, naval, and economic history to prove his point and discovered that the key to British success in achieving its nineteenth-century hegemony was its understanding and application of these principles.

The Mahan theory entered into its period of eclipse once the technical problems of land transportation began to yield solutions to the internal combustion engine, hard surfaced highways, railways, and the airplane. Today, although naval might is yet a powerful element in world politics, the pure form of the sea-power thesis has few defenders.

Mackinder and the Heartland. The 'Heartland' doctrine is intimately connected with Sir Halford Mackinder, the British geographer, who was most influential after 1920. Mackinder thought of the land masses of the world as having a relationship to each other and out of this relationship grew the controlling forces of world politics. He considered the Eurasian continent, plus Africa north of the Sahara, as the heart of the world, and termed it the 'World Island.' Here was gathered the great bulk of the man-power and resources of the globe and here everything significant in world politics took place. The remainder of the land of the world he considered as satellite islands surrounding the World Island. The Island itself he divided into two parts. The first was the center, or 'Heartland,' which was beyond the reach of sea power, was protected by many natural barriers from the coastal areas, and which possessed human and material resources superior to those of any other region. The remainder of the World Island he called the 'Rimland'; its dominant characteristic was its division into many small states.

Within the Heartland proper there was a further geographic division of men and resources; eastern Europe was the critical area. From this breakdown he derived his famous summary of the lesson of geopolitics: 'Who rules East Europe commands the Heartland; Who rules the Heartland commands the World-Island; Who rules the World-Island commands the World.'

Later scholars have disagreed with Mackinder's granting of actual and potential supremacy to the Heartland and have challenged both his minimizing of the United States and his underestimation of the strength and power of self-determination of the Rimland states. He made some later modifications in his theory in the direction of meeting these criticisms. Nevertheless his evocation of the geographic fundamentals of politics has had permanent influence. Unless and until his judgments are overturned by later technological developments, they promise to continue to serve—as they do today in the cold war—as determinants of much of the foreign policy of major and minor states alike. This is especially true of American policy toward the Soviet, which draws much of its inspiration from Russia's Heartland position and the requirements for coping with it.

POPULATION AND MANPOWER

Size of Populations. International politics, like any social study, is concerned with people; quite naturally, therefore, the human resources of any state bear directly upon its national power. A state must have a minimum number of inhabitants before it can aspire to major status; the tasks of modern political life are so numerous and so varied and are performed upon such a great scale that a really small population is not able to do them all. Both industrial production and manning a modern military machine require vast numbers of people.

The exact size of the minimum necessary population to form the base for a major power is of course indeterminate; we may gain some inkling, however, by correlating present and potential great powers with population levels. The United States, the Soviet Union, India, and China all have populations of over one hundred million, while such formerly great states as Great Britain, France, and Italy are unable to play really strong roles with populations in the neighborhood of fifty to sixty million. Under present conditions it would seem that the critical number lies somewhere between the two figures. Power calculations involving manpower judgments proceed from the general assumption that the larger the population, the greater the power.

Quality of Populations. This is subject to more refined analysis, however, in terms of the quality of the population. Certain criteria are apparent: sex distribution, age distribution, and general health and vigor. Clearly a population of fifty million of which thirty-five million were women, children, and aged would be less of a source of strength than one of forty million which contained eighteen million men in the military and productive age groups. Other less obvious considerations must be taken into account. The 'efficiency' of the population in terms of education and technical training (treated below in more detail), popular habituation to the tight organization and close contacts of modern society, and cohesiveness in accepting a common leadership and set of values, all bear directly upon the contribution that the population will make to the potential and actual power of the state.

Trends in Population Development. It is vital in making long-range power calculations to estimate the trends of population development. Demographic science has progressed to the point where projections of future population can be made with a reasonable degree of accuracy. These trends are constant in their effect unless upset by radical change in the conditions of life in a given society, such as technological revolution, epidemic disease, birth control, or war.

When the demographic history of all states is examined with a view to determining the cycle of population development, a striking relationship appears between population and industrialization. A three-stage process seems to be common.

Stage I, the pre-industrialized era, is characterized by a stable population kept virtually at the maximum supportable by the food supply. Birth and death rates are high and balance each other, the life expectancy and life span are low, and the population is concentrated in the younger age groups. This is the present state of the populations of India, China, and south east Asia generally.

Stage II occurs when industrialization and urbanization appear and make their effects felt in the society. As modern technology is applied to the problems of health, food supply, and industrial production, death rates drop rapidly. Since the society, by the increased production or exchange of commodities, can sustain more people, birth rates continue high, the life span increases significantly, and the population grows most rapidly. This results in a continued concentration of people in the younger age groups and at this time the state's manpower situation is at its peak. Eventually, as the life span continues to grow longer and the standard of living maintains its rise, the rate of increase in the birth rate begins to fall. Although the population continues to grow because death rates drop even more rapidly, the population begins to age perceptibly and the manpower situation is deteriorating. The United States is often regarded as being in the latter part of stage II; the Soviet Union is only well into it.

Stage III is the period of stabilization or decline in population. Birth rates fall until they match death rates; both continue low and the population no longer increases. Instead, it concentrates more and more in the older age groups and eventually birth rates may drop below death rates and an absolute decline sets in. France and several other western European states exhibit the characteristics of this state of affairs.

By these calculations the USSR and eastern Europe generally are due for great population increase in the near future. followed later by an even more extensive increase in Asia. On the contrary the United States and western Europe are in a relatively and absolutely unfavorable situation, with only a slight increase in prospect before the onset of stabilization. Even the last ten years, however, have provided evidence that these population trends are not inflexible and that social patterns can and do change. The United States birth rate, after many years of decline, reversed itself during World War II and the 'baby boom' thus created has caused all projections of American population to be sharply revised upward. France, by a deliberate government policy, has halted the drop in the birth rate and made large families fashionable once again.

These efforts are cumulative in their effects (since an increased birth rate produces larger numbers of prospective parents) and can completely alter the future prospect in the space of a single generation. In like manner any major technological change, such as that promised by atomic energy, could make all population predictions obsolete and begin the cycle all over again for many states.

RESOURCES

Modern national power is largely industrial power, and modern industry consists of the application of energy to raw materials. Resources of energy and raw materials are of great importance in national power and their lack proved fatal to the great power aspirations of such states as Italy and Japan.

Resources alone are not the key to power—many states with great re-source endowments are not very important in world affairs—but great power without guaranteed access to adequate raw materials is unthinkable. The key resources of modern times are coal and iron.

Coal. Coal is the principal source of energy for industrial processes and states without ample supplies are hard put to it to improvise substitutes. Petroleum, hydro-electric power, wood, and other energy sources occupy an important place in the hierarchy of raw materials but they cannot replace coal. There is much informed speculation about the eventual replacement of coal as the principal energy source by atomic power. There remain many formidable technical difficulties with which to deal, but if atomic energy should become a major source of industrial power many contemporary political judgments would have to be revised.

Iron and Steel. Iron and steel are the fundamental components of the great part of modern industrial production. The age of steel demands pro-duction of many forms of steel products as the inescapable prerequisite for national power. If a state lacks either coal or iron it seeks to acquire adequate supplies by one means or another; if it lacks both it is likely to be doomed to inferior power status.

Following coal and iron there come a long list of raw materials of strategic or critical significance, most of which (notably petroleum) are important because they impinge upon the coal-iron technology. Substitution for them is sometimes impossible and always difficult; however, they are seldom re-quired in such large amounts that it is out of the question to stockpile them.

Food. Food is another class of raw material relevant to power. The extent to which a population is able to feed itself at a level sufficient to maintain productive and military efficiency contributes to its power position. Here it is necessary again to recognize variations between societies. A people ha-bituated to a high standard of living will, even in time of crisis, demand that more of the state's resource endowment be devoted to civilian purposes than would a population inured to privation. The diet of the Japanese people during World War II, although adequate to sustain life, would have been intolerable to Americans.

The Impact of Technological Change. It must also be added in general that the list of key raw materials changes as technological demands evolve. A century ago petroleum was largely a waste product; today it is one of the half dozen really critical materials of the world. Magnesium is a metal whose true value is only now being realized. We are all familiar with the global search for fissionable raw materials now going on; uranium, plutonium, and thorium are everyday words. The successful synthesization of rubber during World War II has virtually removed natural rubber from the list of critical raw materials.

Technological change may alter a state's resource position drastically, as also may the depletion of its reserves. Most mineral raw materials are irreplaceable; once any particular source is exhausted a new one must be found. The rate of consumption of industrial raw materials in time of war is so rapid that certain states of the world today (including the United States) face early disappearance of a large part of their proved resource endowment as an outcome of the two great world wars. When projecting power calculations into the future, statesmen must take into account the possibility of exhaustion of reserves and the time and effort necessary to bring new reserves into effective utilization.

INDUSTRIAL AND AGRICULTURAL PRODUCTION

Without raw materials a state cannot mobilize great power; the same is true of industrial production. Modern war is a struggle of machines, and a state without the means to produce the machines of war is under a major handicap. Control over their own destiny or a large role in world politics is impossible for any people unless they possess a solid and balanced productive power. The modern age is the era of industry, in international politics as in other areas of life.

Industrial Criteria of Power. The optimum pattern of industrial production for national power is impossible to isolate. Certain criteria, however, are frequently used as devices of measurement and comparison. Total production forms one standard for judging a nation's industrial power; other things being equal, greater productivity equals superior power. One must ask further questions, however. How is the production distributed? Where is the major productive effort normally made? Some states are foodstuff and agricultural producers, others specialize in extractive industry, others concentrate upon manufacturing alone, while a few are able to diversify their production into all these areas. From the point of view of the relative contributions to national power, the types of economy are listed in ascending order.

Again, however, the areas of manufacturing specialization operate unequally in their contribution to the total power of the state. Capital equipment ('heavy') industry making 'hard' goods (steel, machines, and so on) is more of a source of immediate power advantage than is 'light' industry producing consumer goods. We must also consider the efficiency of the industrial plant, in terms both of the output per worker (furnishing a guide to probable production if the labor force were contracted or expanded) and of the general level of quality (one good rifle, for example, is often more effective than two inferior ones).

When projecting into the future one must consider the flexibility of the economy under conditions of crisis. Can production be converted from one line to another in a situation of stress? If so, this gives the government an opportunity to direct the flow of production in terms of a changing situation and thus to gain maximum power advantage from the economy. Can productive capacity be expanded? Is the technological and resource position of the state sufficiently advantageous to permit it to divert men and material from the production of finished goods to the creation of new plant facilities? World War II demonstrated that no state in the world can match the United States in the flexibility as well as in the total productivity of its industrial plant. During the war, goods flowed from the prewar American productive machine in enormous quantity and at the same time great industries were converted in short order to war production and entirely new ones (synthetic rubber, magnesium) were created.

Agricultural Criteria of Power. Much the same criteria are applicable to agricultural production. Total production, diversification, convertibility, and expandability are pertinent in considering the strength added by a state's agricultural activity.

Normally food is the most important agricultural product from the point of view of national power, and adequate production to eliminate or minimize dependence upon outside sources is regarded as desirable. But there are other critical agricultural products, including rubber, fibers, oils, and natural chemicals.

Often states have a problem apportioning the claims of agriculture and industry for manpower and materials. Each is obliged to work out the answer in terms of its own particular international and domestic situation.

MILITARY ORGANIZATION

The most obvious and immediately available manifestation of national power is military power. Here is the visible arm of the state and the one that is used to serve the most important policies. Much effort is expended by statesmen upon the analysis of military power and power judgments are often phrased in military terms.

In attempting to give military strength its just place in the totality of national power, particular care must be taken to distinguish between power-in-being and total potential. No state remains permanently in total mobilization: every government seeks to keep immediately available that portion of its total military power which would protect it while it organized its potential reserve. The sliding relationship between actuality and potentiality and the time required to go from one to the other are constant modifying factors in all military power analyses.

There are at least three major heads under which a state's military organization should be considered: size, organization, and development; quality and the strategic and tactical theory governing the employment of the armed forces.

Size, Organization, and Deployment. The sheer size of the armed force of a state is not an authentic determinant of its military position, but obviously a large military establishment is superior to a smaller one of equal efficiency. As a matter of fact, most states do seek to maintain as large a military machine (actual and in reserve) as their situation will permit.

The organization of the armed forces includes the basis upon which men and materials are distributed among the various land, sea, and air branches and how they are further subdivided within each major service. A state invulnerable to sea power would have little to fear from a much more powerful neighbor whose major military strength was in its navy. A state that emphasizes interceptor aircraft in its air arm is less of a menace to its fellows than one stressing strategic bombardment. There are few states in the world whose geographic, manpower, and industrial situation permits them to maintain a high level of power in all branches of the armed forces. Most must specialize in some area and minimize others, depending upon their over-all strategic judgment.

The deployment of the armed forces automatically conditions their mission and tends to strengthen some aspects of the state's position and to weaken others. Wide deployment in dispersed bases limits their ability to defend the homeland; concentration upon home defense reduces their global effectiveness. If, as in the case of the totalitarian states, the armed forces serve as instruments of government by controlling the population, they are less effective for either foreign or defensive warfare since in normal circumstances they may not be withdrawn from their governmental role without endangering the safety of the regime.

Quality. The quality of the military organization is determined by several factors of varying concreteness. The most important of these are the state of the equipment, including such things as mobility, fire power, and efficient supply; the effectiveness of the leadership corps; the morale of the troops; the type and amount of support given the military establishment by the civilian elements of the government.

Perhaps no aspect of national power is more difficult to measure that the quality of the armed forces and judgments on this point consume a great deal of time of statesmen. In the last analysis the quality of the armed forces of any state can be tested only in battle. However, an estimate of the battle effectiveness of a given military machine is usually sought most vigorously before combat, at a time when statesmen are calculating the expediency of risking a war. This is why 'small' wars, such as the Spanish civil war (1936–), the Italo-Ethiopian war (1935–7), the Russo-Finnish war (1940), and the Korean conflict (1950–3), are watched so closely by the leaders of all nations. In these relatively limited situations much valuable information about the tactical worth of men, materials, and plans can be gathered against the day of large-scale struggle.

It is easy to see how the quality of military power can offset mere size;

indeed, military policy in democratic states usually concentrates upon the maintenance of a relatively small force of extremely high quality backed by ample reserves in contrast to the larger (and presumably less efficient) establishment kept in being by dictatorships. By keeping in existence only a minimum core of strength adequate for emergency defense of the homeland and by conducting constant research and development in the interests of higher efficiency, a state is able to mobilize at full strength in terms of the latest and best equipment instead of 'fighting this year's war with last year's weapons.'

Strategic and Tactical Theory. A state's strategic and tactical theory has a broad influence upon the role its military power will play in its policy. If a state is wedded to a strategic concept of the defense of fixed positions, any judgment of its military strength will be affected by this fact. If, on the other hand, the prevailing notion in a state involves a war of movement, with armored and motorized warfare dominating military thinking, such a state is less powerful in a situation in which broken terrain and logistical difficulties figure. A state that considers air power as the decision-forcing weapon is at a relative power disadvantage when confronting an opponent which offers few strategically valuable targets. Since no state is able to mobilize enough military power on a grand scale to cope with every possible contingency, every government must make these basic strategic decisions which largely govern all military planning.

Although most states would usually prefer to keep these decisions secret, the information usually becomes available to other states, often in incomplete and garbled form, and becomes in turn a part of their power judgments. An instructive example was provided by the hearings held by the Armed Services Committee of the United States Senate looking into the circumstances surrounding the ouster of General Douglas MacArthur as Supreme Commander in Korea in 1951. As each participant in the discussions sought to justify himself, the details of American strategic and tactical planning were exposed for all to see. By the time the hearings were concluded the entire American plan and the power judgments upon which it was based had been communicated to all interested states.

INTANGIBLE FACTORS OF POWER

There are a great many intangibles of power; indeed, we have already seen that most of the tangible factors already examined have intangible overtones that affect their impact. These intangible elements of national power prevent the subject of power analysis from being an exact science. If geography, manpower, resources, industry, and military force were all there was to national power, its analysis and manipulation would be both easier and more accurate. The non-specific and non-quantitive aspect of power, however, constantly intrude upon and upset any judgment based purely upon measurable phenomena; in order to make any power analysis as realistic and valid as possible it is necessary to evaluate and make due allowance for the effect of less visible but real influences.

Although there are countless intangible factors that impinge upon national power, we shall confine our description and analysis to four broad categories: the political, social, and economic system of a state; its level of technology and education; its national morale; and its over-all international strategic position.

POLITICAL, ECONOMIC, AND SOCIAL SYSTEM

In spite of the propaganda of the disciples of one or another ideology, from the point of view of national power there is no political, economic, or social system that is everywhere preferable. The pattern of institutional arrangements a society affords is peculiar to itself and may be worthless for another. The only valid point of inquiry in this connection is whether the political, economic, and social system which a state has is in fact a source of strength or a source of weakness, and in what direction the society is evolving.

The Political System. As an area of power analysis, the 'political system' of a state refers to the structure and functioning of the government and its relation to the people. Whether the government is autocratic or democratic, totalitarian or limited, mild or ruthless, is in the strictest sense irrelevant. It is a myth that free men always fight harder than unfree men, and that a free society is inherently stronger than a police state: a myth that is comforting to the group psyche of democratic peoples but has no basis in historical fact.

The examination of the relation of government forms to national power may proceed upon any of several bases, all of which have in common a lack of concern with whether a government is morally good or evil. Certain questions are always asked when making such an analysis. Is the government rooted in the culture? Does it reflect the prevailing scale of political values of the people? Is it efficient in its administration and does it use techniques of governing appropriate to the situation and the goal sought? Does it have support from popular concensus, or is it imposed by force upon a recalcitrant people? How extensively does it rely upon violence and terror as methods of maintaining its power, and does the use of such disorderly measures indicate a latent or active resistance among the masses? The answers to these questions will throw much light upon the capacity of any government to perform its mission.

Although no political system is the best in all ways in its contribution to national power, each major contemporary type has advantages unique to itself. Dictatorships and other authoritarian governments concentrate decision making and executive power in a relatively small group and thus obtain greater speed and—presumably—efficiency of operation. The various parts of the government are kept in close relation to each other and greater co-ordination and economy of effort thus result. Democratic governments lack this advantage. Their decision-making personnel are numerous and the relationships among them are usually more vague. Decisions often require popular ratification by the legislative branch, with probable delay and much wrangling.

Democratic government, however, grounded in a more active consent of the people, is able to withstand stress and defeat with much more elasticity than a dictatorship. Well-established democracies are much harder to overthrow than are autocracies, and their tenacity in the face of adversity often creates strength that offsets the superior efficiency of dictatorships. Furthermore, recent studies seem to indicate that dictatorial efficiency is not so great as had been painted; fear, suspicion, hostility, and bureaucratic inertia at the lower levels vitiate effective decision-making at the top. This was certainly the case in Nazi Germany, and a strong suspicion exists that it is true within the Soviet government.

The Economic System. By the 'economic system' of a state is meant that group of fundamental principles which govern the conditions of production and distribution. Modern economic life is complicated and there are many ways of arranging the productive process.

As in the case of the political system, a series of questions will bring out the sort of information that bears directly upon the role of the economic system in national power. What system of ownership is the economy based upon: private property, state capitalism, a mixed economy, or communism? How and by whom are the decisions made regarding what shall be produced, in what quantity, and how the goods shall be distributed? What is the nature of labor-management relations? Is the system self-regulating or does the government play an active role in controlling the economy? If the latter, how extensive is government control? Is the decision-making process in economic affairs of a type to permit conversion and expansion of all or a part of the economy with relative ease and speed?

It must again be emphasized that the answers to these questions must be as objective as possible if the judgment reached is to be trustworthy. The only valid criterion to apply is that of efficiency. If the economic system is such as to produce the maximum of the right type of goods or services that the resources of the state can provide, then the system is a source of strength.

As we said earlier, no state can direct all its economic activity into narrowly 'political' channels. It is not sufficient that the population be kept at a bare subsistence level; all populations demand some of what they deem to be the niceties of life. It is a test of the economic system for a government to be able to strike the optimum balance between the competing claims of the civilian economy and the military and associated demands.

Many of the observations made about the political system are applicable in this connection also. Some states are more efficient under a vigorous system of government control of all aspects of the economy, while the United States during World War II blended government control with private initiative to produce the greatest outpouring of goods in history.

The Social System. Underlying both the political and economic systems of a state is its social system. This set of relationships has a less immediately perceptible influence upon national power than the previous two, although it occasionally emerges as the most critical factor in the power position of a state. From the point of view we are assuming in this analysis, that social system is best for power purposes which is the most homogeneous and united behind the state's leadership and which embodies the minimum amount of stress and tension. To the extent that a society is marred by internal division the state is weakened; if it be united in support of a given value system the state is strengthened.

In attempting to determine the degree of unity and agreement in a society, one must examine the rigidity or fluidity of the class structure, the extremes of high and low income, the urban-rural balance and whether it causes stress, and whether there are dissatisfied minority groups in the population. If so, they must be identified and their influence estimated. If the society is in a transitional period of shifting values there is more likely to be a conflict between the believers in the new order and the defenders of the old. Any such struggle, no matter how happy its eventual outcome, cannot help but represent an element of weakness in any state while it is going on. No state involved in a fundamental internal social conflict is in a position to muster very much power in support of a vigorous and expanding foreign policy.

Examples of states in this situation are numerous; two from recent history are Bolshevik Russia from 1919 to 1939 and India since 1945. In both cases the domestic social revolutions through which the states were passing demanded much effort and attention from the governments. As a result both states sought international stability as an important objective of policy.

LEVEL OF TECHNOLOGY AND EDUCATION

A state among whose people there is a wide diffusion of technological skills is in a preferred power position. There are many tasks the effective performance of which provides sources of strength for any state. The greater the percentage of the population the government can call upon for these specialized functions the better off it is. For this reason, the level of technology and education of a people is regarded as an important factor of power.

Literacy. Concern with the level of education begins with a consideration of such a basic fact as literacy. A population of which only a small portion is literate is difficult to organize for the purposes of national power. As modern civilization grows more complex everyone is finding it necessary to read more and write more. One of the most valuable devices of government today is the printing press. It is significant that when their rulers set about seriously to elevate such states as Japan, the Soviet Union, China, and India to great power status, one of their initial steps was a campaign to eliminate illiteracy. Rules, directives, propaganda, and policies can be most efficiently disseminated to large numbers of people by means of the printed word. It therefore seems logical to assume that a population that cannot be so controlled because of its illiteracy represents a serious weakness in the power position of a state.

Tool Skill. As basic as literacy to national power is the distribution of tool skill throughout the people. It is trite but true to say that modern power is machine power, and a population unfamiliar and unskilled with modern machines affords a real obstacle to that state's rise to power eminence.

There is considerable evidence that a time lag exists between the introduction of modern machinery into a hitherto non-industrialized society and the enjoyment of the full advantage that such a technological change ultimately brings. The operation at peak efficiency of a modern machine, whether a turret lathe, an automobile, a machine gun, or a typewriter, requires a particular mental and emotional orientation in an individual as well as an awareness of the public and private requirements placed upon members of a technological society.

The question of how widely tool skill is dispersed among a people is therefore one of the slower-changing factors of national power. A state which has a population habituated to machinery will continue for a reasonably long time to enjoy this advantage over a state just introducing industrialization.

During World War II, the United States discovered that nearly any American soldier could be trained to operate complicated military machines because virtually all of them had come from backgrounds where they had been surrounded by machines and had thus gained the basic familiarity with mechanical processes. In contrast, it is reported that the Communist government of China has found that so few Chinese have any mechanical orientation whatever that a truck driver in the Chinese army is a rare specialist whose safety is jealously guarded. Machines are indeed the measure of modern power, but it is sometimes forgotten that human beings operate the machines. How well they perform that task may spell the difference between national success and failure.

Scientific and Technological Knowledge. At a somewhat more specialized level, the state of scientific research and technological and engineering skill has a direct role in a state's power.

Under more relaxed conditions in the nineteenth century, scientific and technological advances became common property as a matter of course and it was not a vital concern for each state to carry forward on its own in this respect. Today, however, when so much of social life is politically pertinent, this concept of the brotherhood of science is anachronistic and every state must depend for the most part upon its own efforts in the discovery of new scientific truths and technological processes. Since many of the greatest scientific discoveries and technical advances have been made as a result of the intensification of research during wartime—atomic energy is an example —every state of any stature today is making great efforts not to be left behind in the race to discover scientific principles of military and power significance.

As a power factor pure and simple, the level of science and technology is measured in terms of certain criteria. How extensive is the program of research? What is the relation between basic and applied research? How numerous are the scientific and technological personnel, and what is their social and economic status? Is the program subject to non-scientific restraints (as in the USSR) or are the scientists granted 'freedom of the laboratory?' What facilities exist for the training of replacements for the present scientific and technological personnel and for increasing their number? How adequate are these facilities? These and many other questions that concern the level of science and technology help reveal its role in national power.

Specialized Non-scientific Learning. Finally, the state of learning in the whole area of human knowledge other than the scientific bears upon national power. Although many of the subdivisions of knowledge are highly specialized and seemingly remote from political concerns, no one can safely predict that any information will be valueless to the state. The United States, for example, has had to call upon the services of many specialists in out-of-the-way fields in order to meet its rapidly expanding responsibilities in foreign affairs. Strange regions, populations, and problems call for the extensive assistance of those few people who are acquainted with them in order to advise the government upon conditions and to recommend policies. Such is the breadth of the international political process that all areas of intellectual interest have a place in it.

National Morale

Definition. Morale may be defined in terms of the extent to which a people are united in a belief in the rightness of their cause, in the integrity and ability of their leaders, and in the certainty of their eventual triumph. When a people have a high degree of unity in these terms, their morale is viewed as good; if such unity is lacking their morale is poor. Since any great mobilization of power by a state requires the active aid and support of the mass of the people, a high state of morale is indispensable if any great part of its power potential is to be made effective.

National morale is compounded of a variety of elements whose enumeration would make a list beyond the scope of this chapter. It is largely a mass emotion and is closely associated with the promptings of nationalism. Like any such popular sentiment it is subject to wide variations in response to seemingly slight stimuli.

Good and Bad Morale. Any government must make a constant effort to keep itself informed about the state of the morale of its people and to raise it if it is low, to keep it high if it happens to be so. Generally, policy makers feel that the people should be kept ignorant of unfavorable news lest it damage morale, or at least that bad news should be broken gently; on the other hand, if morale is low because of national complacency (a common complaint about the morale of the American people), bad news may have a salutary effect, as may also 'fear propaganda.'

The problem of how to handle public relations in the interest of optimum morale is a continuing problem of leadership for all statesmen. No single formula is best for all states or even for one state all the time.

An indication of popular morale may often be found in the subjects and quality of public discussion. In any state some dissatisfaction with the way affairs are being ordered will always be present; statesmen learn to recognize and discount this. But when discontent passes this safe level a prudent leader takes warning and initiates some form of remedial action. When public discussion ceases to confine itself to the debate of the wisdom of the moves taken in implementation of policy and begins instead to question the policy itself, the objective the policy is designed to achieve, the motives and abilities of the leadership, or the prospects of ultimate success, popular morale is at a low ebb.

Government Morale Policy. Such a state of public opinion limits the extent of popular effort in support of any policy and serves effectively to tie the government's hands. If the drop in morale is traceable to a small and discoverable group of dissentients, punitive action against these few individuals may halt the undesirable trend. If lack of information is the source of the difficulty, a deliberate policy of 'taking the people into the confidence of the government' may be the remedy.

Often morale is raised by making an example or a scapegoat out of an unpopular official or two, or an unpopular group in the population. Most commonly, on the general principle that 'nothing succeeds like success,' governments with morale problems will seek policy victories that they can present to their people as a justification of their stewardship. Diplomatic or military offensives are often undertaken for no reason other than the need or the desire to prop up sagging morale.

If these measures fail and support for government programs remains low, serious policy modifications must be considered. The government must make the recapture of mass confidence its first order of business, and its policy steps in that process must be guided by what the people demand, or at least by what they will accept. This may mean either a contraction of objectives or their expansion; in any case the statesmen concerned must do what is necessary in order to re-establish the intimate contact between themselves and the people without which morale cannot be high. Failure to do so might possibly result in the collapse of their policy and at the least would make it weak and vacillating.

INTERNATIONAL STRATEGIC POSITION

Allies and Their Effect upon Power. The final factor affecting the power position of a state is its strategic role and position in the world community. A state whose over-all situation, objectives, and policy are such as to minimize its dependence upon other states is therefore at an advantage; a state unable for any reason to operate extensively upon its own is for that reason weakened. The explanation for this is found in the very nature of international politics.

States determine their objectives for themselves, taking into consideration exclusively the egoistic demands of national interest. When they decide that any particular objective is both necessary and beyond their capacity to attain it alone, they seek allies to assist them. When any state enters into an alliance with another, it gives up some of its freedom of action, whether in regard to its ally, toward the common object of the alliance, or toward some other aspect of international politics. This cannot help but to serve as a limiting and occasionally weakening aspect of its over-all power position.

It may therefore be said that a state's power is affected directly by the extent to which it stands in need of other states and to which its freedom of action is circumscribed by its pattern of agreements with other states. Naturally, the working out of the process of international relations results in periodic increases and decreases in the needs of any state in this regard. Any particular state may at one time be following a policy well within its power capabilities and thus be free from extensive reliance upon allies; at other times it may require agreements with many states in order to be able to achieve its objectives.

In this, as in so many other areas of international politics, technology often plays a decisive role. Great Britain for many years was able to dispense with allies upon the European continent. When technology destroyed the impregnability of the home islands Britain found itself obliged to secure binding commitments upon the continent, thus being drawn into the main stream of European politics and depriving itself of the free hand British policy had enjoyed for such a long time.

Military Significance of Allies. Of course the crux of the question of allies is a military consideration. A state needs allies in order to defend itself against a more powerful neighbor who might be planning an attack, or else to be in a position to make such a successful attack itself. The more conducive to war is the climate of international affairs, the more important it is for a state accurately to assess its status and make such adjustments in its international understandings as seem necessary and expedient.

As was pointed out in Chapter 3, the finding of allies is contingent upon the discovery of other states whose interests, objectives, and policy are in close enough harmony with those of the state seeking the alliance to make joint action feasible. If the alliance is of sufficient immediate importance, states often hastily settle some of their long-standing disputes with a would-be ally; at the very least they cease to press disagreements with the same tenacity in the interest of harmony upon a larger issue. In the interest of forming a common front against Imperial Germany in 1902, Great Britain and Czarist Russia buried some of their most persistent points of dispute, including especially their quarrel over their rights and privileges in Persia.

Many relatively weak states have driven very hard bargains when their aid was being sought by greater powers in a time of crisis. The state which more strongly needs the assistance of allies is inevitably in a weaker position than the one which is being requested to join the common cause. In other words, the passive state, without doing anything to merit such superiority, enjoys a significant power advantage over the state wishing the alliance. As long as the alliance endures upon its original terms this situation will continue.

A clear illustration of this relationship is afforded by the history of the negotiation of the North Atlantic Treaty in 1948–9. The United States was the most active participant in the discussions, feeling a strong necessity to create a defensible entity in western Europe. The European states, naturally enough, placed a higher value upon their adherence to the alliance than one would have expected from their relatively weak power situation. There was very little American negotiators could do except to accede to European demands. The preferred position of the European allies continued as the cold war progressed. Their position seemed to be one of 'you need us more than we need you'; there has been a constant threat in their attitude that if the United States pressed them too hard they migh listen sympathetically to any propositions the Soviet Union might make. Thus the American need for European allies weakened the United States power position in Europe.

Allies as a Source of Weakness. In still another way dependence upon allies often works out to be a factor of weakness. If a state must have allies in order to cope with its enemies, it can never be absolutely assured of their support even after the strongest and most binding agreements with them.

States join alliances because of a mutuality of interest; if the interest of any ally changes it is in logic free to shift its allegiance to the side where it feels greater advantage to itself to be found. Whether or not it does so depends upon considerations of power. If it is sufficiently powerful, a state is able to compel adherence to itself by smaller associates. How effective this is depends largely upon the type of support that is needed. If the ally is valuable because of raw materials it controls or strategic territory it occupies, forced allegiance may be as efficacious as voluntary; if, however, the ally's role is one calling for large-scale military or productive effort, obligatory co-operation is usually unsatisfactory to the coercing state.

Some statesmen have felt that it is better for a state to stand alone than to be plagued with a reluctant or inept ally. Very probably the Nazis had many occasions to regret the fate that threw their destinies in with Mussolini's Italy during World War II. It is a maxim of statesmanship that the power to make binding decisions must be kept in one's own hands and not conferred upon an untrustworthy ally. All states that enter into any alliance at all make some such concession to a certain extent, since all allies must be considered as potentially untrustworthy; however, good statesmanship makes a serious attempt to keep as much control of the situation in the hands of one's own government as is possible.

5

Dynamics of International Politics

U P to this point in our study we have concentrated upon the individual state as an entity and upon the way it plays its role in the world society. We have examined the nation-state itself and have considered some of the basic notions that give form and content to state action in international relations: national interest, national policy, and national power. Since we already know that our subject matter concerns itself primarily with the relations states have with each other, the next stage in our inquiry logically demands that we consider the international scene as a going concern. We shall attempt to discover what happens when the various states of the world, each of them possessing the common characteristics of statehood and each equipped with an interest, a policy, and a certain amount of power, come into contact with one another. It is out of these contacts that international politics arises.

The relations of states with each other may assume a broad variety of forms. A government may at the same time be fighting a war with one state, carrying on a diplomatic dispute with another, maintaining close and friendly relations with a third, and virtually isolated from a fourth. War, crisis, friendship, and isolation are all equally 'normal' forms of international intercourse; each arises out of appropriate conditions. This range of possible types of interstate behavior serves to complicate the study of international relations.

From the point of view of the casual observer, the international scene appears to be one of unrelieved confusion. There seems to be no underlying body of principles which govern the conduct of interstate relations, and crisis follows crisis with no apparent causal relationship except the will of statesmen and the workings of blind chance. States sometimes give the appearance of wandering aimlessly in the pursuit of haphazardly selected objectives and to be continually surprised and taken aback as events work themselves out.

To seek to predict the course of international politics is often a frustrating and unrewarding waste of time and many a citizen has given up the task in disgust. Yet the international order is not as unorganized as might appear at first glance. There are a number of principles, of varying degrees of formalization, which to a large extent actually govern the policies of states and the conduct of statesmen.

The Two Categories of Principles. As we shall consider them in this chapter in an attempt to outline a working hypothesis of international politics, they fall into two broad categories. The first group consists of those that arise as logical deductions from the nature of the nation-state system and which impose certain conditions of existence upon all states. These give international relationships much of their distinguishing character and provide the framework within which all state policies must fit themselves. The second body of rules includes those principles of action which statesmen follow in carrying on policy as they attempt to adjust to the society of states. Generally they may be thought of as the procedural techniques by means of which policy makers seek to insure the survival of their states and the attainment of the practical maximum of their objectives. In this chapter we shall consider these two sets of principles in order.

Dynamism and the Trend toward Disorder. The nation state system is composed of sixty-odd states of the type we discussed in Chapters 1 and 2. The society they make up imposes certain requirements of behavior upon all of its members. These rules of organization and procedure are really logical conclusions derived from the assumptions upon which international society is constructed, and are largely independent of the policy of any particular state or of the decisions of any individual statesmen.

The premises of international life are many, but in their effect they may be reduced to two: first, the assumption of the monolithic state as an entity complete and whole, implying if not specifying a legal and/or organic reality; second, the assumption that all the states of the world stand in a relationship of sovereign independence and equality to each other. When states embodying such assumptions enter into intimate and continuous relationships with one another, there are certain consequences that immediately arise. These combine to produce the fundamental rules of interstate life.

The system that emerges has two fundamental characteristics: a condition of constant dynamism and change, and a general trend toward disorder. In other words, 'normal' international relations—by which is meant a situation in which states follow the logic of their existence—is always changing and is always at least potentially disorderly.

Operation and the Techniques of Control. Despite the compelling logic of the conclusions drawn from the nature of the state and the state system, it is nevertheless clear that the course of international politics is not governed entirely by a near-mechanistic determinism. We know from Chapter 2 that the assumptions of the anthropomorphism and the sovereign equality of all states are simply not objectively valid. Human beings, possessed of both reason and will, alone reach the decisions and operate the controls that make governments and states act in world affairs. Consequently, the second set of rules which we must consider delineates the principles that govern the decisions and actions of human policy makers. It is true that their conduct is frequently inhibited by the impact of the conditions of state existence within the society of which they form a part; nevertheless, considerable leeway is permitted human choice in carrying on international relations.

As a result of the necessity with which statesmen are faced of carrying on policy in a potentially explosive context, a set of more or less systematized generalizations have been developed with which all successful policy makers are familiar. These aim at specifying the techniques that must be employed if statesmen are to achieve any degree of success in their policies. These derive from the nature of the state system. In general they are attempts to soften the impact of change and to minimize the trend toward disorder.

Not only have men tried to discover a means of existence within the frame-work of the society of states; going farther, statesmen for centuries have been seeking to capitalize upon the basic forces of international relations and to turn them to the advantage of mankind. No such effort has yet been completely successful, but each of several of them has had marked influence upon international life in general and upon the course of events within a particular era or eras of history.

THE LOGIC OF INTERNATIONAL POLITICS

THE MOVING INTERNATIONAL SCENE

An appropriate first premise in the syllogism of international politics is that the relations of states with each other are in a state of constant evolution and change. All social studies that have man as their central object of concern must take account of the notoriously dynamic nature of the human species, but international politics is particularly subject to this caution.

The study is complicated by the relative lack of institutional restraints upon the subjects of its examination, the states themselves. As a result, the student must accept the fact that he is to some extent shooting at a moving target and must adapt his techniques of analysis to that condition. Let us first examine some of the factors that produce this situation of permanent dynamism.

The Evolution of National Policy. We pointed out in Chapter 3 that the course of action pursued by a state in attaining its objectives is termed its policy. Although any state is constant in its devotion to its policy, it is not so obvious that the concept of policy is itself dynamic. The pattern of objectives and procedures followed by any state is in constant evolution. The policy the United States is following today is not the same in all its details as that with which it was concerned yesterday; the same is true of all other states with which the United States maintains relations. All the factors that enter into any policy decision are subject both to normal evolution and to sudden change. National interest, national objectives, and national power all defy being frozen into any set pattern.

The Impact of Other States. Another element in the policy process which brings about frequent policy revision is the impact of the actions of other states. We saw earlier how much effort and time any statesman must invest, not in the deliberate pursuit of his own objectives, but rather in devising effective responses to steps taken by his associates in other states. A policy that may be satisfactory so long as it meets only limited resistance often must be drastically altered when it meets firm opposition. The injection of a new issue which requires that corrective action be taken to deal with it serves also to cause policy modifications.

Domestic Developments. Another factor which also contributes to the constant evolution of national policy might be termed domestic developments. Pronounced political, economic, social, or psychological change within a state inevitably finds expression in foreign policy, thus adding still another variable. In all these and other ways, we find that policy in a state of permanent evolution is the first explanation of the dynamism of world affairs.

The Climate of World Politics. A final variable in world affairs is what we might term the prevailing 'climate.' International affairs, like all forms of politics, is materially affected by the milieu in which events take place and by considerations of time and place. Particular epochs may be favorable to bold and venturesome policies, while others may permit success only to cautious and conservative defenses of the *status quo.*

For example, the period immediately following World War II was one of disorganization and unrest throughout much of the world. This condition of society is usually advantageous to a policy of expansion by a strong power and the Soviet Union moved rapidly to take any opportunity to capitalize upon it. Much of its postwar success can be explained in these terms.

Beginning about 1947, however, the general temper of world opinion had changed. After that time, the defensive policies of the United States began to prove effective in countering Soviet aggrandizement; by 1955 it appeared that the USSR had gone on the defensive. Not only do such changes in 'climate' often occur for unpredictable reasons, but they often take place with relatively little warning and succeed each other with considerable rapidity in today's interdependent world. The state system is an intricate and finely attuned mechanism which reacts with great sensitivity to changes in external conditions.

The Impossibility of Preventing Change. Movement and change are of the essence of the international political process. Failure to recognize and to take account of this essential characteristic has rendered futile many otherwise well-conceived ventures in foreign policy by statesmen of all nationalities. Statesmen have proved to be disposed to fall into this error particularly in the period immediately following a successful and important venture. At the very moment when they have finally achieved an objective of great worth after a long and often perilous struggle, there seems to be a tendency to relax: to assume that the circumstances which produced the victory will endure forever and that it is unnecessary to take any action to perpetuate them. So long as the nation-state system retains its present characteristics, international politics will not submit to being thus frozen. We need only reflect upon the outcomes of both the great world conflicts of this century to discover historical verification of the persistent dynamism of world affairs. Following the war of 1914–18, the victorious Allies constructed with great effort a structure of world relationships which they hoped would guarantee them the permanent enjoyment of the fruits of their victory. Germany and the Central Powers were defeated and reduced either to impotence or to definitely subordinate status; in the League of Nations, furthermore, there existed an instrument which might be used to maintain that relationship. In the immediate postwar period Britain and France (particularly the latter) stubbornly refused to make any but the slightest alterations in the terms of the peace settlement. It was only later that they learned to their sorrow that the forces of international politics may be temporarily suppressed but that they eventually break forth with all the greater violence. Economic depression, resurgent nationalism, and technological advance all combined to render obsolete the settlement that had been won at such cost on the battlefield.

The same general pattern re-established itself after World War II. This time, Germany was crushed and dismembered and all its allies had thrown themselves on the mercy of the victors. So complete was the triumph that many people throughout the world felt that at last the forces of freedom and democracy had gained a permanent ascendancy. This dream was dissipated even more rapidly than had been that of 1919. By 1946, the dynamics of international politics had again reasserted themselves and the world was off upon another round of shifting alignments and recurrent crises. Statesmen who seek successful policies must be ever aware of the impossibility of gaining permanent and rigid stability.

THE RELATIONS BETWEEN STATES

Participants in World Politics. We stipulated earlier that the sovereign nation-state is the component element of the world society, and by far the greatest number of the contacts that compose international politics take place between them. In appropriate circumstances, however, other forms of political organization figure in the process. These are of sufficient inherent importance to merit mention at this point, although we must keep in mind that their appearance in the international arena is a periodic rather than a regular matter.

Initially we might mention non-sovereign political entities (not, be it noted, 'non-sovereign states.' There is a considerable body of opinion which claims that this latter term is contradictory; to constitute a true state, a political group must be sovereign). These include members of the United Nations such as the Ukrainian Socialist Soviet Republic, creations of the United Nations such as the Free Territory of Trieste, and such *de facto* governments as those of

Indonesia and Israel before the international recognition of their independence. For limited purposes, these groups play a direct part in international affairs and carry on relations with sovereign states.

The second category of special participants in interstate relationships is formed by international organizations of all types. The principal example is of course the United Nations. Although the organization includes many states, each of which has a policy of its own, the United Nations acts frequently as a single entity and conducts affairs with individual states. Often these latter states are United Nations members themselves and thus a single state may appear upon both sides of a negotiation. The 'specialized agencies' of the United Nations (UNESCO, the International Labor Organization, and so on) also carry on direct relations with individual states and thus fall into the same class.

The third group includes blocs of states each of which acts as a unit in pursuing an objective which the members hold in common. If the alliance is sufficiently close and well organized, these states form a single entity and any relationship between the group and an outside state is as if only two states were involved. The European Coal and Steel Community and the North Atlantic Treaty Organization are two examples of such blocs which in reality deal with non-members upon a state-to-state basis. Whenever any of these special organizational types do have contact with sovereign states (or with each other), the following general principles apply as completely as in the case of only two states. The fundamental nature of the interstate relationship undergoes no change.

The Nature of the Interstate Relationship. In earlier chapters we have outlined the characteristics of the state as a participant in international affairs. Let us now briefly examine the principal features of the relationship that arises between such states.

In the first place, each participant in world politics is proceeding in response to internal motivations; interest, objectives, and policy all arise in response to stimuli the origin of which is within the state. Secondly, each state possesses certain increments of power with which it supports its policy. Third, the society in which states move and carry on their relations is structurally incomplete. Large areas of state action are completely free from institutional regulation, while such rules as exist are often vague or else lack mechanisms of enforcement. A fourth factor which affects this relationship is the fact that there is no agreement today among all states upon any single moral code by which to judge the propriety of state action.

The relationship between states which derives from these conditions necessarily reflects them. States approach each other as free agents with no inherent reason for mutual confidence. Each is required by the system to view the others as actual or potential competitors; each is prepared to advance its own cause at the expense of the others and to seek to prevent them from doing the same. Agreement is based upon a coincidence of interest and may be great or small, long-lasting or temporary, depending upon how extensively and how long the respective national interests happen to remain in harmony. Which of the states gains the bulk of its objectives is determined largely by the interplay of power factors.

It must be stressed that within the present structure of the nation-state system, the criteria of morality and justice which we in the Western world accept as guides to private conduct are to a great extent irrelevant. States, by the very circumstances of their existence, are obliged to accept different standards.

It is true that the relations between particular pairs or groups of states have often been friendly for long periods of time and real harmony has marked their contracts. The great degree of cordiality in Canadian-American relations since the middle of the nineteenth century is a good example of this type of relationship. Even this felicitous arrangement, however, when examined closely, reveals the characteristics mentioned above. With the best will in the world, even such similarly situated states as Canada and the United States have been unable completely to escape the logical consequences of their existence as sovereign political entities. Disagreement and occasional open dispute between them upon numerous issues serves to remind us all that each is a sovereign state with the primary goal of serving its own best interest.

The Forms of the Interstate Relationship: Hostility. The relationship between states covers a wide gamut of forms in its constantly changing evolution. At one extreme is the relationship of extreme hostility, including war. This is rooted in a direct clash of vital interests between the states involved, and is marked by the open, direct, and usually unlimited mutual application of violence.

It arises when states have been unable to discover a formula for settling a dispute, and the only means left open to them in such a situation to achieve their objectives is to attempt to coerce their opponent into submission. If war exists between two states, hostility extends to every point of contact between them and no other basis for supporting a relationship is possible. If, on the other hand, conflict does not reach the point of violence, relations between the states may be hostile only in certain areas and upon certain issues, while remaining cordial and even friendly in others.

The Forms of the Interstate Relationship: Friendship. At the other extreme, an interstate relationship may be friendly and marked by close policy co-operation. In this case, an identity of interest exists, either upon a particular issue or upon a more broadly based general program. At the very least, friendly relations between states indicate a lack of fundamental disagreement. Co-operative affirmative action is more likely when active agreement exists upon an issue sufficiently important to motivate concrete policy steps, but friendship may be just as close if it arises out of a mere lack of grounds of disagreement. In any case, hostility or friendship between states is directly proportional to the degree to which their interests conflict.

The Forms of the Interstate Relationship: Balance. Somewhere in between the two extremes are found most of the actual relations of states. Clashes of interest are normal, but so is some degree of agreement; the result is some form of dynamic balance which reflects the conflict-agreement mixture. States prosecute their differences with other states, but the lengths to which they will go in the struggle are limited by such agreement as exists upon other policy matters. The converse is also true; co-operation upon the basis of identity of interest is usually incomplete because of the existence of other areas of controversy.

THE WEB OF RELATIONSHIPS

The State in the Multi-state System. The state, as we have already pointed out, exists within a system along with all its fellows. Let us for a moment consider how it fits itself into this framework.

Each state has a policy derived from its national interest and consisting of a set of objectives and a program for their attainment. It also has a certain amount of power with which to gain those objectives. Each state determines for itself which objectives it will seek, in what priority they will be arranged, how it will go about attaining them, and the power commitments necessary and appropriate for the purpose.

So far can it go on its own. From this point forward the degree of success or failure it enjoys is determined to a large measure by the fact that it is one among a number of similarly minded states. Once a state decides upon a policy and sets it into motion, it immediately comes into contact with many other states, each doing the same thing. With each of these an interstate relationship is established whose general characteristics we have already seen. As each state pursues its objectives with regard to all its fellows, it attempts to arrange matters within each of these relationships to its satisfaction. This necessitates paying close attention to each of them, making advances toward its goal when possible, standing fast when desirable, and retreating when necessary and expedient. A state that finds itself at a power disadvantage in a particular relationship must usually either give ground there or weaken its effort elsewhere in order to gain the additional power necessary to stabilize the first situation; a state that finds its opponent weakening may increase its own pressure so as to force a victory or else may reduce its own effort, restore the balance, and employ the ensuing surplus of power elsewhere. If the last course is chosen, new situational changes are thus brought about which call in turn for new corrective measures.

It must be remembered that each state maintains some sort of relations with nearly all of the other seventy-odd members of the nation-state system, and in doing so it exerts pressure upon and receives pressure exerted by each of them. The multi-state system is a complex and intricate web of dynamic relationships, each materially affecting all the others. As a result, the task of any statesman is to pick his way through these complexities with skill and direction sufficient to gain the practical maximum of his policy objectives.

Relativism is the keynote of interstate relationships. Absolute success in international politics is so rare as to be practically nonexistent. No state can do more than come close to reaching its policy goals; the system itself intervenes to prevent most solutions from being truly clear-cut. Any state in seeking the objectives it has laid down for itself is beset by so many interruptions and irrelevancies—most of which arise from the nature of the system—that it is seldom that it can devote itself single-mindedly to the fulfillment of its own plans. All states must therefore devote considerable amounts of their energies to the basic problem of maintaining their existence in the dynamic and unstable nation-state system.

The Chain Reaction of Policy Change. The results of even a minor policy change by any state usually extend far beyond the immediate issue.

As soon as any state makes a modification in its policy as it affects any other state, the latter seeks to bring its own program into harmony with the new situation. This in turn presents other states with different circumstances, which they in turn must meet by making policy shifts of their own. Still other states are affected at this point and more policy alterations take place—all of which reminds us of the concentric ripples that radiate out from the point at which a dropped stone struck the surface of a placid pool of water.

In this way each policy change tends to touch off a chain reaction of adjustment to it. Some of these may be slight in the first place, but so delicately must statesmen calculate in allocating their available power that the effect of any policy modification tends to increase in a geometric proportion.

Further affecting the nature of international politics is the fact that many such chain reactions are taking place simultaneously. Each state involved in any of them—and in today's interdependent world nearly every state is ultimately drawn into the process—meets each such set of new conditions one at a time and in a way determined by its own situation and the demands of its national interest. The changes follow each other, often with bewildering rapidity. What is more, these chain reactions often affect each other. Sometimes they neutralize each other and particular states may be able to adjust to new conditions without making any significant policy changes at all; sometimes they double up in their effect and states must execute virtual policy reversals in order to keep abreast of a drastically altered set of conditions.

Most of the time the interaction of the various patterns is not so clear or so extreme as has been suggested. Instead, their impact is relatively intensified or diluted as the result of their concurrence. In any case, the nature of international politics is such that each state must always be prepared to modify its policy in great or in small measure in response to changes in circumstances brought about in the first instance by a policy change made by some other state.

United States Trade Policy and the Chain Reaction. Let us illustrate this idea with a concrete example, chosen from American policy in the cold war. In 1951, the Congress of the United States enacted the Battle Act, designed to cut off trade between the free world and the Soviet sphere by denying American aid to any state engaged in trading with Iron Curtain states. This was actually an intensification of an already decided policy—an increase in the power we were exerting upon our allies. This policy change set in motion a chain reaction.

Each of our allies, faced with this new move on the part of the United States, sought to react to it as best it could in terms of its own situation. Great Britain, for example, found the new American attitude distinctly unfavorable to itself, both in the area of Anglo-American relations and in dealing with the Soviet. Consequently British policy attempted to redress the balance. Diplomatic representations were made to the United States; consultations were held with other adversely affected states; the possibilities of an entirely new line of procedure based upon the termination of American aid were explored. All of these moves added up to a counterbalancing increase in the power Britain was in turn applying to the United States. Britain adjusted to a new American policy, and its programs in other policy areas were in turn affected. Its Soviet policy was modified, its relations with its fellows in the alliance of the free world were overhauled and made closer under the stimulus of a common problem, and its economic policy sought to make up for the loss of its trade behind the Iron Curtain.

The states affected by the last group of derivative policies were in turn confronted by new conditions in dealing with Britain. The Soviet Union, for example, redoubled its efforts to split the Western alliance by tempting Britain with ever more attractive offers of trade agreements; in doing so, however, it was in its turn obliged to prepare itself to modify its economic relations with its satellites and to soften much of its propaganda campaign against Britain.

And so the process continued, involving all the states initially affected by the passage of the Battle Act; each state reacted to new conditions by policy adjustment.

There is no need to go into further detail at this point about the specific issue: it seemed to have reached resolution of at least one phase in late 1953 and early 1954, when the United States government officially relaxed the ban on trading in non-strategic materials behind the Iron Curtain. The incident illustrates the fact, however, that the consequences of a single policy change by any state cannot in practice be kept confined. Reaction to change is inevitable, and its ultimate ramifications are almost impossible to predict. It is for this reason that every government keeps a watchful eye upon all developments in the whole global arena of world politics. Even if it is only remotely concerned at the moment, all new situations eventually may result in changed circumstances which would necessitate policy revisions by each state.

THE ANARCHY OF INTERSTATE LIFE

The society in which the sovereign state has its existence is one that by its very nature is potentially disorderly. In contrast, a domestic social life is marked by orderly behavior, the promulgation of generally accepted rules, and the progressive elaboration of the institutional structure. These characteristics are only partly present in the contacts that states have with each other. Consequently, the nation-state system moves according to a different set of principles from that of private society. To draw analogies between domestic and international life is deceptive and misleading unless the differences between the two systems are kept clear.

Philosophers and political scientists use the term anarchy to describe a situation within a society in which there is no government, no agency to enforce order, and no universally applicable rules of behavior. In interstate life, although rudimentary forms of social control do exist, the logical necessities of statehood are such that their role is usually a relatively minor one. It is therefore analytically defensible to generalize that the society of states is an anarchic one.

The Limited Effect of Institutions. The institutions of international life— the formalized agencies that embody moral principles and rules of conduct— are incomplete and of limited effect. International organizations of many types exist which include states as members and which pursue their particular objectives with varying degrees of success. Membership in these is voluntary on the part of any state, however, and each member in practice determines for itself the degree to which its conduct is affected by the dictates of the organization. One need recall only the uneven response given by members of the United Nations to the call for military action in Korea to become convinced that the organization is not yet the controlling element in international politics.

International law as an institution is also relatively weak and feeble compared to its domestic counterpart. The scope of the law is restricted; several critical forms of state conduct do not come within its provisions. Its enforcement mechanisms, when present at all, are weak and comparatively inefficient. States obey international law upon the occasions and to the extent that it conforms to their national interest to do so. Settlement of international disputes by formal judicial process is infrequent and exceptional.

Even the institution of diplomacy, the formal mechanism of interstate contact and communication, draws its validity from its expediency rather than from its institutional maturity. When a state chooses to employ some other channel of communication and has the power to make itself heard, it is free to do so; no automatic sanctions exist to prevent or punish the violation of the institutional framework.

It would therefore appear that states are not in any fundamental way restricted in their international conduct by the existence of any institutional structure, but instead feel themselves to be legally and morally free agents— a basically anarchic point of view.

The Absence of a Sense of Community Obligation. There is no logical reason for a state (considered as a collective entity) to feel any real sense of fundamental obligation or respect to any entity outside itself. The law and the philosophy of statehood in international relations make the state form an end in itself. There is no room in the concept for any higher or outside loyalty.

In a real sense it is questionable to think of the terms 'international society' or 'world community' as having any meaning when applied to the sovereign states in the world (in Chapter 9 we shall see that the 'international community' is made up of individual people, and not states). For a society or community to exist, there must be some form of concensus, some form of recognition of a mutual obligation to the group. There must be a willingness on the part of individuals upon occasion to submerge their private concerns to the appropriate requirements of the society. There must usually also be some agreed-upon authority to enforce decisions in the name of the collective whole.

In the relations between sovereignties, no such sense of community obligation can logically be presumed to exist, The notion of the national interest is an all-inclusive one which demands the complete commitment of the state to its service. Each state is therefore so immersed in the service of its own interest that little room is left for a sense of duty to be applied to the whole group.

The pattern of international politics offers many examples of this idea. One of the most recent is afforded by the question of European unification, which has been a major issue since 1945. The idea of a unified Europe is one of great logical force and has the additional advantage of being in harmony with existing conditions.

Between 1947 and 1955, aided by pressure from the United States and a common fear of the USSR, progress toward European unification was made in a number of areas. Nevertheless, each member of the West European bloc, although recognizing the extent to which all of them were involved in a common enterprise and would inevitably share a common fate, was repeatedly driven to endanger and possibly to sabotage the whole undertaking in the service of its particular national interest. Each of them has tended to make the satisfaction of its own special desires the price of its participation in the movement which alone can save all of them.

France has been obstinate in obstructing the plans because it feels that its interest demands military supremacy over Germany; Italy seeks satisfaction of certain territorial claims; West Germany is ever raising the question of German unification; Britain refuses to become a full partner in Europe—thus impeding and almost stopping further advance—because of its reluctance to give up its area of independence in world affairs and its position as leader of the Commonwealth of Nations. All have been eager to gain American support for their own policies and have given some measure of consideration to American interest in European union in order to earn United States backing in return. But the limited success of the European movement up to the present—despite the fact that its ultimate prospects are bright—is due primarily to the inability or the refusal of the European states themselves to recognize a duty or a loyalty to anything greater than themselves.

Self-help. In a highly organized society there are institutions to assist the individual in coping with situations beyond his strength. Through law and by means of private organizations, the social group guarantees to private citizens a measure of rights and freedoms and stands behind him if these are invaded. No such situation can be assumed in the state system. The only logical method open to a state to attain its objectives and to secure redress of injuries is to employ its own strength.

Self-help in crisis situations, unusual in private life, is a common and routine procedure in international politics. The only rights and freedoms in the possession of which a state can feel truly secure are those it is physically capable of defending. This necessarily means that the power inequalities of states are usually faithfully reflected in their respective areas of rights and freedoms. Futhermore, each state may determine for itself what measures are appropriate in any situation and—despite some attempts at formulating legalistic restraints—no institution presently exists which effectively limits that freedom.

It has sometimes been claimed, for example, that the United Nations Charter has made war illegal. Even if this point be granted, however, there still remains the unsolved problem of how this judgment could be enforced against a possible violator without first winning a war against it. Many of the rules of international conduct were themselves initially laid down by powerful states in a moment of victory with the basic objective of legitimizing a policy that had proved successful. Such were the rules making aggressive warfare a crime punishable by death which were handed down by the 'war crimes' tribunals in Germany and Japan after World War II. This fact tends to make international affairs a demonstration of the ancient thesis that 'might makes right.'

The central feature of the anarchy of international politics is the right of the state to go to war any time it decides such action is expedient. The employment of force without limit in order to coerce other states into agreement is a logical derivation arising from the nature of interstate relations. War is therefore considered to be a normal—although often undesirable and unwise —technique of policy.

All attempts to organize international relations upon a basis of order and stability have up to this time come to grief upon this central idea. As long as states feel that they can not trust any outside agency to give them complete fulfillment of what they deem to be their legitimate interests, they are not going to give up their power to enforce their rights themselves. In this way, the power of states and their willingness and ability to use it becomes the ultimate determinant of most international intercourse, particularly in times of crisis.

When states disagree, the only procedure that will produce definitive solutions within the peculiar framework of the state system is the mutual application of elements of power by the states involved. No external mechanisms that the world has thus far seen have proved capable of ending such a struggle in any clean-cut way.

Hobbes's Vision of Anarchy. One of the most famous evocations of the consequences of anarchy was made by Thomas Hobbes, the seventeenth-century British philosopher. In *Leviathan* (1651), he sought to justify the institution of civil government as the only way by which man could escape chaos. To make his point more effective, he drew a vivid picture of what human social intercourse would be like if there were no civil authority to enforce order. This 'state of nature,' as he termed it, would be a miserable existence; he called it a 'war of all against all.' Man, driven by his appetites and an instinct of acquisitiveness, would be engaged in constant conflict with his fellows. Self-preservation was the basic human motivation; that accomplished, man would turn to the service of his physical and psychic well-being. He would have only his physical strength and his native wit to aid him in this purpose. He could turn for assistance neither to organized society (which would not, under these conditions, have any existence) nor to his fellows (except for those particular designs which coincided with the interests of certain other individuals, and then only for the duration of such agreement). There would be no rational basis for any relationship of trust with his fellow men, for all would be competitors for the same rewards. The result would be incessant hostility. Each man would enjoy such personal security and rewards as he was powerful enough to gain and retain, and each would be racked by fear of violence and death as he eked out his allotted span. From this unhappy existence man could be liberated only by the creation of a central governmental authority to protect all against all.

Without stretching the analogy, we can discover a close resemblance between Hobbes's classic vision of anarchy and the theoretical premises upon which international politics are built. The assumption of hostility, arising from the absence of a common ground of understanding and procedure, underlies much of the basic approach of states to each other. No central governing body, no generally respected rules, and no all-inclusive moral code control sovereign states. The principle of action inherent in the state system is *sauve qui peut*—every man for himself.

The unstable system that results from this condition is becoming more and more difficult for individuals to endure. Statesmen might well ponder the conclusion that Hobbes himself drew and perhaps might discover it to be applicable to the anarchy of interstate life: that only by the erection of a central civil government is it possible for men to escape from the consequences of uncontrolled power.

POWER POLITICS

The system of states, being a regime posited upon a partly systematized anarchy, takes its driving force from the only principle of action appropriate in such a society. With no socially sanctioned principles of right and wrong to provide guides to correct procedure, the international political process can be and often is summed up in a single simple phrase: power politics. The germ of the idea is expressed in the aphorism: 'States do what they can and suffer what they must.' This is the lesson of power politics.

The Determination of Policy. Each state determines for itself both its policy objectives and its techniques. There are no objectives that are in themselves wrong or immoral in any absolute sense; a state is free to attempt world conquest or world revolution with no sense of moral restraint, provided only that its people feel that such action is in the national interest. The selection of appropriate techniques for attaining objectives is also done unilaterally; any means that promises success may be adopted, up to and including total war.

It must be stressed that these decisions about objectives and techniques are reached within the framework of government of each state. In international politics there are no external agencies, like those in private life, whose impact must be taken into account in every such decision. The law that always prohibits antisocial objectives and the policeman who punishes antisocial action are equally minor in their effect upon states. Prospects of success or failure, interpreted in the light of the national interest, provide the guides to policy which states actually follow.

To say that the selection of objectives and techniques goes on entirely within a state is not, however, to say that it takes place in a complete vacuum. All statesmen recognize and act upon a set of restraints. These are never wholly concrete and usually are not verbalized, but they nonetheless delineate the real area of freedom enjoyed by a state in making any policy decision. These restraints are represented by the existence of all other states, each of which is engaged in the identical process of seeking the achievement of its objectives and the satisfaction of its national interest. This means that any policy decision made by a state will inescapably meet some degree of resistance from a number of the states affected by it. Any action program involves as an essential part a judgment of the power necessary for success.

The probability of meeting superior hostile power serves as an immediate limitation upon the freedom of choice of states. Superior power is still the only final arbiter in the state system and it serves as one of the controlling mechanisms in shaping the course of world politics.

The Settlement of Disputes. The principles of power politics are seen at their clearest in the settlement of an international dispute. When two or more states become involved in a controversy, the final resolution of the dispute is arrived at in terms of power. The merits of the respective cases and considerations of legal or moral rights are irrelevant to the final outcome, except in so far as they themselves are factors of power on one side or the other.

No questions are actually settled in any rational sense by the operation of the state system except those involving power. World War II, for example, did not prove that Hitler was morally or legally wrong, nor did it prove that the United Nations had fought in defense of a set of absolutely applicable moral precepts. Nothing was finally decided about the relative merits of dictatorship and democracy, or of authoritarianism and freedom. All that was established was that the military machine commanded by Hitler and his associates was insufficiently powerful to withstand the onslaught of the forces arrayed against it. This verdict, although clear-cut and providing a base for future policy, was independent of the emotional involvements of individuals and of any moral judgment binding upon the collectivities called states. The haste with which the former enemies have resumed close relations and with which the victorious alliance dissolved after the war serves to underscore this verdict.

Power politics means in practice that international disputes tend to be settled in terms of the relative power applied by each party. If a sufficient preponderance of power be mustered by one state, a fairly clear victory is gained; if the opposing forces are sufficiently well balanced so as to make a forced triumph impossible or inexpedient, some compromise is arranged which reflects the relative strength of the disputants. This generalization is equally applicable to a violent conflict or to a diplomatic controversy.

THE COMPETITIVE SYSTEM

The Competitive Approach. The logic of the state system necessitates that states approach each other in an atmosphere of competition. Competition and conflict may not be evident in any particular interstate relationship, but they underlie all of them and serve to govern the strategy and tactics of states in conducting their policies.

The principle cause of the competitive approach of states is found in the egocentric nature of the state institution which we noted above. Each state plays its part in world affairs as a means of satisfying its own desires and acts in any situation in such a manner as to turn it to the maximum advantage.

A second premise which adds to this atmosphere of competition is that most national objectives are logically absolute. States are by nature insatiable; there is no rational end to a policy of security, prestige, or ideology except world domination. Later in this chapter we shall see how statesmen seek to discover and lay down practical limits to these absolutist drives. For the moment, however, it suffices to point out that the nature of the interstate relationship makes it inherently a competitive one.

A striking example of how states react to new situations in a competitive way was furnished by the rapid sequence of events in Iran during August 1953. The internal political convulsion through which that state passed represented one of the sudden and unexpected twists of history which require immediate adjustment on the part of nearly every state. All the major powers analyzed the *coup d'état* of Prime Minister Mossadegh, the flight of the Shah, the almost immediate counter-revolution, the return of the Shah, and Mossadegh's arrest in terms of the impact of these events upon their own long-range and absolute objectives. Some states gained an advantage by the turn of events, some were injured; most were unable to discover immediately how they had fared and consequently avoided making over-hasty commitments.

The relations of the major powers to each other were materially affected. The United States found the change in Iran's government to its liking; with a pro-Western ruler once again in command there, the United States could withdraw some of the power with which it had been supporting its Iranian policy and use it to increase the pressure it was exerting upon the Soviet world.

Great Britain, hoping for an end to the annoying dispute with Iran over the expropriation and nationalization of the Anglo-Iranian Oil Company looked to an end to that quarrel and to the opportunity to play a larger role elsewhere in the Middle East. This improved position would strengthen it hand with the Soviet on the one hand and the United States on the other. The accuracy of British judgment seemed to be confirmed when, a few month later, diplomatic relations were resumed with Iran after a long period of suspension. The oil dispute was finally settled during the summer of 1954.

The USSR, on its part, found itself at a disadvantage as a result of the change of government in Iran. The new ruling group was clearly anti-Soviet (Mossadegh had been, at least, benevolently neutral in the cold war). Russian policy was obliged to face the alternatives of employing direct coercion upon the new regime or else permitting a significant impairment of its position in Iran and the entire Middle East. In either case its position with regard to the West was weakened. Each of the three major powers analyzed the Iranian crisis in the light of its own objectives and policy and sought to extract the maximum advantage for itself.

Conflict and Agreement. We already know that the guide followed by each state in international politics is its own concept of national interest. When the national interests of any two states fix upon the identical objective and each seeks its attainment, a situation of international conflict is created. When interests do not clash but instead coincide, harmony and agreement exist.

Because of the absoluteness of national interest and the inevitably competitive pursuit of national objectives, we should logically expect conflict to be the most common climate of international relations. To take just one example, so long as each state conceives security as an objective to be unilaterally attained, no other relationship than conflict is possible as each state seeks to achieve security on its own terms.

Competition, our economists assure us, is the life of trade; in international relations it is the life of politics as well. It is the basis upon which the system is constructed. Were some other factor the governing force in the constant intercourse of states, the story of international affairs would be entirely different.

Competition in Practice. States do not, in their corporate capacity, 'trust' each other as do individuals; each of them regards all the others as competitors and potential adversaries. The logic of national sovereignty does not allow any state to view with equanimity the progress of any other state toward the attainment of any of its absolute goals. All must be concerned over any increase in the power of any of the others. No matter where such improvement in the status of any state may be directed at the moment, there is no reason for any of its associates to assume that this increased power may not some day be pointed at them.

Consequently, as soon as any state succeeds in improving its position in any perceptible and signficant way, one of the chain reactions we discussed earlier immediately sets in. Every other state in a position to do so strives either to strengthen its own position in proportion or else to weaken the newly powerful state in some other way so as to restore the relationship to something like its former dimensions. All of the available resources of policy are usually thrown behind this attempt at readjustment; it is a matter of great urgency for most states and becomes often the first order of business. The possible means are many: military (rearmament), political (new alliances), economic (discriminatory trade practices), or psychological (propaganda campaigns). If it proves to be impossible to redress the balance, all the states involved must thereupon make major policy changes which reflect the altered power relationship.

Competition and Atomic Control. The postwar maneuvering of the major powers on the question of the international control of atomic energy and atomic weapons provides an instructive example of this process. At the end of the war in 1945, the United States enjoyed a 'monopoly' of atomic knowledge, at least as far as the manufacture of militarily feasible atomic bombs was concerned. The United Kingdom and the USSR, to say nothing of the rest of the world, were disquieted by this development; despite our assurances of good intentions, they found American leadership in atomic weapons to be a cause of insecurity. They undertook several policies in an attempt to rectify the situation.

All sought some form of international control over atomic energy which would have freed them from the danger of American employment of the bomb as a policy weapon, and at the same time would have given them access to American technical information and production techniques. The United States, in its turn, refused to part with its information without gaining some corresponding policy advantage over both Britain and the Soviet. We advocated a form of international control (the 'Baruch plan') which would have permitted us to construct bombs until such time as world-wide atomic regulation would have forbidden the use of atomic power for military purposes. The adoption of this proposal would have enabled us to maintain our continued power advantage over the USSR and Britain.

This was totally unacceptable to the USSR, even though the fundamental harmony of interest between Britain and the United States persuaded the British to accept it. The Soviet Union and the United Kingdom both intensified their own research and development programs following the failure of this initial effort to discover a formula of control; by 1951 both had exploded bombs of their own. Now it was the turn of the United States to be disturbed.

Although American leadership was yet unchallenged, the fact that other states had mastered the scientific and technical problems of bomb manufacture necessarily represented a weakening of the United States power position. The search for international control over atomic power thereupon took on a new dimension for Americans; it was no longer a problem of confining the USSR to a position of inferiority, but instead one of seeking to neutralize a growing power factor in the position of the principal adversary of the United States. As a result, in 1953 the United States made a new proposal for international atomic control, focused upon the peaceful exploitation of atomic power instead of upon its military aspects; the American government kept urging its adoption during the next two years. An international conference on the peaceful use of atomic energy, in which Communist and free world scientists exchanged information, was held in Geneva in the summer of 1955. This was the first concrete result of the new American policy.

In the meantime, the lesser states found themselves trapped in a steadily deteriorating situation as the great powers made more and more progress in atomic weapons. There is no logical reason for small powers to trust any o the three world leaders with atomic bombs, or any one of them more than the other two. Accordingly, they have reacted in several directions.

In the first place, many—notably India—have redoubled their efforts to create some effective form of international control. Secondly, several of them —including especially France—have been devoting increasing amounts of money and manpower to a feverish research program of their own. In the third place, those in a position to do so have attempted to use their bargaining power to secure some rectification of the atomic balance. France, for example, attempted repeatedly to make its inclusion in the atomic power pool a price for its approval of German rearmament.

The problem of atomic energy is only one manifestation of the competitive nature of world politics; it is a basic characteristic of the system in which any advantage gained by one state sets off a search for compensating gains by the others.

The Pressure–Counter-pressure Relationship. The state of relations between any two states is therefore determined by the interaction of two opposing currents of force. We have already seen that states approach each other competitively and that no international institution exists which can guarantee the outcome of any particular dispute. As between any two states, there is a two-directional flow of power. Each state is engaged in a constant process of applying power to all its associates—in some cases direct and in considerable quantity, in others indirect and in small amount—and at the same time it is itself the object of power applied by all other states. The balance that is struck between the two flows of power and the resistance each meets determine the over-all climate of relations between any such states.

Of course, it is impossible to measure the mutual relationships of the different factors of power with anything like mathematical exactitude. Too many imponderables enter into the judgments of statesmen and no policy maker is able to govern his conduct exclusively by the power exerted upon him from beyond the boundaries of his state. The existence of the pressure–counter-pressure relationship, however, provides the point of departure in the process of policy making by all rational statesmen.

Power in War and Peace. This dichotomy applies in all international relationships. It is of course most obvious in time of war, when each combatant uses all the political, economic, psychological, and military power at its command in order to force compliance with its wishes. The verdict of war is delivered clearly in terms of the relative power applied. The only significant difference between a warlike relationship and a peaceful one, however, is the particular means employed. The mental orientation, the objectives, and the principles of action are identical: to coerce the opponent into agreement. Nonviolent struggles do not go to the extremes of war, and compromise upon the basis of relative commitments of power is usually easier to arrange. Nevertheless, what the free world has come to call 'cold war'—a state of diplomatic controversy in which states combat each other with every weapon at their command except armed violence—is different only in degree from 'hot' war at one extreme and from more routine international contacts at the other.

Intra-alliance Relationships. In international politics there are many close and 'harmonious' relations between particular states, but even these are susceptible to the influence of competition and mutual pressure. Mutuality of interest explains co-operative action. No international agreements in history have been closer or more binding than some of the defensive alliances worked out by states that have felt themselves menaced by a common enemy.

The greatest and most inclusive of these was the United Nations Organization, the 'grand alliance' of World War II. Yet even this one—among the most successful international groupings of all time—was marked by constant bickering among its members and was not able to survive to make a lasting peace. A single overriding interest—a fear of the common enemy, the Axis powers—brought together a number of otherwise ill-assorted states. Agreement of interest upon one point, however, even such an important one, did not carry with it agreement upon all. Each member of the alliance was in the war for its own purposes and was pursuing its own future advantage. Each had its own version of what it wanted the postwar world to be like, and each attempted to influence the conduct of the war in that direction.

Great Britain, for example, sought to persuade the other allies to make the major European effort of the war in the area of the Balkans in order to preserve its own influence and power there after the fighting ended. The USSR insisted upon a second front in Europe long before the West was prepared for such action; this would have relieved some of the pressure upon the Red armies and simultaneously weakened the West in the postwar world. The United States, seeking the earliest possible end to the European phase of the struggle so as to be able to shift its emphasis to the Pacific, insisted upon a cross-Channel invasion as the cheapest and most direct method of destroying the enemy. Other allies—France, the Netherlands, China, and others—also sought to influence strategic and tactical decisions to their own advantage.

The alliance proved unable to outlast the crisis that had brought it into existence. Once the single common purpose of all the various governments had been accomplished by the defeat of the Axis, the national interests of the allies fell again into their mutually competitive relationships, and the alliance disintegrated. It was replaced by new alignments more in harmony with the situation that prevailed after the war. It is a truism of diplomacy that a military alliance endures only as long as the crisis responsible for its creation continues to concern the states involved.

Degrees of Competitiveness. Although logically the requirements of the state system demand that states be absolutely competitive in their relation

with one another, in practice the level of intensity of the actual conflict between them varies among different states and between the same states at different times. The competition between states waxes and wanes in direct proportion to the degree to which their interests clash. If no conflict of interest
obtains, relations are either nonexistent (a logical but improbable condition)
or harmonious. At times, harmony of interest upon particular issues may be
so great as to enable states to forego their normally competitive approach. It
was, for example, to the real interest of the United States that its European
allies be strengthened after 1947. On the other hand, if a direct collision involves matters of vital importance to both states, the inevitable conflict may
reach the peak of war. As concepts of interest held by states in executing
their policies evolve in response to internal developments and the course of
history, the degree of competitiveness between particular states may change,
either intensifying or relaxing. Sometimes long-standing hostilities dissolve,
as was the case between Britain and France after 1900 as both were menaced
by an expanding Germany. Sometimes new hostilities are born as interests
expand; the suddenly emergent conflict between the United States and the
Soviet Union after 1945 was the direct outgrowth of the radical expansion in
interest which both states experienced as a result of World War II.

TECHNIQUES OF STABILITY

In the preceding section we attempted to demonstrate that the assumptions upon which the state system is grounded operate upon states to direct
their activities in particular directions. However, even after it is admitted that
constant dynamism and a trend toward disorder are the theoretical principles
upon which the system depends, it remains obvious that in fact international
relations do not always display these characteristics in any extreme measure.
Movement, evolution, and change do actually take place in the relations of
states, but in practice it is rare that they occur as frequently and extensively
as is theoretically possible: instead, both their pace and their direction are
subject to considerable control.

The trend toward disorder is usually confined within fairly clear limits
through the efforts of statesmen. The collapse of orderly international relationships—an event logically to be expected to occur often in terms of the
theoretical base of the state system—is instead today viewed by most people
as a catastrophe whose avoidance is a matter of first importance. Indeed,
when one considers the inescapable first principles of international life and
the possible consequences that might flow from them, the relatively high
incidence of peace and orderly process which obtains in international relations is a tribute to the dedication and ingenuity of most of the statesmen
who guide the destiny of states.

In general their task of preserving order may be thought of as a limiting
one. If the logic of international relations should be permitted to reach its

ultimate development, the relations between states would resemble the Hobbesian concept of anarchy. The dynamic forces of international life cannot completely be eliminated so long as the state system retains its historic bases of organization. This being the case, the rational statesman seeks to work out the details of his policy in harmony with these postulates. He attempts to capitalize upon those factors in the international situation which operate to his advantage and to control and limit those which are unfavorable. The impact of change is thereupon minimized and the greater share of interstate contacts gains a reasonable degree of systematization.

It might almost be said that the forces of international politics are self-neutralizing. The closer disaster comes within any particular context, the greater the effort put forth by statesmen to ward it off. In this endeavor they have several techniques of stability to aid them.

The Rule of Expediency

Perhaps the best—and certainly the most enduring—of all the guides to practical statesmanship ever written is *The Prince* (1513), by the Florentine Renaissance figure, Nicolo Machiavelli. Although written early in the sixteenth century, his maxims of prudence and force are as applicable to contemporary conditions as they were to the era of the Renaissance. The general lesson taught by this little book is the first of the great techniques which all statesmen must respect and apply. It may be termed the 'rule of expediency': always to do what is expedient and to refrain from doing what is inexpedient. No more inclusive and efficacious imperative could be imagined for insuring state success in international relations and the preservation of the structure of peace.

To comprehend the nature of expediency, it is vital that a policy maker be sensitive to all situational factors that affect him and his government. Often statesmen misjudge the expediency of a particular course under existing conditions and thus they err about where the maximum advantage for their state lies. In such cases international crises occur with potentially disastrous results. Sometimes the impact of other political or psychological forces leads them to ignore practicality in policy and to undertake risky and adventuresome programs. Nevertheless, the rule of expediency is perhaps the most revealing single idea aiding in the comprehension of the behavior of statesmen.

The Relativism of International Politics. We have already touched upon the fact that in international politics there are virtually no absolute values except the existence of the state and the satisfaction of its interests. The state is morally its own excuse for being in any international sense; it requires no moral justifications other than those which it provides for itself. The only concepts of 'good' and 'bad' which have any relevance to the international conduct of the state are relative to its success or failure in attaining its ob jectives. Any policy that succeeds in advancing national interest is a good policy; any policy that, for whatever reason, fails to reach its objective is by that fact a bad one. No more relativist philosophy could be imagined.

It has proved particularly difficult for Americans to grasp this idea, because it runs directly counter to our native political philosophy, the doctrine of natural rights. Our ideology is grounded upon a series of premises which we hold to be true and of universal moral application. This absolutist doctrine has served us well at home; accordingly, we tend to assume that international politics also is organized upon a series of absolute dogmas of morality. Many of the rude shocks which we have felt since 1945 have been due to our natural expectation that the principles of political democracy would be applicable at the international level. This has simply proved not to be the case; instead, the conduct of states is determined by a highly flexible relativism.

Part of the confusion to which many individuals are subject in thinking about world affairs is due to the fact that they fail to realize the irrelevance of private moral principles in considering the relationships of states. In point of fact, the corporate state does not govern its international conduct by the Judiac-Christian code of ethics to which most individuals in the Western world subscribe. It might be a better and more orderly world if states did so, and perhaps we shall know stability only when statesmen apply the same standards to their official policy that they do to their private lives. In practice, however, states do not seek to accomplish the absolute moral right and to flee the wrong as these concepts are formulated by any ethical-religious code. Whatever they may be attempting to accomplish at the moment is 'right' and 'good' at that time; whenever a new line of policy is selected, it becomes 'right' and 'good' in its turn.

This is not to say that governments never espouse the cause of private morality; indeed, many of them often do. When a state's policy leads it to advocate policy in harmony with principles of private right and justice, however, it does so because of its belief that such action is in service of the national interest. When interest diverges from morality, few statesmen hesitate. They usually continue to adhere to the guide of interest, and abandon (although sometimes regretfully) the teachings of the private moral code.

It would be inaccurate to imply that the state is a completely amoral entity with no concern for any moral principles. Actually, in international relations the state serves as the creator of a morality of its own, and its policy is shaped by the teaching of a doctrine of which it is the principal architect. This 'state-morality' is, as Machiavelli pointed out, logically disassociated from private ethics. The objectives of the state organization are different from those of private persons and its conduct must therefore be measured by different standards.

In modern political life, the state form looms large in the activity sphere of individuals, and it is inescapable that under such conditions state-oriented and state-manipulated codes of behavior should come to gain wide acceptance despite their seeming conflict with the standards of right and wrong which we accept for our private lives. Most of us never seem to question the existence or the validity of such a double moral standard. Acts immoral within private moral judgment become sanctified if done in the name of the state by someone armed with its authority.

The Notion of Expediency. It is within this relativist and (by private standards) amoral situation that the political notion of expediency is applicable. The idea means in practice that a state should always select and act upon that particular policy which is most likely to advance its interest in the given context. The only constant is national interest; all else is relative to the situation. Great decisions and small alike are made in the light of this principle. The most pressing question of our age—whether or not there is to be a total war which might well wipe out our civilization—will be in the last analysis answered according to the same general criteria that would determine whether or not a state should ratify a proposed treaty for the regulation of cod fishing.

We already know that in the process of selecting the most expedient from all the possible courses of action, a statesman always balances the advantages to be gained from any particular policy against the possible disadvantages arising from any certain or expected opposition by other states. War, for example, becomes expedient when two factors are present simultaneously in the situation facing a state: (1) an objective which is sufficiently important to justify the risks and inescapable destruction of combat and which cannot be attained by any lesser means; (2) a power advantage which offers a sufficiently strong likelihood of winning the military test and of gaining the objective. If both factors are present, a statesman can confidently accept war as a policy technique; if either is absent, war is inexpedient and probably will not be resorted to. All alternatives of policy are analyzed in the same way: the statesman 'balances the desirability of the possible with the possibility of the desirable' and strikes the best practicable compromise between them.

The Influence of Circumstances. Two elements of the foregoing discussion require some further consideration. The first is the influence of situational factors in any policy decision; the second is the critical importance of maintaining the maximum number of alternatives of policy.

Although every state seeks to follow the dictates of national interest and designs a policy to chart a consistent course toward its objectives, these permanent and relatively fixed 'principles' of policy exercise only a partial control over the actual maneuvering of the state. Circumstances affect the conduct of international politics more than is often realized. The long-range policy of any government is subject to a constant buffeting of conditions which force major modifications. Among these can be included the action of other states, unexpected historical 'accidents,' and the impact of domestic policies.

As a statesman seeks to advance national interest in the face of all the rapidly changing circumstances he deals with, he has no other guide but expediency. He must be willing temporarily to abandon a long-range policy in order to seize a short-run gain, if such be the true course of expediency; on the other hand, he must not be overly short-sighted in analyzing the expedient, or else he runs the danger of doing permanent injury to long-range national interest in the pursuit of the immediate. Always, however, he finds that the formalized policy statements of his government provide an insufficient guide to action; he must be ever alert to recognize the extent and the form of the influence which conditions exert upon his policy.

A good illustration of this problem is provided by the course of American policy toward Yugoslavia since 1945. Up until 1948, the United States attitude toward the government of Marshal Tito was controlled by the general policy principal of opposition to the dogma of communism and to its visible manifestation, the Soviet sphere of influence. This idea was formalized in the policy known as 'containment,' which involved hostility to everything and everyone inside the Iron Curtain. Then, in 1948, there occurred the first break in the monolithic structure of the Soviet world: the expulsion of Tito from the councils of the communist elect.

Here was a circumstance that made much of our former policy obsolescent. No longer was it possible to consider communist ideology and the Soviet empire as being synonymous or coterminous. We were obliged to choose our real enemy from between the two in order to frame a policy that would be in harmony with the circumstances. If we were primarily interested in fighting communist doctrine we should then attempt to destroy Tito's regime, which, alone and friendless, would have proved no formidable obstacle; if our true enemy was really Russian national power and imperialist policy, our course would then be to ally ourselves with Tito on the ground of identity of interest and thus to gain added strength for the bloc of which we were the leaders.

We chose the second course. All Americans know that national interest dictated our policy of co-operation with Yugoslavia which dates from our decision at that time. Such a policy is greatly at variance with our former doctrine of ideological purity. It was not a happy choice that was forced upon us; many Americans are yet restive in any close relationship with a communist dictatorship, even an anti-Russian one. Circumstances no longer permitted us, however, to follow our previously applicable principle. The new policy represented merely the selection of the most expedient course open to us under the conditions.

The Concept of Equilibrium

Dynamic Equilibrium. Although the dynamism of world affairs is apparent, it is not so immediately clear that they are constantly tending toward equilibrium. This point—a great cause for encouragement about the ultimate prospects of man—requires some analysis at this time. So powerful are the forces of movement and change that this equilibrium can never, under our present system or organization, become static and permanent. A 'dynamic equilibrium' in international relationships, however, not only is possible but is frequently attained.

This condition of relative balance between states is the principal means by which the world is spared the scourge of war in most crisis situations. Even when it exists, much change and modification in the relationships of states continues to take place. The trend toward equilibrium usually confines the movement within the limits of safety, however, and non-violent resolutions are worked out for the problems that come up during the period of its effectiveness. Equilibrium breaks down and war comes only when the dynamic forces become too strong to be any longer confined.

The Limits upon International Action. Relations between any two states and within the system of states take place within a broad range from relaxation to tension. Measures appropriate to a happy state of affairs are out of place in a time of tension, while extreme measures (violence and war) become practicable only in situations of great crisis. In other words, if the state mechanism possessed the ability to prevent international crisis from passing the danger point of tension, the inclination to resort to violence would be lacking and greater reliance would instead be placed upon more orderly procedures. Confinement of international politics within 'safe' limits would deliver man from at least the worst consequences of his inability to organize society upon a supra-national basis.

Although in no sense an automatic mechanism and of no guaranteed efficacy—failures have been many—factors do exist in world affairs which frequently serve as confining elements to state action in a crisis. The closer the world drifts toward war in the course of an international dispute, the greater the number of factors that appear to seek to halt the trend. Perhaps the most influential factors supporting this thesis are the growing hazards of war for all states and the decreasing possibility of meaningful victory for any.

Techniques of Equilibrium. Several techniques for bringing about equilibrium have been developed by diplomats in earlier eras and are being applied today.

The device of the sphere of influence, by means of which competing states mark off their respective areas of hegemony and each guarantees to respect the other's prior rights, repeatedly has proved capable of ending disputes and is today governing great-power relations in such territories as the Balkans.

The technique of the buffer zone also has had a great effect in restoring and preserving equilibrium by separating contending states by a neutral zone. Revival of this idea in the present day was indicated by the numerous proposals (mainly by Russia and France) looking toward a permanently neutralized Germany which were made during 1954 and 1955.

Collective security, discussed briefly earlier and in more detail below, may also be considered as a technique of equilibrium.

Perhaps the most elaborate system for the creation and maintenance of dynamic equilibrium is the balance of power. This idea is also considered in detail later in this chapter, but at this time we may point out its essential characteristic: at attempt to capitalize upon the inherent dynamism of world politics by creating a self-neutralizing situation. How this is done we shall see later.

Factors Making for Equilibrium. Why is it becoming easier for the crises of world politics to be neutralized short of breakdown? Why are the factors making for equilibrium growing steadily stronger? To answer these questions fully would necessitate retelling the diplomatic history of the past fifty years, but some few general reasons may be suggested.

(1) The growing reluctance of states to resort to war. This subject is considered in the next section, but it may be said here that evidence is plentiful that states today are much less willing to accept war than they formerly were. This circumstance gives the neutralizing forces greater opportunity to do their work.

(2) The difficulty of isolating and confining war if it should occur. War, under contemporary technological conditions, is tremendously contagious, and no state can be unconcerned about an outbreak of war anywhere in the world. The best way for a state to avoid being drawn into a war in which it has little real interest is to help prevent that war from ever starting.

(3) The growing unwillingness of individuals to undergo the hardships of war for any but the most important of reasons. States passively endure provocations today that would have been unbearable a few years ago because statesmen feel that they cannot ask their people to die for any but the most vital of interests.

(4) The increase in the number of expedient alternatives to war. As these continue to expand their area of effectiveness, more and more of interstate relations is coming within their scope. War becomes a less attractive means of accomplishing national purposes when there exist several other devices that offer promise of attaining the objective without the stresses and disruptions required by war.

THE AVOIDANCE OF WAR

War is generally admitted today, by statesmen and laymen alike, to be a course of last resort adopted only in desperate situations permitting of no other remedy. There is little of moral revulsion in this evolving attitude, little idea that war is inherently wrong and evil. Instead it is, as are most of the decisions of statesmen, grounded primarily in considerations of practicality and expediency. Nevertheless, the growing reluctance of states to go to war is in itself a factor of stability which serves to make international politics somewhat less dangerous and unpredictable.

The Inexpediency of War. War is daily growing more inexpedient for most states. We saw above that war is selected as a technique of policy by states if two factors are present: an objective worthy of the effort, and a reasonable probability of victory. On both counts war is today becoming less attractive.

Modern war is incredibly destructive. Modern 'total' weapons, with entire civilizations as their targets, are capable of wreaking great havoc upon any state in the world. In addition to the physical damage that war brings, organizing a nation to fight today involves a wholesale disruption and uprooting of the entire structure of social and economic life. Even a state which, like the United States, escaped the physical destruction of World War II, suffered a great social and economic upheaval whose effects will continue to be felt for generations to come. From the point of view both of the probable destruction and of the certain social and economic upset, war necessitates a tremendous effort on the part of any government and its people.

The Difficulty of Victory. A further factor makes war less expedient: the diminishing possibility of meaningful victory. Modern weapons are offensive weapons, and the best defense against them is the capacity for immediate reprisal. Thus any statesmen calculating the desirability of a war must gamble upon the possibility of a quick victory to end the struggle before it settles down to a grim process of mutual pulverization.

To gain this quick triumph requires an overwhelming preponderance of power. In earlier days, when the outcome of a military defeat was merely a loss of territory or the payment of an indemnity, a policy maker might often be tempted to risk war upon nothing more substantial than a fairly good prospect of victory. Today, when the penalty for losing a war may be national obliteration, this margin of advantage is insufficient. Great superiority is necessary and, at least among the major states, it is a near impossibility to achieve it. Even the two great powers whose bitter controversy has earned the name of the 'cold war,' the United States and the Soviet Union, have been scrupulous not to present each other with ultimatums that might leave only the alternatives of capitulation or war.

Avoiding War by Compromise. Statesmen seek to avoid war by compromising disputes upon the basis of relative involvements of interest and power. A given object of controversy may be a matter of deep interest to one party and of only minor concern to the other. If the relative involvements can be diplomatically determined and if the objective is one permitting such a technique of disposal, a compromise reflecting the differences in commitment is often not too difficult to arrange.

In theory this process would make wars forever obsolete. If power judgments could be made in an atmosphere of perfect rationality, statesmen could conduct their affairs like chess players. Calmly and soberly they would analyze their relative positions and power dispositions, foresee the inevitable end of the struggle, and either claim victory or accept defeat without any necessity of fighting the war at all. Such detached objectivity is more than most statesmen are capable of, however, in the hectic atmosphere of international and domestic politics. It must also be admitted that the rigidity of the two-power world after 1945 made the diplomatic compromise a much less effective substitute for war than it might otherwise have been.

Avoiding War through Institutional Alternatives. A second basis for avoiding war is the settlement of disputes by an institutional instrument of some sort, the best known of which is the United Nations. The institutional approach to the avoidance of war has not prospered in the post-1945 era, and at the present time it is of limited applicability. Nevertheless, if most of mankind has its way, the day will come when the United Nations or some similar organization will be given effective power to enforce the rules of peaceful settlement. Today, with war growing daily less expedient, the long-range possibility of such a development is brighter than at any time in the past.

The Bases for Accepting War. Perhaps it is not too much to say that no war is inevitable. Somewhere along the chain of events that precede an outbreak of hostilities, one of the statesmen involved must make the critical choice. Should he select a different policy alternative, war over that issue can be avoided. Perhaps the choice is made unknowingly; the fact remains, however, that in the course of every dispute there is a 'point of no return.' Once the final step is taken, there is no way out but war. Realizing this fact, most policy makers walk ever more warily as they near the point of the irrevocable decision.

A statesman chooses to resort to war in one of three circumstances: when he is under pressure from an inflamed national opinion which reckons not with possible defeat or rational goals of victory; when he recognizes a threat to his state's vital interests that is so intimately bound up with national existence that in its defense the people would fight even a doomed war; or when he calculates that war in any particular situation is expedient.

Miscalculating the expediency of a war is one of the most common dangers to peace. Once a leader decides that his power situation is such that he can safely risk a war, he tends to commit his state so deeply as to make withdrawal impossible if it should later become clear that he has made a mistake. It must be kept in mind that in any dispute war may be inexpedient for both parties, or for either one; it cannot be expedient for both. Unless deprived of free choice by some irrational force, a state in a condition of actual power inferiority to its opponent does not accept war unless it is unaware or unconvinced of its weakness.

In modern world politics, such a miscalculation often brings complete disaster. One need look no further than the consequences of Germany's misjudgments of Great Britain in 1914, of the United States in 1917, and of Great Britain again in 1939 and 1940 to find corroborating evidence. Communist leadership also apparently miscalculated United States reaction in 1950 at the time of the commencement of the war in Korea. In all of these cases, war originally thought expedient proved not to be so because of an analytical error.

Contemporary Techniques for Avoiding War. The present structure of world politics affords several interesting examples of the techniques employed by states to avoid war. Remembering that modern war, to be practical, must involve a great power superiority over any enemy, every state has sought to escape from positions of inferiority to any probable foe. In doing so, most of them have fled to the protection of the great blocs led by the United States and the Soviet Union. These massive alliances confront each other today in a state of baffled hostility. Exactly how much each alliance has contributed to the strength of the United States and the USSR as regards each other is open to question; certainly neither has won any great victories over the other since the alliances came into being.

It is nevertheless clear that within at least the Western alliance there is much working at cross purposes. American policy makers have viewed their group as added support for United States policy in the cold war against the Soviet Union and have assumed that our allies are motivated by the same purposes as we have been. On the other hand, many of the associates of the United States joined the group as a means of reducing the possibility of their being drawn into a war, and they would consider a war begun by the United States and serving American national interest as being just as undesirable as one begun by the Russians. As a result, there is a constant controversy going on within the Western bloc.

More recently this concern with their own vulnerability has led some of the smaller states to join a new grouping led by India. This bloc has not formalized its status by written agreement, but its over-all position is clear. It rejects both alliances as being equally war-minded and is establishing for itself a position of neutrality and mediation between them. In this effort the Indian (sometimes called 'Arab-Asian') bloc seems to have gained some support from many people now included in one of the bipolar groupings. For example, in the debates in the United Nations during August 1953 dealing with the details of the final truce in Korea and the proposed political conference to be held there, several allies of the United States, including Australia and the Philippines, deserted the American position to side with India. The neutral bloc's position grew more strategic as the cold war relaxed during 1954 and 1955. All this maneuvering has at its root a desire on the part of each of the weaker states not to be caught in a position of such weakness as to make war upon it expedient on the part of a stronger neighbor.

THE DEVELOPMENT OF INSTITUTIONS

A final technique of stability in international politics remains to be considered. This is the development of international institutions. Although we know already that the institutional structure of interstate life is incomplete and of limited effectiveness, formalized institutions are nevertheless significant in themselves and of great importance as possible harbingers of the future.

The present generation is not the first to discover that international politics is logically anarchic and provocative of tension and crisis. The student is struck by the long history of man's attempts to discover a route of escape from this condition. One of the principal methods employed has been the deliberate creation of new international institutions and the strengthening of existing ones. These institutions have developed by drawing analogies with private civil life.

In highly organized private society, the institutions that surround us are constructed upon predictable behavior patterns of individuals. We know, for example, that private citizens will not normally settle their disputes by violence but will have recourse to the courts. This tends to make interpersonal relations more orderly and stable and provides a greater measure of personal security. Indeed, without the institutional framework ordering individual relationships, social life would be nearly impossible to endure.

If some such institutional framework were to be created for control of sovereign states, much of the anarchy of international life would be eliminated. Therefore, international institutions seek to prohibit certain modes of state conduct as being antisocial and at the same time to provide adequate alternative procedures for the satisfaction of the legitimate desires of states. Up to now, their impact upon world politics has been peripheral; if they should succeed in materially increasing their scope, the shape and texture of interstate relations would be improved.

The Institutions of International Life. The analysis of the institutions of the world political community will be undertaken in later chapters. At this point we need only name and briefly characterize the more important of them.

International law is a body of rules and principles that specify the rights of states and lay down the procedures to be followed by states in dealing with each other. It includes mechanisms for the settlement of interstate disputes upon the basis of legal right as well as techniques for the redress of injury. Much of international relations is already within its scope, and the attempt to enlarge its area of effectiveness is a continuous one.

International organization is the term applied to permanent associations of sovereign states which have become sufficiently formalized to acquire an international status. The United Nations is one with a generalized multi-purpose mission; hundreds exist with more specialized purposes. Through these organizations states develop regularized procedures for co-operative action, and in the aggregate a remarkably large proportion of international contact takes place within the institutional structure.

The third international institution that merits our attention is supra-national government. Only in the present generation has this concept transcended mere abstract speculation and entered the stage of significant development. It involves the partial merging of the sovereignties of the member states to create new instruments of government with real, though limited, powers. For the special purposes of the organization, the participating states forswear their sovereign independence and full authority is exerted by the new authority. Of the many proposals for such organizations made since World War II, by the end of 1955 only the European Coal and Steel Community had entered upon its operations, but its success and the logic of its organization promised that several others would come into early existence.

ORGANIZING AND OPERATING CONCEPTS

In the preceding section we considered the techniques employed by statesmen to enable them to accomplish their mission within the requirements of the state system. We now turn to an analysis of a somewhat more formalized development of the same general idea: the various concepts that seek to provide general organizing and operating hypotheses for the entire structure of international politics.

These all seek to bring a higher degree of order and predictability into the international relationships by establishing single principles upon which to base all political action. Each of them is dynamic, in the sense that it accepts the inevitability of change in interstate life. Each has at one time or another been asserted to be the single route to stability and peace that the world must follow; each has had its more or less successful application at particular periods of history, and each has undergone its periods of ineffectiveness and failure. We shall examine four of them in some detail: the concept of the great powers, the concept of the concert of power, the concept of the balance of power, and the concept of collective security. They all share a common preoccupation with the phenomenon of power and the need for its control; each attempts the solution of the problem in a different way.

THE GREAT POWER CONCEPT

The Role of the Great Powers. The first principle is the idea of the great powers. It owes its origin to a factor mentioned in Chapters 2 and 4: despite the legal equality which states pretend to enjoy, there are actually wide variations in their power and thus in their relative ability to achieve their ends. One group of states that individually encompass great concentrations of power and collectively dominates world politics has come to be called the 'great powers.'

Historically, the shape of world affairs has been determined by the relations of the great powers to each other. The present pattern of international relations has been laid down by these few states simply because they have had available the power to support their pretensions to superior status. The great powers have determined the standards of international conduct; they have asserted the right to be consulted upon any question in which they take an interest; they have created world-wide empires; they have repeatedly redrawn the map of the world; they alone have been able to force the entire world to go to war. Their superior position has enabled them to concentrate their attention upon their relations with one another, dealing with small states by means of considerations of status and prestige instead of by raw power.

Such has been their dominant position that most smaller states have found it impossible to remain aloof from great-power politics. The majority have found it expedient to attach themselves at one time or another to the protection of one of the great powers upon the latter's terms, and then to work out their further policy within this framework.

The Group of Great Powers. The number of great powers has varied from time to time but has always been relatively small. During most of the nineteenth century all of them were European. Austria, Prussia, Great Britain, and Russia were the 'Big Four' of the Congress of Vienna in 1815, joined shortly thereafter by France as the Napoleonic issue diminished in importance. Later in the century Italy was accepted as an additional member and Germany replaced Prussia. Around 1900 the European monopoly upon great power status was broken with the maturing of the United States and Japan. World War I resulted in Austria-Hungary's disappearance from the group and the temporary eclipse of Russia and Germany. World War II shook up the membership seriously and it has not again stabilized. Japan and Germany were crushed temporarily and the terms of their reacceptance have not yet been decided; Italy and France were so badly injured that their return to full status in the group at any time in the future is most doubtful; Great Britain was grievously weakened and has been so far unable to meet all the requirements of a great power.

The United States and the Soviet Union emerged from the war as the only survivors of the old group. Indeed, their power position was improved not only relatively but absolutely; so great was their margin of superiority that a new term was coined and some called them the 'super-powers.' Today the United States and the USSR still dominate the scene; Great Britain, Germany, France, and Japan are hoping to recapture their former eminence while two new aspirants for membership, China and India, are seeking to qualify.

The Decline of the Great Power Concept. The great-power principle—that only the great powers matter and that their decisions are binding upon all states—has been to a great degree weakened by the rise of nationalism. The upsurge of national spirit in the smaller states has given rise on their part to a reluctance and a great resistance to being taken for granted. Populations of smaller states, especially those that have only recently won their independence, feel that their national objectives and aspirations are just as valid and worthy of consideration as those of the people of a great power. In order to escape from great-power domination and to devise means to make their independence effective, small states often concert together.

One of their favorite techniques in recent years has involved the use of the mechanism of international organization. Much of the history of both the League of Nations and the United Nations can be told in terms of the more or less successful attempt of the small states to avoid being mere pawns of the great powers. For half a century the most eloquent spokesmen for the philosophy of international organization have come from the ranks of the lesser powers; contemporary figures include Herbert Evatt of Australia, Carlos Romulo of the Philippines, Paul-Henri Spaak of Belguim, Sir Leslie Munro of New Zealand, and Trygve Lie of Norway, the first Secretary-General of the United Nations.

The great-power principle has been seriously compromised by this outbreak of resentment and resistance among the citizens of the lesser powers, and no longer can it be successfully argued that only the foreign policies of the handful of great states are of any real importance. Small states, either through the identity of their policies with mass opinion throughout the world or through their total power when they combine forces, represent points of view which the great powers watch carefully and take due account of.

This may be a portent of a fundamental change in the character of world politics, or it may be only a temporary loss of position by the great powers. It is beyond doubt, however, that the principle of the great powers today has little relevance to the current world situation. The remainder of the world would simply refuse to be disposed of by any small group of states.

THE CONCEPT OF THE CONCERT OF POWER

A second concept of organization is the concert of power. The idea received its greatest formalization at the time of the Congress of Vienna in 1815, although it is actually much older. Put briefly, the notion has at its root the idea of the privileged role of the great powers and goes on from there to postulate that these few states have the right and the duty to concert together and to arrange all international affairs to suit their common convenience. It may thus be thought of as a technique for making the principle of the great power more effective.

Historical Incidence. During the period of reaction in Europe which followed the final victory over Napoleon in 1815, the concert of power sought to suppress the bogey of revolution wherever it might appear. The leading members of the concert were Austria, Russia, and Prussia; France was a later adherent and Britain an irregular participant. Under the leadership and guidance of Austria, the major states held several formal conferences to deal with specific revolutionary crises and in between maintained close contact with each other. Throughout the remainder of the nineteenth century the concert, including all the European great powers, functioned fitfully; effectively in 1856, 1878, and 1905 and unsuccessfully in 1827, 1848, and 1870. Its final failure was its greatest: it proved unable to ward off war in 1914.

In disrepute during the interwar period, the principle was made respectable again during World War II. The various 'Big Three' and 'Big Four' conferences at which Roosevelt, Churchill, Stalin, and other leaders shaped joint strategy represented a renewal of the old idea. The privileged position given permanent members of the Security Council of the United Nations is another example of the contemporary validity of the concept; under the Charter and the rule of great-power unanimity in the Security Council (the 'veto'), the major states collectively exercise a virtual monopoly over questions involving the maintenance of peace.

Strengths and Weaknesses of the Concert. It cannot be doubted that at particular moments the concert of power has proved to be most effective in preserving or restoring international peace. It is nevertheless painfully clear that the concert has failed in as spectacular a fashion on other occasions, and that its current manifestations, either in the Security Council or in the 'Big Four,' have proved unable to end the long crisis that grips the contemporary world. The reasons for the dramatic successes of the concert principle and its equally dramatic failures are found in the basic assumptions upon which the whole idea is grounded. There must be substantial agreement among the members of the concert—or at least among the preponderant majority of them—upon a general line of policy before the concert technique can produce significant results. This is why the concert is most effective in protecting the *status quo*. When the members of the concert are satiated and have a common interest in the perpetuation of what is for them a desirable arrangement, they can easily unite to subdue any potential upsetting force as being equally a threat to all of them. When there is no consensus upon the desirability of the *status quo* but instead a sizeable proportion of the great powers is more interested in altering the distribution of rewards, then the concert cannot succeed.

It breaks down when revisionist states are powerful and united enough to make the risk of breaking the peace worth taking. In other words, the agreement underlying an effective application of the concert of power is no different from any other type of international agreement. It comes into being as a result of an identity of interest among states and endures only so long as the interests coincide.

It seems obvious that the concept of the concert is of only remote significance in the world today, because the type of situation in which it is the most effective does not exist. The great powers today do not share an 'area of agreement' regarding the over-all structure of world politics and thus the essential precondition to an effective concert is lacking. Before the principle can again become effective, an identity of interest must develop not only between the United States and the Soviet Union but also among all the other states that qualify as great powers. Although great-power discussions were begun again in 1955, it is scarcely overpessimistic to predict that the full-fledged revival of the concert is still a long way in the future.

THE BALANCE OF POWER

General Theory. The principle of the balance of power is somewhat better known than are the first two. It has as its ideal a state of international equilibrium arrived at not by confining relationships into a set pattern but by accepting the dynamisms of world politics and utilizing them to secure peace. It enjoys one great advantage over the concert. The latter usually necessitates basic agreement among participating states in order to operate; the balance instead can function in a situation of conflict and disagreement. This makes the balance applicable in a somewhat broader variety of circumstances.

The balance has at its center an idea to which we have earlier alluded: a statesman will not normally resort to war when the odds are heavily against him. In operation, the balance of power is supposed to arrange matters so that any state which seeks to upset the peace will automatically have ranged against it sufficient power to persuade it of its folly.

Prerequisites: Dispersal and Fluidity. To be effective, the balance mechanism requires a relatively wide distribution of power among the states of the world. It is self-evident that when a single state or a small group of states enjoys a near hegemony, a much greater temptation exists on their part to attempt adventuresome policies backed by a willingness to go to war. Only when power is widely dispersed can the peace be preserved by the balance because only then is the international situation sufficiently fluid to permit states to move with the requisite freedom.

The regulatory mechanism of the balance of power therefore cannot be

DYNAMICS OF INTERNATIONAL POLITICS

effective unless international alignments are flexible and states are comparatively free to select the most expedient course in each situation as it arises.
Concentrations of power and rigidity of relationships are the twin phenomena
which the advocates of the balance recognize as the greatest dangers to peace.
Accordingly, dispersal and fluidity are regarded as indispensable prerequisites
for its operation.

Prerequisites: the Holder of the Balance. Most states are concerned lest
they be menaced by superior power and therefore do what they can in the interest of guaranteeing its effective distribution. It can thus be argued that all
states employ the balance principle in framing their policies. Upon a wide
basis, however, the concept is significant only when a single state or bloc of
states makes the preservation of the balance the major component of its
policy.

The 'holder of the balance' must be relatively powerful in its own right
and have the preservation of peace as a matter of fundamental national interest. It must therefore be a highly satiated power with a vested interest in
the *status quo*. If it meets the requirements and plays its part with resolution
and firmness it can be the key to the entire international situaion.

An essential in a state's manipulation of the balance is the freedom of action it is able to exercise; in preserving international fluidity it must always
guarantee itself the maximum practical number of alternative courses of action. In practice this requires that, in so far as possible, such a state avoid
binding commitments to others and that it be prepared to rid itself of any
that become unduly restrictive. The balancing power must therefore eschew
any obsessive moralisic or legalistic concern in its policy, since these tend to
impose a rigidity of thought and action that is fatal to the policy of the balance. Diplomats following the strategy of the balance must be extremely skill-
ful, have a clear idea of the requirements of such a policy, and possess the
courage to make unpopular decisions.

The Balance Principle in Operation. If the international situation is ap-
propriately fluid, the holder of the balance can move with some confidence.
Relieved of major commitments or absolute objectives, it is free to preserve
the condition of dispersed power and to impede the creation of hard-and-fast
alignments tending toward dangerous concentrations of power. An impending crisis calls for the holder of the balance to move with determination. As
the lines of the dispute harden, the balancing state decides which of the disputing parties (if either of them) is willing to carry the dispute to the point
of war. In practice this is usually the stronger party, since only for it would
war be expedient.

The holder of the balance then places itself unreservedly and promptly in
support of the peaceful side and thus presents the potential warmaker with
the practical alternatives of military defeat or the abandonment of its aggressive policy. If the peaceful side becomes bellicose in its turn as a result of the

increased strength arising from the balancer's support, the latter must be prepared to shift its allegiance to the original aggressor, and continue to move back and forth until both are convinced that any war started by either of them would have to be fought against superior force. Once the crisis passes, the balancing state resumes its independent role until a new situation arises to call it into action again as a peacemaker.

Britain and the Balance. The balance of power is generally identified with the name of Great Britain. During several centuries British diplomacy self-consciously sought to create situations favorable to British exercise of the role of holder of the balance. Its success was considerable, and British experience is most instructive to any state aspiring to follow its example. European peace was the dominant British interest (desirable to enable Britain to concentrate its attention upon its overseas empire).

In pursuing the strategy of the balance, the British attempted to avoid being drawn into binding arrangements with any European power which might prove restrictive. British policy minimized moral absolutes and concentrated upon a realistic version of national interest. Britain therefore systematically obstructed any policy aimed at domination of the European continent by any state. Despite its lack of moral or legal justification, the balance principle under British direction succeeded in creating and maintaining one of the longest periods of comparative peace in world history.

The balance failed to head off World War I because the necessary conditions for its success no longer obtained: the lines of alliance in Europe had become rigid, and British strength had become dissipated to the point where its joining the Entente in 1912 made little difference. The scales were not so decisively tipped by British action that the Central Powers would call off the war.

Between World War I and World War II, Britain made some attempts to renew its policy of the balance, but the serious worsening in its power position ultimately persuaded its leaders to seek to appease the dictators. After 1945, Britain sought again for a brief period to hold the balance between the United States and the Soviet Union. Unable to maintain the requisite independent policy, the British government soon recognized the futility of any such program. Today Britain is in no position to play its traditional role, although much of its present policy (for example, its relative reluctance to join in the movement for European unification) undoubtedly looks forward to the day when conditions will be again favorable for a renewal of the role of holder of the balance.

The Balance in the Future. There is a body of informed opinion in the United States today that contends that only by the reapplication of the balance principle can the stalemate of contemporary world politics be broken. If by that they mean that the United States should recognize the dangers inherent in any overconcentration of national power and should work to break up any such concentration, and that Americans should not allow concern with private morality to obscure the national interest, it is impossible to disagree with them. If, however, these evangels of the balance are proposing that the United States take upon itself the free-wheeling course followed by Great Britain during the previous century, there is little that can be said in their defense. The United States could not become the holder of the balance without breaking nearly all its binding commitments and assuming a role close to that of our nineteenth-century isolation. This is a policy whose outcome would be perilous in the extreme. Furthermore, no matter how willing the United States might be to manipulate the balance, it would be a hopeless task to attempt to do so until the rigidity of the two-power world has been further relaxed. The balance is a dynamic concept that draws its strength from movement, and so long as the two giants keep the world locked up in great armed camps, the freedom of choice which the principle demands simply does not exist.

The two-power world may be in a process of breakup, as some qualified observers feel; even so the United States could not assume the role of the holder without sacrificing its place as leader of the free world. This last alternative is one which many observers are not yet ready to advocate. If the two-power world no longer existed and the situation were again ripe for the application of the balance principle, it is probable that some other power or power bloc than the United States would emerge as holder of the balance. American commitments are too widely dispersed and our involvements are too deep to permit us to free ourselves without causing chaos.

India and its allies constitute a strong candidate for the future balancer; the Indian policy of avoiding fixed arrangements with either camp and the demarcation of a distinct third position between them gives clear evidence that the Indian government is thinking in these terms. Another conceivable nominee is China, if it could free itself from Russian control; so is united Europe after the current trends toward consolidation have reached sufficient maturity.

It is possible to entertain a cautious optimism about the future of the balance principle. Obviously it remains an academic concern so long as the only ponderables on the international scene are the Russian bloc and the American bloc. It is self-evident, however, that the smaller states are growing increasingly restive under their manipulation by the great antagonists, and that resentment is now beginning to be reflected in concrete policy.

If the Afro-Asian-Arab bloc led by India continues to gain strength, cohesion, and new recruits from the other camps, the possibility exists that it might be able, on a limited scale, to hold the balance between the United States and the USSR. In that way the new group might keep the two alliances from one another's throat long enough to permit irritated nationalisms to cool and the adjustments of policy to take place which are necessary for continued co-existence. If the balance principle could neutralize the most dangerous aspects of the cold war, it would more than justify the most extravagant claims made in its behalf.

COLLECTIVE SECURITY

In Chapter 3 we referred to collective security in connection with other objectives of policy. At this point let us consider it as one in this catalogue of the organizing and operating concepts of international politics.

We know already that as a scheme it involves primarily two components: the exchange of security guarantees by all participating states, through which the security of any is protected by all, and the creation of mechanisms to make these guarantees effective. Many proposals have been advanced to implement the idea, their number and the rapidity with which they have been suggested increasing in recent years as war has grown more dangerous for all states. In the present day, the idea of collective security continues to exercise a great attraction of statesmen and private individuals alike, as new weapons, tactical theories, and techniques for warfare make an outbreak of war a progressively more frightening prospect.

Requirements for Collective Security. For collective security to be an effective base for international action, two requirements must be satisfied.

In the first place, there must be general acceptance on the part of all states involved that the maintenance of peace is a vital interest. In other words, none must be pursuing an objective of such great importance that it is willing to go to war over it. All must be willing to accept non-violent solutions to such conflicts of interest as arise among them. Generally speaking, a state may be brought to the recognition of the critical importance of the maintenance of peace for either of two reasons: either the state is generally satiated and hence is willing to forswear further military adventures, or else the state is in such a vulnerable position that, despite the urgent promptings of national interest, to seek to accomplish its ends by war might prove fatal. In today's world, it is not too much to say that all states fall into one or another of these categories, with many more in the second than in the first. Many governments, however, have not recognized this.

The second requirement for successful collective security is the existence of acceptable alternative procedures to substitute for war. Any system that is founded upon the sovereign state must provide outlets for the dynamism of interstate relations and failure to do so makes the search for peace fruitless. Stability in international politics cannot be reached by attempts to freeze the relations between states; it must take the form of the dynamic equilibrium we discussed earlier. What collective security seeks to accomplish is to insure that inevitable change takes place peacefully.

Regional and General Systems. In theory, collective security in the true sense is applicable only to the entire state system, since only then would the peace it would bring be general. Up to the present time, however, general collective security has not been made into a reality. The principal defect in such essays as have been undertaken has been the failure to meet the first requirement mentioned above: the recognition of the maintenance of peace as the *summum bonum* of interstate life. It is a peculiarity of collective security as an idea that peace is attainable only by being willing to fight for it, and both before and since World War II, many states have proved unable to grasp this notion. Total peace necessitates total commitment of all states to its preservation, and as soon as any considerable portion of the membership of the state system abstains from the mutual guarantee, the collective character of the idea disappears.

Under the League of Nations system and within the United Nations, many states have indicated that they did not and do not believe in the indivisibility of peace and in the necessity of taking joint action to prevent a successful aggression. Passive disapproval of expansion by force, even when delivered with near unanimity, has proved to be insufficient to make collective security a reality. General agreement upon positive action is necessary.

Although collective security upon a general basis has been beyond attainment up to the present, much greater success has been obtained in the application of the principle to geographically limited areas. In such arrangements, the participating states mutually guarantee each other's security, both as regards the members of the group and as regards outside states. In addition, mechanisms are usually provided by means of which alternative nonviolent procedures are stipulated to govern the relationships between the members.

Perhaps the best known of the many recent examples of regional collective security arrangements is the North Atlantic Treaty (1949). In this document, the fifteen participating states first agree to settle all disputes arising among themselves by pacific means. In later sections it is stipulated that an attack upon any one of the signatories would be deemed an attack upon all, and that all would thereupon concert together in order to decide upon and to take appropriate action. We can see that these two notions sum up the entire heart of the concept of collective security.

The Case of Korea. Perhaps the most impressive test to which collective security has been put was the intervention of the United Nations into the fighting in Korea between 1950 and 1953. The reasons for military action on the part of the seventeen nations represented there involved both the collective concept of the maintenance of general peace (the necessity of punishing an aggressor) and the individual concern with self-defense. It is unnecessary at this time to discuss the Korean operation in detail; certain features about it, however, bear directly upon the question of collective security in the mid-twentieth century.

In the first place, the unequal contributions made by the membership of the United Nations to what was declared to be a common operation showed the unequal extent to which the idea had taken hold. Some states saw in communist military aggression a threat to the fragile fabric of peace and reacted promptly and with determination, others contributed only few forces and those grudgingly; still others remained aloof.

In the second place, the common military venture in Korea could not be interpreted as setting a definite precedent in the event similar situations arose in the future. The United Nations decision to act was taken as promptly as it was only because of the accident of Soviet boycott of the Security Council during the summer of 1950; once returned, the USSR demonstrated its willingness to veto any further moves to implement the original directive. So long as the Soviet-Western split continues, general collective security through the United Nations will be limited in its application to those few points upon which East and West agree.

Third, despite the foregoing criticisms, the Korean matter proved that collective security as a concept was workable and indeed a necessary idea if peace is to be the lot of mankind. Only by making certain that the will to peace of men will find expression in action can aggression be curbed. When all is said and done, it may well be that future generations will find the decision of the United Nations to intervene in Korea to be the turning point in the history of man's attempts to control the drift toward self-destruction.

II

International Conflict and Its Resolution

6

International Conflict

IN the preceding chapter we pointed out that international politics is characterized by movement and change. States pursue their policies in an active fashion, come into contact with other states doing the same thing, and readjust their relationships accordingly. Sometimes these contacts reflect a coincidence of national interest and the ensuing relationship is harmonious and co-operative. More frequently national interests disagree and there develops a situation of international conflict. It is the purpose of this chapter to examine in detail the phenomenon of international conflict, the situations out of which it arises, and the techniques of conflict used by states.

The Inevitability of International Conflict

International conflict is an inevitable feature of world politics. Although it is too much to say that conflict is perpetual, it recurs so frequently in international affairs as to make justifiable the claims that it is a thoroughly normal relationship between states. No state can hope to escape conflict with other states in the accomplishment of even its minimum policy objectives.

A Competitive System. In the first place, the nation-state system is inherently and intensively competitive. States, insistent upon the universal recognition of their political independence and their freedom of choice and action, find themselves trapped by the converse of the proposition: they must grant every other state the same freedom and independence and hence cannot trust anyone but themselves. They must seek salvation by their own efforts and maintain a suspicious and distrustful attitude toward every state with which they have relations.

Security, the ubiquitous concern of all states, can be absolute only when a state controls more power than the remainder of the world combined. Every state feels that this would be a desirable situation for itself; however, when any one takes a step, no matter how small, toward the attainment of this objective all other states feel less secure with respect to the one gaining strength. They in turn seek to gain some corresponding advantage to redress the balance.

In this generally competitive situation conflict becomes inevitable. Any state, feeling itself a free agent, will oppose any other state that is following a course thought to be inimical to its interest.

The Absolute Character of Objectives. A second factor tending toward conflict in international politics is the absolute character of so many objectives of national policy today. As we said earlier, a limited objective that is spelled out in concrete terms is capable of achievement; an imprecise and absolute objective tends instead to involve the state seeking it in continuous inconclusive struggle. The promotion of national ideology, the enhancement of national prestige, the augmentation of national power: these are absolutist objectives that attract controversy because of their very lack of rational content and clearly defined limits. Even such concrete objectives as territorial integrity and political independence have been on occasion conceived in such absolute terms as to bring conflict in their train that would otherwise have been avoidable. The nation-state system, emphasizing the freedom of action of the individual state, is constructed in such a way as to make international conflict likely.

Nationalist Conflicts. Policy conflicts reflecting disagreements of national interest are common enough, but another type of international conflict adds greatly to world tension. This is the struggle between embattled nationalisms, a phenomenon of increasing familiarity.

Conflicts of interest usually have in their background some basis of rational and realistic calculation by statesmen; the same cannot be said for nationalist controversy. By definition nationalism is an emotion and hence is irrational; its contribution to world politics has largely taken the form of reducing the rational content of policy. Modern nationalism is no longer content with securing the political independence of the nation; in many societies it has acquired a missionary zeal to spread its message beyond the state's boundaries and to secure converts by persuasion and force. When two such expanding ideologies come into contact, no outcome is possible except an immediate bitter hostility.

Nationalism is often an effective instrument used by statesmen in support of rationally determined policy, but it is not susceptible to being turned on and off as political conditions dictate. It persists in holding on to its emotional patterns of attachment and hate long after any rational reason for either emotion exists. Many states have become involved in conflicts with others with which they had no quarrel of interest merely because of the promptings of an outraged nationalism.

THE TWO TYPES OF CONFLICT

Of course no two international conflicts are alike. Each participant brings to the struggle a different policy, power position, and degree of involvement, and a state caught in a controversy today will go at it differently from the way it would have yesterday or would tomorrow. It is nevertheless possible to distinguish between the two major types or categories of international conflict upon the basis of the principal techniques relied upon by the disputing parties. Violent conflict, the first type, involves the use of physical violence by each participating state as the primary means of accomplishing its policy objective; in non-violent conflict on the other hand, major reliance is placed upon other means.

Violent Conflict

War. The most common form of violent international conflict is war. War (as we shall see in a later chapter) is a legal status as well as a means of executing policy, but in the present connection we shall consider it only as a condition of international relations featured by the use of organized and unlimited violence as a means of securing agreement among states.

War is an instrument of policy, used by states when it is appropriate from the point of view both of the objective sought and of the strength of the prospective enemy. It is the ultimate form of settling disputes in international affairs and is the only means now available to obtain a final solution to an international problem.

Is War Inevitable? In the literature of international politics no subject is more frequently debated than the inevitability of war. Many arguments are advanced to support the thesis that violent conflict is an inescapable part of interstate life; the combativeness of man, the competitive instinct, the theory of evolution, the incompatibility of diverse cultures, and the sacredness of ideologies are only a few chosen at random from among the strong views on this subject. Some philosophers, such as Nietzsche, Sorel, and other apologists for Fascism, have conjured up the theory of what might be called 'therapeutic war'; they argue that 'war is the health of the state' and see in violent interstate conflict a desirable and elevating custom that raises civilization to its highest peak. Those who deny the inescapability of war, on the other hand, point to the progressive elimination of violence from human social life in other areas as proof that there is nothing immutable about the institution of international violence.

From an analytic point of view we may conclude that under the prevailing conditions of interstate life conflict is as close to an inevitability as anything human ever is; the system and the character of the participants combine to make disagreement as normal and much more common than agreement. But conflict is not synonymous with war; private citizens have their conflicts under a legal order without resorting to violence. The decision whether or not to choose violence as the technique of international conflicts is usually a deliberate one, made by statesmen upon the basis of the particular situation and the position in which the state finds itself. Conflict itself is inevitable, but no particular war is inevitable. When an objective not worth the trouble of violence is in dispute, statesmen do not resort to war, nor do they rationally select it when they know in advance that it will be a losing effort.

Can War Be Eliminated? Since the decision to make war is based upon the importance of the objective sought and the probability of victory, the logical route to the abolition of the institution would seem to lie through an attack upon the conditions that make war profitable. If all the objectives in whose behalf war is undertaken were attainable by non-violent means, or if there were no objectives worth while enough to justify violence, there would be no point in fighting. If all statesmen knew that any resort to war would be greeted by the united and implacable opposition of a vastly superior force, the acceptance of war would be clearly inexpedient.

These are substantially the arguments of the advocates of collective security and world government. If the legitimate desires of states were satisfied by peaceful and co-operative means, and an overwhelming preponderance of the states of the world guaranteed each other's security against a potential aggressor, violence in international affairs would disappear as completely as it has gone from private life. Individuals in domestic affairs still occasionally run amok and make use of indiscriminate personal violence, it is true; society has created means of coping with them, however, administering punishment for their violation of the social rules.

There also would remain the possibility in a world government of an irrational resort to violence; it would be the responsibility of the group to devise techniques of control and punishment for this form of antisocial behavior. Thus, even the disciples of world government cannot and do not guarantee a completely non-violent system of international relations, even if their proposal should be adopted. The best summary view on the inevitability of international violence seems to be that war is not truly inevitable, but that under present conditions of international life it is an omnipresent possibility and sometimes an overpowering probability.

The Objectives of International Violence. War is, as Clausewitz's classic phrase has it, 'the continuation of policy by other means.' The object of any policy is the attainment of the objective sought, and war as a policy technique must be measured in terms of its effectiveness in gaining the real objectives of the state.

Military textbooks define the object of warfare as the destruction of the enemy's will to resist, and this is ample for the battle captain. The statesman contemplating a war, however, must ask himself what happens after the enemy has ceased to resist. The first cause of war is always some form of international disagreement and the reason war is undertaken is to secure the compliance of the enemy. This means that any war worth the effort must be in the service of an attainable set of objectives. This is true of any foreign policy, but it is particularly apposite in regard to such risky and destructive business as modern war. If a war is undertaken without any clear idea of what will be done with victory, even glorious success on the battlefield becomes a hollow triumph when the final results are analyzed.

No more devastating criticism can be made of American participation in the two world wars than this last point. In both struggles great national efforts were made that culminated in military victory, but both wars left the American people frustrated and the United States government bewildered because the only objectives for which the wars had been fought had been moral principles and emotional slogans. These defied being pinned down in specific terms and hence were unattainable in the postwar world.

The major fault to be found with 'unconditional surrender' as a policy objective in World War II was that it carried a strong implication that once battlefield victory had been gained the concern of the United States with the problems that had precipitated the war would end. When the fallaciousness of this idea was discovered by Americans, they reacted strongly. In 1919 the United States attempted to withdraw from a world that Americans considered beyond salvation; since 1945 we have 'played by ear,' improvising policies in reaction to an imperfectly understood situation that forced itself upon our attention. The experience of the United States underscores the basic principle that the object of war is to obtain a policy objective of great importance, and to fight a war without such an attainable objective is dangerous and may prove suicidal.

Furthermore, the violence of war should be proportional to the objective in view. The complete destruction of the enemy, however satisfying to nationalist appetites, often redounds to a state's embarrassment. The question of Germany, for example, was not eliminated from international relations by the crushing defeat of the Nazis in 1945; on the contrary, Germany's former enemies have been required hastily to rebuild its power and to seek its assistance. With the clarity of hindsight the free world understands today how much better it would have been to have applied only enough military pressure upon Germany to destroy the insanity of Hitler and then to welcome back a strong but free Germany into the body of nations. Instead we created the power vacuum in central Europe that has proved to be so troublesome.

Another example is furnished by the course of the Korean struggle after 1950. Part of the uncertainty that gripped United Nations leadership throughout 1951 and 1952 arose from a widely held conviction that a military victory there would not necessarily achieve the objectives sought in the first place. To contradict a famous general, in war there *is* a substitute for military victory: the attainment of the political objectives for which the war was undertaken. Too much battlefield success may be as great an impediment to the attainment of a state's real interest as too little.

Limited war. The most clear illustration of the foregoing generalizations about violent conflict is afforded by what we might call 'limited' war. Such a struggle is fought for precise and well-understood objectives by both sides;

the violence used is controlled as strictly as possible, with only those measures being taken that contribute directly to the attainment of the objectives of the belligerents; the war is broken off at the moment the objectives are attained or when either party realizes that further struggle is useless because the objective is unattainable; and the conclusion of peace is followed by the restoration of normal relations between the former enemies. This is the 'classic' form of war, developed during the formative days of the nation-state system and founded upon fairly general recognition of its implications by all the participants in world politics.

Limited war is not necessarily mild or restrained; it may be extremely destructive and bloody. What makes it distinctive, however, is that destruction and bloodshed are undertaken not for their own sakes but only after a deliberate decision that such measures are necessary to the accomplishment of the political objective.

The most famiilar illustration of the efficacy of the technique of limited war is the series of wars undertaken by Prince Bismarck in the nineteenth century while he was engaged in the process of creating a unified Germany. The Danish war of 1864, the Austrian war of 1866, and the French war of 1870–71 were all necessary steps in his program of erecting a single German government. With amazing detachment he precipitated each struggle, fought until his objective was reached, broke off the war upon that basis, and moved forward to the next step in his policy. No other statesman of modern times has been able to match Bismarck in his understanding of the role of war in national policy, except possibly Count Cavour of Italy. The latter involved his state in the Crimean war of 1856, with the issues of which he had no concern, for the single purpose of gaining a place at the peace table in order to advance his policy from that advantageous position.

Total War. The improvements in the technology of warfare and the increasing demands of nationalist hysteria have given war a new outlook in the modern day. At least as far as major powers are concerned, limited war as just discussed has been largely replaced by a new concept, 'total' war.

Technologically it is no longer possible to apply violence with near surgical precision; new weapons and techniques are those of mass destruction and are particularly applicable to civilian populations. Armies now form only a part of a nation's military force; every citizen is forced to play his part in the conflict. In such a situation statesmen are required to invoke the most extreme nationalist reactions from their people in order to gain the necessary high degree of commitment from all individuals, and super-patriotism and bitter hatred of the enemy become the normal order of the day in a state engaged in a total war.

Thus technology and nationalism join forces to make this type of conflict a struggle of peoples against peoples. In this combat, no objectives are conceivable except total ones; nationalist attitudes are not satisfied with anything less than the complete destruction of the enemy. His territory must be occupied, his government extinguished, his ideology repudiated, and his state leveled and remade in the image of the victor. These objectives—irrational and imprecise—make any war likely to become a war of annihilation. If a government is losing a limited war it is good sense to give serious thought to calling an end to the struggle, since its leaders realize that peace would be made in terms of specific objectives and the defeated party would be allowed to continue its national existence. In total war, defeat necessarily involves capitulation. Since a government knows that to surrender places it completely at the enemy's mercy, there is no particular advantage to ending the struggle as long as any capacity to resist remains. Thus total war tends to require total victory.

New weapons—the atomic and hydrogen bombs, guided missles of tremendous destructiveness, supersonic aircraft, and so on—and the different psychology of warfare have created something of a revolution in strategy. No longer is the principal target of military power the armed forces of the enemy; since armies today are mere rabbles without ample supply and energetic high command, the enemy's productive machine and his political and social morale become objectives of primary concern. The atomic bomb is relatively ineffective against dispersed troops in the field, but has high efficiency when exploded in a crowded urban area. So it goes with other weapons; there is some doubt about the tactical worth of atomic artillery. Some wit has remarked that the safest place to be in any future war is alongside an infantryman in a front-line foxhole. So much will the enemy be concentrating upon the destruction of civilian society behind the lines that the combat soldier will be left in relative peace. This jocular exaggeration conceals a profound truth. International conflict of the total war variety has ominous implications for every individual everywhere.

If World War II may be taken as a fair example of a total war, there is much doubt about the efficacy of this technique in attaining national objectives. It is only under rare and extreme circumstances that any state's real national interest would be served by securing the complete destruction of another state, even if it were possible completely to wipe a modern state off the face of the earth. The lesson of the last war (for at least some students) is that total war in and of itself makes it impossible to achieve any but a small portion of the concrete objectives sought by the victorious state. As soon as the nationalist apparatus sets to work emotionalizing and moralizing the issues of the struggle the conflict transcends rational control.

The grand alliance of World War II won as complete a military victory over the Axis as any that modern history can furnish, and yet the real advantage gained by the victors as a result is minimal as compared to the damage they suffered in the struggle. Total war may yet revolutionize international relations, either by causing such havoc as to destroy modern civilization or by precipitating a popular revulsion against war by world public opinion that will bring about effective world organization to prevent it.

Statesmen generally realize the irrationality of total war. Charged as they are with the necessity of advancing the interest of their respective states, they cannot afford the luxury of indulging in the nationalist excesses that are involved in the concept. But nationalism plays its part in even the most detached policy judgments, and the tendency to think in terms of a 'showdown' by force with a stubborn enemy is always present.

The course of the Korean war after 1950 reveals how nationalist sentiment in the United States built up great pressures looking toward the transformation of that sharply limited conflict into a total war with communism. Yet, policy makers are usually anxious to avoid being swept into total war. The great powers of the contemporary world tend to move quickly, if sometimes at cross purposes, to end the little wars that flare up between smaller states before rival nationalisms get hold of them and begin to agitate for the totalization of the struggle.

Violence Short of War. Before quitting the subject of violent conflict some mention must be made of the use of violence in disputes that do not go to the point of open war. The exact dividing line between war and violence short of war is sometimes hard to draw except in terms of the legal formalization of conflict.

Raids, large or small, by the military forces of one state upon the territory of another with which it is technically at peace are not unfamiliar events in international politics. 'Punitive' expeditions, such as that dispatched by the United States into Mexico in 1915, are usually full military campaigns with battles and bloodshed, but are not synonymous with legal war. In certain circumstances international law holds that a blockade is a violent but not a hostile act. Many shades of difference in this technique exist, but their essential common characteristic is that the utilization of violence in terms of one particular problem area does not lead to all-out war.

Police Action. Under the aegis of the United Nations the armed forces of many states fought a series of major campaigns in Korea from 1950 to 1953 Much of the public opinion of the democratic states found it difficult to distinguish clearly between the Korean affair and a war. Technically, from the United Nations point of view the struggle in Korea was a new form of international violence which is called, somewhat exaggeratedly, a 'police action. The use of this term depends upon an analogy with a civilian police force which is authorized and ordered to use violence in the apprehension of antisocial criminals. The police use their power in the name of the whole society and to serve a social purpose; they do not engage in combat with criminal in the service of their own private interests. Such is the idea that supported United Nations military activity in Korea.

The various states that fought there were not primarily advancing a specific and egoistic concept of national interest; they were attempting instead to restrain and punish antisocial behavior on the part of the aggressor nations. From the point of view of the private citizen the police action in Korea was a war pure and simple. His private life was disturbed and his political duties magnified exactly as if a fully legalized conflict were being fought. Both from the point of view of international law and of the precedent such action sets, however, there was a vast difference between Korea and the clash of national interests which underlies most wars of the traditional type.

NON-VIOLENT CONFLICT

General Characteristics. Non-violent conflict includes the great bulk of international conflicts: those that do not reach the point of organized hostility and the employment of force. At the outset it must again be stressed that the only real difference between violent and non-violent conflict is one of technique; in all other respects they are exactly similar. Both grow out of the same types of situation, both are marked by the attempt of the participants each to coerce the other into agreement with it, both are characterized by the application of elements of national power by each disputant upon the other.

Non-violent conflict stops short of violence because of the absence of the set of factors that otherwise would make war expedient: either the objective is not worth fighting about, or one or both parties lack the requisite power advantage to make a war sufficiently attractive. Because of the unique role of violence in bringing about absolute solutions to international quarrels, non-violent conflict tends to be inconclusive and productive of only partial victory or partial defeat. We shall see in detail in the next chapter the great frequency with which the discovery of a mutually attractive compromise is the most frequent means of ending such a struggle.

Methods of Non-violent Conflict. Non-violent conflict is marked by the application of all the techniques of policy listed in Chapter 3 except that of full-scale war. Diplomacy, economic pressures, and propaganda are used by all parties singly and in such combination as is appropriate to the situation and to the participants. So pervasive is conflict of this sort and so much is t a part of the routine conduct of foreign affairs of a state that often the population and sometimes the government are not aware that the international contacts they are engaged in are of such a nature as to be formally termed conflict.' Yet disagreement is a common thing in relations between states and the process of securing agreement almost always involves the application of measures of a coercive character.

Diplomatic procedures cover a wide gamut of alternatives of action. In one case a state may confine itself to persuasion and discussion; in another more forcible representations may be made and a 'battle of notes' may ensue. Other diplomatic techniques include the communication of threats of violent action, either veiled or open. We saw earlier that the diplomatic instrument of policy is confined in its effect to the responsible statesmen of other states and to that extent it is limited in its applicability.

At other times the application of measures of economic coercion may be likely to produce the desired results, as typified by the various stages of American policy toward Japan from 1939 to 1941, during which time the United States revoked its commercial treaty with that state and then instituted a series of embargoes on the shipment of critical materials.

Another example of the use of economic measures in non-violent conflict is furnished by the great bulk of United States policy in the cold war. Here the object of struggle between the United States and the USSR has been the allegiance of the undecided people of the world and the greatest ready weapon of the United States has been its capacity to satisfy their economic needs.

Interestingly enough, the Soviet Union, unable to match American economic power, has relied primarily upon the third great category of non-violent methods, that of the psychological instrument. By vigorous anti-American propaganda and the effective dissemination of its messianic ideology it has succeeded in offsetting much of the economic effect of United States policy. Psychological techniques in conflict may be aimed at the people of the other disputing state, at one's own people, or at neutral public opinion.

Subversion. Another method of international conflict merits attention in its own right. Since the end of World War I a new dimension has been added to international politics with the elevation of organized subversion to the place of an accepted method of foreign policy. Before 1914 statesmen could confidently expect that although they might be hard put to cope with the pressures exerted by foreign states, these would at least be of a familiar nature and be applied through recognized channels. For the past thirty years, however, it has become a normal procedure for a state to seek to enlist individuals and groups in other countries as its supporters and to set them to work clandestinely to undermine their government and, if possible, to overthrow it.

This goes far beyond mere intelligence and espionage activity, which has long been recognized as a standard procedure. Nazi Germany in Europe and imperial Japan in Asia raised this technique to new heights of effectiveness before 1939; the Soviet Union has picked up where its predecessors left off. Today the USSR has a world-wide apparatus of Communist parties who are engaged in constant combat with their home governments in the interest of the Russian state. In self-defense the Western world, led by the United States, has set about taking similar counter-measures to subvert the Iron Curtain governments and to weaken their grip on their peoples. Thus far the communists have proved more adept in their use of this new weapon.

Effect of Subversion on World Politics. Subversion as a method of international conflict has had at least three perceptible effects upon world politics.

In the first place, it is only by the extensive use of a seductive ideology that a state can win converts and supporters in another country upon a scale broad enough to be worth while. As a result, it has been necessary to tailor ideologies for export in order that they prove sufficiently attractive to peoples of vastly different cultures and attitudes. Current ideological lines of major states therefore place more stress upon fundamental human values and less upon the emotional manifestations of any particular nationalism; failure to make this alteration by a government often renders nugatory the ideological message. The communist propaganda that serves as a great ferment throughout much of south and southeast Asia is a far cry from the sophisticated economic principles of Marx and Engels.

Second, the singular importance of winning adherents abroad for purposes of subversion has made it necessary to aim the propaganda activity of major states at particular targets abroad. The United States, in its 'Voice of America' propaganda behind the Iron Curtain, has directed much of its effort toward the social groups in eastern Europe that are known to be centers of disaffection, in the hope of convincing them of the necessity of resisting their own governments. Likewise, the USSR makes particular effort to win supporters among the minority groups in the United States who might have reason to be resentful and willing to listen approvingly to Russian propaganda.

In the third place, the severity of the threat from subversion has forced virtually all governments to take strong measures to guarantee their own internal security. Subversive groups have already demonstrated their effectiveness unless protective measures are taken, and every government in the world is alert to the danger. There has thus been imposed upon free peoples the unfamiliar and unpleasant task of seeking to check subversion by investigating the loyalty of their own citizens. In the United States this necessity has to some extent played into the hands of a groups of obscurantists and super-patriots who seek by this device to destroy all dissent and to impose a dead conformity.

Forms of Non-violent Conflict. There are two general forms of non-violent conflict. The first is concentrated upon a single object of controversy and is independent of the relations of the states concerned in other policy areas. If the struggle is serious enough it may dominate the relations of the states and culminate in a war; most non-violent conflicts, however, are carried to resolution without destroying normal relations between states.

Single-objective conflicts may arise suddenly out of unexpected crises or turn of events, or they may involve a policy disagreement whose origins are found far back in history. Great Britain engaged in quarrel after quarrel with

Russia for a century and a half over the issue of the Straits—the Bosphorus and the Dardanelles, connecting the Black Sea with the Mediterranean. It remained a sore point between them—indeed, it remains so today—despite normal and occasionally close relations on many other issues. Other long-standing disputes in world politics involve the status of the Saarland, the frontiers of Poland, the Zionist movement for an independent Israel, and extraterritorial rights in China.

The other form of non-violent conflict is familiar to the contemporary world under the name 'cold war.' This type goes deeper than any particular policy objective of the states concerned, and involves a fundamental opposition between them on every issue that arises. It has roots in a basic disagreement of national interest that leads the states to conflict at every turn. There seems to have been, at least in the current major manifestation of this form, an unspoken 'agreement to disagree' which has required that both the United States and the Soviet Union ground their respective policies upon the assumption that the other will object and seek to nullify it. In a 'cold war' every issue becomes a matter of struggle and every technique short of war is used.

CONFLICT OF POLICIES

It was pointed out above that conflict arises either from a clash of national policies that reflects a competition of national interests or from a battle of nationalisms the basis of which is not necessarily any divergency of interest. The first is much more common in international politics, but the second, though quantitatively rarer, is potentially more disruptive.

Policy clashes are among the daily occurrences of international affairs. They occur over great questions and small, and involve matters either of vital interest, peripheral interest, or no real interest at all to one or both states. They cover the whole range of international politics, involving at one time a security question, at another an economic issue, at still another a legal question of jurisdiction or state rights. Despite the variety of conditions of struggle, it is nevertheless possible to stake out certain general situations from which international policy conflicts arise. They differ from one another primarily in terms of the policies the disputing parties are following at the time they became involved in the controversy. Each type of conflict situation produces a different result because of the variation in the pattern of objectives the different states are seeking.

There are at least three clear types of international-conflict situations involving purely policy considerations: first, a conflict arising out of a clash between two states or blocs of states, each of which is following an active expansionist or revisionist policy; second, a conflict between a state seeking to upset the *status quo* and one whose policy is designed for its preservation; third, a conflict involving two *status quo* policies.

CONFLICT OF EXPANDING POLICIES

Historically a conflict arising between two states both of which are following policies of expansion or revision has proved to be the most dynamic and potentially dangerous to peace of all policy-conflict situations. Usually both parties are driven by powerful motivations and internal stresses in undertaking a policy that they know will produce strong opposing reactions. When a revisionist policy encounters resistance, there is a tendency for the government to increase the pressure. When two such states conflict, the quarrel is usually marked by the rapid increase in the power each commits to the objective it is seeking and a swift development of tension and crisis. Revisionist states also find it extremely difficult to reverse or even to halt policies short of their ultimate objective because of the great internal and international pressures developed.

It is often quite difficult to bring a conflict between two expanding states to a peaceful close. Driven by profound compulsions and often today backed by an aroused nationalism, such states always give serious thought to the expediency of a solution by violence before they will abandon any policy short of its goal. They usually do not choose war as the means of ultimate resolution, but the choice of some other course that involves policy change is always a difficult one.

Examples of this type of conflict are numerous. One of the most common historical sources has been the struggle between expanding colonial empires. Perhaps the most famous instance of this sort of controversy is the Fashoda incident of 1898. British imperialism, expanding southward from Egypt to the headwaters of the Nile, clashed with France, expanding eastward across Africa. The overt incident that brought on the crisis occurred at Fashoda on the upper Nile. Neither side was willing to relinquish its position and for some weeks there was serious talk of war between Great Britain and France. Finally the difference was adjusted, French expansion was directed elsewhere, and the crisis abated.

A more recent example is found in Russo-German relations before World War II. Nazi Germany was wedded to a policy of expansion from the moment the regime was established and Hitler never made any secret of his intention to extend Germany's frontiers and influence into Russian territory. What he overlooked was the fact that by 1938 the USSR had solved most of its internal problems and was in turn planning to expand westward. The Nazi-Soviet pact of 1939 could not restrain the rival empires; by 1941 fundamental disagreements had multiplied to the point where war was a natural outcome.

For over half a century, Russo-Japanese relations in northeast Asia have constituted another continuous struggle between two expanding policies. The Czarist empire and the Soviet government each in its turn sought to consolidate Russian possession of eastern Siberia and to penetrate economically and politically into Manchuria and north China. Japan was at the same time seeking to carve out an empire on the mainland of Asia in the same general area. Conflict, often violent, between the two states has raged steadily for fifty years; the principal events were the Russo-Japanese war of 1905, Japanese penetration into Siberia after 1917, the undeclared war on the Manchurian frontier from 1931 on, and Russian revenge on Japan in World War II.

Duration of Such Conflicts. A further comment on this type of conflict is suggested by the examples cited. If the expanding policies that conflict are the results of cold and realistic appraisals of the respective national interests, the conflict is unlikely to be of short duration. Solutions to any particular incident of the struggle are temporary, and the deep-seated problem will continue to flare up again and again until one of the disputing states modifies its policy in some basic way.

The Russo-Japanese quarrel is illustrative. Already over half a century old, no one feels that the conflict is ended; it will be resumed whenever Japan feels that it has recovered adequate strength to make the effort. Both states feel that their national interest is fundamentally involved and each has so far accepted any setback as a mere temporary reversal.

If, on the other hand, an expanding policy that clashes with another is not so clearly identified with a particular interest of a state and does not involve such heavy commitment of emotion and power, the prospects for permanent resolution are a good deal brighter. It is much easier in such circumstances to devise a settlement that will definitely remove the problem from the area of controversy. Such was the outcome of the Fashoda incident. France had no deep-seated interest in the upper Nile per se—France was pursuing imperialism as an anodyne for defeat in the Franco-Prussian war—and the French government was satisfied to relinquish its claims in exchange for British recognition of a French sphere of influence elsewhere in Africa.

REVISIONIST POLICY VS. STATUS QUO POLICY

A more frequently recurring type of conflict situation is that in which an expanding policy collides with the interests of a passive, *status quo* state. Whereas in the preceding type the motives of the disputing parties were basically identical, both seeking to reach the same general objective of an expansion of their authority, in this situation the objectives of the respective states are complementary. The revisionist state seeks to take away from the passive state some particular object of advantage, while the latter, seeking nothing, attempts only to retain that which it already has. The possible objects of such a controversy are limitless; practically any aspect of international political life may serve as a pretext.

Differences in Approach. The expanding state always takes the initiative, seeking by any appropriate means to detach the passive state from its control of the objective; the latter restrains its action to defensive measures, countering each affirmative step of its adversary as it is taken. For the *status quo* state, an inconclusive end to the conflict is really a victory, since any such outcome leaves it still in possession of the object of the battle. As a result the passive state is ready at any time to terminate the conflict upon the basis of the *status quo* ante.

The advantage, assuming the power position of the two states is approximately equal, lies of necessity with the defensive state, since a drawn battle is a victory for it; it need only devise tactics that neutralize the policy of its opponent without necessarily gaining any counter superiority of its own. The lot of the active and expanding state is not so happy. It must be always on the move, actively pressing its policy, or else its whole cause may be lost. Any revisionist state seriously entering into a conflict with a satiated state must have an extraordinary power preponderance before it may contemplate victory, or else be willing to risk the hazardous course of a *blitzkrieg* in order to shatter its opponent's resistance before its power can be mobilized.

Impact of World Conditions on Such Conflicts. Conflicts between *status quo* and revisionist powers are to a great extent influenced by the general socio-political climate. When the international order—or at least that segment of it which is involved in the dispute—is relatively stable and there is general satisfaction with the way affairs are arranged, the satiated state enjoys a comparative advantage. At such a time potential aggressors are likely to encounter a hostile public opinion in neutral states. It is therefore more likely that a *status quo* state will gain aid and support from other like-situated states in this situation. On the other hand, in times of great social change, ideological unrest, or personal insecurity, when accepted value systems are crumbling, strong and aggressive states are more likely to succeed in altering the existing political patterns. The satiated state is less able to count upon support from its associates—many of whom are likely to be having some difficulty in keeping their own houses in order. The climate of world affairs is an important element in determining whether or not a conflict of this sort leads to war.

Other factors may enter in also, including those that always impinge upon any decision of war or peace: the importance of the objective to the states concerned and the probability of victory if war were undertaken. It is almost always the aggressive state in this situation that forces the choice of war or peace. The satiated state, having in its possession the disputed objective, has no reason to fight unless such a course is forced upon it by the policy of the other state. The actual first blow may be struck by the state that had been on the policy defensive, but unless some additional complicating factor enters the picture the ultimate responsibility for such a war rests upon the expanding state.

The Cold War. Perhaps the greatest and most striking example of the conflict situation we have been discussing is that furnished by the cold war of the post-World War II era.

At the close of the war the United States was in most ways a perfect example of a 'have' state. Its enemies were crushed, its power was unmatched, its ideology was triumphant; it asked for nothing more than to be let alone to execute its self-imposed mission of repairing the damage and destruction caused by the war and of creating a new day of freedom and peace. Its national interest was satisfied to repletion and it had no quarrel with any other state.

On the other hand, the Soviet Union entered the postwar world bent upon a revisionist course. Although its power position and its role in international affairs had improved tremendously—from world pariah to one of the two global giants in a space of twenty-eight years was an amazing advance—it was moved by ideological, historical, political, and military considerations to embark upon a course of upsetting the distribution of power to its own advantage. This policy naturally brought it into conflict with the United States, whose interest in the *status quo* was global and diametrically opposed to that of the Soviet Union. The cold war was the natural result of such a clash of fundamental interests.

The course of the cold war in every way has matched the general description of such passive-active conflict given above. The only difference is one of degree; instead of the struggle being fought over a single objective, the stake is, ultimately, which way of life and point of view is to prevail. Everywhere in the world the USSR went on the attack and the United States on the defensive. Such instances as furnish examples of American initiative in the cold war—for example, the network of American alliances with the states of Europe—have been always tactical for the purpose of gaining a better defensive position. Those respective roles are imposed upon the two states by the requirements of their world policy and the nature of the conflict. American policy must be defensive; popular demand that the United States 'seize the initiative' was based upon a misapprehension of the problem of American foreign policy.

As it was the USSR that began the cold war, so it must be the USSR that ends it. The United States is prepared at any time to call a halt if it were assured that a real change in Soviet policy were in effect, but so long as the fact remains clear that any slackening in our countermeasures would result only in increased Soviet pressure, the cold war must continue. The choice of war or peace must remain in Moscow. The United States has nothing real to gain by initiating a 'hot' war since its basic interests are fully satisfied by peace. It is only the Soviet Union that can see any prospect of real advantage by electing a war, and the decision on that question will be made, as it always is, on grounds of expediency. When in 1955, it appeared as if Russo-American relations were improving, it was the USSR that took the initiative.

Other Historical Examples. Other historical examples of the dynamic-static conflict are common. Hitler, the aggressor, clashed with satiated Britain and France during the 1930's; bent upon avoiding war, they sought to appease him but only delayed the eventual conflict. Japan's expansion in Asia during the same period ran afoul of the interests of the 'have' states in the area—Britain, the United States, France, and the Netherlands—and since Japan was unwilling to limit its objectives war resulted in that case also.

At earlier times in history we find other instances of the would-be conqueror coming into conflict with passive, satisfied states: examples are Napoleon, Frederick the Great, Louis XIV, Charles XII of Sweden, Henry IV of France. In each case the resulting struggles, whether of long or short duration, conformed to the general pattern.

CONFLICT BETWEEN TWO PASSIVE POLICIES

Less obvious because less of a spectacular threat to peace is the third type of policy-conflict situation. When two *status quo* states, at least in their relations to each other, disagree on great matters or small, international conflict arises. These struggles are seldom so dramatic and never so difficult to handle as the two preceding categories, but altogether this third group constitutes the great bulk of all disagreements in international affairs. In this type of conflict all the parties in dispute share a certain consensus and as a result the struggle only rarely becomes a matter of major policy concern. It remains confined to limits that permit its being dealt with without injury to the over-all programs of the disputing states. As a true policy clash, however, it conforms to the general framework of international conflict and is handled in the same way and according to the same principles.

What marks off this type of situation from the other two described is the attitude of the disputing states toward each other. For whatever reason—and there are many possible ones—the states involved are basically satisfied with the general relationship that exists between them and any dispute arising out of this situation will be settled far short of the point where it would menace such harmony of interest. For this reason such conflicts are unlikely to involve an objective of vital interest to both parties since if this took place, the dispute would almost automatically be converted into one of the other two types. If one state's interest is deeply involved the other state's probably is not, and an adjustment can easily be reached upon the basis of the relative interests of the parties.

Conflicts of this type are more likely to be procedural in character, involving questions of how relations are to be conducted, rather than the substance of what the relations should be. Being primarily procedural, they are peculiarly amenable to settlement by the more formalized international techniques which employ the rules of international law: mediation, arbitration, or judicial decision. When such a dispute arises out of a deliberate policy decision by one state, it is the least likely of all conflict situations to lead to war. It usually culminates in a mutual adjustment of policies after only the most nominal power clash. This type of struggle is the most 'normal' since it is the inescapable accompaniment of the execution of policy by any state.

Of the innumerable examples of this situation only two need be cited. Anglo-American relations since 1945 have been extremely intimate and have proceeded upon the joint assumption of an identity of interest. The United States and Great Britain have worked in close partnership in all areas of the world in executing projects of great importance and delicacy. This has not, however, eliminated conflict between them; indeed, Anglo-American disagreement upon specifics has been almost as obvious a feature of the partnership as has agreement upon general principles. On such questions as the recognition of the communist government of China, the partition of India, the partition of Palestine, the Schuman Plan, international trade policy, and the European Defense Community, disagreement and struggle between Britain and the United States has been marked. Yet—and here is the point— in no single instance has conflict been prolonged to the point of creating a rupture in the close alliance. Each single dispute has been settled or dropped before it has become critical, since both states agree that harmony and co-operation are more important than any single point of disagreement.

A like course was followed by Britain and France during the twenty-five years preceding the coming of World War I. As the German threat developed, Britain and France, being equally endangered, were drawn together. Although both recognized the seriousness of the coming crisis and the value of co-operation, each was loath to give up the independent policy it had been following. Although conflict between them had been frequent in the nineteenth century, the historian today can detect a growing inclination on the part of both states between 1900 and 1914 to minimize their differences and eliminate their disagreements in the interest of constructing the basis for future co-operative action.

CONFLICT OF NATIONALISMS

It was pointed out in an earlier chapter that nationalism, as an inescapable aspect of political life, has a great influence upon the foreign policies of states, and that statesmen seek to control nationalist sentiment and use it in the service of rationally determined objectives. It was also mentioned at that time that contemporary nationalism tends toward the runaway variety and often pushes policy makers into conflicts with states with which they were few, if any, real differences of interest.

Hysterical nationalism as a cause of international conflict is the catalyzing element in far fewer international disagreements than is the making of a rational policy decision by a state, but today it constitutes a graver danger to peace. The crisis areas of world politics in the contemporary world are all characterized by a battle of embittered nationalist attitudes. Statesmen find such situations extremely rigid and difficult to control.

It must be admitted that the dichotomy between policy and nationalist conflict is to some extent a false one, since political leadership is everywhere alert to mobilize fanatic popular opinion in its support; but many conflicts are also forced upon statesmen by nationalism and go forward by their own emotional momentum without very much calculated direction.

Characteristics of Nationalist Conflict. By definition a nationalist attitude is constructed of stereotypes—we earlier called nationalism 'a sense of unity' —and it represents a formula for feeling rather than a blueprint for thought. Nationalism as a mass emotion is heedless of what it considers to be the niceties of international politics, and uninformed about the details of the policy either its own government or the government of its enemy is following. It is impatient; once mass emotions are aroused they demand an outlet. When popular hatred is focused upon a particular state, great pressures are brought to bear upon the government demanding that direct and forceful measures be taken against the offender. It is by its very nature moral in its outlook and imprecise in what it wants except in terms of moralistic and emotional slogans.

When two states each embodying such a vigorous nationalist attitude become involved in a dispute, no one can confidently predict the outcome. The relative probabilities of war or peace, which in a situation under the control of statesmen are calculated soberly and realistically, are largely beyond ascertaining. All sorts of intangibles enter into the situation. The personality and character of the various leaders; the extent to which they can control and, if necessary, oppose public opinion in their respective states; the degree to which the conflict of nationalisms is at the same time serving the real interest of one or both parties: all of these factors are beyond measurement but they contribute to the ultimate resolution of the struggle.

Often wanting clear cut objectives, nationalist conflict tends to be waged in ideological terms. This connotes necessarily a battle of slogans which sum up the attitudes and aspirations of the rival groups. Ideologies are always moral, absolute, and mystical; they carry with them an assumption of the unquestionable truth of the propositions they embody and therefore an arrogation of superiority to all who believe over all who do not.

Nationalist conflict thus usually takes the form of the attempt of one group to prove its moral, intellectual, or cultural superiority over another. If the other people accept the challenge and seek to do the same in their turn, a battle is joined that is especially bitter because compromise on moral issues is impossible. It is when the respective governments join in, and the propaganda conflict is matched by official policy steps, that a dangerous situation immediately becomes a crisis. With populations egging on their governments and the governments in turn stimulating their peoples to new heights of frenzy, it frequently requires a near miracle or at least inspired statesmanship to prevent a war.

Often such a war is fought for no rational objectives and culminates with both sides exhausted and badly injured, nationalist hatreds deeper than ever, and the situation no nearer resolution than it was at the beginning of the whole controversy.

The termination of a nationalist conflict by any other means than war is a difficult and often impossible problem. Nationalist hatreds are notoriously unpredictable and a quarrel of peoples may continue for generations, inventing pretexts when no real object of controversy exists. On the other hand, such a conflict may slowly and gradually disappear after a diminution of intensity over many years, it may suddenly be abandoned with a shift in popular concern to new problems, or it may quite inexplicably evaporate for no perceptible reason.

The Forms of Nationalist Conflict. In the contemporary world several major types of nationalist conflict can be distinguished. Some are two-sided, with both nations displaying the hatreds and the unyielding attitudes that mark the more pathological variety of nationalism. Other conflicts are one-sided in that one state is on the psychological offensive and energetically prosecutes nationalist agitation while the other does not make use of such techniques and attempts to confine its relations with the nationalist state within a more rational policy framework. Some of these nationalist struggles have a long history and some are of more recent origin. Some are fought out upon a broad front while others are concentrated within a single overriding issue.

Whatever their special characteristics, however, they are all prosecuted in a highly emotional atmosphere, are fought in ideological terms, and are oriented to an imprecise pattern of objectives. Let us examine at least some of the more conspicuous types of such conflicts.

HISTORICAL ANIMOSITIES

Much of the foreign policy of many states is governed by nationalist animosities that have a long history. Their origins shrouded in obscurity, they have become to the people a familiar and expected part of the way of doing international business, and governments count upon their continuation in framing their policies. They may lie dormant for long periods, only to flare up at critical moments. Their existence imposes great restraint upon a government seeking for practical reasons to establish a closer relationship with the state that is the object of the popular hatred. Most are reciprocal, although some few are unilateral.

Franco-German Animosity. The most conspicious example of such a historical nationalist disagreement is that of France and Germany. This hostility has its origins in the ninth century and virtually each generation since has witnessed events that have furnished reasons for the mutual enmity to be deepened. Today, irrespective of concrete issues, it is axiomatic for many Frenchmen to hate and fear Germans and for many Germans to hate and despise Frenchmen. With this general public attitude to build upon in both states it has been no difficult feat for governments to discover problems that served to intensify the tension. In the postwar world, the status of the Saar and the question of German rearmament have been the principal points of dispute, but such is the basic unreasonableness of the attitude of the two people— mainly, in the period since 1945, of parts of the French population—that had these issues not presented themselves others would have been found.

Particularly disheartening to men of good will on both sides of the Rhine is that the overriding realities of European politics in the present day make close and intimate Franco-German co-operation a sheer necessity. French public opinion today is divided; some groups recognize the necessity of abandoning their cherished Teutonophobia if France and the French way of life are to survive, while others find their traditional hatreds a familiar comfort in an uncertain world and stubbornly refuse to adopt different attitudes in the face of crushing necessity.

Although nationalist opposition has slowed the pace of European unification it has not been able to stop the movement entirely; barring a sudden crisis that might recreate the old hatreds in full force, we may look forward to Franco-German nationalist animosity fighting a series of bitter and losing battles with the forces of history and common sense. By 1955, when West Germany was admitted to the NATO, Franco-German hatred seemed no longer to govern policy in the two states.

Other European Antipathies. Western Europe, the birthplace of modern nationalism, affords many other examples of long-lasting nationalist quarrels whose impact upon the states concerned and upon world affairs generally has been of great importance. Their roots are varied; fear, religious and cultural differences, the course of history, economic rivalries, and differences in status all have played a part in particular situations. Many of them are receding under the soothing influence of time and the imperatives of contemporary political life. Some, however, retain much of their original strength today.

One of the well-established nationalist animosities in Europe is that between Russia and Germany. Originating in basic political differences and buttressed by centuries of bickering, the relations between the governments are often tense and never completely relaxed. Periods of co-operation between the governments (which have been infrequent) have come about only as a result of overpowering compulsions, and have proved usually to be short-lived. Today the Soviet seems more genuinely concerned about the

prospect of German revival than about any other postwar political development, while German Russophobia is so great that even in communist East
Germany the Soviets have had a difficult time maintaining working relations
with the population.

Other areas of nationalist tension in Europe which might be mentioned
include the relations between Germany and Britain, between Britain and
France, and Britain and Italy (although the feeling, at least in Mussolini's
day, was much stronger on Italy's side than on Britain's).

Anglo-American Animosity. Less spectacular than either of the foregoing
examples is Anglo-American hostility. Born of the American Revolution and
aggravated by a number of contributory factors including the large number
and great influence of Irish immigrants into the United States, it underlies
much of the day-by-day relations between the two states. A sizable segment
of the populations of both countries is always ready to seize upon any pretext to provoke a nationalist *crise des nerfs* (called in the United States
'twisting the lion's tail'). Many realistic policy decisions of the two governments have to be modified or deferred in deference to this attitude.

Today, the American state of mind toward Britain is made more critical
by United States assumption of the burdens of British policy in many parts
of the world, by the repeated subsidies given to Britain by the United States,
and by what many Americans feel to be a lack of proper gratitude and humil-
ity in Britain in return for American aid and leadership. On the other hand,
Britain also has a sensitive nationalism. It is restive under Britain's subordinate position (vignetted most sharply for many Britons by the ignominious
spectacle of an American admiral in the NATO commanding British naval
forces), by the dependence of Britain upon American largess, and by what
they feel to be an American inability or refusal to live up to the requirements
of world leadership. These are minority attitudes in both states, it is true; but
every individual policy disagreement between the two governments is magnified out of its true proportion by these nationalist predispositions with a consequent real effect upon the course of world politics.

The Balkans. No discussion of historical nationalist hatreds would be
complete without the mention of the complex of nationalisms in the Balkans.
Here is found a mixture of national groups, each fired by a frantic patriotic
zeal, and each hating and fearing all the others. Balkan relations have been
violent and bitter for three quarters of a century and the rival claims to local
predominance and for disputed bits of territory have served to keep Balkan
politics a synonym for intrigue, betrayal, and conflict. In the postwar world
the normal confusion of the area has been heightened by its inclusion in the
critical zone of the cold war.

Bulgaria, Romania, and Albania are Soviet satellites; Yugoslavia was
formerly an adherent of the Soviet Union but fell from grace; Greece and
Turkey remained in the western sphere. To historical nationalist hatreds were

added the complications derived from ideological differences, made more complex because Titoist Yugoslavia, anti-Russian and forced into a pro-Western orientation, nevertheless remained true to its Marxist-Leninist philosophy. Early in 1953 it appeared that history had scored another victory over nationalism when Greece, Turkey, and Yugoslavia concluded a mutual defense pact under Western auspices; Balkan alliances of an earlier day, however, had proved to be short-lived and notoriously susceptible to the disruptive pressures of nationalism. Whether this one would prove an exception is yet to be seen.

COLONIAL REVOLUTIONS AND THEIR AFTERMATH

Another type of nationalist conflict that is common today has its origin in a successful colonial revolution. No subject people can become free of alien control without first developing a keen sense of nationalistic particularism and making the achievement of independence the primary order of business. Once the revolution has been accomplished, the hatreds created by the struggle live on and form a significant part of the foreign policy of the new state.

Sometimes the predisposition toward conflict is directed entirely toward the former imperial master; more often it is a broader attitude, which encompasses all states that are associated with the former ruler or that have similar policies. The Asiatic revolutions of the postwar period have left the new states with a very strong anti-white and anti-imperialist nationalistic bias. That these attitudes are not unique to the generation that accomplished the revolution but may be transmitted for many years until they become a matter of historical tradition is indicated by the persistence of the anti-British feeling both in the United States and among the Boers of South Africa.

The Impact upon World Politics. The aftermath of a colonial revolution is often such as to make the re-establishment of close relations and policy co-operation between the former ruler and the new state difficult or impossible. Newly won independence is a cherished thing; even its insignificant external manifestations are made much of and new states are peculiarly sensitive to real or imagined slights. The pride of the people who have recently gained independence often forces them to demand foreign policies from their government that run counter to basic requirements of the state.

Modern colonial revolutions do not end with the termination of political relationships; they often involve wholesale uprooting of long-standing economic and cultural ties as well. This serves to make affairs somewhat chaotic within the new state; the people, finding that freedom is not the unalloyed boon they had expected it to be, discover in their former sovereign a convenient scapegoat upon whom to vent their frustrations. Often this latter state is the one in the best position to take remedial action to the mutual advantage of everyone concerned, but the barriers of nationalist opposition prevent this from happening.

What is true for the formal rupture of political imperialism applies also in cases where the independence acquired is economic in nature, or merely the freedom from informal tutelage. Some of the states of the Middle East have been technically independent for over a generation, but Arab nationalism is a fairly recent growth since World War II. Its target has been British and French economic domination of the area and the destruction of the privileged role of Britain as 'adviser' to the Arab governments. Although the situation has many local peculiarities, the general tenor of Arab anti-British feeling is exactly what one would expect in a people recently freed from colonial status. The Arab governments often follow an anti-British course even when the reverse would clearly be to their real advantage. This has served to complicate United States relations in this region, since the close Anglo-American partnership serves, in Arab minds, to contaminate the United States with the virus of colonialism also.

Asian Nationalism. In the modern world the major colonial revolutions have taken place in Asia. Although the colonial powers who saw their empires shrink and disappear in the backwash of World War II—Great Britain, France, the United States, and the Netherlands—varied in the alacrity with which they recognized the new situation and in the degree of resistance they offered to the trend toward independence, none of them displayed very much nationalist animosity toward their departing subjects. The hatred was all on the other side, and has continued almost unabated to the present. By and large the populations of the new Asiatic states are suspicious and hostile toward their former masters—least of all are the Filipino people toward the United States—and in addition their colonial experience has colored their over-all *Weltanschauung.* In their foreign policies and particularly in the United Nations they tend to band together into an anti-imperialist bloc aimed at preventing any renewal of white imperialism in Asia and at the continued rapid destruction of imperialism elsewhere.

Much of the Western world feels this is a mistaken emphasis. The free democracies of the West fear that the newer states, in their determination to destroy European-style imperialism and to bring independence to everyone, overlooked the real threat to freedom everywhere represented by Soviet-style imperialism.

British-Indian conflict is a pertinent example of this sort of nationalist struggle. Although the leadership of the Republic of India is sophisticated enough to appreciate the extent to which its destiny is tied up with Britain and the Commonwealth, Indian nationalism, fed by the memory of the long and bloody struggle for freedom, insists upon flaunting India's independent status. Even such an innocuous symbol as dominion status proved insupportable to sensitive Indian spirits and India rather petulantly shrugged off the Crown and proudly asserted its unfettered republican status. It should be noticed, however, that India nevertheless remained a member of the Commonwealth.

The government of the United States has discovered that its close association with Britain has made it an object of suspicion in Indian eyes also; even policy steps taken by the United States on its own, without previous collaboration with Britain, have met hostile receptions. Indian nationalists have proved very alert to discover indications, even when none existed, that American attempts to organize the non-communist world for defense were really elements of a plot aimed at the re-enslavement of India.

The relations of Indonesia with the Netherlands have followed much the same pattern. The Dutch were probably the most reluctant of all Asiatic colonial powers to part with their colonial possessions, and the struggle for Indonesian independence was marked not only by bloodshed but by a barrage of accusations of bad faith on both sides. Freedom for Indonesia was achieved only after United Nations intervention, which finally persuaded the Dutch to yield to the inevitable.

Since 1949, when the formal creation of the Republic of Indonesia took place, relations of the native state with the Netherlands have ranged from the frigidly distant to the excitedly tense. The Indonesians simply do not trust the Dutch and feel that, given the opportunity, the latter would immediately seek to recapture the islands. As a result Indonesian policy has kept itself noticeably aloof from the Netherlands (and their Western allies as well) and has found its closest associates in like-minded states of the Arab-Asian bloc, among which Indonesia has been a leader.

As in India, the government has been more aware of the requirements of world politics than have the people; in 1952 an Indonesian cabinet fell from power as a result of its willingness to ratify a Mutual Security agreement with the United States. Popular objection destroyed the government and forced repudiation of the pact. Such pro-Western moves as the government has made since that time have been undertaken almost by stealth, and only after disguising their true import so as to make them acceptable to the hypersensitive nationalism of the people.

RACIAL, RELIGIOUS, SOCIAL, AND CULTURAL ISSUES

Another group of nationalist conflicts that plague contemporary world politics arises out of a complex of causes that we may generalize as racial, religious, social, and/or cultural. In this type, the issues are often trivial in themselves, and if rational analysis were applied to them satisfactory solutions usually could quite easily be worked out. The specific objects of controversy are often merely symbols of ideological differences. Settlement upon the basis of compromise would, in the minds of the people, involve concessions upon points of fundamental moral significance. This they generally refuse to consider. No conflict situation is more difficult to deal with, either by the statesmen concerned who wish to keep it within bounds and directed toward valid policy objectives or by the outside states seeking to end the struggle in the interests of peace. Such a conflict tends to run its own course, whether short or long, and seldom ends suddenly. The termination of such struggles comes about usually because one or both of the nationalisms involved finds other issues to become concerned about and the one that caused the trouble is simply abandoned.

Racial and Religious Conflict. An apt example of a racial root to a nationalist controversy is the dispute between India and the Union of South Africa, involving the treatment of the Indian population of the Union.

South Africa's recent racial policies are a matter of world concern, but only India has had the opportunity to join the battle directly. The conflict, although officially waged in a restrained manner through the formal channels of diplomacy and in the United Nations, has been a matter of profound nationalist conviction on both sides. India sees in this dispute the culmination of years of resentment toward the claims to superiority made by the white race; the Union of South Africa claims its policy is the only way possible to preserve the peculiar values of white civilization against the encroachments of other races. In such a conflict there can be no middle ground and compromise involving such basic considerations appears out of the question.

The involvement of religion in nationalist disputes is all too common both in history and in present-day international politics. Western hostility toward the Ottoman Empire in the nineteenth century was to a large extent the result of Christian hatred of Mohammedans; Irish Anglophobia is the partial product of religious differences; Argentine spurning of 'Yanqui' policy is buttressed by a distrust of a predominant American Protestantism; the Middle East crisis of the past few years has been intensified by Arab-Jewish religious disagreement. It is seldom that a religious issue is the principle admitted cause of a nationalist conflict (although for millions of Americans the most damning charge that can be made against the Soviet Union is its promotion of atheism and its semi-official attitude that 'religion is the opiate of the masses'), but it is often a contributory element and has a strongly moving effect upon the emotions of a people. It is no wonder that the injection of a religious issue into a nationalist conflict is usally the signal for an immediate increase in tension.

Social and Cultural Conflicts. Social and cultural questions also contribute their share to nationalist disagreements. Involving as it does the whole matter of a 'way of life,' this last category is the most vague and lacking in specific terms of all the classes of conflict.

Europeans generally have had an unfavorable reaction to United States leadership in the cold war. Barred by their pride from a candid recognition that European weakness itself is the reason for American entry into European affairs, they have discovered an outlet for many of their resentments in a nationalist campaign against the intrusion of American cultural standards into their society. The United States is castigated as the home of a 'Coca-Cola' civilization, as materialistic and insensitive, as worshiping wealth, size, and strength to the exclusion of intelligence, creative and critical ability, and sophistication. American civilization is claimed to be mass-produced, mediocre, and destructive of all the civilized amenities.

Americans, on their part, often consider Europeans soft, decadent, corrupt, and incapable of ordering their own affairs. There is a tendency in the United States to feel that the historical roles at last are reversed and that the time has come for Europe to discard its pretensions and to learn the lesson of freedom and democracy from its new master, the United States.

Of course neither set of arguments deserves to be taken seriously on its own merits, but one must realize that this cultural conflict has seriously colored United States relations with the states of western Europe. The pernicious effect of these nationalist attitudes has reached government circles on both sides of the Atlantic with unfortunate policy results.

Incomplete reports indicate that something of the same controversy is going on inside the Soviet empire. Russian pan-Slavism has always argued that the Russians are the 'great Slavs' and thus the natural preceptors and protectors of the 'lesser Slav' peoples. Implicit in this attitude is the assumption of the superiority of Russian cultural values over those of the smaller states. Since 1917 this historic point of view of the Russian people has been strengthened by the 'monopoly of truth' which Marxist-Leninist-Stalinist ideology purports to possess.

Since the war, Russian cultural pretensions have been impressed upon the European satellites in no subtle fashion; it has long been clear to the minor partners of the USSR that they are expected to make themselves over into exact copies of the Russian state and society. This has met with great, although *sub rosa,* opposition by the peoples of eastern Europe. They have proved to be remarkably stubborn in clinging to their own ways of life. Although the Soviet-controlled government apparatus has succeeded in producing external conformity, the constant program of purges, propaganda, and disciplinary action that goes on in the satellite world is strong evidence that Soviet cultural imperialism has so far proved to be an incomplete success.

EXPANDING NATIONALISMS IN CONFLICT

A final situation out of which nationalist conflict grows is that which makes so much of today's world politics tense and threatening: the clash of expanding great-power nationalisms. When a people with a "universalist" outlook on the world happen to occupy a state having great power resources, a powerful dynamic element is injected into world politics. When two such states are simultaneously in existence, each supporting its nationalist aspirations with power, even an inexperienced observer could accurately forecast serious and long-lasting conflict.

This situation has recurred not infrequently. French and British nationalism clashed in the Napoleonic era (and many times previously); Austrian and Russian nationalisms in the latter part of the nineteenth century. Today, the rival nationalisms, each with its own imperialistic overtones, are the Russian and the American. We have no need at this point to inquire into the factors responsible for these attitudes, except to say that Soviet nationalism is a product of its peculiar ideology, history, and political situation, while the American version today is derived from the tensions of the past thirty years plus the particular frustrations and insecurities felt by Americans when their hopes for a peaceful world faded after 1945. What is more important for our purposes in the effect that this clash of nationalisms has upon the over-all course of international politics.

The Policy Consequences of Nationalist Conflict. Of course the cold war is more than a pure nationalist disagreement. Earlier in this chapter we pointed out that the Soviet-American conflict was an inevitable outcome of the particular policies adopted by the two states after the defeat of the Axis. Nationalist attitudes intensify the struggle, however, and tend to perpetuate it; the concrete policy disagreements are often lost sight of and largely forgotten in the preoccupation of both groups with the nationalist battle. Policy conflicts are difficult or impossible to resolve as long as each side indentifies itself with virtue incarnate and its opponent as the personification of evil. So long as this nationalist orientation is maintained on both sides the lessening of the tensions of the cold war is scarcely to be expected.

The existence of the rival nationalisms has served to block the attempts of each ideology to achieve universal acceptance. Prevented by Russian propaganda from convincing the Russian people of the inherent superiority of the United States, American nationalism has shifted its sights and concentrates instead upon proving the same point to the other states of the free world. The results of the forcible Americanization of Europe and free Asia were alluded to earlier: an immediate resentment and resistance on the part of the people of the other areas, followed by a demand for policy reorientation by their governments in order to escape from American domination.

Soviet nationalism has had the same experience. Unable to find fertile ground to spread the message outside the Iron Curtain, it has perforce been obliged to preach Russian supremacy to its own allies. One such ally, Yugoslavia, broke away rather than subscribe to the dogma; another, China, has already displayed its lack of enthusiasm. The remainder of the Soviet satellites have been too weak to make good their desire to escape, but much of the reservoir of good will the Soviet Union created for itself at the time it liberated eastern Europe from the Nazis has been dissipated by the program of Russification and has been replaced by passive dislike or active hate.

No sober or neutral analyst could reach any other conclusion than that imperialist, expanding nationalism is a self-defeating policy. Not only has neither the Soviet Union nor the United States convinced the other of the correctness of its ideology, the strength of its institutions, or the inevitability of its eventual triumph; instead both discover today that outside their own borders there are fewer people who believe in the claims of either or both of them than there were before they set about trying to convince them. An expanding nationalism serves usually to inflame the nationalist attitudes of other states and to stir up animosities that had not previously been active.

A growing impatience with the recklessness and dynamism of both great powers is already apparent in many parts of the world. Whether this will culminate in a concentrated effort to quell the great-power rivalry before it brings the world to war or merely in a futile attempt of other peoples to declare their neutrality as between the two giants, no one can yet tell. One thing, however, is clear; the clash of the expanding nationalisms of the United States and the Soviet Union is the most unsettling and dangerous feature of world politics today.

Conclusions on Nationalist Conflicts. It has become clear throughout the foregoing discussion that the categories of nationalist conflict are not exclusive, nor is the distinction between policy conflict and nationalist conflict always evident. The various types of nationalist controversy shade into one another; racial and religious issues are involved, for instance, in the quarrel between the Netherlands and Indonesia. Nationalism, as a mass emotion, does not lend itself easily to objective analysis, and many of the distinctions drawn in the discussion in this chapter are those of emphasis and degree rather than of kind. But despite the imprecise description of an imprecise phenomenon, the whole subject of nationalist conflict points one great moral. International conflict is susceptible to control when it arises out of the reasoned judgments of statesmen. It escapes from control and may lead anywhere at all when it arises from the interplay of nationalist emotions which call into question the most basic attitudes and beliefs of entire peoples.

The Organization of Power in the World Today

For the purposes of more effective prosecution of policy, the leading states of the world today have sought with some success to organize large multi-state power blocs. This is not a novel development in international politics; as we have seen, very few states feel themselves sufficiently strong to seek to accomplish their ends without assistance. Alliances and power groupings of all sorts have been a feature of world affairs even since the beginning of the nation-state system.

The present basis of organization of power in the world differs materially from that of earlier periods, however, on two grounds. In the first place, contemporary alliances are geographically much more extensive and organizationally more elaborate than at any earlier time. The great antagonists of the contemporary era have attempted to bring all the states of the world into one camp or the other and to bind them there with detailed institutional arrangements. Second, each of the power blocs of the world is organized around a single leader. The relations between the principal member of each group and all its other members are supposed to be those of director and subordinates. This latter condition has not been altogether happy; a constant feature of each major alliance is the internal struggle as each of the lesser members seeks to gain some greater measure of independence of action.

The World Power Structure. The world today is divided into two great-power blocs. Despite the inherent instability of international relationships, which makes each group somewhat less firmly organized than might appear from the formal treaty arrangements, they nevertheless give most of the states of the world a general policy orientation which underlies most of their policy. These groupings are of course the alliance of the 'free world' and the communist bloc. Between them they include the great majority of the people of the world and a clear preponderance of its political power. Not included in either alliance, and seeking to establish a basis for action, are the so-called 'neutrals.' This third group hopes to preserve its independence and to remain upon passable terms with both great alliances.

THE 'FREE WORLD' ALLIANCE

Role of the United States. In the first of the great-power groupings, the alliance of the free (non-communist) world, the United States has played the critical role. The creation of the network of alliances grew in the first instance out of American policy, and the economic, military, and political strength of the United States has provided the organizing and directing force. We have hoped to organize all the non-communist, democratic states of the world into a grouping that could (and would) successfully resist any further expansion of communist power. By constructing such a bulwark against Soviet expansionism, United States policy has aimed at securing the support and assistance of its allies in the prosecution of purely American policies.

The 'free world' is not a monolithic entity; it does not consist of a single massive whole which thinks and acts as a unit. Even if such an arrangement had been possible, it would have been undesirable. The free world meets the Soviet challenge in so many parts of the world and under so many different conditions that it has been better to create a series of alliances, each covering a specific region of the world or designed to deal with a particular situation. Membership in each alignment includes the United States and those states with common interests in the region or the problem. When possible, these

alliances are multilateral; in several instances, however, it has proved necessary to conclude arrangements with individual states. In addition, the United
States has encouraged its allies to negotiate supplementary treaties with each
other and occasionally with other states not directly included within the
American orbit.

The alliances led by the United States are basically similar. They are
almost all 'mutual defense' pacts, which provide for assistance and co-operative action in case of crisis. They also generally provide for mutual assistance
in building defenses against communist pressure; this in practice means that
the United States undertakes to make available to its allies various forms
of aid—economic, military, and technical. Another common feature is the
commitment entered into by the membership that all disputes arising among
them will be settled by pacific means. This serves a double purpose; it insures
peaceful relations among the United States and its allies, and it reduces the
possibility that the communist bloc might disrupt the alliance by exploiting
differences of opinion within it.

The North Atlantic Treaty. Perhaps the keystone of the structure of the
free world, and certainly the most elaborately organized alliance within it,
is the North Atlantic Treaty. This agreement became effective in August
1949, between the United States, Canada, and ten western European states:
Belgium, Denmark, France, Iceland, Italy, Luxembourg, the Netherlands,
Norway, Portugal, and the United Kingdom. In February 1952, Greece and
Turkey announced their adherence; in May 1955, West Germany entered
also. It was hoped that this alliance would bring together the principal allies
of the United States and a number of key European states into a solid and
manageable grouping. It has served as the basis upon which much of our later
policy, both in Europe and elsewhere, has been built.

The treaty is founded upon the principle that an armed attack against one
or more of the signatories 'in Europe or North America shall be considered
an attack against them all.' Here is a clear obligation to co-operate in the event
of war. Other provisions stipulate rearmament through self-help and mutual
aid, and regular and frequent consultation upon common problems. To execute the treaty, there was created in April 1952 the North Atlantic Treaty
Organization (NATO). This is the formal operating agency which carries out
the provisions of the treaty.

NATO is organized at three levels. At the top is the North Atlantic Council, made up of civilian political representatives at the ministerial level. This
body, responsible for over-all policy, is aided by a permanent international
staff headed by a Secretary-General. The next level of NATO includes the
Military Committee (national representatives) and the Standing Group
(military personnel on permanent assignment). These groups are responsible
for detailed plans of operation to execute the treaty. The 'operational' level

of NATO consists of its field military commands, including one for Europe (SACEUR) and one for the North Atlantic area (SACLANT).

A word must be added about the relationship of NATO to the United Nations. The North Atlantic Treaty itself declares that the alliance was created pursuant to Article 51 of the Charter, which recognizes that every member has the inherent right to engage in 'individual or collective self-defense.' It is perfectly clear that one of the inspirations for NATO was a conviction that the United Nations is insufficiently strong to provide a security guarantee against the USSR, and the treaty seeks to fill this deficiency. As might be expected, the Soviet Union claims that NATO is contrary to the Charter, being an instrument of aggression against Russia; more serious is the accusation made by many serious scholars that NATO is not in the spirit of the United Nations. Regional alliances, it is argued, are supposed to supplement United Nations action, not to replace it. In any case, however, there has not been any widely based move to challenge the compatability of NATO and the Charter, although the questions continue to be debated.

The Organization of American States. The Western Hemisphere is also organized regionally into a great alliance. Known as the Organization of American States, the alliance is based upon the Inter-American Treaty of Mutual Assistance, signed at Rio de Janiero in 1947. The Organization itself was created at the Bogota conference of American states in 1948; the Charter went into effect in 1951.

The Rio Treaty served as the general model for the later North Atlantic Pact and it contains the same kinds of guarantees. Collective-security understandings, involving mutual consultation and aid in the event of security threats to a member, form its central idea. There are also included pledges of pacific settlement of disputes arising among the membership and provisions for self-help and mutual aid in building up effective hemisphere defense.

The organizational apparatus of the Organization of American States is not so elaborate as for NATO. In the first place, no unified military commands exist within the Western Hemisphere and therefore nothing similar to SHAPE or SACLANT can be found. The emphasis of the OAS is upon regular consultation and policy co-ordination, rather than upon unified military action by the membership, and consequently the central agency of the Organization is the periodic (every five years) conference of all member states. A central headquarters with a permanent staff is maintained, and various agencies for communication and co-operation in limited fields are now operating.

It is clear that OAS is conceived as a truly 'regional' organization under the terms of Chapter VIII of the Charter of the United Nations (it will be recalled that NATO is not justified under this provision, but rather under Article 51). As such, it is supposed to fit cleanly within the United Nations system and to serve as an arm of the Security Council in settling disputes (or even in enforcement action). The OAS Charter is quite specific in seeking to subordinate the organization to both the letter and the spirit of the United Nations Charter and also provides for various forms of co-ordinated action with many parts of the United Nations system.

ANZUS. A third regional organization was put into effect by the United States in 1952, when a mutual-defense treaty between the United States, Australia, and New Zealand became operative. ANZUS, as the new grouping came to be known, was created as a result of the need to organize the Pacific region to meet the evolving communist threat there. Discussion centered for a time upon the possibility of forming a general Pacific pact, to include as many anti-communist states as could be induced to join, but eventually this idea was rejected in favor of the creation of ANZUS plus a series of bilateral pacts involving particular Asian nations. ANZUS brings together three states whose governments, cultures, and objectives are basically similar, and frees the alliances from the complications that would arise if Asian states, with their complex heritage of colonialism, were included.

ANZUS is organized more or less like a simpler NATO. An ANZUS Council, composed of the foreign ministers of the three states, sets general policy; military and political co-operation grows out of these arrangements. Consultation among military staff representatives and programs of mutual aid in the defense of the Pacific area constituted its major business during its first year of existence.

Bilateral Treaties. The United States has also negotiated several bilateral security agreements with states that, for one reason or another, could not be included within a regional grouping. By means of such arrangements, these individual states have been brought into the general framework of the free world and contribute their particular increments of strength to the common effort. These bilateral treaties are similar in effect to the multilateral ones previously discussed, providing for mutual assistance in resisting attack, for friendship and co-operation, and for mutual military and economic assistance. A considerable amount of American aid has been made available to individual states under the terms of these agreements.

Among such bilateral arrangements is included the Security Pact with Japan, dating from September 1951. The relationship was clouded by the terms of the Japanese Constitution of 1947, which forbade that nation ever to maintain armed forces except for internal police purposes. Accordingly the major provision of the Japanese-American agreement simply conferred upon the United States the right to maintain armed forces within Japan. Later, as it became obvious that the permanent disarmament of Japan was unworkable and undesirable in view of the development of the cold war, the United States initiated programs looking forward to eventual rearmament of its erstwhile enemy. The first such agreement, providing for American aid to Japanese military forces, was reached in August 1953.

Other mutual-defense treaties made by the United States include those with the Republic of the Philippines (March 1952), with the Republic of Korea (August 1953), and with Spain (September 1953). Each of these has its special problems. The Korean treaty, for example, was hammered out during the period of crisis preceding the negotiation of the final armistice ending the Korean war, and tied the United States to a truculent and potentially troublesome ally. The agreement with Spain, on the other hand, is of only limited scope; it grants the United States land for the development of air bases in return for American economic and military assistance to Spain.

SEATO. The most recent regional grouping to become formalized is the Southeast Asia Treaty Organization, which became a reality on 7 September 1954, when eight states signed a mutual-defense agreement covering that region of the world. The signatories included the United States, the Philippines, France, Pakistan, Thailand, Britain, Australia, and New Zealand. The treaty, immediately known in the United States as SEATO, is designed to protect southeast Asia from any attempted aggression.

Although termed a Southeast Asia defense treaty, the list of adherents reveals that only three Asian states participated in framing the document; the rest of the allies are states of Western culture. The greater part of non-communist Asia forms part of the 'neutral' bloc, whose leaders are India, Indonesia, and Burma. These states, as fearful of renewed Western imperialism as they are of the threat of communism, refused to join SEATO until they became convinced that its purposes are genuinely peaceful and in their own interest.

Even so, SEATO is a not as strong a document as many had originally hoped for. It provides for joint action against 'aggression,' but not specifically against communist aggression. This is a gesture toward those states that feared an open provocation to China. Another point of relative weakness would seen to be the provision that each state shall meet a crisis 'according to its constitutional processes'; this would mean that no automatic obligation is assumed by any signatory. Such an arrangement is much less stringent than that of NATO. A third shortcoming is the absence of provisions creating any enforcement mechanisms; action to create such agencies was begun in 1955.

Despite these objections, however, the mere creation of SEATO served to close a large gap in the ring of alliances the United States has attempted to extend around the communist empire. The treaty became a matter of high priority following the Indochina debacle in the summer of 1954, and to get the alliance created so soon after such a communist victory was a diplomatic stroke of much significance. If it proves workable and sufficiently attractive in its economic implications to tempt the Asian neutrals toward the camp of the West, SEATO may yet turn out to be a major stone in the structure of the free world.

The Middle East Defense Command. Though it is yet only a project for negotiation rather than a detailed plan, the United States is attempting to create a Middle East Defense Command. This proposed alliance would tie the United States and Britain with the small states of the region in a single organization for mutual defense. Although prosecuted by the United States for several years, the proposal has not had much encouragement.

Several complications have impeded its realization. Perhaps the most significant has been the continuation of tension between Israel and the Arab states, growing out of the former's successful war of independence. Other obstacles have arisen out of Arab resentment at Britain, stemming from the Israel war, the Anglo-Iranian oil dispute, and the Suez Canal question. Resolution of the last two of these quarrels during 1954 seemed to brighten ultimate prospects for an over-all agreement at some later time. Underlying much of the Arab resistance to the idea is a vigorous nationalism which prefers a recently won—although perilous—independence of action to membership in an organization that would inevitably be under Western leadership. Here again the ghost of a dead imperialism has impaired effective co-operation. Despite these difficulties, however, the United States is continuing its effort to organize the Middle East.

THE COMMUNIST BLOC

The Role of the Soviet Union. Inside the communist alliance there is a much higher degree of unity and centralized control than in the more loosely organized free world. The USSR makes no pretense; it attempts (with uneven success) to reduce its allies to satellites rather than to deal with them as equal partners. It aims at being the only architect of the policy of its associates and in so far as possible to control the maneuverings of the communist bloc in any situation. Furthermore, it has made little visible attempt to develop a policy line that would reflect a synthesis of the views of all the members of its group; instead, it seems to operate upon the principle that 'what's good for the Soviet is good for all loyal communists.' Any associate of the USSR soon learns that the Kremlin feels that the satellite's major contribution to world affairs is to advance Moscow's interest. This bald fact is overlaid with a great deal of Marxist-Stalinist ideological subterfuge, but the true relationship between leader and follower is clear.

It must not be supposed that the Soviet has had its own way in this matter without resistance. Although Moscow has had considerable success in keeping obedient the governments of most of its European satellites, it has had to combat a persistent nationalist resistance in all of them. It has been necessary to institute a steady diet of purges to remove satellite leaders whose loyalty to the Soviet has fallen under suspicion; even so, Marshal Tito of Yugoslavia broke away rather than submit. Moscow's relations with communist China are likewise clouded by nationalist differences.

172INTERNATIONAL CONFLICT AND ITS RESOLUTION

Soviet Alliances in Eastern Europe. When the United States began in 1948 to construct its network of alliances in western Europe, the Soviet Union responded with a program of organizing that portion of the continent which was under its control. It brought all its minor satellites into close relationship with itself and with each other by means of a series of mutual-defense and economic agreements. These small states—Poland, Czechoslovakia, East Germany, Hungary, Bulgaria, Romania, and Albania—were tied to Moscow and to each other in a pattern that brought the entire area under effective domination by the Kremlin. Russian economic, military, and ideological power has sought to transform these states into lesser imitations of the Soviet motherland and to dominate their foreign policy. By the time of the beginning of the Korean war in 1950, the entire region had been brought under subjugation. Under the terms of these agreements, the Soviet Union controls the external relations and supervises and aids the military establishments of its allies. In 1955, the Kremlin proposed to unify the military establishments in a way frankly imitative of NATO.

Mention must be made briefly of Finland and Yugoslavia, which constitute special cases. Finland, although signing a treaty of friendship and mutual defense with Moscow in 1948, has escaped the process of forced communization imposed upon the other satellites and has retained a precarious independence in foreign policy. Although the Soviet does not fear Finland today, neither does it gain any great strength from it. Tito's Yugoslavia, after a brief period of neutrality, has reluctantly accepted aid from the West and today may be counted as a member of the anti-Russian bloc although Tito attempted to regularize his relations with Moscow during 1955.

The Russo-Chinese Alliance. One of the major mysteries of recent world politics is the exact nature of the relations between the USSR and the government of communist China. The victory of the Chinese communists in 1949 was the most impressive increase in communist strength since the 1917 revolution in Russia. The Soviet Union moved swiftly to captialize upon this advantage. In February 1950 a treaty of friendship and mutual assistance was signed in Moscow between the two communist Titans. This original alliance, announced to the world with much fanfare, has been supplemented by other arrangements. Economic agreements which provide for the exchange of commodities and military protocols regarding the training and equipping of Chinese troops have been negotiated. In addition, there is evidence that other, secret understandings have been reached involving co-ordination of policies in particular situations.

Despite the outward appearances of harmony, buttressed by incessant parade of ideological unity, the Western world has come to wonder about the solidarity of the Russo-Chinese relationship. Fundamental points of rivalry and disagreement have never been cleared up, and considerable suspicion remains that China is unwilling to remain indefinitely in the subordinate role Moscow intends for it to play. The death of Marshal Stalin in March 1953 removed the one Russian whom the Chinese recognized as an ideological and political superior, and since then China has asserted its independence more aggressively. The Korean truce of 1953 and the Indochina truce of 1954 were both more in harmony with Chinese wishes than with those of the Soviet.

What the future holds for the Russo-Chinese alliance we can only guess. Disruptive forces are present, but we dare not underestimate the cohesive force of ideologies and of common enemies and dangers. Whether Moscow can sustain a close working relationship with an ally that insists upon being considered an equal remains to be seen. If a viable basis for co-operation cannot be worked out, it is clear that the power structure of the world will undergo a major change.

7

Escape from Conflict: Informal Techniques

THE last chapter stressed the fact that conflict is a normal manifestation of international politics. Disagreement is a frequent outcome of interstate contacts as the states pursue their respective policies. International conflict arises from these disagreements. In this chapter and in the next we shall examine the procedures and techniques employed by statesmen to bring these disputes to an end.

Grounds for Ending Conflict. Generally speaking, any international dispute represents the attempt of the disputing states each to attain an objective. Sometimes these objectives are clear and explicit; at other times they are vague and ill-defined. As a controversy progresses, an alert statesman is always engaged in analyzing the progress that he is making toward his objective. This is important since policy makers reach a decision to terminate any conflict primarily in terms of the objective for which the struggle was begun. This may be done in either of two ways.

The first possible way is obvious: the attainment of the objective. Whether the dispute has taken the form of a non-violent diplomatic battle or an all-out war, whenever either disputing party feels that the objectives it sought in the first place are within grasp, there is no longer any point in continuing the conflict.

It frequently happens that a state takes on new and more extensive objectives during the course of a dispute, and in that case the attainment of the original object of controversy will not in itself necessarily suffice to bring about a change in policy looking toward an escape from the conflict. But regardless of the sequence of events resulting in the final selection of objectives, as soon as a state has obtained satisfaction out of the struggle, its policy undergoes a fundamental change. Instead of seeking further to gain a power advantage of any sort over its adversary and to apply such a preponderance coercively upon the other state, it proceeds to propose bases for settlement, pacific overtures, and suggested compromises upon outstanding points of difference. In other words, having gained its objectives it attempts the early liquidation of the struggle.

The second possible basis upon which a struggle may be terminated is just the opposite of the first. Whenever a statesman becomes convinced that the

174

power situation facing him in any conflict situation is so unfavorable that he can never gain his minimum objectives with the resources he has available, and if no convenient way exists for him to alter this basic power inferiority, he usually seeks to escape from a struggle that has become unprofitable.

Thus we see that there is both a positive and a negative aspect to the termination of a dispute. Either because the objectives have been attained or because they are unattainable, a conflict may become no longer worth the effort required to continue it. The converse of the proposition is also true: when a disputing state has not obtained its minimum objectives but still retains hope of ultimate success, the dispute is destined to continue until such a situation changes.

From the point of view of sheer speculation it is possible that an international dispute could be concluded upon the basis of the attainment of the desired objectives by both sides, and perhaps an example of this happy circumstance could be found. Such even balancing of forces, however, and such a neat outcome, if they occur at all, happen only rarely.

The two most frequently occurring bases of settlement of an international dispute are both based upon an inequality of power. One party to the conflict may attain all its objectives at the expense of the other, or the power relationships may be so evenly balanced that neither side is able to reach its intended goal and the controversy is ended upon a note of compromise. The second is much more common than the first, although many historical instances exist of states that have won complete victories over their opponents. By far the greatest proportion of international conflicts, however, is brought to a close more or less inconclusively, with each party obtaining a portion of what it set out to achieve. As we saw in Chapter 5, these settlements are usually in fairly close relationship to the power commitments made by the disputing states.

One of the most common difficulties that complicate the process of terminating an international conflict is the problem of persuading both parties of the desirability of such a step. If one state has attained its objectives it must discover a means to convince its opponent of the futility of continuing. This is a ticklish problem at best. It is made far more troublesome when nationalist pressures are involved; statesmen themselves may be capable of the rational acceptance of their own defeat, but the nationalist credo of most peoples refuses to admit any such possibility.

Even more difficult to bring about is the mutual understanding on the part of conflicting states that the dispute in which they are engaged cannot be won —in the sense of the attainment of their objectives—by either side without making more of a power commitment than the objectives are worth. Defeat is unpleasant but at least is understandable; stalemate, draw, or compromise is often an even more bitter pill to swallow for a proud people.

Anyone who lived in the United States during 1951 and 1952 can testify to the frustrating effect of a struggle in Korea that dragged on with no victories to cheer and no defeats to inspire heroic reprisals. The ultimate basis for ending the battle, reached in August 1953, was equally uninspiring. The goals of the United States in the war were vague to the popular mind, and while to go on fighting indefinitely was unthinkable, to accept anything less than victory was an abomination. And yet, this realization of the mutual impossibility of victory must be obtained before most of the disputes that occur in world politics can be ended. Otherwise they would be prolonged beyond all reason and would tend to break down into war much more often than they do.

The Two Methods of Escape from Conflict. There are two general methods by which disputing statesmen may translate into actuality a mutual desire for an end of the conflict. They differ from one another largely in terms of whether or not the participants call upon the services of an external agency of some sort to expedite their search for a route of escape from the controversy, and also in the extent to which formalized and institutionalized procedures are employed.

The first method, which in this book we term informal, involves only the disputing parties themselves and has very few formal and procedural requirements. The major instrument used between the parties in settling the dispute is the medium of diplomacy. Any settlement that is mutually agreeable to the disputing parties serves to end the struggle regardless of how it was reached and what its terms may be.

The second method is the formal one. It of necessity involves the entry of a third party into the dispute, who, in a variety of ways, is instrumental in bringing the conflict to an end. The intervening party has many possible courses of action open to it, ranging from the mere provision of physical facilities for negotiation between the disputants to the handing down of a ruling that both parties are bound to accept. In most of the formal techniques of escape from conflict, procedure is highly detailed and standardized. Depending upon the specific terms of reference of the neutral party, its duties, rights, and powers are clearly understood in advance by everyone concerned. Much of the procedure is governed by the rules of international law, which is quite specific and binding on this point. Each of the two methods has its place and each is used by states under appropriate conditions. In this chapter we shall concentrate our attention upon the informal techniques; in the next we shall examine the formal.

ESCAPE FROM VIOLENT CONFLICT

THE LEGAL STATUS OF WAR AND PEACE

War (violent conflict) produces a basic alteration in the legal relationship between states. While at peace, states may engage in conflict with one an other, but by and large they continue to operate within the same framework of legal rights and duties whether or not they are involved in a controversy. A policy dispute between two states does not preclude the maintaining of more or less friendly relations between them in other policy areas. Neither does a peaceful (non-violent) conflict alter the legal relationships of the disputing parties with other states.

When war as a legal condition occurs, however, new relationships are created and new statuses appear. The states engaging in organized hostilities become belligerents; as a result they assume new responsibilities, gain new rights and powers, and must perform new duties. Under the role of a belligerent, a state is authorized to do many things that it is forbidden in time of peace, most of them being derived from its newly acquired right to employ violence upon its enemy; at the same time it is forbidden to do other things (such as the maintenance of diplomatic representation at the capital of its enemy) which it was empowered to do under peaceful conditions.

Likewise the status of all states not engaged in the war as belligerents undergoes a major alteration. They are now neutrals; as such they, too, acquire new legal rights, duties, and powers. They must refrain from showing any official partiality in their treatment of the belligerents. The states that are fighting each other find their relations affected at every turn by the new legal condition. Technically they maintained 'friendly' relations before the war; they could conflict in one matter and be harmonious in another. Now, being at war, all their relations are by that fact 'hostile.' No official contact between them is possible except one of conflict and controversy accompanied by violence. In every area and in all possible circumstances, the legal condition of war exercises its influence.

Beginning of War. Within this legal framework the conflict of organized violence is prosecuted. The classic law of war assumed that the legal status preceded in time but always accompanied armed hostilities. In the modern day, however, when the advantage of surprise is so great as not to be lightly thrown away, there has appeared an increasing tendency either to launch organized attack without warning or else to conduct full-scale military operations without bothering to formalize the hostile relationship by a declaration of legal war.

Japan followed the latter course in 1931 and 1937 in its operations against China; the North Korean government likewise refused to accept the fighting it precipitated in 1950 as being legally war. Examples of armed attack previous to a declaration of war are numerous. In 1935 Italy attacked Ethiopia without a declaration; Germany struck Poland in 1939, the Low Countries in 1940, Yugoslavia in 1941, and the USSR the same year, all without any formal announcement. Japan attacked the United States in 1941 in the same way.

The Hague Convention of 1907 provided that even if a formal declaration of war were not made, 'previous and explicit warning' of the imminence of attack should be given. In some of the cases mentioned above such informal declarations were made, but often they were delayed until too late to permit th state attacked to prepare adequately in any way. In 1939, Russian troops invaded Finland the day after the Soviet Union declared itself released from its treaty of non-aggression; in 1940 Italy invaded Greece after a three-hour ultimatum. Thus hostilities that create legal war may exist without or prior to the formalization of the status. In such a case, states sometimes formally 'recognize the existence' of a state of war instead of creating one by a declaration.

Hostilities and 'War.' In like manner, legal war may continue long after hostilities have ceased. In World War I, the fighting ended on 11 November 1918, but the official end of the war was delayed for many months. The United States remained legally at war with Germany until 1923. World War II required even more time to liquidate. V-E Day was 8 May 1945; V-J Day 2 September 1945. Peace arrangements were made with the various satellites in 1947, with Japan in 1951, and (for the Western allies) with Germany in 1952. Germany was not admitted to be fully sovereign until 1955. During these long periods between the end of hostilities and the formal end of the war, relations between the former enemies were most anomolous. No longer actually hostile, with all major points of difference removed by the verdict of the battlefield, they were nevertheless obliged by the legal requirements of the situation to refrain from any officially friendly actions and to treat with each other upon the basis of conqueror and conquered.

The Legal Termination of War. Just as war is a legal condition that causes major alterations in the status of all states involved, both belligerent and neutral, so also is the re-establishment of peace. Although some wars in history have been terminated by a simple cessation of hostilities, today peace comes about only by means of a formal agreement between the belligerents to end the war and to resume normal relations. It is undertaken normally through the medium of an international treaty, duly negotiated and ratified by the participants. It is a curious aspect of international legal procedure that war may be—and almost always is—initiated unilaterally by one state, but requires joint action by the belligerents crystallized into a written agreement to end it. The effect of the treaty of peace is to restore relations between the states to their normal ante bellum friendly status, subject to such special limitations as may be included in the treaty.

NEGOTIATED PEACE

A negotiated peace is the name applied to a peace settlement arrived at by the belligerents at a time when the military outcome of the conflict is unclear. Neither side has won a clear advantage over the other and neither feels confident of its early prospects for obtaining such a victory. When this state of a fairs prevails and both sets of belligerents have decided, each upon its own, that the termination of the conflict is expedient and desirable, the situation is ripe for a negotiated peace. The decision may be made at any point in the war: before major contact has occurred, after an initial test of strength, or, most commonly, after a fairly long-drawn-out struggle.

Preliminaries to Peace. In modern international politics, the most common means of initiating steps leading to a negotiated peace is for one side to make tentative proposals to the other and then to await its reaction. This may be difficult or easy depending upon the particular circumstances.

Sometimes it has been possible to deal directly with the enemy, either on the battlefield or through formal channels; on occasion, as was the case in the early stages of the protracted negotiations in Korea, radio broadcasts or public speeches serve to convey the offer. This latter procedure has one particular advantage: the state making the first move does not lay itself open to an official and calculated rebuff if its proposals are not accepted. More frequently, however, the first contact looking toward peace between the belligerents occurs through the utilization of some unofficial intermediary. This usually involves a neutral state. Either the diplomatic corps of the neutral (which normally maintains representation at the capitals of both belligerents) is used as the medium of transmission for the first proposals and the reply to them; or diplomats from each of the belligerents may meet in a neutral country to which both are accredited and in that way communication is established.

In any event, the opening of these first hesitant and tentative negotiations and their favorable reception give the signal for serious reflection on the part of the leadership of both combatants, as they prepare to transfer the scene of the conflict from the battlefield to the conference table. Innumerable technical details remain to be worked out, however, centering largely upon the minimum acceptable basis for peace.

Armistice. An armistice, according to international usage and the laws of war, is an agreement providing merely for a temporary cessation of hostilities; the implication is clear that if both sides wish to resume the war they are free to do so. Recent experience indicates, however, that once an armistice is agreed upon, it produces such a slackening in international tension and in morale among the respective populations that a resumption of the war would be extremely difficult for either party. It was in order to avoid this 'let-down' that the truce negotiations in Korea during 1951 and 1952 were carried on amid continued battle operations. Of course, no state still capable of exerting a military effort would agree to a complete cessation of hostilities (surrender) without some knowledge of what the general terms of the final peace settlement might be.

Some armistices in modern times have attempted to provide more than a mere cessation of hostilities. The agreement for a cease-fire in World War I, signed 11 November 1918, contained many detailed provisions whose cumulative effect definitely was to end the war upon the basis of an Allied victory and to foreshadow the eventual shape of the peace treaty. Likewise, the Korean truce negotiators during 1951 and 1952, although ostensibly striving only to discover terms upon which a termination of hostilities could be arranged, were also seeking on both sides to score political victories in the bargaining and to precondition the nature of the final terms of peace.

Sometimes a formal armistice has been followed by a preliminary arrangement between the belligerents intervening before the treaty of peace. Such was the case in the Franco-Prussian war of 1870–71: a first agreement was reached in February 1871; the final treaty was not signed until May of the same year.

Negotiation and Ratification of the Treaty. The negotiation of the actual treaty of peace in this situation is a problem differing only in its details from the reaching of any international agreement. The parties must, if they are to make peace, adjust their conflicts of interest and differences in policy. Presumably they will be in a more compromising mood than usual because they have already attempted a military solution to their problem and have abandoned it as unsatisfactory. Each party to the negotiations can be expected to make its own estimate of the power situation and the optimum advantage it can hope to extract from it.

Sometimes, when the struggle has been confined to only two participants, the negotiations proceed almost in private, either at the capital of one of the belligerents or at a neutral site. If the war involved several states or alliances, a general peace conference may be convened. Such was the case in 1814–15 at the Congress of Vienna, and in 1856 at the Congress of Paris.

Here negotiations usually become multilateral and often the wartime alliances weaken and dissolve in favor of new arrangements involving former enemies. This was Talleyrand's great success at the Congress of Vienna. Despite France's complete military defeat, he was able largely to destroy the victorious coalition and succeeded in maneuvering France into the key position in Europe by playing upon the mutual rivalries and suspicions of his opponents. In any case, the hammering out of the details of the peace treaty calls for the exercise of diplomatic skill of the highest order and may turn out to be a very protracted process.

After agreement upon the terms of the treaty, it must be ratified by the respective states according to their own constitutional processes before it goes into effect. If negotiations have proceeded under the terms of an armistice, that instrument may have contained provisions providing for its denunciation; if the treaty proves unacceptable to either party hostilities could be reopened. It would be a great surprise, however, if either state in such circumstances would seek to begin again to make war; the mere fact that both had agreed to negotiate peace terms in the first place demonstrated a real interest in peace.

As soon as formal ratification is accomplished, individual and political relationships revert to their normal form and the actual war is ended.

DICTATED PEACE

A dictated peace is the device used to terminate a war in which the military struggle has resulted in a complete victory for one side. Today a dictated peace is the most logical outcome of a total war, but in earlier periods in history this form of peace settlement came about merely as the result of an abject surrender by one of the belligerents. In any case its essence is that its terms are imposed in all their details by the victor upon the vanquished; the latter has no true negotiatory function but merely waits to learn the fate its conquerors have in store for it. It is a settled rule of international law that the defeated state in such a situation has no appeal from the terms imposed by the victor. Once a question has been put to the test of armed battle and a decision reached, no machinery exists to review it.

Dictating Peace by Treaty. Although in the past some dictated peace terms have involved the obliteration of the defeated state and the annexation or partition of all its territory (such as the outcome of some of Napoleon's wars, of Italy's against Ethiopia in 1936, and of Hitler's upon Poland in 1939), most imposed peace settlements have preserved the fiction of a peace treaty. Of course, a treaty in international law is held to be an agreement between states that are equal because both are sovereign. No one pretended for a moment, however, that when Germany was forced to sign the Versailles Treaty that it was the act of a political equal. But for the purposes of the law, both international and internal, as long as a corporate entity called Germany existed, it was necessary that the state of legal war between Germany and the Allies be formally ended by treaty. Germany was thereupon required to sign and ratify a punitive treaty in the drafting of which the German government had had no part.

Nevertheless peace treaties created in such circumstances have often been claimed to be as binding as if they had been brought into existence by means of full and free negotiation. This argument was made much of by writers on international law before the twentieth century. Scholars in a more leisurely day found it easy to claim that the punitive terms of a dictated peace treaty were really voluntarily accepted by the defeated state as an alternative to complete destruction. Since acceptance of the treaty was a voluntary act, it was therefore a binding one.

This casuistry did not explain away the fact that many governments and populations—for example, France after 1871—did not feel any legal or moral obligation to honor a treaty they had been coerced into accepting. The Treaty of Versailles likewise never had any real moral or legal effect upon the only state forced to accept it, Germany. At the very time of signing the treaty, the German emissaries made clear that they were submitting to superior force and not to a rule of law. In such a situation, the continued existence and binding effect of the treaty would depend not upon its (questionable) legality, but instead upon the political and power relationships of victor and vanquished in the postwar period.

Terms of a Dictated Peace. Of course, if the victory of one side in a war has been complete, there are no restraints upon the terms of peace imposed except those of morality and of expediency. Often these are most clearly expressed through world public opinion. Dictated peace today flows from victory in a total war and the defeated state surrenders completely. In World War II there were no armistices; the Axis powers surrendered, unconditionally, each in its turn. Germany was crushed completely; Italy had largely disintegrated at the time of its surrender; Japan abandoned the struggle under the whiplash of atomic bombardment while still a formidable fighting entity. In each case, however, they threw themselves completely upon the mercy of their conquerors and left the determination of peace terms to the councils of the victors.

Military Occupation and Reparations. Certain terms of peace have become almost standard in this situation. Military occupation of all or a part of the territory of the defeated state is customary. There are several reasons for the prevalence of this practice. Sometimes the concern of the victor is to insure the payment of reparations and indemnities, while at others it is to destroy the old government and to remake it in a new form. Occasionally the reasons are strategic. Frequently the occupying state has an ideological objective or is motivated by a desire for revenge or prestige.

The imposition of reparations—either in goods or in cash—is a familiar aspect of such peace terms. Cash indemnities were usual for centuries; for example, France paid five billion francs to Germany after 1871. The invention of new weapons of mass destruction caused much greater devastation in World War I and modified the theoretical basis for reparations. Germany's reparation bill was ostensibly to pay for the damage of the war. It was to be paid in gold—all thirty billion dollars of it—and proved to be impossible to collect.

After World War II, a different philosophy of reparations was invoked. The Allies abandoned the unrealistic idea of payment in cash and set about collecting it in goods. These commodities were of two sorts: 'reparations in kind' and reparations out of current production. The first category included capital equipment of all sorts: factories, machinery, railroad equipment, and the like. The second category covered a much broader variety of commodities, ultimately including all varieties of finished goods. These were supposed to be delivered to the Allied states in proportion to the extent to which each had suffered from the aggression of the Axis.

Although the failure to make a final peace between the Allies collectively and the Axis powers prevented a final total reparations bill from being

formulated, payments 'on account' were begun by all of the defeated enemies. They were continued until the pressures of the cold war removed Germany, Italy, and Japan from their condition of helplessness and instead made
them valuable potential allies for either side in a new struggle. Once it became important to have the former Axis states as strong allies all attempts
to levy reparations came to an abrupt halt.

Seizure of Territory. Another normal and familiar element of a dictated
peace is the transfer of territory from loser to winner. It would be difficult
to discover a war of modern times that ended without some alteration in
national boundaries; many such have been of major proportions. Often these
have involved colonial possessions; indeed, it may almost be laid down as a
general rule that a state losing a war must count upon being deprived also of
most if not all of its colonies. France lost an empire to Britain in the eighteenth
century and Mexico lost outlying territory to the United States in the nineteenth. In our day, Germany was stripped of its colonial empire after World
War I and both Italy and Japan lost theirs as a result of World War II.

Often of more significance to future developments, however, is the alienation of portions of the homeland of the loser. This often has the effect of deepening the hostility between the states and serves to inspire in the state being
deprived of territory a burning desire to recapture it as soon as it gains sufficient strength.

Examples of this sort of irredentism in world affairs are abundant. Perhaps the most famous is the territory of Alsace-Lorraine, which has changed
hands in every recent struggle between Germany and France. It remains a
sore point regardless of which happens to possess it. The Saarland is another
territory whose destiny has been to be moved back and forth across the
Franco-German border. Eupen and Malmedy on the German-Belgian
frontier, Schleswig-Holstein on the German-Danish border, and Upper
Silesia on the Polish-German border are examples. The 'Polish corri-
dor,' carved out of German territory in 1919 in order to give Poland access to
the sea, as well as the anomalous status of the adjacent city of Danzig, both
proved to be causes for war in 1939. The various struggles in the Balkans
have also resulted in many transfers of territory with the usual results.

Sometimes a seizure of territory has been accomplished in such circumstances as to make it permanent, as in the case of the final expulsion of Great
Britain from any foothold upon the mainland of France in 1558; more commonly, however, forcible transfers of territory among great powers are followed by attempts at their reversal.

Political Reconstruction. World War II produced on a large scale a relative innovation in the terms of a dictated peace. Part of the postwar program
of the Allies involved the re-education and reorientation of the populations
of the defeated Axis and the political reconstruction of their governments into
forms that would prove more acceptable to the victors. It was hoped that the

new governments would be 'free' and 'democratic,' and the occupation policies of the Allies were aimed initially at making impossible any future aggression by their former enemies.

Unfortunately for the planners of the program, however, the rapidly developing cold war prevented any systematic and co-ordinated program of re-
education and reconstruction from being carried out in Germany. That unhappy land became the scene of a major East-West struggle for German
allegiance and was ultimately divided between the adversaries. The primary
objective each side has had in Germany has been to win support from the
portion of Germany it controls. Italy and Japan were allowed to remain in
the orbit of the West and some far-reaching reforms were consummated
there. The overpowering need for allies, however, has forced the United States
to minimize its efforts at reconstruction and to concentrate instead upon
the rapid development of the maximum strength in both Italy and Japan.

Escape from Non-violent Conflicts

Escape from a conflict that does not involve either the extreme commitment of power or the legal complications of a war does not offer so many
procedural difficulties as the formal making of peace. War is an irrevocable
step and the new relations created by it affect the whole course of the dispute.
Non-violent conflict of whatever sort, as we saw in the last chapter, is a much
more varied and multi-formed area of international activity and its resolution
may be correspondingly much more elastic in its terms and in the procedures
used in reaching it. Indeed, since the legal relationships of states do not
change as a result of a conflict short of war, there are no legal limits to the
settlement that might emerge from any particular controversy other than
the ordinary regulations governing international intercourse. Although it was
possible earlier to detail certain rules and techniques that largely govern the
process of ending a war, it is impossible to be so specific in the case of non-
violent international conflict. The most that can be done is to make some
general observations about the whole problem and to provide examples of
the way specific controversies have been liquidated in the past.

Prerequisites to Settlement

If the states involved in a dispute lack the willingness or the ability to seek
a final settlement to their quarrel by force, they must discover some other
means to adjust their conflicting concepts of interest. In this section we shall
first examine some of the prerequisites to the discovery of a non-violent escape from international conflict.

An Understanding of the Nature of the Conflict. The first prerequisite to
the settlement of a dispute is a willingness on the part of all states involved
to end the struggle. In international relations, unlike private life, it does not
require 'two to make a fight.' One state, by refusing to negotiate except upon

terms totally unacceptable to the other, can keep a dispute going indefinitely. Granting that a desire for termination of the conflict is held by both sides, the major remaining problem is the discovering of the terms of settlement. This calls for the exercise of the optimum skill of the diplomatist and will be considered later in this chapter.

From the point of view of either state, the discovery of a formula for settlement necessitates that the real nature of the conflict be understood by all concerned. The objectives each state is pursuing must be made clear; the actual status of the struggle and the probable future course it will take are equally vital considerations. Only by a thorough realization of exactly what has been involved in the dispute on the part of both sides can the search for a basis of settlement proceed with any hope of success.

No more clear illustration of this point can be found than the course of the cold war. From the very beginning of Russian-American hostility after 1945, there has been great disagreement in the United States about exactly what the Soviet Union has been attempting to do. Some American policy makers have proceeded upon an assumption of purely aggressive motivation on the part of the Kremlin; others have been equally sure that Russian policy has been essentially defensive; still others have found a mixed causation but have been unable to discover the proportions of the various ingredients. Some Americans see in every Russian action a step in a meticulously worked-out policy (or plot); others feel that the USSR was surprised by the course of postwar events and has reacted almost instinctively to the pressure of circumstances without ever confining its actions within the dimensions of a planned program. Since no one has been sure of what Russia is seeking, no one has been able confidently to lay down a policy guaranteed to be adequate to meet the problem.

Russian interpretation of American policy has been in many respects as incoherent as American analysis of theirs. The Russians seem to feel that the United States is simultaneously plotting to ensnare the world in a capitalist trap, reacting emotionally without conscious plan, and attempting to stave off the coming collapse of capitalism; that these are mutually contradictory has seemingly escaped the attention of the Kremlin. Much Soviet policy confusion has reflected an inability to comprehend American motives. Obviously when neither side knows what the other is doing or why, the discovery of an acceptable basis for ending the conflict is very difficult. The United States, on a number of occasions, has attempted to explain to the USSR the detailed reasons for some of the steps of American policy. This has been for the purpose of convincing the Russians that the United States means what it says and that if the Soviet should wish an end to the cold war, they would thus be acquainted with the general pattern of American objectives within which any settlement would have to be fitted.

Adequate Power. Often a state has sufficient power to continue a dispute but is in an insufficiently sound power position to accept a settlement. This arises most frequently when the state involved has not won any of the objectives for which it entered the struggle or when it is losing the dispute. A prerequisite to settlement must therefore be the possession of enough power, either committed or potential, by either state so that it can contemplate the achievement of at least its minimum objectives as an outcome of any resolution. Both sides in a dispute must feel that they will obtain enough out of it to make the end of the dispute worth reaching. If one side feels it will not, the conflict must continue; sometimes the unfavorable situation of a state caught in this way has left it no recourse but to plan for war.

A case directly in point is the policy of the United States toward Japan from 1939 to 1941. As the crisis in the Far East worsened during the late 1930's, there was a genuine disposition on both sides thoroughly to explore any basis for an end to the dispute short of war. The attempt at a peaceful settlement failed because there was one problem American policy makers never could solve. Japan possessed certain power advantages in her Asiatic policy that the United States could never offset, at least in any way short of war. Despite the tremendous potential power of the United States it was impossible to bring direct pressure to bear upon Japan in sufficient quantity to force a change in policy. As long as the Japanese-American struggle remained non-violent, the United States was unable to secure a sufficiently advantageous settlement from Japan. Ultimately, the American government chose the only course of action open to it if it wished to halt Japanese expansion: it presented Japan with a near ultimatum and the die was cast for war.

In like manner the Anglo-French alliance in 1938 and 1939 found itself insufficiently powerful to work out a peaceful solution to the controversy with Nazi Germany. Their disadvantage was such that no non-violent means existed to halt the Nazis and war was necessary if Hitler's ambition was to be balked.

Disposition to Compromise. A vitally necessary prerequisite to settlement, and the catalyzing agent that produces the final agreement, is a disposition toward compromise on the part of both states. It is self-evident that most disputes that do not go to the point of war cannot be counted upon to produce complete victory for one side. This has happened upon occasion, however; perhaps the most famous modern episode of this sort is the ill-fated Munich Agreement of 1938 wherein Britain and France prostrated themselves before Hitler and gave him everything he demanded in exchange for an illusory promise of peace.

Normally, however, the outcome of a non-violent dispute is partial victory for both sides. One side, that with the greater relative power committed to the dispute, usually obtains the bulk of its objectives, and the weaker state gets only a smaller share; each side, however, must come away with something to show for its efforts. Inasmuch as the points involved in the dispute are often the ones that both sides insist upon, extensive give-and-take is a sheer necessity if a viable arrangement is to be worked out.

Of course, no state is going to compromise away what it feels to be a vital interest. The statesman must realize that compromise is possible only in terms of the non-vital concerns of both states. If the conflict is entirely in terms of issues relatively minor to both states, he may anticipate reaching an understanding with relatively little difficulty. If vital interests clash, however, he must calculate the power situation in terms of the ability of his state to resist coercive pressure and to apply such pressure in turn upon the other state. If compromise is not possible and the power situation does not permit of non-violent coercion of one state by the other, settlement of the dispute is, for the time being and in existing circumstances, impossible. The only possibilities open are a continuation of the struggle at its existing level, its inconclusive abandonment by tacit agreement, or its intensification, possibly to the point of war.

Assuming that the analysis of the situation indicates that compromise is possible, the search for the formula is undertaken. This is the province of diplomacy. The role of diplomacy in the settlement of disputes is discussed in detail in the last part of this chapter, but some remarks may be in point at this time. In working out a compromise formula, diplomats keep three criteria in mind.

A good compromise settlement—that is, one that endures—must first satisfy the minimum requirements of both sides. Of course, both parties must be realistic in stating the least they will accept, but if they do so and these minimums do not overlap and conflict, compromise upon a lasting basis is possible.

Second, a good compromise represents a reasonably accurate reflection of the actual power situation. Any proposed settlement that does not do so stands little chance of being accepted; if by some accident it were to go into effect, the side that felt itself wronged would be constantly seeking its amendment and thus would be likely to reopen the dispute. If the disputing states approach the negotiation with a clear comprehension of the power realities, it is more likely that due consideration will be given to them.

In the third place, the compromise settlement must be of a sort that saves the prestige of both sides. The level of nationalist identification with foreign policy is at its highest at a time of international conflict. Questions of pride and prestige are everywhere involved in any conflict and unless a means can be discovered to save the 'face' of the governments, popular resentment may well prevent the acceptance of any formula of settlement. It is of great importance that no agreements be demanded that involve the capitulation of one state to another. Defeat, even on unessentials, rankles bitterly to a highly nationalist populace. Not only is it necessary that both sides avoid the appearance of humiliation and defeat; each must receive adequate rewards upon which to base a claim of victory. The people of major states today demand nothing less.

REACHING THE SETTLEMENT

The actual process of negotiating such a solution to a dispute proceeds in a fashion unique to the particular situation. The actual procedure is undertaken tentatively, usually through diplomatic channels. Negotiation then proceeds—sometimes expeditiously, sometimes haltingly. Ultimately the final shape of the agreement is determined, most frequently representing an accommodation of the two policies that had been in conflict. It may be kept secret, or nearly so; often the world has remained ignorant of the terms of settlement of a dispute long after the struggle had ceased. It may, on the other hand, be made public for all who will to see and draw conclusions therefrom. Usually, particularly if the controversy has been prolonged or serious, the final terms of agreement are formalized in some documentary form; sometimes states go so far as to enact a treaty. Most commonly the result is an official joint statement reflecting the newly harmonized policies. In any event the dispute has been officially ended and relations between the states concerned go forward upon the new basis.

THE BERLIN BLOCKADE—A CASE STUDY

The dispute that took place during 1948 and 1949 between the USSR on the one hand and the United States, Great Britain, and France on the other, involving the status of Berlin, furnishes an informative case study of the general observations made above. Beginning in early 1948 and continuing for over a year, the controversy brought East-West relations in Europe to a crisis closer to war than at any time before or since. Tension was high throughout the summer and autumn of 1948 and the conflict was settled peacefully only as the result of patience and skill on the part of Western diplomats. As we examine each step in the dispute, beginning with the first clash of policies, proceeding through the period of mounting tension and stalemate, and culminating in the discovery of the formula that permitted each side to disentangle itself relatively unscathed, we shall see how the governments concerned acted always in general accordance with the requirements for settlement that we have discussed. The Berlin crisis endured until all the prerequisites for agreement were realized and then the controversy was speedily ended.

Background of the Dispute. The origins of the Berlin crisis lay in the general problem of postwar Germany. The theory of the Potsdam agreement (1945) for the administration of the inter-Allied occupation of Germany envisaged a single occupation policy for the entire state, run from a four-power headquarters in Berlin. It was in accordance with this idea that the Western powers were in Berlin at all, since the city lay a hundred miles within the Soviet zone of Germany. As the cold war intensified during 1947 and the

United States sought a positive way out of the German dilemma, Western policy abandoned attempts to unify Germany and concentrated its attention upon the stabilization of the three Western zones.

Here inflation and economic and political disunity had caused serious problems. Under American leadership, late in 1947 steps looking toward the economic unification of the American and British zones of Germany (called 'Bizonia') and later incorporation of the French zone ('Trizonia') precipitated Russian protests and the beginning of pressure upon Berlin. The Berlin problem was complicated by the vulnerability to Russian blockade of all surface means of transportation to the West. Such agreements as existed to guarantee access to the city were verbal in nature and general in terms, failing to specify details in written form. The West was later to have ample cause to regret its failure to obtain such guarantees during the early postwar period of inter-Allied amicability.

First Steps in the Crisis. The Berlin dispute began to grow intense in March 1948, when the Western powers began to clarify their objectives for West Germany. It became clear that economic unification of the three zones was insufficient and that political unification was necessary—in other words, an independent West German government. This was unacceptable to the Soviets; on 20 March 1948, the Soviet Union's representatives walked out of the Allied Control Council (the four-power governing body for Germany) on the grounds that American policy had destroyed the Potsdam agreement. This marked the beginning of the acute stage of the struggle.

Soviet policy at this stage was concentrated upon forcing the Allies to quit Berlin. The Russian argument ran as follows: Since the only reason the West was in Berlin at all was to co-operate with the Control Council, and since Western policy had destroyed the framework of co-operation by the creation of an independent government for West Germany and a policy of partition, there was no longer any reason for the West to remain in the city. Always the Russians offered the Allies the option of abandoning their plans for West German unification and the re-creation of the Control Council upon Russian terms. The Allies, on the contrary, refused to consider leaving the city, viewing the dispute as a major test of strength with significance transcending Berlin itself. Soviet policy first took an openly hostile turn in April, when the initial restrictions upon transportation were declared; in May and June further regulations were promulgated as the Russians began to increase the pressure in hopes of forcing concessions. By this time, Berlin had been split into two hostile cities, each under the control of its occupying power.

The Currency Issue. The precipitating cause of the major crisis was the long-contemplated currency reform in West Germany (announced 18 June 1948), which wiped out the ruinous inflation there almost at one stroke. The new, Western-backed currency was not at first introduced into West Berlin as the Allies hoped for four-power currency control in the whole city. The

Russians disagreed and attempted a currency reform of their own which was to include all of Berlin. The Western powers then forcibly introduced their new 'Deutsche Mark' into their sectors. At this point the issue was squarely joined. The USSR cut all surface transportation into the city, effectively blockading not only Western military forces but the entire civilian population of West Berlin.

The West responded by the initiation of the famous 'airlift' and the establishment of a counter-blockade. The currency issue, actually only peripheral to the major problem of the East-West clash in Germany, became the critical point of controversy (just as did another minor point in Korea three years later—the issue of voluntary repatriation of prisoners of war). Open Russian-Western hostility was clear. The Soviet maintained and increased the pressure of the blockade; the West improved its airlift and counter-blockade. At this point, July 1948, the focus of attention shifted from Berlin itself as the negotiations proceded at a higher level.

The Moscow Negotiations. A three-power protest to Moscow about the blockade ended with a Western refusal to 'negotiate under duress'—that is, the Western powers felt that the lifting of the blockade must precede any resumption of the discussions about the future of Germany. The Soviet reply stated Russian policy with great frankness. The blockade was admitted to be in simple retaliation for Western policy in organizing West Germany and would be continued until the West either scrapped the proposed West German government or abandoned Berlin. The Russians refused to consider the lifting of the blockade as a precondition to negotiation; they further insisted that the problem of Berlin was inseparable from the problem of Germany and urged the reopening of the whole question at the highest level.

Turning with reluctance to direct negotiations, the Western powers held conversations with Stalin and Molotov and pressed their case. Ambassador Walter B. Smith of the United States emphasized the willingness of the West to negotiate about Germany, but again refused to consider doing so under duress. Stalin himself, on 2 August, proposed a compromise—the blockade should be lifted in return for the introduction of East German currency into all Berlin—and did not demand the formal abandonment of plans for a West German government. During the remainder of August more discussions were held with Molotov on the proposed Stalin plan. The Russian proved to be difficult to pin down. He insisted that in return for Soviet control of the currency throughout all of Berlin, only the transport restrictions dating from 18 June need be lifted; if any others were to be abolished additional concessions would have to be made by the West. He also stressed again the issue of West German unification as an obstacle to agreement.

Eventually, losing hope of securing any acceptable proposals from Molotov, the Western ambassadors returned to Stalin on 23 August. He proved unexpectedly co-operative. He met all the fundamental Western demands:

their right to be in Berlin, the binding effect of their decisions on western Germany, unconditional lifting of the blockade, and adequate four-power control of the Russian currency in Berlin. If these points were granted, the Western powers were willing to renew four-power discussions upon the problem of Germany as a whole. With this to build upon, the negotiators drafted the directive of 30 August. This called upon the military governors in Germany to work out the practical details regarding the simultaneous lifting of the blockade and the introduction of the Soviet currency into all Berlin.

It would be well to recapitulate the story up to this point. The Berlin dispute had its roots in the fundamental conflict of interest on the part of the great powers in regard to Germany. The precipitating cause was the Western decision to proceed toward the economic and political unification of West Germany and its permanent partition from East Germany. The dispute opened upon a relatively restrained note and its early stages consisted of the mutual attempt by both parties to employ persuasion in order to bring about alterations in policies. This having failed, the Russians initiated coercive action, the West refused to yield, and finally full pressure was applied by the Soviet through every channel short of war. The airlift (a defensive measure) and the counter-blockade (an offensive gesture) constituted the Western reply. This brought the struggle to the stage of equilibrium.

At this point the search for a formula of settlement was undertaken. The first step, as we have seen, actually consisted of each side's frankly and fully informing the other of its objectives and, by implication, of the minimum terms of settlement it would accept. Amid much maneuvering to ascertain clearly the relative power situations, it appeared that the Russians were aiming at a reopening of the whole question of Germany at the four-power level and the West was insistent upon the preservation of the structure of unity in West Germany that it had undertaken to construct. The directive of 30 August seemed to ratify the preliminaries of agreement and to set the stage for rapid end of the struggle.

The Failure of the Directive. When the military governors set about implementing this document they ran into a famiilar morass of contradictions and accusations of bad faith. The Soviet commander in Germany, Marshal Sokolovsky, discovered novel and legalistic ways to interpret the language of the directive in what appeared to the West to be clear disregard of the Moscow agreement. The Soviet government supported its representative and accused the United States of distorting the meaning and sense of what had been agreed to the previous month. In any event it became clear that the Soviet was not ready to reach a solution to the crisis; it had been unable to halt preparations for the creation of the West German government, nor had it been able to force the Allies out of Berlin. This, to Moscow, was no time to compromise.

From the Russian point of view it was necessary that the struggle continue until a more favorable basis of agreement could be discovered.

The Crisis before the United Nations. Baffled in the dealings in Berlin and despairing of reaching any agreement by direct negotiation with Stalin, the United States then undertook to exert some coercive pressure of its own. It chose to do this in an area in which it was as much at an advantage as it was at a disadvantage in Berlin—the United Nations. American policy makers, joined by Britain and France, had no illusions about the probable effects of their action. They expected that no concrete solution would emerge as a result of United Nations treatment of the controversy. Their purpose was to try the case before world public opinion and to extract the maximum propaganda advantage from it.

A complaint was thereupon lodged with the Security Council on 29 September charging that Soviet actions in Berlin constituted a 'threat to the peace' under Chapter VII of the Charter and calling for action to redress the situation. This was dangerous; the USSR might have walked out, thus destroying the United Nations, or else might have precipitated violent action leading to war. Western policy, however, was founded upon the assumption that the issues of the Berlin crisis were not worth a war to the Russians and that a walkout would not serve their purpose. The Soviet Union sought to prevent the consideration of the dispute upon several legalistic grounds but was defeated in the test vote.

Mediation by the 'Neutral Six.' At this point an interesting development took place. Five of the members of the Security Council—the three Western Allies, the USSR, and the Ukrainian SSR—were directly involved in the dispute. The remaining six states (under the leadership of Juan Bramuglia of the Argentine, the president of the Council) formed themselves into an informal compromising body to work out an acceptable agreement. After an arduous round of negotiation, on 22 October they produced a compromise formula which called for an immediate end to the blockade, the introduction into all Berlin by 20 November of the Russian currency under four-power control, and an early meeting of the Council of Foreign Ministers to take up the German question. The Western powers agreed not to press for action condemning Russian policy on the Berlin question.

The Russian Veto and Stalemate. It was clear that the difference in dates between the lifting of the blockade and the introduction of the Russian currency into Berlin would be unacceptable to Moscow although the compromise formula as a whole was approved by the West. Mr. Jessup of the United States bluntly asked the Soviet Union what it wanted. He insisted that if the aim was simply to drive the West out of Berlin, it would fail; if Russia wished concrete attack upon any of the real problems inherent in the currency situation it could obtain such action at any time simply by lifting the blockade.

Undaunted, Mr. Vishinsky vetoed the compromise on 25 October and the whole proposal fell.

Although other attempts at United Nations mediation were made during the next month, the constructive action for the session had ended. The Western Allies had scored a notable propaganda victory by forcing the Soviet Union to veto a compromise which included concessions to the Soviet position. World public opinion clearly turned against the Russians at this point. The United States was content to let affairs drift for a while; the airlift was working smoothly and by this time the only way the Soviet could drive the West from Berlin was by a war. The danger of such extreme action had receded sharply from its high point of the previous summer. As the edifice of a West German government continued to grow, the Western position became stronger; the Soviets could not help but become the victims of stalemate.

The Break in the Crisis. In January 1949, there occurred the first break in the Soviet position. Stalin, in replying to a series of questions posed by an American reporter, indicated that if the Western powers would postpone the creation of a West German government until the Council of Foreign Ministers had reopened the question of Germany as a whole, there would be no Soviet objection to a removal of the blockade. The next month, in a private and unofficial conversation at the United Nations, Mr. Jessup asked the Soviet delegate, Mr. Malik, if there was any significance to the fact that Stalin had failed to mention the currency issue as a factor in the blockade. In March Mr. Malik reported that Stalin's omission was 'not accidental' and that a reciprocal lifting of the blockade and the counter-blockade could take place before the Council of Foreign Ministers met, providing a date for its convening were stipulated. Rapid exploitation of the Soviet concession was undertaken, the dates for the end of the blockade and the meeting of the Council of Foreign Ministers were set, and on 5 May a four-power communique announced the end of the blockade. The restrictions on transport in both directions were to be lifted on 12 May and the Council of Foreign Ministers was to reconvene on 23 May. The crisis had ended. That the foreign ministers proved unable to reach any sort of agreement on the broader issues of Germany is not a part of this story but of the larger history of the German question.

Conclusion on the Berlin Blockade. From the foregoing analysis certain conclusions may be drawn. The conflict fell into two stages. The first was the period of clash and the mutual application of power pressures by each party, culminating in a condition of stabilization (or, more accurately, equilibrium). Once this was realized by both sides and it became clear that neither could accomplish anything further by coercion, short of war, each set about salvaging the maximum it could out of the now stalemated situation. The second stage, overlapping the first to some extent, was featured by the long and complex course of the negotiations that eventually eased the tensions and removed Berlin as a threat to peace.

The outcome of the crisis was a major defeat to the Russians. Forced by Western tactics into taking unpopular positions, such as vetoing United Nations proposals and imposing hardships upon the civilian population of Berlin, Russian appeal to the German masses was drastically reduced. The USSR appeared to the world as insensitive either to the demands of the world for peace or to the pleas of common humanity. Russian prestige suffered a blow from which it never recovered in Europe. This has had a clear influence upon subsequent Soviet policy.

In the same way, the specific objectives sought by the USSR during the dispute proved unattainable. It became clear that the Soviet had an alternative program throughout the entire crisis: to force the West to abandon the project of a West German government or, failing in that, forcibly to eject the West from Berlin. The counter-measures that Western policy devised stalled the effective progress of the Soviet Union toward either of these goals and ultimately the Russians were obliged to settle merely for an unproductive meeting of the Council of Foreign Ministers. The controversy in Berlin had dragged on so long that American plans for West Germany had matured beyond the capacity of the USSR to stop them and the Soviet gained nothing concrete and lost much as a result of the whole affair. To a revisionist state, a dispute that terminates in a draw can never be considered as anything but a defeat.

The Western Allies were caught more or less off guard by the rapid development of the crisis and during the spring and summer of 1948 seemed at a loss how to proceed. They permitted the Russians to mount a full-scale political offensive backed by the blockade before they were able to devise a counter-strategy. Even then they contented themselves with neutralizing Russian pressures and engaged in unproductive direct negotiations for many weeks before taking the initiative themselves. The submission of the dispute to the Security Council and the trial by public opinion that ensued put the Soviet Union on the defensive for the first time. Once having gained the upper hand the West was willing to relax and to permit the multiplying pressures upon the Soviet Union to bring about the final easing of the tension. The eventual solution was not ideal from the West's point of view—the Berlin currency question remained unsettled and the city was broken into two parts —but the over-all outcome of the controversy was far more in accordance with Western desires than with the Russian.

The Berlin controversy demonstrated the typical 'fever chart' of a non-violent international conflict. A disharmony of interest brought about a policy clash, the conflicting policies were backed by commitments of power, each side went as far in seeking to force a settlement as it thought the issues were worth, and the final settlement could not be reached until both sides were convinced that further pressure would produce no concrete results. The ultimate outcome was a negotiated compromise in rough harmony with the real power disposition.

In these details it closely resembled other disputes that have culminated in the same way. Particular issues and circumstances and the fact that it was part of a larger 'cold war' pattern provided peculiarities, but, in the main, detailed study of the Berlin crisis and its resolution serves to throw much light upon the problems and the procedures involved in the liquidation of a serious international conflict.

EFFECTIVE VS. INEFFECTIVE DIPLOMACY

It has been repeatedly pointed out that the resolution of disputes by means of a formula of accommodation is a function of diplomacy, perhaps its most important function. Diplomacy is a convenience in the execution of normal international intercourse and extremely useful in prosecuting policy, but it is an instrument of vital importance when it becomes desirable for states to terminate a dispute. Diplomatic skill is a primary requisite for statesmen involved in the fast-moving process of international politics. It calls for the exercise of all the talents of negotiation at their highest point of development. Failure to utilize the unique advantages of the diplomatic process may deprive a state of hard-won power advantages, while to a considerable degree diplomatic ability may offset power inferiority. The process of diplomacy bulks large in any study of statesmanship. It is therefore desirable now to analyze some of its characteristics as it enters into the settlement of international disputes.

Generally speaking, 'good' or 'effective' diplomacy in this connection is the conduct of negotiations so as to secure the maximum advantage for one's state. This is a constant criterion, regardless of the situation. In conflict situations, good diplomacy has an additional task: that of securing an end to the dispute upon the best possible terms. 'Bad' or 'ineffective' diplomacy fails to secure the maximum possible share of the state's objectives within the terms of a particular situation or else does not succeed in its peacemaking task. In this section we shall examine the characteristics of good diplomacy and analyze some of the reasons for its failure to be more effective in contemporary world politics.

EFFECTIVE DIPLOMACY

From the point of view of the diplomatic process proper, the characteristics of a good and effective diplomacy restate the prerequisites to settlement discussed earlier in this chapter, but phrase them in terms of the conduct of individual negotiators. It was pointed out earlier that before a dispute could be resolved, three attitudes must be present in the policy of both states: a realistic understanding of the nature of the controversy, an awareness of the power positions of the disputants and the extent to which each was committed in the conflict, and a disposition toward compromise. Effective diplomacy in any conflict situation displays all three of these characteristics. We shall examine each of them, considering them under the general headings of realism, forcefulness, and flexibility.

REALISM

Approach in Concrete Terms. Successful diplomacy must be realistic; that is, a diplomat must deal always with the human beings with whom he is in negotiation and concentrate upon the tangible elements in the situation he is confronting. Only by reaching understandings with actual persons upon concrete problems can disputes be liquidated.

An obsession with moral absolutes, such as 'justice,' 'honor,' 'face,' 'peace through law,' or 'self-determination,' serves often to obscure the diplomat's vision and to render difficult or impossible the achievement of agreement. The pursuit of such lofty abstractions to the exclusion of concern with the demands of national interest phrased in concrete terms is a luxury which no diplomat may permit himself if he is to serve his state effectively.

The problems with which diplomats are called upon to deal are seldom, if ever, purely moral in their nature; even when a clear moral issue is presented to statesmen, it can never be successfully solved in the abstract. Moral problems in international politics must be handled in terms of the tangible factors in the context in which they arise. No statesman who seeks 'justice' in absolute and abstract terms can achieve any goal other than frustration and defeat, but justice for a particular state or people within a given set of circumstances not only is realistic and attainable but may also be in harmony with the most practical dictates of national interest.

Realism and Morality. The defense of 'realism' in diplomacy is not for the purpose of establishing a false dichotomy between morality and power or of discounting the real impact of morality upon international politics. In any particular situation moral force may be, and often is, an element of real power significance. Shrewd diplomacy recognizes this fact and seeks to take advantage of it. An invalid distinction between morals and power has been drawn many times in history and always with disastrous results. Hitler's complete failure was in no small measure due to his incapacity to comprehend this relationship; communist policy today likewise fails to recognize the political power represented by widely shared moral convictions.

Whereas ignoring the role of morality and concentrating instead only upon considerations of naked force produces one variety of unrealistic diplomacy, seizing the other horn of the dilemma is equally fatuous. Viewing international politics as the cosmic struggle between the forces of good and the forces of evil results in an entirely erroneous picture of the world political process. Statesmen who succumb to this fault, in their eagerness to smite sin and to exorcise the devils they find in international life, find themselves unable to cope realistically not only with moral issues but with all others as well. In addition to systematically deluding themselves about the nature of the task before them, they often do irreparable harm to the policy they are pursuing and the states whose servants they are.

A particularly apt example of the consequences flowing from this orientation in a political leader is provided by the course followed by President Woodrow Wilson at the Paris Peace Conference in 1919. Mr. Wilson's views on world politics were such that he was never able to rid himself of the basic idea that World War I was a struggle for the achievement and realization of a set of absolute moral principles of interstate life. The victory of the Allies in 1918 was in this light a triumph of right and virtue over wrong and evil; to him the problem of peacemaking consisted merely in the execution of these principles and their establishment as settled procedures in world politics.

At the peace table, therefore, he sought constantly to bring about the acceptance of these general propositions—political democracy, self-determination, international organization, open diplomacy—to the exclusion of the more immediate and concrete issues that crowded in upon him from less high-minded statesmen than he. Such issues as reparations, boundary adjustments, trade requirements, and the like he either disregarded as being unworthy of the new edifice of world politics of which he was the principal architect or else sought to have deferred until after his moral principles were accepted as binding rules of international conduct. He left Paris frustrated and defeated because of his inability or his refusal effectively to come to grips with the actual issues in the terms in which they presented themselves. As a result, his moral code never exerted the influence he had hoped and the specific problems with which he disdained to deal were to rise up again in an even more virulent form and to subject the world to another and a greater war.

Perhaps—as many astute thinkers today believe—it was Wilson himself who was the true realist and sanity can come to the world only when international affairs are governed by the moral law. The states of the modern world, however, are led by men who do not share Wilson's faith. The working diplomat serves both his government and all mankind by recognizing and acting upon the current primacy of the concept of national interest. If he admits that international conflicts are rooted in concrete situations and that only in concrete terms can solutions for them be found, he has taken the first great step toward the restoration of peace and equilibrium in any conflict situation.

Recognition of Other Points of View. A realistic diplomat is of course thoroughly aware of his own point of view toward the crisis with which he is dealing and is determined to win its acceptance. If his negotiations to that end are to have any success at all, however, he must recognize also that other points of view exist and that the men he is to deal with probably subscribe to these others. If he is ever to make contact with his adversary in terms that are meaningful, he must know what the other diplomats are seeking, why they are seeking it, and how important it is to them. Without some such knowl-edge, it is most difficult to estimate in advance what a state's reaction would be to any proposed solution.

It is often impossible even to have any idea of what kinds of subjects are open to discussion and compromise. No more infuriating and unsuccessful diplomat exists than the one who blithely assumes that any attitudes other than his own are either nonexistent or so completely misdirected as to be be-neath serious notice.

The United States government, for example, completely failed to com-prehend the real pressures to which Japan was subject during the period be-fore the war in 1941 and which impelled it in the direction of Asiatic expan-sion. American attitudes summed up Japanese policy as merely impudent ag-gression prompted by sheer malevolence, and were unable to take it seriously. Any hope of averting the war was doomed when the Japanese failed to get their point of view across to the United States. Conversely, the United States after 1945 found the Soviet Union to be as impossible to convince of the seriousness of American policy. The Russians persisted in viewing the United States as engaged in a hysterical and inevitably futile effort to stave off the global victory of the proletariat. It was only after such American successes as the Berlin dispute that Moscow came to realize that there was an American point of view which merited and demanded attention.

If a diplomat hopes to achieve any of the goals he is seeking by the use of non-violent means, he must start from a recognition that the states with which he deals have policies, attitudes, and points of view to which they are attached as firmly as he is to his own. Only then can he proceed to make the realistic judgments and agreements without which diplomatic success is im-possible.

FORCEFULNESS

Successful diplomacy is forceful. This necessitates that a diplomat have a thorough understanding of the role of power in international politics, an ap-preciation of the power situation as it affects him, and a willingness to use such power advantages as he may possess to press vigorously for a solution in his favor. Diplomacy that fails to use all the aspects of power in its service is not going to gain very many successes nor is it going to serve as an effective agent for the solution of conflicts. A diplomat must be aware of the extent to which world politics is power-dominated and must govern his conduct ac-cordingly.

The National Interest. The starting point in a forceful diplomacy is the concept of the national interest. A diplomat is the servant of his national in-terest and his every action must be in its defense. He knows that the interest he is charged with advancing is a matter of profound identification with his people and that to promote it his government may call upon the property and lives of all its individual citizens. His awareness that he is pursuing a matter of great interest to his state and all its people serves to strengthen his hand immeasurably. Failure to comprehend the current concept of national interest is fatal to any negotiator.

For an example we may return to President Wilson: by the time he reached Paris, he no longer represented the prevailing American idea of national interest. American public sentiment, recorded in the Republican victory in the Congressional elections of 1918, had turned against him and the approach to foreign policy which he exemplified. The other statesmen at the conference realized this better than he; the result was a complete loss of force from his arguments, since his adversaries realized that he was unable to back them up at home. Without the knowledge that he is advocating true national interest, a diplomat cannot gain even nominal success; being mistaken about it, as was Wilson, is almost as dangerous.

Supporting Interests with Force. Once his position is identified with the national interest, the diplomat must be able to support it by the collective power of his state. He must stipulate the points upon which he himself will not yield and make it clear that he is willing to go the limit in their defense. He must be prepared to exert pressure unerringly upon his opponent where the opponent is weak and he is strong. He must retain an understanding of the role of armed force even in 'peaceful' international affairs and be willing and able to employ threats of violence and even armed demonstrations when such techniques do not run too great a danger of involving him more deeply than he cares to go. Perhaps forceful diplomacy is demonstrated most clearly when one state offers another the clear choice between compromise settlement and war.

The earlier discussion of the Berlin blockade furnished concrete instances of the use of forceful diplomacy by both sides in that struggle. Throughout the entire first stage of the dispute, up to September, 1948, the Allies, negotiating from relative weakness, were unable to alter the basically unfavorable situation in which they found themselves. Once the dispute reached the United Nations, however, the diplomacy of the West grew more forceful as they discovered a power instrument of their own and obliged the USSR to combat a world public opinion that was growing steadily more hostile. Ultimately the Soviets found their power resources inadequate to cope with the worsening situation and they accepted the best possible compromise. A comprehension of the advantages of force in international politics, an understanding of the limitations upon its efficacy, and a willingness to use it where its application is appropriate are all hallmarks of the successful diplomatist.

The Policy Role of the Military. The diplomat who is aware of the significance of force in diplomacy must be constantly alert to see that the armed forces of his state remain the servant of his policy and not its determinant. Particularly in a democracy, there is a general fear of the 'military mind.' Whether or not such a thing exists, it is undeniable that a professional soldier views every international situation initially in terms of its strategic and tactical implications. This may, under certain conditions, exert an unfortunate influence upon the policy decisions of a government. Military analyses, made in terms of bases, supply routes, possible allies, and similar factors, may tie the hands of the political policy makers so as to prevent the making of the most attractive and expedient arrangement.

The wise and prudent statesman sees to it that the armed forces of his state are kept in such a relation to the non-military elements as to make them available for commitment and use when such action is in the national interest, but not to make them free agents with the power to make policy independently.

The Japanese cabinet that was in office before 7 December 1941 was destroyed and its policy repudiated simply because the uniformed armed services were able to take action without consulting or even informing the Premier or the Foreign Minister. Prince Konoye, the former Premier, had been following the policy of attempting to secure a compromise settlement of the Japanese-American dispute; the military branch, acting without effective control by the political leadership, attacked Pearl Harbor and precipitated the war. No diplomacy would be successful in such circumstances.

In like manner much of the diplomacy of the cold war has been materially affected on both sides by the limitations of military calculations. The United States, for example, has been led by its search for military support against the USSR to enter into working understandings with some strange bedfellows. Being in alliance with such autocratic governments as Portugal and Spain (to say nothing of communist Yugoslavia) makes United States defense of democratic principles somewhat less convincing to many peoples. In the Pacific, American espousal of Japan since 1949 has caused much concern in the minds of many Asian peoples who were subjected to the rigors of Japanese occupation during the four years from 1941 to 1945.

FLEXIBILITY

The chief characteristic of effective diplomacy is its flexibility. No matter how realistic his analysis of the situation or how shrewdly his position is supported by power, no diplomat is going to achieve permanent solutions to problems unless he is prepared for considerable give-and-take. Compromise is of the essence of diplomacy; good diplomacy differs from poor diplomacy in that the former knows when and upon what issues to reach agreement and when compromise is impossible or useless. The great diplomats of all time have been noted for their flexibility and their ability to cope with sudden changes in the situation. Talleyrand, Palmerston, Bismarck, and Clemenceau all avoided the danger of over-rigidity in their conduct of affairs and as a result they scored a high percentage of diplomatic successes. On the other hand, negotiators whose policy cannot be altered to meet new circumstances always either fail entirely or at best do not capitalize upon all the advantages inherent in their position.

Compromise upon Nonessentials. Diplomacy cannot get anywhere by a rigid insistence upon the letter of every policy; endless controversy would inevitably follow and solutions would be possible only by force. Equally suicidal, however, is the policy of agreeing with an adversary merely for the purpose of ending the dispute. Compromise must be confined to the nonessentials, to those more or less peripheral interests of the conflicting states which are the ones most frequently involved in disputes. To compromise away vital interests in pursuit of an illusory harmony is not only destructive of the policy of a state but instead of ending dispute only invites more.

Every successful negotiation involves intelligent compromise. Perhaps its key role in securing smooth international relations can be demonstrated by citing two conspicuous examples of the lack of it.

During the early postwar period after 1945, United States policy toward the Soviet Union represented a desire for agreement at almost any cost. As a result all disagreements between the two states resulted in American concessions, often involving a bargaining away of real advantage, in return for imprecise Soviet promises of co-operation in the future. This period—ending in 1947—furnished an example of over-willingness to compromise which did not actually result in any lasting understandings or thorough settlements.

On the other hand, Soviet diplomacy has failed to come up with many significant achievements through negotiation because of its great rigidity. Russian diplomats have developed a technique of the endless reiteration of a set position without ever giving any consideration to possible adjustments except the most inconsequential ones. Their Western adversaries have come to understand that to propose compromise is viewed as weakness by the Soviet and results only in greater Soviet firmness, while to remain as adamant as the Russians is frustrating and maddening.

The most effective device thus far discovered by the West to undermine Soviet inflexibility has been to interject some new element into the negotiations that catches them by surprise. Such action always results in a cessation of discussions while the Russians integrate this new element into their policy line. In the subsequent readjustment of policy that takes place at this time, the Soviet often yields ground formerly contested. American-Russian relations during the first ten years of the postwar period reveal a common inability to understand the function of compromise and its role in securing agreement. It will require a major reorientation of the popular and official attitudes of both states before either provides a very good example of diplomatic flexibility.

The Need for Alternative Policies. An essential requirement for a flexible diplomacy is the avoidance of a position so firm that no retreat is possible.

A prudent diplomat does not put himself 'on the spot.' He instead seeks always to provide an alternative policy or bargaining point to fall back upon in case the maintenance of his original line becomes impossible or inexpedient. The amorphous character of so many international relationships would seem to preclude any overly firm stand upon any but the minimum essentials of national interest. Even the cold war—an example of the worst type of international rigidity—has not stood still but has continued to evolve and to create new conditions. A diplomat who commits the power and prestige of his state to a single firm position discovers himself to be without any leverage when the situation suddenly changes.

American espousal of Chiang Kai-shek's regime in China, for example, was a valid position during the period before 1949, when he was a real factor in Asiatic politics. His fall from power, however, came so suddenly that American policy was unprepared for it, and as a result the United States, tied tightly to Chiang, has lost much of its ability to control affairs in Asia. Our bargaining power is sharply reduced as long as we remain unalterably committed to the support of Chiang and his regime continues to be a negligible factor in the Far East. We can see now that it would have been far better if the United States had left itself an escape route by means of an alternative program.

Soviet policy, although by nature given to extreme and rigid positions, has on occasion proved itself capable of utilizing escape routes. For all its insistence upon ideological purity, for example, it has been able to maintain effective contact with the noncommunist government of Finland and at the same time to expel the Sovietized government of Yugoslavia from its councils. Nevertheless, it remains vulnerable to sudden changes in circumstances and this has on occasion resulted in real diplomatic defeats.

Freedom of Maneuver. A flexible diplomacy sees to it that the maximum freedom of maneuver is retained. This necessitates that the diplomat engaged in negotiation have the support of all branches of his home government, especially the armed forces. He must be certain that any agreements he enters into will be honored at home and that no one but he is able to commit his state with regard to the particular subject under consideration. Binding agreements of his state must of course be adhered to, but no obligation that is not a clear source of advantage should restrain his actions.

Particularly should he not be subjected to the decision-making power of a minor ally. It is sometimes necessary for a powerful state to allow a minor partner to commit it to a course of action, but such arrangements are entered into only in cases of overwhelming necessity. Always an alliance of this sort operates as a galling restraint upon the bargaining power of the large state.

During the Berlin blockade, for example, American policy makers were forced to move slowly and sometimes ineffectively because of the fundamental United States decision to work only in concert with its British and French allies. Although no serious crisis developed in interallied relationships, much of American policy was affected by the particular and special interests of Britain and France.

Some doubts about the wisdom of the North Atlantic Pact have arisen among serious students because of the possibility that one of the European associates of the United States might provoke war and invoke the pact over an issue that American policy might not feel to be worth such an effort. Much effort has been already expended by the United States to minimize this danger.

These dilemmas, however, serve only to illustrate more clearly the task of the diplomat in the modern world. He must negotiate, maneuver, bargain, and compromise within an international framework grown increasingly rigid. Ideological combat, the bipolar world, hysterical nationalism, and the specter of total war make the function of diplomacy today more modest than formerly. Yet if the tensions of our time are to find final release short of violent outbreak and the possible end of our civilization, the way must be through the medium of diplomacy and its harmonizing and adjusting effect. Under present conditions the conduct of diplomacy is of such a character as to make its success in this role doubtful. Let us examine some of the shortcomings of diplomacy in the contemporary world.

THE INEFFECTIVENESS OF DIPLOMACY TODAY

Rigidity of the Two-power World. The diplomatic instrument of policy has proved ineffective to resolve the basic policy and power conflicts of the cold war. This failure of traditional procedures has caused many pessimistic observers to forecast the future of world politics as an uninspiring and endless power struggle among totalitarian states. The only escape from interminable cold war, they argue, is either the dreadful catharsis of total war or a fortunate accident of some sort to deliver man from his frightening dilemma. The 1984-like vision overlooks both the lessons of history and some fundamentals of human psychology.

The most important single reason for the failure of diplomacy to find a way out of the cold war is the rigidity of the international scene today. Diplomacy, with its emphasis upon freedom of maneuver and the necessity of compromise, demands a situation of relative international fluidity to achieve its effects. Under the bipolar organization of present-day world politics, this fluidity is lacking.

This immobility of policy is not, however, the outcome of historical forces of cosmic significance; it does not represent any concatenation of tendencies all beyond human control. Rather, it came into existence as the result of specific and concrete policy decisions on the part of the governments of the two great powers. It is of human origin, and can be terminated by the same people that brought it into being. The United States and the USSR initiated the policies that have led to the present stalemate in hopes that they would lead to the attainment of sought-after objectives. To a great extent today these policies cancel each other out; the objectives are therefore unattainable, at least under present conditions. To break the deadlock and once again to free the diplomatic instrument of policy for effective use, all that is required is a series of new and different decisions made by both governments.

This is not to say that such a reversal of contemporary trends is either easy or likely in the immediate future. There are great obstacles to be overcome before diplomacy can again operate freely. The difficulties are not insurmountable, however, and good will and determination could, in the end, remove them.

There was some hope that such a fundamental reconciliation was in the making, following the death of Stalin in March 1953, when the Russian attitude toward the West softened perceptibly. During the subsequent two years, the Soviet line fluctuated but gradually grew more flexible. In early 1955, the Kremlin took action to end the impasse over Austria on terms favorable to the West, and made unexpectedly conciliatory moves on two troublesome questions: the unification of Germany and a formula for disarmament. Although the major states of the free world moved swiftly to exploit the opportunity for meaningful diplomacy with the USSR, many people throughout the world retained their doubts.

'*Open Diplomacy.*' One of the unfortunate inheritances of the contemporary world from the era following World War I is a popular faith in 'open diplomacy.' It had its origin in a popular revulsion against the 'secret treaties' of the war of 1914–18 and was given great currency by its inclusion as the first of President Wilson's 'Fourteen Points.' The world generally misunderstood, however, what Wilson meant by 'open' negotiation. He was not arguing for the conduct of all relations in public, but merely condemning the assumption of treaty obligations by governments without first informing their peoples. Nevertheless, the League of Nations experience and the conference diplomacy of the interwar period served to convince millions of people everywhere that there was an inherent virtue in the conduct of diplomacy in the bright light of publicity.

In the period after 1945 this practice was carried on both in the United Nations and in various forms of international conference. The intensification of nationalism, earlier remarked, served to make every diplomatic exchange a matter charged with heavy emotional content and sharply limited the efficacy of negotiation. Concession is interpreted as weakness and compromise as defeat ('appeasement') by sensitive public opinion.

In this way the diplomat is severely inhibited in the selection of subjects upon which he is free to compromise and in the concessions he may make in the interest of agreement. This has tended to make the conduct of public diplomacy only a succession of speeches primarily for domestic propaganda purposes, and the search for agreement has been a foredoomed futility. So long as the nationalist frenzy of peoples makes them unable to comprehend the compromising aspects of diplomacy, the conduct of negotiations in public cannot be expected to accomplish anything.

It is revealing that the most important diplomatic agreements reached in the postwar era after 1945 were arrived at in privacy and near secrecy. The negotiations leading to the North Atlantic Treaty and the arrangements for the lifting of the Berlin blockade are only two examples. Until diplomacy goes back into privacy, where there will be again the freedom to engage in the give-and-take that is necessary for any agreement, its success will continue to be negligible.

Popular Ratification of Decisions. Intense nationalist concern with the conduct as well as with the outcome of diplomatic negotiations has produced another grave difficulty. Diplomats constantly keep an ear attuned to the demands of their own people and tend to take their cue from nationalist demands. No decision is reached unless the diplomat is convinced that his people will accept it, regardless of its relation to true national interest. This leads to a view that is all too common today: diplomatic procedures are thought of as being primarily valuable as vehicles for the dissemination of nationalist propaganda.

Of course, all sympathizers with democracy approve in principle of popular ratification, formal or informal, of foreign-policy decisions made by a government. But it would be far more in keeping with the democratic idea if such approval were given in terms of a reasoned concept of national interest instead of the more irrational aspects of nationalist emotion and prejudice. This seldom happens today. American nationalism often conceives of any concession to Russian policy as 'appeasement'—one of the most overworked words of our time—and indignantly rejects any international solution that does not imply that a judgment of moral turpitude is being passed upon the Soviet. Similar attitudes are demonstrated by the Russian people, at least as far as it is possible for the West to determine their reaction.

Nationalism is rigid, and popular decision upon foreign-policy questions tends today to be rendered in terms of a narrow and particularist point of view. In this connection again, the freedom of action of the diplomat is restrained and his usefulness correspondingly diminished.

Loss of Sense of Proportion. A final outcome derived from the injection of nationalist values into diplomacy must be mentioned. When every difference in policy is materially augmented in size and importance so as to appear a quarrel of fundamental values, all sense of proportion tends to be lost. Each issue is as important as any other, and compromise and/or concession is thought of as equally immoral no matter what the specific terms. Of course this is unrealistic. Some items of dispute between states actually do involve basic aspects of policy and diplomats dare not lightly dispose of them, but these represent only a small part of the total business of international relations. Most international controversies are of vastly less importance and can be handled with relative ease provided their true relation with the overall policy of the state be kept in mind.

But when, as in the case of much of the cold war, nationalist attitudes find everything the other state does to be suspect and motivated by sheer viciousness, the preservation of an accurate perspective on the part of diplomats becomes a near impossibility. Minor questions are argued heatedly while major issues go unregarded, and agreement upon an entire broad problem may remain in suspension while interminable wrangling goes on upon a petty question of procedure or prestige. The refusal of diplomats to come to grips with many of the real questions of our day is a major cause of the failure of diplomacy to perform its special function of the adjustment of conflicts.

Conclusions upon Ineffective Diplomacy. Diplomacy has proved inadequate to resolve the majority of the conflicts of the cold war because of one great central reason and several subsidiary ones. The core of the problem is the nature of international relations today. The rigidity of the bipolar world, brought about by deliberate policy decisions on the part of the major antagonists, has frozen the pattern of world relationships so as to deprive diplomats of much of the freedom of maneuver and of choice among alternatives without which they are helpless.

In addition, the hypertense nationalism of most of the world today has caused people to identify every policy dispute with fundamental nationalist aspirations and thus has led to the conduct of negotiations in public and a loss of any sense of proportion as among issues. Thus both government policy and popular attitudes contribute to the cycle that keeps diplomats baffled and impotent. If any break in this pattern is to result in renewed use of powerful diplomatic techniques, both government policy and nationalist sentiment must relax and give diplomats another opportunity to exert their be found to break the stalemate of world affairs.

8

Escape from Conflict: Formal Techniques

Formal techniques for the resolution of international conflict differ from the informal methods described in Chapter 7 in at least two distinct ways. In the first place, the formal method is characterized by the active participation of a third party—usually a state not involved in the controversy—along with the disputing states in the process of reaching agreement and settling the dispute. The specific role played by this third party varies according to the particular procedure adopted, but it is always an important one. Second, formal techniques are marked by a high degree of procedural and substantive control by means of mutually understood rules. The disputing states and the neutral third party are alike subject to controls, and the failure to follow them often vitiates the whole undertaking.

It is not an overstatement to claim that the entire world political society has an interest in the outcome of the application of a formal technique to a conflict situation. The manner in which the discussions proceed and the decisions are reached, as well as the general nature of the eventual settlement, is watchfully controlled by the third party, who often symbolizes the desire of all other states that the problem be disposed of peacefully and expeditiously. Formal techniques thus involve both the appearance of a third party and the reaching of the agreement in accordance with predetermined rules and principles.

The solutions to disputes reached through the application of formal techniques have a high degree of permanence. When a controversy has been disposed of by means of one of these devices, statesmen have come to feel that they may safely count upon its total and permanent disappearance as a source of international conflict. This has led to a considerable degree of misunderstanding about the nature of these formal procedures. Many people feel that if means could be discovered to give them wider—preferably universal—applicability, all or most of the instability and recurrent tension of world politics would be removed. Analogies are drawn with the rule of law in civil societies and it is argued that the establishment of similar arrangements in international life would reduce the incidence of violence there to as low a level as that of violence in civil life.

To argue this way is to ignore most of the realities of both civil and international political life. In the first place, formal techniques are invoked only by the active or tacit consent of the disputing states themselves, and even then they are appropriate only in certain circumstances. We shall see later how the Charter of the United Nations attempts to deprive states of some of their freedom of choice in this matter, but in practice it cannot yet force the employment of any of these devices of pacific settlement. Furthermore, many of the disputes engaged in by states—perhaps the majority—are not amenable to settlement by formal means. Being clashes of policy, they are not reached by the mechanism of formal settlement.

PRECONDITIONS TO EFFECTIVENESS

There are several conditions upon which the effectiveness of any of the formal techniques depends. All of them must be present together in the situation; the absence of any one of them prevents the employment of any but the informal methods of diplomatic negotiation. It frequently happens that all but one of them will be present and the dispute will languish unresolved until the situation develops to the point where the missing one appears. At that time the formal mechanisms go into action and produce the solution.

Desire for Settlement. The first prerequisite for the effectiveness of the formal techniques of settlement is a desire on the part of the disputing states for a solution. Of course, this is a necessary precondition for the termination of any international dispute by any non-violent means, formal or informal. It has a special connotation, however, when a formal technique is to be used. Although the extent to which this is true varies from one procedure to another, to a considerable degree a state that submits a dispute to resolution by formal procedures loses control over the eventual outcome. The mere existence of a third state in the mechanism of settlement reduces by that much a state's ability unilaterally to produce a solution in harmony with its own position.

Even more of a restraint upon a state's freedom in securing its objectives is the fact that the settlement of the dispute is often subject to the rules and the practices of international law. This means that before a state agrees to the utilization of formal techniques in the resolution of a dispute affecting itself, it must be prepared to face the prospect of a decision being rendered in the determination of which it had only a minor part.

There are only two possible reasons why a state will accept such a set of conditions. The first arises when the state is so certain of the merits of its case that it is willing to stand or fall upon an objective judgment of the controversy. The second comes about when a state has abandoned hopes of winning a victory by its own efforts and prefers to end the controversy as gracefully as possible even if it loses all of the points for which it has contended. A state, in other words, accepts formal procedures either when it is almost certain of victory or when it is fully prepared to face defeat.

Normally, therefore, formal techniques do not gain acceptance until relatively late in the course of a dispute. Driven by the compulsions of national interest, a state will always seek by every convenient means to gain a victory by its own efforts. The decision to relinquish the hope of unilateral success and to trust to an agency that is, for the most part, externally controlled is usually made only after the thorough exploration of all other possibilities. This is to say that a state will not accept formal methods to resolve a dispute until the liquidation of the quarrel upon almost any terms has become an objective of high priority. Finally, it must again be pointed out that the desire for settlement upon formal procedures must be mutual and shared by both disputing states.

Failure of Direct Settlement. A second prerequisite for the effectiveness of formal procedures is the non-susceptibility of the dispute to informal settlement. It was pointed out above that states prefer to keep the maximum control themselves over all situations in which they are involved. It therefore follows that they always attempt to settle controversies among themselves by direct, informal, means. Formal procedures do not ordinarily make their appearance until the best efforts of the disputing parties at direct negotiation have proved fruitless.

There are many possible situations with which informal procedures are incapable of dealing but which are peculiarly suited for formal solution. Three such may be cited as examples.

In the first place, a dispute may have at its core a question of fact, upon the determination of which both sides ultimately agree the final solution must rest. Such a controversy was that between Russia and Great Britain in 1904 in the dispute known as the Dogger Bank incident. In such circumstances no negotiations can compromise the facts, which usually speak for themselves; formal fact-finding procedures become the only efficacious means of terminating the dispute.

A second type of controversy that would defy solution by informal techniques but would yield to formal ones centers about a question of international law, either procedural or substantive. If direct negotiation reveals that both sides are willing to stand or fall upon an authoritative pronouncement of the law, further informal approaches are pointless. Formal procedures involving legal determination provide the only way to dispose of the controversy. Among many famous disputes of this sort one need only cite perhaps the *Alabama* claims arbitration between Great Britain and the United States in 1872. After a long dispute carried on at the highest diplomatic level, the issues between the two states were reduced to a short series of legal points, neatly disposed of by an arbitral tribunal. The judgment of the court was rendered and the indemnities were paid with no further ado.

A third class of dispute which baffles diplomats but is resolvable by formal means is one arising from a certain type of intense nationalist clash. If popular tensions surpass a minimum level, gaining acceptance for even a good compromise settlement becomes impossible and permanent stalemate threatens. But in a situation in which a people refuse to make even minor concessions to a state they hate, they might be much more amenable to pacifying proposals emanating from a neutral party, preferably one of high prestige or one representing a considerable body of public opinion. In this way retreat from an extreme position would be interpreted not as a defeat but as a voluntary and high-minded act in the interest of world peace.

The Influence of Delay. A further factor of advantage inherent in the formal approach is particularly in point in this connection. Formal procedures, involving as they do many arrangements of an almost ritualistic nature, often serve to slow down the pace of a dispute once they are invoked. Long periods of waiting ensue while preliminary arrangements are being made and hearings or investigations undertaken. These periods, during which the struggle is often suspended, serve to cool the ardor of nationalism which earlier had been heightened by a rapid succession of events leading to crisis.

United Nations intervention into the disputes in Indonesia and Palestine had this clear effect. Once the mounting tension began to relax with the cessation of open dispute and its transfer to the council table, the respective populations became much more willing to accept less than the maximum they had once claimed.

Appropriateness of the Dispute. It was pointed out above that only disputes of a certain type are susceptible of resolution by formal means. Since many of the formal and procedural techniques involve a reliance upon and extensive employment of the rules of international law, a dispute that is not reducible to legal terms is very difficult to cope with in this way.

This includes the great majority of policy conflicts between states that involve fundamental differences in national interest and broad policy orientation. Such a basic hostility as the cold war, arising as it does out of deep seated antipathy rooted in divergent outlooks upon the world, simply cannot be reduced to a disagreement over one or two points of law. Legal differences abound in Russo-American relations, but their resolution would not in itself create harmony in the place of controversy. Nonjusticiable dispute cannot be resolved by legal procedures in international relations any more than they can be in private life.

Not all formal techniques, however, are narrowly legalistic in their principal focus. The whole field of conciliation does not presume a legal settlement but instead emphasizes the expediting of informal solution of the controversy upon any expedient basis. But even here, where the third party involved assumes the role of a catalyst to speed up the process of negotiation many disputes defy solution. If the policy clash goes sufficiently deep to call into question the honor or vital interests of both parties, the application of formal techniques is either impossible or useless.

We may therefore conclude that the only disputes which by their nature are resolvable by one or another of the formal means are those which (a) are justiciable or (b) involve a policy clash of non-vital interests between the disputing states. These, and these only, offer a fertile field for the use of the formal methods.

The Necessity of Institutional Machinery. A final requirement for formal techniques to be effective is the existence, or at least the creation in time to be of use, of adequate institutional machinery. Formal techniques require that some concrete agency be created to function as the peacemaking force. Conciliation proceeds through a mediator, a commission of inquiry, or a good-offices agency; adjudication through an arbitral tribunal or a permanent court. Without the institutional arrangements, it is impossible to use the formal techniques.

It has often happened in history that the incompletely organized structure of international life has proved unable to produce new institutions in sufficient time during a crisis, and the world lost an opportunity for the successful application of formal peacemaking devices. The diplomatic crisis preceding World War I furnishes a striking example. Simultaneously with the march of events leading to war during July 1914, there was a frantic attempt led by Sir Edward Grey of Great Britain to extemporize machinery to deal with the Austro-Serbian dispute while it was still local and resolvable by pacific means. He lost the race; before any of his proposals could be implemented the struggle had reached the point of world war. This is a constant problem in connection with these formal devices. If the machinery created is to be of any use at all it must be in existence in time to perform its functions.

Later in this chapter we shall examine in detail the way these formal techniques have been employed by the United Nations. Its record of success is creditable; not the least of the reasons for its effectiveness is the fact that it is in constant existence as a forum to which problems may be brought while in an early and less acute stage. It may prescribe which of the available techniques is best suited to the particular conflict and proceed immediately to the creation of the appropriate machinery. Its use of mediation, inquiry, and good offices in each case has been marked by a high degree of promptness in getting the chosen instrument into operation on the spot.

It also has the advantage of having available within itself the International Court of Justice, a permanent court of law, to deal with cases that fall within its scope. Indeed, with the creation of the United Nations the world now enjoys the greatest variety, the most rapid application, and the most complete organization for formal peacemaking that it has ever known.

THE ROLE OF INTERNATIONAL LAW

Before we examine in detail the various techniques of formal settlement of international conflict, some understanding of the role of international law is necessary. Not only do some of the formal devices operate completely within a legal framework, but the pattern of relationships reflected by international law governs, or at least materially affects, the application of all of them. Much clarification of many of the problems inherent in later consideration of the resolution of disputes is possible if the fundamental characteristics of the law of international affairs is kept in mind.

DEFINITION AND CHARACTERISTICS OF INTERNATIONAL LAW

Although definitions of international law differ in details almost as widely as do definitions of some of the other terms we have discussed, there is pretty general agreement that international law consists of the body of legal rules that actually govern the formal relations between states. If we view international law in these terms, certain of its characteristics become immediately apparent. In the first place, there is no universal agreement on its content; states differ from one another in detailing their legal rights and duties. In the second place, it is not enforced in the sense that municipal law is. There is no socially sanctioned institution whose function it is to secure compliance with the law and to punish disobedience. Each state is its own law-enforcement agency as against other states.

The United Nations Charter seeks to replace this anarchic system with at least a partial recourse to collective law enforcement, but the uneven response of the sovereign states constituting the membership to the Korean operation —its most ambitious venture in this field to date—reveals to what a small extent this idea has taken hold.

A third characteristic of international law arises from the nature of the state. Obedience to the law in any situation is a voluntary act on the part of the state. Of course, a small state is frequently coerced by a larger one into obeying the law, but even so, its obedience is voluntary; it could, if it preferred, instead suffer the punishment for disobedience. In such a situation the small state is not obeying the commands of an abstraction called 'the law,' but is yielding to the superior power of another state.

A fourth characteristic of international law has already been mentioned: international law does not apply to all forms of international contact, but covers only a part of them. This means that international relations go on partly within the scope of the law and partly outside it. Many international relationships of critical importance are completely irrelevant to the legal system and go forward without any restraint or control from that source.

Sources of International Law. The first source of international law is international custom. This, the most productive source, includes all the practices of international intercourse which states have found to be convenient and mutually advantageous, and which have gained sufficient currency of acceptance to attain the status of general rules. This part of international law is the most influential in its effect and is the most generally obeyed.

The second category is international legislation. This term refers most specifically to the great multilateral law-making treaties of the nineteenth and twentieth centuries. In these instruments a group of states, more or less numerous, drew up a statement in the form of a treaty which decreed the state of the law on a particular subject or subjects. Sometimes, as in the case of the Geneva Convention of 1864, adherence to the agreement was so nearly universal as to constitute a true general rule; sometimes, although only a few states entered into the agreement, they were so powerful as to force the acceptance of the rules by other states.

The movement for international legislation gained its greatest impetus with the creation of the League of Nations and the United Nations. The drawing up of agreements by these bodies and their ratification by a sizeable majority of the membership gives them a truly general character. The General Act for the Pacific Settlement of Disputes by the League in 1928 and the Universal Convention of Human Rights by the United Nations in 1949 (the latter not yet ratified) are only two examples.

International legislation, in other words, bears roughly the same relationship to customary law that statute law does to common law in Anglo-American jurisprudence. It amplifies and fills in custom, it sometimes supersedes it, and it fills in the gaps created by technological change. The term 'international legislation' is also used occasionally to describe bilateral treaties, in which states lay down special rules which they will obey in their relations with each other.

The third great source of international law we may call international morality. Owing to its theological and philosophical origin, international law has always had a greater moral content than the majority of the other legal systems with which Americans are familiar. The first two sources—custom and legislation—reflect modes of conduct that states actually follow; the 'positivist' school of thought argues that that is all there is to it. There is another group which contends, on the contrary, that there is a normative standard of international behavior. International law which expresses such a code has 'natural law' at its root. This self-evident body of law, discoverable by reason, determines not what states actually do but what they ought to do. Over the centuries many of the moralistic precepts of this system have influenced the development of a good deal of positive law.

Evidences of International Law. How can one determine the rule of law in any international situation? The determination of a legal rule requires the examination of several jurisprudential fields, some of which were discussed above. Article 38 of the Statute of the International Court of Justice specifies four categories of law which the Court shall apply. These are listed in something like descending order of importance: first, international conventions, whether general or particular, establishing rules recognized by the contesting states; second, international custom ('as evidence of a general practice accepted as law'); third, the general principles of law recognized by civilized nations; fourth, judicial decisions and the teachings of 'the most highly qualified publicists' of the various nations, 'as subsidiary means for the determination of the rules of law.' Thus the critical elements in international law, from the point of view of the supreme judicial body dealing with the subject, are formal agreement, custom, reason, and the writings of private persons.

THE SUBJECT MATTER OF INTERNATIONAL LAW

Although the body of international law is considerable and goes into great detail with regard to specific points, it is possible to reduce it into three great classifications of subject matter. Always in this sort of classification the lines between the categories are unclear; nevertheless, they do furnish a convenient and not inaccurate way to summarize the content of the discipline.

The Law of Statehood. The first field is the law of statehood, dealing with the legal personality of the state and the duties, rights, and privileges appertaining thereto. This includes the assumption of statehood through international recognition, state succession, and the loss of statehood. It covers also the acquisition and alienation of territory and analogous topics. It gives legal definition to such evidences of status as equality, the responsibility of a state for actions on its territory and by its nationals abroad, and jurisdiction.

The point of jurisdiction merits particular emphasis. Territorial jurisdiction, although theoretically complete, has many conditions in practice. Jurisdiction over marginal seas (the three-mile limit) is limited by the right of 'innocent passage' and extended by the right of 'hot pursuit.' Foreign vessels are accorded certain rights in the seaports of a state. International rivers and the law of the air both furnish many borderline cases of jurisdictional conflict between states.

Jurisdiction over persons calls into question the issue of nationality and citizenship. No universal rules regarding citizenship exist; *jus soli* (law of the soil—citizenship is acquired by place of birth) and *jus sanguinus* (law of the blood—citizenship is acquired by the citizenship of one's parents) are both practiced in the world today. Most states lean toward *jus soli,* but the United States and several other large states employ both. The international law of nationality includes also grants of jurisdiction to a state over its nationals abroad, over aliens resident within its territory, and provisions covering naturalization, denaturalization, stateless persons, and exemptions from the personal jurisdiction of a state.

The Law of Peaceful International Intercourse. The second category may be termed the law of peaceful international intercourse. We may break down this classification into its three major components: the law of diplomacy, the law of treaties, and the law of the pacific settlement of international disputes.

Diplomatic law prescribes the powers and privileges of the various classes of diplomatic agents and details the protocol affecting the way in which diplomatic business is carried on. It also governs the subject of diplomatic immunity, which exempts most of the members of a diplomatic mission from the local laws of the state in which they are stationed. Consular law is also part of this section.

The law of treaties is an important part of international law. The tests of a valid treaty, the rules of interpretation, and the process of termination of a treaty are some of the more significant subclassifications. With regard to termination, at least two major doctrines have been in conflict for centuries. *Pacta sunt servanda* holds that treaties made in good faith must be honored until expiration or until abrogated by mutual consent; *rebus sic stantibus* confers the right upon a state to denounce a treaty unilaterally if the basic conditions under which it entered into the agreement have changed. Most practice today leans to the former doctrine.

The law governing the pacific settlement of international disputes controls the various procedures used to settle international conflict peacefully. The techniques, discussed in detail below, are good offices, inquiry, mediation, arbitration, and judicial settlement.

The Law of War. The law of war is the third subject-matter classification. It deals initially with the legal concepts of belligerency and neutrality. Belligerency grants a state many legal rights it would not enjoy while at peace, including generally the right to impose its will upon the enemy by violence. It also requires a state to obey the laws governing the conduct of warfare. Neutrality confers certain rights upon a state enjoying the status, principally the maximum immunity practicable from the effects of the war. In return a neutral must behave in a prescribed manner, acquiescing in certain belligerent rights, abstaining from certain acts, and preserving strict impartiality.

Neutrality is not necessarily synonymous with non-belligerency, as United States policy during 1940 and 1941 demostrated. It should also be mentioned that neutral rights have verged upon extinction with the increasing totalization of war.

The law of war also includes the rules for the conduct of warfare. Most of these have been brought into existence through major law-making treaties of the last hundred years. Included are distinctions between combatant and non-combatant elements of a population, rules for the treatment of prisoners of war, the prohibition of certain weapons, protection for the sick and wounded, and rules governing such irregular military elements as guerrillas and spies.

Various other provisions of the laws both land and sea warfare are aimed at mitigating the horrors of war, in harmony with the classic aim of doing the minimum harm to the enemy commensurate with the achieving of the military objective. The experience of World War II, however, reveals that total war and mass destruction make many of these rules irrelevant to present-day conditions.

INTERNATIONAL LAW AND INTERNATIONAL POLITICS

Just how much influence upon the conduct of international politics does the body of jurisprudence just described actually exert? This is a question of more than academic significance; it is apparent that law has a great stabilizing and order-bringing effect upon civil society, and some index of the relation between order and disorder in international affairs may be arrived at by an estimate of the actual impact of legal rules. Furthermore, if the 'rule of law' and peaceful process is ever to become the normal mode of behavior in world politics, we must first know the extent to which law serves its purpose today as well as where it fails.

Applicability in Normal Situations. Although international law is subject to many frontal attacks by self-styled 'realists' who see nothing in law except coercion, sanctions, and punitive enforcement, there is no evading the central fact that the great bulk of normal and routine international contacts does take place within the framework of international law and according to its rules. Rooted either in expedient custom or in co-operatively formulated legislation, this *corpus* of law actually governs international behavior to a great extent. The conduct of diplomacy, the rights and duties of states, and the negotiation, ratification, and applicability of treaties all occur within a pattern of general provisions that are universally understood and possess a high degree of predictability. Even in crisis situations, so strong is the effect of these rules that most of them are meticulously observed. Despite the bitterness that accompanied the outbreak of World War II, for example, the legal requirements of diplomatic immunity were adhered to and the various missions were returned safely to their home states.

The Sanctions of International Law. It is true that these rules do not possess fully developed techniques of enforcement. The absence of effective and automatic coercive sanctions is the greatest shortcoming of international law. But sanctions are not entirely lacking.

Perhaps the greatest of all is expediency; states conform to the rules because of a positive advantage arising therefrom and this outweighs any gain that might arise from violation.

A second sanction is habit or inertia. Psychologists know that obedience to law by a private person is often a conditioned response; he obeys simply because he and the rest of the society of which he is a part are by training 'law-abiding citizens.' Thus it has been with states. So universal has been the acceptance of most of the rules of normal intercourse that it never occurs to most statesmen to disobey; barring exceptional compulsion most statesmen order their conduct accordingly.

A third sanction, related to the previous two, is public opinion. Although it is deceptively easy to overestimate the extent and the power of public opinion, there is no doubt that the inarticulate demand of men in all parts of the world for a release from unforseeable and recurrent crisis serves to influence statesmen in the direction of orderly behavior. World reaction today is immediately hostile toward any state that flamboyantly breaks the law. Of course, a state that is sufficiently powerful and sufficiently determined can flout public opinion and follow its own course; nevertheless it is obvious that many a would-be violator of international law has been restrained because of fear of a hostile public reaction outside its own national boundaries.

The Relative Strength of Procedural Law. It must be pointed out in this connection that the provisions of international law upon which there is the most general agreement are procedural in character. Procedural, or adjective, law is much more highly developed than is substantive international law. The latter specifies certain concrete rights of states; the former deals with the process by which rights are established and guaranteed. What we are saying is that the 'how' of international law is much clearer than the 'what.' For example, although a state is secure in its right to maintain diplomatic relations— a procedural point—there is no sure guarantee that it will not become the object of such diplomatic pressure from a more powerful associate as substantially to deprive it of its substantive right to independence. The process of seeking redress for injury is clear, but obtaining it is quite another matter. This is the reason for much of the cynicism about international law. People sometimes view it as a hollow set of forms without substance, within which states move in a sort of ritual that is devoid of any significance.

Breakdown in Situations of Crisis. It is at a moment of crisis that the incompleteness of the international legal system is most obvious. Whenever the national policies of states come into direct conflict over an issue deemed of vital interest to both, the law provides today no automatic restraints to prevent them from going to war. In private society, on the other hand, if two individuals become so incensed that they seek to settle their differences by violence, both are equally guilty of an antisocial act and an offense against society, and machinery exists to exact punishment. We pointed out earlier how a test by force between two states does not decide the issues in terms of which of them was on the side of legal or moral right, but instead merely which possessed and was able to apply the greater amount of power. Far too often for logical consistency, new interpretations of international legal rules have been enunciated by the victor in such a conflict. These principles of 'victor's justice,' although solemnly propounded and as solemnly accepted at the time by everyone concerned, survive only as long as the relations of conqueror, conquered, and neutrals continue as they were at the immediate end of the war.

The Right to Resort to Force. This medieval concept of law—that the victor in a trial by strength is automatically on the side of justice and law—is a heavy blow to the claims of many of the defenders of international law. A jurisprudence whose borderline issues are decided on the basis of *force majeure* cannot offer much hope to a world seeking order and peace.

A further factor of breakdown was alluded to above. Despite the elaborate procedural paraphernalia of the law, a state always possesses the right to use force as an alternative to obedience to it. This makes international law a largely voluntary system, since no obligatory conformity to its regulations exists.

The United Nations has sought to make war 'illegal'; despite learned and ingenious interpretations of the Charter, the 'principle of sovereign equality' upon which the organization is founded remains unimpaired. What the sovereign gives, the sovereign can take away; no other interpretation squares with the facts. As long as international law remains what it is, a body of rules governing the relations of sovereign states, no legal system can abolish the right of a state to go to war if its national interests so demands.

The recurrent crises of the twentieth century have all been marked by a rupture of the fabric of international law at moments of fundamental decision when statesmen chose illegal action rather than to restrain their national policies. Bethmann-Hollweg, the chancellor of imperial Germany in 1914, was a bewildered realist who failed utterly to comprehend the concern of the Western states with Germany's violation of the treaty guaranteeing the neutrality of Belgium—that 'scrap of paper,' as he is said to have called it. Likewise, Adolf Hitler, never noted for his social-mindedness, precipitated the Second World War by his course of systematic destruction and violation of not only the obligation of treaties but also the general rules of international conduct. Without either the social sanction or the machinery for collective enforcement, the injured states in both cases had no recourse but to meet force with force.

Unilateral Interpretation of the Law. Another weakness of international law at crisis points has to do with the tendency of states to interpret undefined or borderline issues to suit their own policies. This is of course especially true of the major states, which possess the power to back up their arguments. Thus there may be at any time several interpretations of identical points of law emanating from as many states, and no agency exists to give an authoritative finding that everyone must accept. In a time of tension and conflict, states are thus able to choose the rule of law most in support of the particular policy each holds and in that fashion to gain whatever advantage accrues from having the law on its side. Not only is there often an oversupply of conflicting rules in a particular situation, but these nationalist interpretations of the law demonstrate an ability to change to meet the evolving requirements of a state's policy.

The recent history of the doctrine of neutral shipping and contraband is an instructive example. The United States, during World War I, insisted upon the maximum freedom of the seas for neutral shipping and the most circumscribed definition of contraband; the British, possessing great naval power and an interest in cutting off trade to Germany, defined contraband loosely and exercised great initiative in the interference with neutral shipping.

Thirty years later the power position of the two states had reversed and their policies on neutral trade had followed suit. Naturally enough, each claimed the law to be on its side; what was ironical was that the United States was now denying the freedom of the seas it had formerly defended, while the British were substantially maintaining the position formerly held by the United States. Many other examples of such reversals of position could be cited.

INTERNATIONAL LAW IN THE SETTLEMENT OF DISPUTES

This rapid survey of the nature, content, strength, and weakness of international law has been for the purpose of arriving at some general understanding of the effect of the international legal system upon the settlement of international controversy. Certain points are immediately evident. International law furnishes many clear and precise procedures for the settlement of disputes and implementation of claims. There is also a considerable body of substantive law which lays down rights and duties of states in their relations with one another. Much of this is sufficiently well accepted to furnish a guide to the liquidation of many controversies. Furthermore, when a dispute has yielded to resolution in legal terms, it is likely to be settled permanently. Very few exceptions to this rule can be found.

Limitations on its Effectiveness. On the other hand, international law suffers from several serious limitations; some of them have appeared previously in this analysis, but pulling them together here will serve to round out the point.

In the first place, only a few of the international conflicts that take place are legal in character and therefore susceptible of solution in legal terms. Many serious controversies arise as a result of a clash of policies in the pursuit of which both parties are acting in a perfectly legal manner. In this situation legal remedies are entirely inappropriate.

A second limitation upon law in the settlement of disputes is the voluntary character of its jurisdiction. Each state is free to accept or reject legal determination of its rights. This has the effect of confining the impact of law to only those disputes which the states concerned feel to be relatively innocuous.

The third major limitation upon international law refers to the lack of sufficiently elaborate institutional machinery for the application of the law. The arrangements that exist are incomplete; when a dispute arises for the solution of which existing institutions are inadequate, time and effort must be expended in the improvisation of new ones. This often handicaps or actually prevents the application of existing legal rules to the particular situation.

Conclusions on International Law. Some general conclusions, based on the foregoing analysis, would seem to be in order at this point. International law is much more effective in specifying procedures than in prescribing rights. Its effectiveness is limited by the very nature of the nation-state system; the course of world politics also results in international law's falling short of its theoretical potential, limited though that might be.

The further development of international law will probably take two related, though dissimilar, directions. In the first place, there will probably be a greater refinement and clarification of the present vague and controversial rules in the direction of making the system applicable in a broader variety of circumstances; in other words, the actual effect of international law will be closer to its theoretical maximum. Secondly, legal relationships will develop reflecting the trend toward supra-national governmental units. The self-contained state is no longer the only participant in the international legal and political process; individuals (as in the Nuremburg trials) and international organizations (the United Nations, the European Coal and Steel Community) form a small but growing part of the international community. As this continues, the unrestrained freedom of action of the individual state will be further circumscribed as collective enforcement agencies multiply and one may at least hopefully anticipate the day when international affairs move within the legal framework of more real vitality and meaning.

CONCILIATION

Conciliation and Adjudication. At this point we turn to the examination of the several formal devices for the settlement of disputes. As discussed in this chapter they fall into two major groups. One, which we call conciliation, includes such a third-party procedures as good offices, inquiry, and mediation; the second, adjudication, covers arbitration and judicial settlement. The differences between the categories as well as among the various techniques will become clear as we proceed.

CONCILIATION IN GENERAL

All the formal techniques that are grouped within the general classification of conciliation possess a number of common characteristics. In each of them the actual effectiveness of the agreement is dependent upon its acceptance by the parties themselves; the role of the third party is always an auxiliary one. As a result the conciliatory devices themselves aim at expediting the elimination of the differences between the disputants and at urging them to reach amicable agreement by their own act.

No Single Form of Agreement. The primary object of all techniques of conciliation is the liquidation of the dispute. In their application it is therefore of the first importance that the eventual agreement be acceptable to both parties. Consequently there are no limitations upon the type of agreement or the provisions of the final settlement, provided only that it serve as a basis for the end of the controversy. It may—and usually does—conform exactly to the provisions of international law; it may be extralegal and hence have no relationship with legal rules; in special cases it may violate them. It may represent a victory for justice and morality or it may be transparently unjust. It may conform to public opinion or it may fly in its face.

All of these considerations are beside the point. In the last analysis, conciliatory techniques may produce a settlement of any form at all; only the disputing parties are intimately concerned and whatever satisfies them serves the public interest as well.

Some scholars cast serious doubt upon conciliation. Their argument seems to be that a settlement reached independently of the law is *per se* inferior to one reached through legal procedures and upon the basis of legal rights, both as regards its own merits and as a contribution to the *corpus* of international law. This position has been dealt with earlier; we have seen that many international disputes are non-justiciable in their terms and hence cannot be resolved by the law. It should also be pointed out that many states prefer to submit to conciliation rather than to adjudication in a particular quarrel. In the former, they retain a veto over any proposed final settlement, while in the latter they are bound in advance to accept the solution that emerges from the workings of the tribunal.

In the postwar world conciliation has proved a far more useful device than adjudication. Not the least reason for its relatively greater success has been its flexibility in terms of the final product. The devices of conciliation have proved capable on occasion of producing solutions that take account of diverse concepts of national interest, conflicting nationalisms, and the existence of the cold war. As such, this family of techniques has brought to an end controversies that, if allowed to run unchecked, might have spread out of control.

It is true that conciliation cannot, by its very nature, produce precedents of binding effect; however, it would seem to be possible to argue that the settlement of a thorny controversy is at least as important and socially justifiable as the futile and unheeded reiteration of an ignored legal principle.

The Role of the Third Party. The third party whose intervention into the dispute gives conciliation its particular form has a somewhat amorphous and often thankless task. Most noticeable is the fact that the third party has no coercive or mandatory power whatsoever. Its principal purpose is to expedite the reaching of a solution by the disputing parties themselves. It may do this by merely providing facilities for negotiation, by objectively determining the facts of a situation, or by taking the initiative in proposing solutions. But in all of this it acts as the agent of the disputing parties and it has only so much real effect upon the ultimate outcome as they choose to give it.

Of course, much depends upon the power and prestige of the third party itself. If a great and powerful state assumes the task of conciliating a quarrel between two smaller ones, and if it throws its weight unreservedly behind a particular approach to a solution, it is more likely to exert a major effect upon the final outcome than a smaller state acting as the third party, or a great one whose approach is restrained or reserved. Several smaller states have sometimes banded together to form a collective third party—such was the mediation of the 'ABC powers' (the Argentine, Brazil, and Chile) between the United States and Mexico in 1914.

One of the reasons for the relative success of conciliation in the postwar world has been the entry of the United Nations as a collective third party into a number of troublesome controversies. This organization, backed by the collective prestige of all its members, is able to apply much more pressure of a non-coercive sort in its conciliating role than any one of its members could. It purports to speak for peace-loving people everywhere and thus escapes the accusation sometimes made that a truly neutral conciliating power is impossible to find. Even the United Nations' use of conciliation, however, has not altered fundamentally the scope of action of the third party in the process. It remains an auxiliary and expediting one; the disputing parties must themselves assume the primary burden of reaching a solution.

The 'Cooling Off' Effect. Not the least valuable aspect of the techniques of conciliation is their dampening effect upon the intensity of any conflict in which they are used. Almost inevitably, the acceptance of conciliation brings in its train an attitude of coolness, detachment, and relative objectivity which acts as an unguent upon the irritated nationalisms of the parties. The atmosphere, formerly charged with tension, becomes instead judicious and less agitated; the current of thinking in both states shifts from the planning of ever more provocative acts to the consideration of possible formulas of settlement. This effect, being psychological, is difficult to measure exactly but its influence is apparent.

Of more specific character is the calming influence of delay. As we said above, the application of formal procedures involves considerable time. This is often pointed to by critics as a weakness of the system. The true fact of the matter, however, is just the opposite; the very delay necessary to set up the machinery and to operate is so as to produce a solution often turns out to be one of the strengths of the method. When two disputing states have accepted conciliation, good faith demands that they at least explore the possibilities of a solution by this means. The dispute then goes virtually into suspension until the machinery is ready and does not again get the opportunity to build up to a high pitch. In this way popular sentiment, usually cooled off by the change of approach brought about through the mere acceptance of conciliation in the first place, does not receive the stimuli needed to get it aroused again. By the time the final solution is announced, many people are wondering why they became so excited in the first place. Several examples of this effect will be given below.

Of course, this is true only in a situation in which conciliation is successful. The technique is not automatic in its effect; the procedures have broken down upon many occasions when nationalist attitudes proved sufficiently strong to withstand the effect of the cooling-off period.

The good-offices procedure of the United Nations in the dispute between the Netherlands and the Republic of Indonesia finally failed and it was necessary to replace it with stronger measures; United Nations mediation in the Palestine controversy likewise missed collapse on several occasions only by a narrow margin before an armistice was finally arranged. The principal failures of the technique of conciliation, however, take place before the machinery is even created. Conciliation falls down most often because its use is voluntary and states need not accept it even when the dispute is one perfectly suited to such a resolution. This means that the initiation of conciliation is itself an augury of eventual success; no state even participates in the process unless it can at least imagine itself accepting a settlement reached by this means.

The Forms of Conciliation. Conciliation assumes one of three major forms. Which of the three is used and upon whose initiative procedures are begun depend upon the particular circumstances of the dispute. The three differ from one another in terms of the role played by the third party.

The first form is known as good offices. In this procedure the third party offers its services as an expediter of negotiations between the disputing parties but plays no direct part itself in them. The burden of reaching a settlement rests entirely upon the disputants, with the third party offering only such limited assistance as it is called upon to give.

A more affirmative role is played by the third party in the procedure of inquiry. Here the purpose is the clarification of a disputed question of fact, upon the determination of which the disputants will presumably be able to resolve their problem themselves. The machinery created for this purpose differs from occasion to occasion, but the neutral party obviously plays the critical part in the entire process.

Finally, in mediation, the third party has the duty of devising proposed solutions and then attempting to persuade the disputants to accept them. In this mission all of the skills of the diplomatist are required and some of the greatest efforts ever demanded of statesmen are put forth in this task. The award of the Nobel Peace Prize to Dr. Ralph Bunche in 1950 was a just tribute to his efforts in mediating the Palestine controversy on behalf of the United Nations.

GOOD OFFICES

The technique of good offices is discussed first in this category because it represents the least extreme commitment on the part of the third party, and the smallest scope of its action. The role of the state that tenders its good offices in the resolution of a dispute is confined to the maintenance of contact between the disputing powers. It may never take an active part in the proceedings itself.

Procedure. The procedure of good offices is undertaken either at the request of one of the disputants to the intervening state or else upon the initiative of the third party itself. In no case is the offer of good offices to be considered as an 'unfriendly' (legally hostile) act; one or both of the disputing parties may refuse the proffered assistance but may not legally retaliate against the would-be conciliator.

If the offer be mutually acceptable, the intermediary state goes into action, with the primary purpose of assisting the disputing states to reach a solution themselves. Its exact functions vary, of course, with the particular circumstances of the conflict with which it is dealing. It may serve as a medium of communication between states that are no longer in direct contact as a result of a rupture of diplomatic relations or other reasons. It may provide facilities for bringing such parties back into direct negotiations with each other, including furnishing a neutral meeting place, secretarial and technical assistance, and the provision of transportation facilities. It may give advice to one or both parties and urge both to a more rapid resolution of the problem. It may serve in any capacity the disputing states care to use it for, so long as it refrains from an active part in the negotiations.

Two of the best-known instances of the employment of good offices merit mention here. President Theodore Roosevelt's intervention into the Russo-Japanese war of 1905 at the suggestion of the Japanese government was decisive in bringing that conflict to an early close. When Russia accepted his offer of good offices, he arranged a meeting place for the full-dress peace conference (Portsmouth, New Hampshire) and served as the medium of communication between the two states until the peace conference actually got under way. He served as an adviser to both states and applied considerable pressure upon them to speed up a solution, but he never served actively as a negotiator. The actual terms of peace were determined in the give-and-take bargaining by the Russian and Japanese representatives; President Roosevelt himself had nothing officially to do with the specific arrangements arrived at.

A more recent example of good offices took place with regard to the Netherlands-Indonesian dispute of 1946-9. This particular situation was unique because the United Nations itself was the good-offices party and the three-power commission that actually did the on-the-spot work served only as an agent for the Security Council. The action taken by the United Nations in the Indonesian dispute will be considered in more detail later in this chapter, but some features of the use of the good-offices technique should be pointed out here.

When, in August of 1947, the Security Council took cognizance of the Indonesian dispute, it immediately issued a cease-fire directive to both parties. Its next move was to offer its good offices, which offer was promptly accepted by both the Dutch and the Indonesians. The work was done by a three-state committee, chosen in the way arbitral tribunals often are: each party to the dispute selected one member and these two together selected a third. The Netherlands chose Belgium, Indonesia chose Australia, and the two nominees decided upon the United States for the remaining place. The committee forthwith removed to the scene of the struggle and opened negotiations with the leaders of both sides. They provided facilities for the signature of a detailed truce agreement—aboard the United States transport *Renville*—in January 1948. This argument prescribed the principles upon which a permanent settlement would be based.

From this point on, the committee's role was largely that of an observer. It reported regularly to the Security Council upon the breakdown of the truce. When, in January 1949, the Security Council decided to take a more active part in the settlement of the dispute, it passed a resolution recommending a specific solution. In doing this the United Nations was transcending the mere use of good offices and the committee was transformed into the United Nations Commission for Indonesia. Its powers were expanded and the resolution of the controversy passed into a new stage.

INQUIRY

Inquiry is a formal procedure in which an international body, including a third party, seeks out and publishes an authoritative and accurate statement of the facts of a dispute. The commission of inquiry has no power to decide the controversy upon the merits of the facts it has discovered. It may, if requested, make recommendations, but these have only such effect as the parties choose to give them.

History. The Hague Conventions of 1899 and 1907 provided specifically for the use of commissions of inquiry by states adhering to these agreements. Ordinarily these were to have five members, chosen from the disputing states and including a neutral member or members playing the key role. The scope and procedure of the commission (including the specific facts it was to determine) was to be stipulated in advance. The Dogger Bank incident, referred to earlier, was a great success for the technique of inquiry; later, certain other disputes (principally of maritime origin) came under examination at the hands of Hague commissions. In the United States, Mr. William Jennings Bryan, as Secretary of State (1913–15), negotiated some twenty bilateral treaties with Latin American and European states providing for the reference of disputes to such commissions. Although hailed as a great forward step at the time, none of these twenty treaties ever served to expedite the settlement of any disputes. Many more such treaties were worked out after World War I, both bilateral and multilateral, with equally small effect.

Inquiry and International Organization. The use of inquiry has been most effective at the hands of international organization. The League of Nations discovered that the appointment of a multi-state commission to investigate the facts of a dispute was very effective. The 'cooling-off' effect was particularly apparent in this connection.

Perhaps the most famous, although futile, use of the device was the case of the Japanese aggression in Manchuria in 1931. The League appointed a commission of inquiry, known as the Lytton Commission, to investigate and to report the facts. It did so; Japan refused to accept the report and withdrew from the organization in protest. In one sense the commission failed; Japan remained in control of Manchuria. Nevertheless its report crystallized much of the world opinion against the aggressor, a handicap from which Japan never recovered.

The United Nations, although not confining itself to a purely investigative function in any one case, has on several occasions appointed special groups whose primary mission was the determination of facts upon which the entire organization could base further action. The United Nations Special Committee on the Balkans (UNSCOB—1947), the United Nations Special Committee on Palestine (UNSCOP—1947), the United Nations Temporary Commission on Korea (UNTCOK—1947), and the commission chosen to investigate the question of the Kashmir (1948) were all originally commissions of inquiry. In all these cases, the groups were later transformed into something different and broader as the United Nations, having obtained the requisite information, set about taking affirmative action. Much of the underlying theory of the whole procedure of inquiry, however, was applicable as ever in the circumstances. As these United Nations groups pointed out the significant facts of the dispute into which each was called upon to inquire, the outlines of the solution most in harmony with both justice and practicality became clearer.

In the use of inquiry by the League and by the United Nations, much of the clear distinction between inquiry and mediation has become blurred. After all, no one is better qualified to recommend positive solutions to a dispute than the group that has done the investigation and is thoroughly familiar with the pertinent facts. The Lytton Commission made recommendations to the League; the various commissions and committees of the United Nations were instructed to include specific recommendations as part of their reports. The United Nations then used these in framing a policy.

Some students prefer the term 'conciliation' for this procedure wherein the United Nations at first investigates and then recommends a solution to a dispute, using commissions of various sorts. The United Nations appointed two different 'conciliation committees' in the Greek dispute following the original report of its special committee. A similarly named body was created in 1949 to help Palestine resolve the questions left undecided following the armistice there. A third commission was appointed to deal with the Kashmir question, possessing a broad area of competence.

The system of nomenclature used in this chapter, however, takes this practice of the United Nations into account. The 'conciliation committees' appointed have, by their terms of reference, a broad scope of power. They may expedite direct negotiations, they may investigate, they may recommend and persuade. They may, in other words, perform simultaneously the functions of good offices, inquiry, and mediation. Instead of being an entirely different technique, conciliation as practiced by the United Nations is what we have termed it in this chapter: a broad category containing within itself a variety of subclassifications.

MEDIATION

Mediation is the most precise of the techniques of conciliation and confers the greatest initiative upon the third party. Its nature has already been made clear: it is a procedure in which the neutral state or organization assumes the active role of proposing solutions and the harmonizing of the differing points of view. It obviously bears a very close relation both to good offices and to inquiry, particularly the former. There is one clear distinction between good offices and mediation, however, that will serve somewhat to preserve their respective identities. Good offices may serve in a dispute upon the suggestion of only one party and accomplish some good in such a situation; mediation, on the other hand must be acceptable to both parties and goes forward only with their consent.

The Hague Conventions dealt extensively with the procedures of mediation and remain the basic law upon the subject. It is explicitly understood that the proposals of the mediator are purely advisory and have no binding character. The conventions stipulated that the acceptance of mediation in no way prejudices the freedom of action of a state in the prosecution of its side of the quarrel by direct means. We have seen that practically this provision is often meaningless; states accept mediation as an escape from conflict and they normally abandon most of their program of affirmative action in the dispute.

Mediation comes to an end either when the dispute is successfully terminated or (in the words of Article 5 of the Hague Convention) 'when once it is declared, either by one of the contending parties, or by the mediator himself, that the means of reconciliation proposed by him are not accepted.' This gives mediation a most uncertain existence.

Automatic Mediation. Mediation is usually an *ad hoc* procedure, extemporized in a moment of crisis to cope with an existing dispute. Ever since the days of the Hague Conventions, however, there have been attempts made to regularize mediation (or, since both inquiry and mediation are involved, to regularize conciliation) by means of bilaterial or multilateral treaties. The usual method is to establish permanent or readily available machinery and to require that all non-justiciable (not subject to legal settlement) disputes be submitted to such institutional arrangements if they defy solution by diplomatic means. The Inter-American Conciliation Treaty of 1929 provides mandatory conciliation of all disputes between the signatories which transcend diplomatic settlement; this obligation has been strengthened with the creation of the Organization of American States. The Locarno Treaties of 1925 and many bilateral treaties between European states are further examples of the many attempts made at the creation of automatic mechanisms of mediation and conciliation. The relatively greater success of international organization in employing these techniques, however, has made most of the bilateral and multilateral treaties of conciliation superfluous.

Mediation by the United Nations. The United Nations, in dealing with the disputes that have come before it, has placed major reliance upon the procedure of mediation. The process has been formalized to varying degrees. In the case of Palestine a 'United Nations Mediator' (Count Folke Bernadotte of Sweden and, after the former's assassination, Dr. Ralph Bunche of the United States) was formally appointed, who personally carried on the mediating mission. In other disputes, notably in the Balkans and in the Kashmir, the United Nations used commissions of several states and combined mediation with inquiry and good offices. In the Berlin dispute the 'neutral six' members of the Security Council attempted a real but informal mediation.

It seems particularly appropriate that the United Nations should serve as a mediator in the contemporary world. It represents a sizable portion of world public opinion and is thus able to speak far more authoritatively in making recommendations than could any lesser combination of states. The Charter provisions for enforcement procedures are also pertinent to the success of these mediation efforts. Now that the United Nations has demonstrated in Korea the willingness of the great majority of its members to back its decisions with force, any further mediatory suggestions on other disputes emanating from the organization will be heeded more carefully by all disputing parties. So long as the United Nations retains its existence and continues to function as effectively as it has in the past, it will continue to be the principal mediating agency in world politics.

ADJUDICATION

We turn now to adjudication. This broad technique, it will be remembered, differs from conciliation fundamentally in terms of the legal or quasi-legal orientation of the settlement as contrasted with the emphasis upon expediency and acceptability found in conciliation. The substantive rules of international law are critical in the determination of the terms of any final settlement. Unlike the procedures of conciliation, which have a tendency to merge in practice or at least for one technique to evolve into another, the different adjudicatory techniques differ sharply from one another and from conciliation as well. The criterion of settlement is legality and the rule of law is paramount.

ARBITRATION

Arbitration is the older of the techniques of adjudication. It dates from classical times and was used extensively in the Middle Ages. The Hague Convention defined arbitration as the settlement of disputes between states 'by judges of their own choice and on the basis of respect for law.' The arbitral tribunal is a court, bound by rules both procedural and substantive; as such, it has the right to make definite finding which both parties are bound to accept.

Arbitration has been unused since World War II but no observer has been so rash as to predict its complete lapse into oblivion. It was far too useful in the past for it to be abandoned in the future. True, it has not been effective in reducing really serious policy conflicts between states; most arbitrated questions have involved issues of relatively minor importance. Many great crises have grown out of issues that were minor on their face, however, and the elimination of some of them by arbitral procedures might have spared the world much trouble.

Submission of a Dispute to Arbitration. There are three different ways by which a dispute may be made subject to arbitration. The first, and most common, way is by purely *ad hoc* procedure. When an international conflict has passed the stage at which diplomacy is effective and perhaps after conciliation has also failed, it is appropriate for either party to suggest its resolution by arbitration. Of course such a suggestion might properly have been made earlier, but usually states prefer to wait until the later stages of a controversy before arbitrating. If the second state chooses to accept, negotiations between them enter a new phase looking toward the erection of an arbitral tribunal. The famous *Alabama* claims arbitration of 1872 was brought about in this way.

A second method of getting arbitration into action arises from the existence of a treaty upon any subject between the disputing states which has as one of its provisions an agreement to arbitrate any dispute arising over its interpretation. This is perhaps the most escape-proof obligation to arbitrate which international practice affords, but as can be easily seen it is of limited applicability.

The third way by which a dispute is referred to arbitration is by means of a 'general treaty.' This type of treaty is one in which, in advance of any particular dispute, the parties make a general commitment to consider the use of arbitration in all quarrels that might arise between them and to make use of it if the conditions are appropriate. The United States has been a leader in the movement for general treaties of this sort. These treaties, which may be bilateral or multilateral, were thought of before World War I as marking a great step forward in the pacific settlement of international disputes. Later experience has shown, however, that no particular increase in either the number or the significance of arbitrations has resulted from them. The treaties are usually designed to cover all disputes that are justiciable and do not effect the honor, independence, or vital interests of the parties.

These exempted categories are so broad and the justiciability of a controversy so difficult to determine in advance that in practice a state retains its right to decide whether or not it will submit to arbitration. In other words, the major effect of the general treaty is to bring before the parties to a controversy the constant possibility of arbitration as an alternative means of settling a dispute; the actual decision to do so or not is made, as it is in other circumstances as well, essentially upon an *ad hoc* basis.

The Compromis. The decision to arbitrate having been reached, the next step in the process is the negotiation by the parties of the *compromis*. This is a special preliminary agreement between the disputing parties, in which such necessary details are stipulated as the composition of the tribunal, the procedural rules to be followed by it, the rules of law upon which it is to base its finding, and other administrative matters. This is obviously a difficult agreement to arrive at, particularly the decision on the relevant legal rules; many arbitrations have broken down despite good will on both sides because the *compromis* could not be agreed upon. Some general treaties of arbitration provide for the formulation of the *compromis* by a disinterested agency, often the tribunal itself.

The *compromis* thus binds the court's hands very closely. It is limited in its scope to the specific points laid down and it may apply only the rules of law agreed upon. Even in the case of disputes submitted to the Hague Permanent Court of Arbitration, where many of the technical points were already settled, the arrival at a *compromis* by the disputing parties was often a task of major proportions.

The Arbitral Tribunal. The definition of arbitration in the Hague Convention pointed out that the disputes were arbitrated by judges of the parties' own choice, and the manner of the selection is really a matter entirely up to them. Certain practices, however, have been standardized. Arbitral tribunals almost always have included in their membership at least one national of each disputing state and always at least one member, chosen by the other members of the court, from a neutral state, whose duty it is to act as 'umpire.' Sometimes the court has only these three members; sometimes each party has two nationals on the court, the total membership thus being five; sometimes the parties each select two judges but only one of them may be a national of the state appointing him. Always, however, the nationally appointed judges select the umpire. As may be expected, national identification holds good normally and in the final analysis the umpire usually casts the deciding vote. There is not so much likelihood of difficulty arising over the selection of arbitrators as there is in the negotiation of the *compromis,* particularly if the procedure of choice is stipulated in a general treaty between the disputing parties.

The Hearing and the Award. Article 63 of the Hague Convention prescribed that the process of arbitration should include two stages: pleadings (similar to the filing of briefs in civil courts) and oral discussions. The oral presentation of the case of each party is under the direction of an 'agent' who supervises a team of counsel. The hearings proceed according to the particular provisions of the *compromis* but usually resemble the court proceedings familiar to Western jurisprudence.

After the hearing the court makes its award. It may, if it choose, make a clear choice between the contentions of the disputants; more often it makes what seems to it an equitable compromise between them. The parties may, if the *compromis* so provides, request later revision of the finding upon the basis of a new fact or facts not included in the original hearing; otherwise the parties are bound to accept the award in good faith. The latter has almost universally been the case. Out of several hundred arbitrations in the nineteenth and twentieth centuries, in only one instance did both parties reject the award; in one another, one party did so. Furthermore, the tendency of an arbitral award to be final and definitive could not help but strengthen the binding effect of the points of law upon which the various tribunals based their decisions.

The Hague Permanent Court of Arbitration. In 1899, after a century of extensive use of the arbitral technique, the first Hague Peace Conference sought to formalize the procedure and make it permanent by the creation of a Permanent Court of Arbitration. The name is somewhat misleading; it is not a court at all, but a large panel of arbitrators from which disputing states may select the judges of their own case. Every state adhering to the convention names four of its nationals as permanent members of the panel. In case of a dispute, each state chooses two members of its court from the list of the panel, of which only one may be its own national. These four chosen name an umpire; if such a choice is impossible because of an equal division, an automatic procedure is prescribed for his choice by other states.

The Court has not been a major influence upon the development of arbitration. Before World War I it handled seventeen cases; since 1920, only two. Arbitrations has continued to develop along bilateral lines and remains, despite the existence of the Hague Tribunal, still largely an *ad hoc* procedure.

JUDICIAL SETTLEMENT

Arbitration vs. Judicial Settlement. Arbitration, although it provides a settlement that is usually reached by means of the application of legal rules, represents only a partial step toward the ideal of a 'rule of law' held by many people. In certain important respects arbitration falls short of pure judicial settlement.

In the first place, in arbitration the disputants select the judges of their own cause; in a truly judicial process the judges are permanent and hear all cases that come before them. Court proceedings in a civil society are studiously impartial. It is contrary to the theory of jurisprudence in most Western societies to insist upon a judge whose primary qualification is his prejudice in favor of one side or the other.

In the second place an arbitral court, under the terms of the *compromis,* is usually limited in the points it can decide and the rules it may use to decide them. A true court is free to use the whole body of law and to rule upon any point relevant to the dispute, regardless of what the parties may think about it.

A third difference exists. Arbitral jurisdiction is entirely voluntary and is founded upon consent. On the other hand, if the rule of law applies in a society its jurisdiction is compulsory. Any disputant may take his case to court and his adversary must submit to the court's jurisdiction.

These limitations upon the legal effectiveness of arbitration have long appeared to be challenges to those statesmen and jurists who have sought to expand the scope of international law. Their proposals have all advocated the creation of a real international court which would overcome the shortcomings of the process of arbitration. In the modern day such a court has come into existence.

The Central American Court of Justice. All of the great 'visionary' schemes of world organization of the past have provided for some form of an international court. The first concrete example of one, however, was the Central American Court of Justice; founded in 1907, it endured for ten years. Five Central American republics formed the membership; the Court consisted of one permanent member from each of the signatories to the convention, and a judge participated in all cases, even those that involved his own state.

The jurisdiction of the Court was very broad, being obligatory in all disputes between the members which were insoluble by diplomatic means and optional as regards disputes between the legislative, judicial, and executive branches of the government of any one state. This latter grant of jurisdiction was, and has remained, unique. The Court was also competent to hear cases brought by a citizen of one state against the government of another state; indeed, five of the ten cases heard by the court were of this type. After ten years and ten cases, the government of Nicaragua withdrew and the Court went out of existence.

THE PERMANENT COURT OF INTERNATIONAL JUSTICE

History. The first ambitious attempts to create a 'world court' was the Permanent Court of International Justice. This tribunal came into existence in 1922, when a majority of the states of the world accepted its 'Statute.' This document had been drawn up by a commission of private jurists under the direction of the Council of the League of Nations. Although a separate international organization, the Court was viewed as a part—perhaps the most successful part—of the 'League system.' It went into operation early in 1922 and, although interrupted by Nazi occupation of its headquarters at the Hague, remained in existence until it transferred its physical property in 1945 to its successor, the International Court of Justice.

During this period the Court heard 79 cases. Of these, 51 were actual controversies involving judgments, and 28 represented advisory opinions given to organs of the League. It attained a perfect record of compliance with its judgments and a high reputation for impartiality and competence.

While the preliminary planning for the structure of international organization for the post-World War II era was going on, there was complete agreement that the tradition of the Court should be kept alive by some new form of judicial body. Thus far in history, at least, international adjudication by a permanent court has proved itself to the point where the existence of some such body is felt to be a necessity.

Composition. The Statute of the Permanent Court was the basic instrument that governed its operations. Fifty-one states—not including the United States—adhered to the document at one time or another. American distrust of the League of Nations extended to the Court and upon several occasions, the last in 1935, the United States Senate refused to permit American adherence to the Statute.

The Court itself consisted of fifteen judges (increased in 1931 from eleven). They were chosen by the Council and the Assembly of the League after a very complicated process of nomination by the 'national groups' of the Hague Tribunal. The Statute provided specifically that the Court should represent the diverse legal systems of the world and that no two judges should be of the same nationality. They were elected for a term of nine years and were eligible for re-election. They were paid out of League funds. The object was to create a truly international judiciary, freed of dependence upon national states. The Statute also provided for 'national judges'; a state not represented on the Court could appoint one of its nationals to sit as a judge for any case to which it was a party. One permanent judge was to be elected president of the Court for a three-year term and was eligible for re-election to that position.

Jurisdiction and Procedure. The jurisdiction of the Court was limited to national states; individuals had no status before the Court. A state might espouse the cause of one of its nationals if it wished, however; several actually did so. Jurisdiction was therefore theoretically and practically voluntary as dictated by the doctrine of sovereignty, except as certain bilateral and multilateral treaties between states provided that any disputes arising under their terms be settled by the Court.

Article 36 of the Statute also included the famous 'optional clause,' which a state was free to accept or not as it chose. This provided for the compulsory jurisdiction of the Court over certain questions arising between two states, both of which had adhered to the optional clause: the interpretation of a treaty; any question of international law; the existence of a fact which, if established, would constitute a breach of an international obligation; the nature and extent of the reparation to be made for the breach of an international obligation. Thirty-eight adherences to the optional clause were registered, but many were for a limited time and were later withdrawn.

In reaching decisions the Court was directed to apply the four classes of international law mentioned earlier in this chapter, and in addition was free to decide a case on grounds of what might be termed 'equity' (*ex aequo et bono*) if the parties agreed. Court procedure was thoroughly in harmony with traditional Western ideas of jurisprudence. Decision was by majority vote and a majority opinion of the Court was written and delivered; dissenting opinions were also given. The Statute specifically provided that the decision had no binding force except between the parties and in respect to that particular case, but inevitably the total of the Court's judgments constituted a body of 'case law.' The judgments were declared to be 'final and without appeal,' although subject to revision on the basis of new and relevant facts.

The Court was also empowered to give 'advisory opinions' to either the Council or the Assembly of the League. These involved questions that were submitted to the Court for legal determination without any actual controversy upon which a judgment was to be rendered. The presumption was that the Court, by making a judicial determination of the question, could guide the organs of the League in making a more rational and effective political decision themselves.

This function was exercised with some frequency and by and large with a good effect. Although the opinions of the Court were advisory and not binding, they tended to be quite authoritative upon the points of law they covered. An organization with the prestige enjoyed by the Court could not help but invest everything it did or said with special significance, and all the pronouncements of the Court, whether advisory or final, contributed materially to the augmentation of the body of international law.

The International Court of Justice

The International Court of Justice, created at San Francisco in 1945 along with the whole of the United Nations system, is the direct descendant of the Permanent Court. It took over all the powers and duties of its predecessor and in nearly every way carries on the identical tradition of international adjudication. There was originally some sentiment in favor of continuing the Permanent Court, but for a variety of reasons it was thought preferable to create a new one. The Statute of the new Court was an annex to the Charter and several Charter provisions deal directly with the Court.

Differences and Similarities between the Two Courts. There are several small but important differences in the two Courts. In the first place, the International Court of Justice is one of the six 'principal organs' of the United Nations instead of existing separately as did its predecessor. In the second place, all members of the United Nations are automatically members of the Court—no separate adherence is necessary—and membership in the Court is open also to non-members of the United Nations under certain conditions. The Statute of the new Court may be amended more easily than could the old. Most of the other salient features of the former Court were carried over unchanged into the new one: the number of judges, the method of their selection, their terms of office, court procedure, and many other aspects of organization and operation are identical.

An important heritage of the International Court of Justice from the old Statute was the optional clause respecting jurisdiction. The provision was borrowed verbatim from the original Statute, listing the four categories of controversies which a state agrees automatically to submit to the Court if the other party also has agreed to the optional clause. Those states whose adherence to the clause in the old Statute was still in effect had their obligation automatically transferred to the new one; there are now 17 such states. In addition 18 other states, including the United States, have accepted the optional clause of the new Statute. In nearly every case such acceptance has been made subject to individually determined reservations and conditions.

Finally, the International Court of Justice, like its predecessor, hands down both judgments and advisory opinions, although it may do the latter now upon the request not only of the Security Council or the General Assembly but of any other agency of the United Nations if the General Assembly approves. This represents a broadening of the scope of the advisory opinion.

The Work of the Court. The Court has not been overburdened with work since its creation. The exigencies of the cold war have been such as to make the times unpropitious for judicial settlement of international disputes, and there has been less of a tendency to go to the Court than the framers had originally expected. Nevertheless the aggregate of work done in the first few years of the Court's existence was not inconsiderable. Half a dozen advisory opinions had been delivered by the end of 1950, most of them to the General Assembly. By early 1952, the Court had delivered three judgments. The first of these handed down in 1949, involved a dispute between Great Britain and Albania; the second, in 1950, between Colombia and Peru; the third, in 1951, between Great Britain and Norway. At the time the third judgment was delivered, five other disputes had been referred to the Court and had begun the process leading to a final decision. Most of these were relatively unimportant but some scholars felt that it represented an encouraging increase in the employment of the facilities of the Court.

The Settlement of Disputes by the United Nations

We have already seen how the United Nations has used all the processes of peaceful settlement except that of arbitration; in this section we shall discover that the techniques of pacific settlement are drastically changed in the hands of a global organization from what they are when used by only one state.

Charter Provisions. The starting point of the United Nations in this entire process is the assumption that there is no longer any such thing as a 'private fight' in international relations. The United Nations speaks for the whole world society in its concern that international peace be preserved. The organization is authorized by Chapter VI of the Charter to take action in the case of any dispute whose continuance is likely to endanger international peace and security. The dispute may come before the Security Council at the application of either party, of any member of the organization, of a non-member in particular circumstances, or upon action of the Secretary-General.

The Security Council has a broad range of possible courses of action. It may first direct the parties to the controversy to seek a solution themselves, either directly or by any of the means discussed earlier in this chapter. If this fails to quiet the disturbance, the organization may then prescribe a particular technique which the parties are urged to use in their search for a settlement and may offer itself as the third party in the proceedings. If this again proves unproductive, the Security Council may begin to play a more vigorous role in the struggle, taking the initiative in recommending the terms of setttlement and applying direct pressure to bring about an acceptance of its formula. If either party (or, conceivably, both) proves intractable and refuses to accept the recommendation of the Security Council, the possibility then arises of action under Chapter VII, which authorizes enforcement measures, including the use of armed force.

The Rise of the General Assembly. The cold war has brought about an unforeseen development in pacific settlement by the United Nations: the rise of the General Assembly to a position of critical importance. At San Francisco the Security Council was thought of as the principal peacemaking organ in the United Nations machinery, and the Charter was written with this idea in mind. The cold war has paralyzed this body much of the time because of the constant threat of a Russian veto and it has proved expedient and wise for the General Assembly to act in a more affirmative manner than was originally contemplated.

In the disputes in the Balkans, in Palestine, and in Korea, for example, the General Assembly took vigorous and effective action and set in motion pacifying or enforcement procedures. Many of the special committees and other such bodies used by the United Nations have been created by and have reported to the General Assembly.

After the Korean war began in 1950, the 'Uniting for Peace' resolutions of that year created a number of new agencies designed to strengthen the peacemaking powers of the Assembly. Under the original rules, it could not discuss a question as long as it remained on the agenda of the Security Council; under the amended procedure the larger body could take jurisdiction over any question upon which the Security Council was unable to reach a decision.

There had also been established in 1947 a 'Little Assembly,' an interim committee composed of a delegate from every member of the organization, which was to remain in existence between Assembly sessions and was to be competent to act at any time in the name of the larger group. In these ways the Assembly somewhat overcame the handicaps of limited competence and periodic meetings. Today the General Assembly and the Security Council form a team which attacks the problem of peaceful resolution of international conflicts co-operatively.

The United Nations has dealt with several important disputes. Among the most serious have been the Indonesian question, the Greek question, and the Palestine question. By examining the way the organization dealt with each of these we shall understand how it functions in settling disputes.

THE INDONESIAN QUESTION

The Good Offices Committee. The issue of Indonesia arose as the result of the revolt of the former Dutch East Indies against the restoration of imperial rule by the Dutch after World War II. Following several false starts, the question was finally taken up by the Security Council in August 1947. Hostilities were going on at the time and the first Security Council action was to call upon both parties to cease fighting. Cease-fire orders were issued by both states, but warfare continued. The Council thereupon offered its good offices; this was accepted and the United Nations Good Offices Committee proceded to Batavia. We have already seen in our study of good offices on page 225 how this group obtained the acceptance of the *Renville* agreement, in January 1948.

The Good Offices Committee made several interim reports to the Security Council, describing the progressive breakdown of relations; in July it reported the final collapse of the negotiations looking toward the implementation of the *Renville* agreement. The Security Council immediately called upon both parties to observe the truce and to proceed directly to a final settlement. On 18 December, the Netherlands denounced the truce and reopened hostilities.

Affirmative Action. The Security Council reacted promptly, calling for a cessation of hostilities and the release of all prisoners (the president of the Republic of Indonesia, among others, had been imprisoned by the Dutch). During January the Committee of Good Offices reported frequently and noticed no improvement in the situation. On 28 January 1949, the Security Council took stronger action. It once again called for a cease-fire, and recommended a specific solution: the creation of an independent and sovereign United States of Indonesia at the earliest possible moment and in any case no later than 1 July 1950. The Committee of Good Offices was transformed into the United Nations Commission for Indonesia with the duty and the power of assisting the parties in carrying out this proposal.

Dutch reaction was rapid. The war was ended, the republican leaders were released, and an early round-table conference at the Hague was proposed to arrange for the transfer of sovereignty to Indonesia. This information was received by the Security Council on 2 March 1949. Later in the month the Commission was instructed to assist the parties in working out an agreement. The meeting was held at Batavia from 14 April to 1 August 1949; all questions were settled amicably. The transfer of military authority from the Dutch to the Indonesians was made under the observation of United Nations military observers. The Round Table Conference, held from late August to early November 1949, in which representatives of the Commission for Indonesia participated, worked out all details and the crisis was over. Formal transfer of sovereignty took place on 27 December 1949—well within the deadline set by the Council in January. The Commission remained in existence in order to observe the implementation of the round-table agreements, but it had nothing to do. The issue was definitely closed as a threat to world peace.

THE GREEK QUESTION

The Security Council. The Greek question arose out of the civil war in Greece in the immediate postwar period and the assistance given the Greek rebels by the three Communist Balkan states of Albania, Yugoslavia, and Bulgaria. When the question was finally taken up by the Security Council in December 1946, its first action was to create a commission of investigation, composed of one representative of each member of the Council for 1947, to make an on-the-spot survey and to report. This body reported in April 1947. The majority found that the Soviet satellites involved were aiding the Greek guerrillas and called for an end to the practice. The minority—the USSR and Poland—rejected the charges. The Council, faced by Russian obduracy, was unable to come to a decision during the summer of 1947. On 15 September it removed the question from its agenda so as to permit consideration of it by the General Assembly.

The General Assembly and UNSCOB. The Assembly, in October, called upon Albania, Bulgaria, and Yugoslavia not to aid the Greek guerrillas but instead to co-operate with the Greek government in the peaceful solution of all frontier, minority, and refugee questions. A Special Committee on the Balkans (UNSCOB) was created to co-operate with the four governments concerned and to observe the extent to which they complied with the resolution. The USSR and Poland refused to participate in UNSCOB and the three Balkan states refused to co-operate with it. The first report submitted by UNSCOB in July 1948 pointed out this situation and confessed a failure in its mission for this reason.

The General Assembly, in November, renewed its appeal to Albania, Bulgaria, and Yugoslavia to terminate their aid to the guerrillas and warned them that a continuation would be a danger to peace. Another resolution called on the four states to renew diplomatic relations and to get to work on the outstanding problems. At the same time an *ad hoc* conciliation committee was created by the Assembly, consisting of the President of the Assembly, the Secretary-General, and two other delegates from neutral states. This group was to devise procedures for the resolution of the controversy and to expedite its settlement. On 19 May 1949, this body reported. Full accord had been reached upon all but one point and a draft agreement was almost ready for signature. The session ended and the conciliation committee went out of existence without seeing this agreement approved.

The Breakup of the Crisis. UNSCOB reported again during the summer. It pointed out that the aid given to the guerrillas by Yugoslavia had decreased (owing to Tito's break with Moscow the year before) but stressed that Bulgaria and Albania were persisting. The report stated that a continuation of this situation would be a threat both to Greek independence and to peace in the Balkans. On 18 November 1949, the General Assembly passed a resolution reiterating the concern of UNSCOB. It declared that any further assistance to the Greek rebels would increase the danger to peace and warned that a special session of the General Assembly might be necessary to deal with the matter.

This veiled threat was sufficient to bring about action. Support of the guerrillas (already weakened by Yugoslavia's defection) collapsed. The outstanding issues were speedily settled. A second conciliation committee, created upon the same basis as the first, had been unable to make any progress during the month before the Assembly resolution; suddenly an atmosphere of reasonableness and restraint prevailed after the passage of the resolution, and the problem largely evaporated. The Yugoslav change of heart, coupled with the determination of the Assembly to move forward one step at a time toward a definitive settlement, had brought this crisis to an end.

THE PALESTINE QUESTION

Background. The Palestine question arose out of the decision of Great Britain to terminate its mandate over the territory and the action of the General Assembly, taken 29 November 1947, of partitioning the territory into an Arab state, a Jewish state, and an international regime for Jerusalem. Even before the end of the mandate on 15 May 1948, fighting had broken out between the Arab and the Jewish communities in Palestine, as each expressed its dissatisfaction with the partition plan. On 17 April 1948, the Security Council called for a truce in that country; on 23 April it established a Truce Commission for Palestine, composed of the Jerusalem-based consuls of France, Belgium, and the United States. This body was to assist in the execution of the 17 April resolution. The people in Palestine paid no attention to the Truce Commission but continued fighting. On 15 May, the day the new state of Israel was proclaimed, the Arab states invaded Palestine and the United Nations had a war to deal with.

Security Council Mediation. On 14 May, aware of the danger of imminent war, the Security Council had appointed Count Folk Bernadotte of Sweden as United Nations Mediator for Palestine. On 22 May, after hostilities had begun, it called for a cease-fire order; on 24 May it called for a four-week cessation of hostilities. The mediator was directed to oversee the execution of this directive, which became effective on 11 June. The truce expired 9 July despite the request of the mediator that it be continued. The fighting began again and the mediator requested more active intervention by the Security Council. This body then, on 15 July, invoked the provisions of Chapter VII of the Charter for the first time. It ordered all states concerned to desist from military action and pointed out that failure to comply would be a breach of the peace and would make the violator subject to United Nations enforcement measures. The truce was to remain in force until a settlement had been reached and the mediator was to supervise its observance. The resolution had its desired effect; the truce became operative in Jerusalem on 16 July and in the rest of the area on 18 July. Negotiations proceeded until 17 September, when Count Bernadotte was assassinated by an Israeli fanatic. Dr. Ralph Bunche of the United States was named in his place.

The Armistices. The truce proved difficult to maintain. Large-scale fighting between Israel and Egypt flared up on two occasions in October in the Negev area of Palestine, to be dealt with by prompt action by the Security Council and Dr. Bunche. On 16 November 1948, the Council decided that an armistice was necessary in order to prevent further outbreaks and directed Dr. Bunche to proceed directly to assist in the negotiation of one. The discussions between Israel on the one side and the Arab states individually on the other were worked out largely on the island of Rhodes and armistices were signed between Israel and the several Arab states between 24 February and 20 July 1949. With this, the military stage of the struggle had ended.

The General Assembly. On 11 December 1948, the General Assembly established a Conciliation Commission for Palestine, consisting of three members: France, Turkey, and the United States. This body was directed to assist the governments concerned to reach a final settlement of all questions. With the signature of the armistice agreements, the Security Council was substantially freed of concern over the issue and the mediator was relieved of any further responsibility. The Conciliation Commission became the principal United Nations agency actively concerned with the problem, although there were other bodies involved in special aspects of the problem. The issues left unsolved by the struggle were numerous and thorny—the question of boundaries, of the status of Jerusalem, of the Arab refugees, any many others—and at the present writing most are still not resolved. Nevertheless the dispute which for a while threatened to grow out of control was calmed down by United Nations action to the point where it became a matter of discussion and compromise instead of armed conflict.

CONCLUSIONS

The three disputes mentioned above do not exhaust the list of those dealt with by the United Nations. Iran, South Africa, the Corfu Channel (ultimately settled by the International Court of Justice), Kashmir, Berlin, Korea: these are some more of the trouble spots of the postwar world whose problems were threshed out before the United Nations. In every case, consideration of the issue by the organization served to set in motion forces that pointed the way toward the final solution.

In no case (except possibly the Korean war) can we give complete credit to the United Nations for the peaceful resolutions of the dispute. Hostile observers sometimes point to the inability of the United Nations to produce neat and final settlements as proof of the 'failure' of the organization. This is more than a little unfair. The organization, in dealing with crisis situations, has as an objective only the preservation or the restoration of peace and security. How it does this, whether by forceful direct action or by gentle stimulation of the will to agree, is immaterial; what counts is the eventual result.

The United Nations has proved to be powerless to take any direct steps toward the easing of the cold war. This inability arises from the very structure of the organization, founded as it is upon the principle of and the belief in great-power co-operation. As a result, the conspicuous successes of the United Nations in the field of pacific settlement have occurred in controversies that were relatively immune from the cold war. The single notable exception is the case of Greece (the Korean war is in another category entirely), and we have seen how a large share of the credit for the happy solution of that dispute must go to Yugoslavia's break with Moscow.

Yet to point out that the United Nations is limited in its scope to disputes that do not involve direct great-power conflict is not to minimize its impact. Any one of the conflicts into which the organization has moved as a peacemaker was a potential source of world crisis, lacking only the identification of the two great leaders with one side or another to create an extremely dangerous situation. In this sense United Nations techniques of pacification have contributed materially to the maintenance of the uneasy peace which the world has continued to enjoy.

III

Alternatives to Conflict

9

The International Community

THE mythology of the national state embodies an implicit assumption that the constituent part of the state, the individual human being, is a 'political animal' pure and simple. Man as citizen is considered to have no interests or motivations other than those that arise from his membership in a political group, and he is supposed to discover complete personal fulfillment in the performance of his civic duties. We have already seen the extent to which this idea finds expression in the nationalist beliefs of most of the established states of the world, including all the major ones. Some such concept is obviously vital to the accomplishment of state goals in a political age.

The facts of human nature, however, run contrary to this operating hypothesis of statesmen. Despite the great increase in the functions of government (most of which have been undertaken in the name of great abundance for the individual), there remains a vast area of individual activity that is 'non-political': that is, it is either untouched by the state or else governmental intervention is unhappy or unsuccessful. Men simply cannot, despite the efforts of the most totalitarian of dictators, live all their lives within the arms of the state. Growing out of this failure of political authority to achieve true totality and as a result of the greater impetus provided by the expanding technology of our time, more and more individuals have had their lives touched by other individuals from different states. Although by no means of equal effect in every case, this increase in private international relationships has served in some measure to diminish the more extreme effects of nationalist bias in many people.

This effect has not been ignored by governments. Those that have had the greatest interest in the perpetuation of intense nationalist rivalry have been most active in attempting to reduce the frequency of private international contacts. The government of the USSR, whose principal domestic propaganda line has been to insist that the Russian peoples have nothing in common with those of the capitalist world, has been the worst offender in this regard, closely followed by the government of Communist China. Nevertheless, despite the cold war and other restrictive policies of governments, private international

245

relationships have been expanding and have grown to the point where they perceptibly affect the political relations of states.

As people representing different states and cultures come into contact in pursuit of common objectives, they frequently discover that the cultural differences between them become less glaring and their common humanity grows in importance. The resulting co-operative attack upon individual non-political problems has been responsible for the creation of many organizations, composed of citizens of different states and oriented toward the mutual satisfaction of private ends. These groups are both governmental and private. Some have lofty objectives, while others are more pedestrian in their goals. They all share one common characteristic: they provide a basis upon which men of differing political allegiance can co-operate in the attainment of a shared objective that is important to each of them.

When an individual is involved in such an activity, he cannot escape undergoing a basic readjustment in his political outlook. He can no longer think of foreign states as corporate entities or political abstractions; Great Britain, France, or Japan ceases to be a monolithic structure but instead is thought of as a collection of individual human beings very much like himself. His acquaintance with particular Britons or Japanese and the relations he has with them serve to modify his point of view of the political group of which they are a part. The multiplication of these individual readjustments exerts cumulatively greater influence upon the foreign policies of governments. So numerous are they today and so different is the orientation of individuals affected by them that it is possible to speak, as we do in this chapter, of an international community.

PRIVATE INTERNATIONAL RELATIONSHIPS

It is one of the many paradoxes of modern political life that the present day, in which the role of the state and the compelling force of nationalism have grown to the highest level in history, has at the same time witnessed the greatest multiplication of private international relationships. As citizens, men are urged on every side to forsake all international identification (except perhaps with those other states with which good relations are temporarily important to their government) and to adhere only to their state and to their own national group. In their private lives, however, more and more of them have experienced some form of personal contact with other peoples. This, to many, serves to make the conflict between private interest and public (national) interest more real and more poignant.

The trend at the present time is unquestionably in the direction of a continued intensification in the conflict, because governments today are not yet ready to relax much of their grip upon the loyalties of men. At the same time, more and more individuals everywhere are being caught up in the ever-expanding network of private relationships that reach across frontiers.

Before proceeding to an analysis of the international-community sense and its impact upon world politics, it is necessary to examine a few of the factors that help to explain the great increase in these contacts.

TRANSPORTATION AND COMMUNICATION

The principal reason for the increase in international contact is the fact that the world has grown smaller. Modern devices of transportation and communication have made any part of the world immediately accessible by radio, telephone, or wire communication, while no portion of the globe is more than a few hours away from any other point by rapid air transportation. A good deal of what has been written and said about man's conquest of space and time either has been hackneyed and platitudinous or else has ignored its broader implications for civilization. Nevertheless, the facts are clear for all to see: many people have taken immediate advantage of these rapid and relatively inexpensive methods of broadening their personal horizons. All areas of human social life are affected by these devices. Economic life has been greatly modified and the social, religious, and recreational activities of individuals in most of the world have been revolutionized by the radio and the airplane.

Transportation. Rapid transportation is so much a commonplace of contemporary life in Western society that most of us realize only vaguely how it has changed the very tempo of our civilization. Today the airplane has revolutionized concepts of distance. In 1952 the British Overseas Aircraft Company placed in service the first scheduled jet passenger airliner; its elapsed time from London to Johannesburg, South Africa—a distance of almost 6000 miles—was just under twenty-four hours. To cross the Atlantic in the eighteenth century required weeks of uncomfortable and dangerous sailing; today modern steamships make the crossing in less than four days and aircraft in only twelve hours. Thus London is closer to New York today than Philadelphia was at the time of the Revolution.

Of only slightly less importance in the development of easy rapid transportation have been the railway and the automobile. There are over 780,000 miles of railway trackage in the world, the bulk in the United States and western Europe; particularly in the latter area has the railway served to expedite the expansion of private international contacts. Since the construction of hard-surfaced highways, the privately owned automobile has also worked major changes in the range of mobility of individuals. In 1949, there were over 62 million automobiles registered in the world, of which 44 million were in the United States.

This means that, granted the curiosity of the human species, more and more individuals will take advantage of the opportunity to travel—for whatever reason—as facilities are improved. Statistics confirm this hypothesis. For example, American airlines (which carry less than half of the total international passenger traffic) steadily increased the total number of international passengers transported from one million in 1946 to over two million in 1952. This constant increase in the employment of air facilities for international travel means that more people are crossing frontiers by air all the time and in the consummation of their business are making the personal contacts and are receiving the impressions that are inevitable. Similar increases are notable in steamship traffic and upon international railways.

Communication. The same story can be told concerning modern devices of communication. Anyone within reach of a telephone can speak with any other part of the world within a few moments, and technical improvements are being made steadily. There are roughly 65 million telephone instruments in the world, scattered over all continents and in most countries, all tied together into one vast network. International telegraph and cable facilities provide another means of rapid communication. By these devices personal communication between individuals becomes extremely easy and rapid; international postal service by air has served again to reduce drastically the time required to exchange more detailed communication by letter mail.

Of equal, although different, significance is the great expansion of the devices of mass, as opposed to individual, communication. The most important of these are the radio and the motion picture. Radio waves know no frontier, and particularly in Europe, where the political units are so small, any regular radio listener is offered a broad international menu of programs to suit his taste. Even in the United States, home radio receivers have become so powerful that to receive broadcasts from Europe, South America, or even Asia is a commonplace for millions of Americans. In 1954, there were approximately 240 million radio receivers in use throughout the world, of which 130 million were in the United States and 67 million in Europe. This obviously represents an enormous audience for broadcasting, the internationalizing effect of which is easy to imagine.

Motion pictures also exert a great influence upon the international attitudes of people everywhere. Latest estimates are that there are throughout the world nearly 100,000 motion-picture theaters with a total seating capacity of over 43 million. The American motion-picture industry has played the leading role in the internationalization of the film. American-made productions go all over the world, into Europe and Asia and Africa, carrying with them their message of the American way of life; revenue from foreign bookings bulks large in the calculations of American producers. Lately the process has been somewhat reversed; films are being made in foreign locations by American companies (largely because of restrictions upon currency exchange) and thus American audiences are furnished visual demonstration of the physical and human backgrounds of foreign countries, all without ever leaving home. The international movement of motion pictures has been made more nearly mutual since World War II as British, French, Italian, German, and even some Japanese films have obtained mass audiences in the United States.

We are not arguing that improved transportation and communication are in themselves necessarily conducive to greater international understanding. It is clearly easier today for many people to establish contact with individuals in other states and more and more people are doing so. Whether this is for good or ill depends of course upon the circumstances of the particular relationship. Indeed, there is a substantial body of American opinion which feels (with some reason) that American motion pictures, although unquestionably presenting a picture of American life that is accepted abroad, are doing the American people and the government of the United States a disservice because of the distortions of the United States which they present.

ECONOMIC INTERDEPENDENCE

The frontiers of states are drawn in response to a number of forces, both historical and contemporary; only rarely do they enclose a territory sufficiently well balanced economically to maintain a high standard of living within the state. Despite the efforts of certain governments in recent years to achieve economic self-sufficiency, the various parts of the world stand in a relation of economic interdependence if the resources of modern industrial production are to be exploited to their maximum advantage for all individuals everywhere. In the face of much political control of international economic life, trade reflecting these mutual needs continues to move; in the process, individuals follow their commerce. No relationship is more universally human than that of buying and selling; in the conduct of international trade some of the closest and most lasting international private relationships are created.

The United States. By way of illustration of the economic interdependence of modern states, let us examine certain aspects of the international economic position of the United States. The data are of the year 1950—not a normal year, but typical of the postwar era. During 1950 the United States engaged in foreign trade in commodities aggregating over 19 billion dollars, of which 10 billion were in exports and 9 billion in imports. It is worth noting that in 1951 the total was nearly 26 billion. Trade relations were maintained with 74 different political organizations ranging alphabetically from Afghanistan to Yugoslavia. The principal customers of the United States were, in descending order, Canada, Mexico, the United Kingdom, Cuba, Western Germany, and Japan; the principal suppliers were, again in descending order, Canada, Brazil, Cuba, the United Kingdom, Venezuela, and Mexico. Trade, in both directions, between the United States and Canada aggregated 2 billion dollars in 1950 and nearly 2½ in 1951.

What does the United States import? It is well known that the United States is one of the best-endowed states in the world from the point of view of agricultural and mineral resources. Yet certain key industrial commodities must be imported in their entirety, while certain agricultural products (food and fibers) must also be procured largely or entirely beyond our borders. In 1950, the import representing the greatest dollar value was coffee—over a billion dollars' worth. Next in value was petroleum in all forms, with a value of 800 million dollars. The range of the key imports can best be indicated by the following table:

SELECTED LIST OF U.S. IMPORTS IN 1950

Commodity	Value (in millions)
Coffee	$1091.0
Petroleum	855.3
Wool (raw and finished)	503.0
Crude rubber	426.6
Newsprint	452.9
Cane sugar	380.5
Copper	243.5
Tin	202.7

A person scanning these data can realize how many parts of the world are represented by this incomplete list. Coffee and sugar and petroleum from Latin America; rubber and tin from southeast Asia; wool from Australia; newsprint from Canada: all of these commodities impinge directly upon the lives of individual Americans and made them, however accidentally, participants in the international community.

Exports tell the same story. Although exports represented in 1950 only approximately 7 per cent of total United States production—the lowest percentage since 1935—the 10 billion dollars' worth of trade they formed was a not inconsiderable factor in retaining the high level of United States prosperity. The principal classes of exports, together with the regions to which they were exported, are shown in the following table.

Where American products go in quantity, there must go also American technicians, salesmen, and other necessary personnel. Thus the process of importing and exporting commodities, made necessary by the economic interdependence of the states of the world, brings people into international contact in two ways. In the first place, products that come from beyond American frontiers or that go outside them play a large part in the lives of those who either produce or consume them; the lives of every one of us would be vastly poorer if we were forced to dispense with all such commodities. In the second place, the exchange of goods across frontiers involves many people in the process, and these individuals participate in the creation of a real working international understanding at a highly personal level.

SELECTED LIST OF U.S. EXPORTS IN 1950

Commodity	Where Exported To	Value (in millions)
Industrial Machinery	Western Hemisphere, Canada	$1561.8
Cotton (raw and finished)	Western Europe, Far East	1251.6
Automobiles and Supplies	Western Hemisphere, Canada	1119.4
Petroleum	Western Hemisphere, western Europe	907.1
Grains (in all forms)	Western Hemisphere, western Europe	833.9
Electrical Machinery	Western Hemisphere, Canada	443.4

Other States. A similar statistical story could be told of most of the other states of the world. Some of the principal participants in world politics must import many more vital commodities than does the United States. Great Britain, for example, imports approximately half of its basic foodstuffs, including meat and cereals; France must normally import the great bulk of its coal; Italy must import both coal and iron ore, in addition to a large amount of food. The more one examines the structure of world economic relationships, the more the lesson of the economic interdependence of peoples is borne home. Politicians may seek, for good reasons or ill, to create self-sufficient enclaves within the borders of their states, but at best this is extremely difficult and possible only at the cost of serious dislocations in the lives of private citizens.

It is a fact of contemporary politics in many parts of the world—especially western Europe—that individuals are growing increasingly doubtful of the wisdom of choosing nationalist autarky over the improved standard of living possible through international economic co-operation. The Benelux customs union and the Schuman plan are only two of the many items of evidence that emphasize the force of this sentiment.

OPENING OF UNDERDEVELOPED AREAS

The Underdeveloped Areas. Closely allied to the general situation of the economic interdependence of peoples as a factor in the augmentation of international private contacts is the special case of the recent opening of the underdeveloped areas of the world to modern techniques. In Asia, Africa, the Middle East, and Latin America, the period since 1945 has witnessed the initiation of extensive two-way contact and communication between these great portions of the world and Western civilization.

Before World War II, the areas that we today term 'underdeveloped' presented certain common characteristics which have affected the role of their peoples in contemporary life. In the first place, most of them were remote from the main stream of either private or public international life; they were largely unaware of what went on outside their boundaries, and the remainder of the world to a great extent reciprocated this ignorance. Secondly, either they were all colonies of imperialist states or, although technically independent, they had never economically or politically emerged from a colonial orientation; that is, nationalist selfconsciousness was only imperfectly developed and self-government was either nonexistent or very ineffective. Third, they uniformly possessed a low standard of living and made only extremely inefficient use of their natural and human resource endowment. Social and economic discontent, although usually submerged, was widespread because of flagrant inequities in the distributions of the rewards of the society.

Since the end of the war these areas have all erupted. Politically and economically they have suddenly broken out into the main stream of world affairs and have attempted, each in its own way, to initiate an attack upon the internal problems it had formerly lived with complacently. It is as if the world political community had suddenly increased its membership by some two dozen states. The 'underdeveloped' peoples refuse to be taken for granted any more and their impact upon international life is already great and will continue to grow.

For Americans particularly, the appearance of these areas upon the world scene has been a revelation. It has become a matter of sheer necessity for us to make contact with peoples of completely different cultures and to learn the requirements for continuing to live in the same world with them. Problems of political, economic, and racial adjustment have pressed upon us simultaneously with the obligation to gain some sort of factual education about what sort of people these are. We have also had to devise techniques for teaching them about ourselves, which has proved to be difficult. Most of our historical contacts with foreigners have been with Europeans, whose value systems and cultural backgrounds spring from the same roots as do our own. Coping with states such as India and Indonesia, Iran and Egypt, all of whom have revolted against Western imperialism, has forced us to re-examine many of our own assumptions in order to discover that approach which will procure a sympathetic hearing for our own case. We shall examine the political implications of the opening of the underdeveloped areas in Chapter 11. For the moment let us look at certain concrete ways in which their entry into the world has increased the individual contacts between their peoples and the individual citizens of other states.

Political Contacts. In the political field, the fact that almost all these states are now executing their own foreign policies with near-belligerent independence has in itself increased their impact upon the rest of the world. India, Pakistan, Burma, the Philippines, and many other similar states now for the first time maintain diplomatic relations with most of the other governments in the world. Natives of these states thus come into direct contact with the governmental machinery and the cultural flow of all Western states, with an accompanying acceleration in the education of all concerned. This effect is heightened by the fact that the diplomats of the new states are all drawn from the leadership class in their homelands and exert an influence out of proportion to their small numbers.

The process of acculturation also works in reverse. Foreign states maintain diplomatic establishments in each of the new states and the citizens of the younger governments come into contact with official representatives of many cultures of which they had previously been only vaguely aware.

In like manner activity in the United Nations has served to speed up this getting-acquainted process in a unique manner; the participation in the Korean war of military contingents from such exotic states as Thailand and Turkey served to bring the peculiar contributions of these peoples to the attention of the world better than any other single action they have taken. It must be repeated that this process of accommodation in the political field is a mutual one. The industrialized West must accept the fact of an independent East that is determined to be treated as an equal, but so must the new states rid themselves of some of their most deep-seated and erroneous antipathies toward Western civilization. The attainment of full political understanding and cooperation can be possible only upon a basis of fundamental intercultural adjustment.

Economic Contacts. It is in the area of economic life that the underdeveloped areas and the Western world have come into the closest and most intimate contact. Before 1941, the economic resources of these territories were, generally speaking, under the direct exploitation of Western capitalists; since then, the inhabitants have to a considerable degree taken over the determination of their own economic destinies. This has been an enlightening experience for everyone concerned. The problems of production, transportation, and distribution of the commodities produced and their exchange for other products in the markets of the world have proved both more complicated and more simple than originally imagined. Technical knowledge of production is often lacking among these peoples, as is also experience in marketing and distributing the goods produced.

The outside world has had in turn to learn the peculiar way of doing business followed by the relatively inexperienced representatives of these areas. The Western world and the underdeveloped areas are coming into wider economic contact than ever before and each has a great deal to learn from the others. It has not been a process altogether easy and happy, but it has been a necessary one that promises to continue for a long time.

Point IV. The program of technical assistance and co-operation with the underdeveloped areas undertaken by the United States—known as 'Point IV' from its inclusion as the last point in a four-part American foreign policy by President Truman in 1949—is perhaps the most ambitious and well-intentioned policy followed by any Western government in dealing with these new states. It is based upon the unquestioned need of these areas for the kind of technical economic assistance that only the West can provide. It proceeds upon a completely voluntary basis on the part of the state requesting the assistance, and includes primarily the furnishing of private investment capital from the United States and the supplying of technically trained experts in various fields to serve the needs of the host country. In the course of its execution, American technicians have aided agriculture in India, mining in Burma, and public health in Thailand as well as many other similar projects.

Many people regard the program as especially hopeful because of its practical application. Instead of involving intergovernmental relationships at a high level, it actually represents individuals engaged in extending a helping hand to other individuals in an attack upon problems that are highly personal in their impact. Some of the greatest failures of the program have come as a result of attempts to impose an American procedure upon a situation completely unsuitable for it; likewise, its greatest successes have accompanied a realization that an agricultural problem in India, for example, may be solved only by the gradual application of Western techniques to a situation that is— and will remain—uniquely Indian. This of necessity has required the modification of many Western techniques of organization, efficiency, and production in order to fit them within the bounds of a differing value structure. In the process of planning and executing many of these projects, thousands of individual contacts of an extremely strategic sort have already taken place between Americans and citizens of the underdeveloped areas which might otherwise never have occurred at all. In this way Point IV has materially increased the sum total of individual international relationships.

OTHER INDIVIDUAL CONTACTS

The principal cause, however, for the increasing amount of individual international contact is the movement of unorganized private citizens in the pursuit of their individual interests. In that part of the world which is still sufficiently free to permit reasonably easy movement by private individuals across frontiers, there is a constant two-way traffic. The reasons for these movements are almost as numerous as there are people moving, but we may at least indicate certain major categories.

Education. International education is an old custom, especially in the Western world. Since the Middle Ages it has been normal for students to seek the completion of their formal education in foreign institutions. This, however, was largely confined to Europe, where a common culture existed of which the universities were among the principal custodians. Thus the movement of students remained within reasonably limited bounds. Today, however, educational interchange upon an international basis includes not only the states of the Western world but representatives of Oriental and other cultures as well.

The United States plays a leading role in this process. As a matter of policy the American government emphasizes private international contact through education, feeling that in this important area real progress can be made toward minimizing intercultural tension. It operates an international educational exchange program whereby foreign students and professors from all over the world may come to the United States to study or teach; in 1953–4 there were over 30,000 such visitors in American institutions of higher learning.

At the same time a many-sided program undertakes to make study abroad available to American students. The largest single such group are the Fulbright scholars, approximately 600 per year, who study in any of some nineteen states in Europe or Asia. They enjoy scholarships provided by the unexpended accounts remaining from United States lend-lease operations during World War II. Similar opportunities exist for American professors, both to teach and to do research abroad, under the Fulbright program.

There are many privately financed international fellowships, including the 32 Rhodes scholarships, the Rotary International fellowships (284 of which were awarded between 1947 and 1952), and the Ford Foundation fellowships for study in the Middle and Far East. All in all, the program of international education exchange is so widespread that foreign students on American campuses, even small campuses, are commonplace; Americans abroad are an equally familiar phenomenon. On the campuses of several large American universities—and in many European universities as well—are located 'International Houses.' These are residence and social centers for foreign students. In this way students from abroad not only learn about the United States, but acquire much sophistication from the intimate contact with other foreign students. Thus an Indian student in the United States may have a Norwegian as a roommate. In this way the process of student acculturation gains a new dimension. Educational exchange between other states is likewise increasing, particularly between Europe and the Orient.

It is particularly important that the lessons of common humanity and sympathetic understanding be taught within the college and university community in all states, because it is from this group that the leaders of the future will come. The attitude toward other peoples held by the current generation of college students in the United States can never be the same as a result of its contact with so many foreign students. When this group of college-age people have matured to the point of taking over national leadership themselves, their views and their policy cannot but reflect the conditioning toward individuals of other cultures that occurred during their student days.

Recreation. The pursuit of recreation leads many individuals into international contact. Before World War II the press made much of the 'international set,' which journeyed from one famous recreational playground to another, but its importance was never great and today is negligible. Of much more significance is organized international athletic competition. The most publicized event of this sort is of course the quadrennial Olympic games, in which athletes from all over the world compete in many different events. But it would be difficult to mention a form of athletics, either professional or amateur, which does not extend into the international arena.

Team sports, such as soccer, football, basketball, baseball, water polo, and hockey have regularly scheduled international tournaments; in addition, national champions in these and other sports make international tours as a matter of course. A noteworthy example of international athletic competition is the annual pursuit of the Davis Cup, for which national teams of tennis players compete in a world-wide elimination tournament. Individual sports —tennis, golf, boxing, wrestling, weight lifting, track and field, and the like—also provide innumerable opportunities for international competition. Indeed, so systematized is international athletic competition that almost any athlete of sufficient talent, regardless of his particular specialty, can look forward to the opportunity of performing in foreign lands and in competition with opponents of different nationalities.

It is difficult, however, to measure the effect of this relationship upon international understanding. An example was perhaps afforded by the 1952 Olympic games in Helsinki. The Soviet Union participated for the first time and the games were marred by ill-tempered disputes about the method of scoring points in the team competition (which was entirely unofficial; all Olympic championships are individual). Despite the Soviet government's desire to make political capital out of the competition and the unfavorable atmosphere of Russo-American relations at the time, American team members reported to the press that they found their Russian opponents to be very pleasant individuals and sturdy competitors. What the Russian athletes told their government we have no way of knowing.

Tourism. Perhaps the most prolific source of personal international experiences, at least for Americans, is tourism. Since the war American tourists and travelers have come to include the entire globe in their itinerary, taking great advantage of the growth of air transportation. The United States government has encouraged this practice for two reasons. In the first place tourist expenditures represent a very considerable transfer of dollars into foreign hands, making it easier for them to purchase American goods. In the second, tourism, being travel for no ulterior purpose, provides an ideal opportunity for Americans to learn about the ways of life in foreign countries. As a result, tourism by Americans has grown to remarkable proportions and the American who has 'been abroad' is no longer a local curiosity throughout much of the United States.

Europeans are almost as great travelers as are Americans and, despite currency and travel restrictions, have covered much of the Western world with their wanderings. In Asia, the smallness of the leisure class and the great distances to be traversed have made travel by Asians less common; however, much of non-communist Asia is regularly visited by tourists from the West and some international contact thus takes place.

The Effects of World War II. This discussion of the increase in private international contacts would be incomplete without a reference to the effect of World War II. Although in no sense pleasant and in most cases involuntary, there was, as an inescapable concomitant of the war and its aftermath, a great increase in the number and the variety of private international relationships. Hostile occupation, the forcible transfer of workers, prisoners of war, displaced persons, refugees, and military comradeship all produced mass international contacts among private persons upon a scale unmatched at any time before or since.

Its effects are still being felt. Many Frenchmen perceived, even in the bitterness of defeat, that the Germans are human beings and that most of them are decent; Germans learned the same about the French. The Japanese, at first despised and then hysterically hated by Americans, turned out on closer acquaintance to be human beings who have the same sort of personal problems as we do but who solve them somewhat differently. Even the Soviet Union felt the impact. The hundreds of thousands of Red Army soldiers who saw the West with their own eyes in Germany and Austria, as well as the Russian slave laborers Hitler forcibly deported to the West during the war, will never again have the same degree of trust in the Kremlin's propaganda about the decayed and dying West.

In this way the world reaped an unexpected harvest of good from the war. The sheer volume of personal contact that developed, ranging from casual acquaintanceships to international marriages, has worked and will continue to work a fundamental change in the outlook of millions of people. The exact outcomes are of course unpredictable, nor do we know when they will appear, but no such mass modification in outlook could be completely without effect.

THE INTERNATIONAL SENSE OF COMMUNITY

The Concept of Community. The term 'community' is defined by sociologists in a number of different ways, but all the definitions include certain common features. There are four essential aspects of a community. First, it is composed of individuals who may or may not be organized into subgroups. Second, these individuals have extensive and habitual relations with one an-

other which are sufficiently well organized to proceed upon a highly predictable basis. Third, there exists within the group a generally recognized
moral consensus that establishes the value system in whose terms certain acts
are demanded by the community, others encouraged or permitted, and still
others prohibited. Fourth, the habitual relations of the individuals and the
value system are both reflected in a framework of institutions. The people
who constitute the community recognize their mutual bonds and order their
behavior accordingly.

The International Community Sense. The international sense of community, therefore consists in the realization shared by an increasing number
of individuals in almost all states of the world that they form part of a group
which possesses most of the marks of a true community. This community
bypasses political organization and political action. Its focus of emphasis is
upon the rough identity of interest shared by its members in their private
lives. In terms of the criteria of a community which we listed above, the international community displays the following characteristics. Its members
are generally organized into subgroups (private and public international organizations), but whether within or without such a subgroup, extensive and
habitual personal relations are carried on. These are developing certain procedural patterns and organization, and predictability in these relationships is
developing rapidly.

The moral consensus that marks a true community is still in the process
of maturation, but its outlines are already clear. It is individual in its emphasis and places primary value upon the dignity of the human being. To enforce its value judgments the international community is developing a set of
sanctions, most of them thus far informal, to prescribe desirable behavior
and to punish antisocial conduct. Extensive institutional elaboration of this
community sense has already taken place and the process is continuing today at an ever-increasing rate.

Nationalism and Technology. Since the creation of the nation-state system
about four centuries ago, the largest political unit reflecting the sense of community shared by its members has been the national state. The state had to
win its victory over other, smaller community units for the prize of the
loyalty of its people. The history of the development of the state in modern
times can be told in terms of the expansion of the community sense of the
people until it actually encompassed the entire national group. Two forces
played critical roles in this process. The first was the development of modern nationalism, which identified the body of citizens with the effective community; the second was modern technology which made the pretensions of
nationalism a reality by making it possible for all people within a state to
maintain close and habitual relations with all the others. The political community of which most individuals feel a part today is coterminous with the

socio-political group called the nation and also with the boundaries within which that nation dwells.

Today these two forces that share responsibility for the state-based community operate in vastly different ways. Nationalism in most societies today draws ever more sharp distinctions between the in-group and all out-groups, and demonstrates an increasing proclivity toward ethnocentric excesses; on the other hand, the advance of modern technology did not come to a halt at the frontiers of the national state but instead leaped over them. The technological frontier now extends to the outermost limits of the entire world. It is an easy matter for individuals to maintain 'extensive relations' upon an organized basis with people in all other states.

In many ways the cruel dilemma of modern man is the result of the contemporary conflict between these two formerly harmonious forces. Nationalism bids him to confine his loyalty and his effective action to the members of his own particular group; technology provides him a world-wide arena for action, with possibilities for good which at present are only hinted at. The international-community sense is most conspicuous among those individuals everywhere who have accepted the implications of a global technology and who have therefore won freedom from the more limited points of view imposed by the more restrictive variety of nationalism.

COMPONENTS OF THE INTERNATIONAL-COMMUNITY SENSE

If the international-community sense is defined as an attitude shared by large numbers of individuals throughout the world, it now becomes appropriate to consider its component parts. Individuals vary in their understanding of what membership in the international community means; many persons pursue an active part in the affairs of the community without realizing the assumptions upon which they are proceeding. Yet we can formulate a reasonably clear outline of the philosophical postulates upon which the international-community sense is built.

Individualism. In the first place, the international-community sense is individualistic in its outlook. It rejects the totalitarian implications of the dogma of the modern state and denies that men have no higher destiny than to serve their governments in all ways that political leadership deems to be fitting. It clearly involves an elevation of the claims of the individual to dignity and worth over the pretensions of the state to absolute dominance. Being essentially a philosophy of individualism it is identified with the classic theory of natural rights and limited government which is also a part of the democratic concept. Since in international affairs the state is everything and the individual has no legal existence, the international-community sense rejects much of international law and almost all of what we know as 'power politics.' In other words, it is a philosophy of international affairs which centers upon the individual human being instead of upon the abstract entity of the state. In this sense it is more realistic than nationalistic particularism, since the individual has objective reality and the state and the nation do not.

It may seem paradoxical that an outlook which emphasizes the prime importance of the individual should seek the broadest possible base of organization. If the state today results in the abasement of the individual, it might be thought odd to urge the creation of a new community to include all of mankind; to change from a large group to one still larger in the name of more dignity and freedom for the individual is a seeming contradiction. But we must remember the influence of technology. The state form of organization, say the apologists for the international community, obstructs the most efficient use of the technological resources of the world in terms of the maximum benefit for individuals; the economies of large-scale production can be best realized by utilizing all mankind in a single body of producers and consumers. Technology leads us to the world community and the greater freedom and dignity of man.

Anti-statism. The international-community sense not only denies the pre-eminence of the state over the individual; its outlook is primarily non-political. Instead of being concerned with problems of national interest, national power, and national prestige, it makes a special point of the highly personal problems of individuals in the economic, social, and psychological areas. It seems to argue that although man unquestionably is a political being, he is first and always a human; as such, he is beset from birth with a host of situations that strike him much more directly than even the most fervent pleas of political authority. He must find food and shelter; he must marry and establish a family; he must combat disease; he must gain enough knowledge of socially useful skills to enable him to cope with the world; he must learn the formal and informal rules of social organization so that he can fit himself meaningful into the group of which he is a part. This is the stuff of human life; political organization today does not adequately solve these problems for millions of people.

The international-community sense concentrates upon these aspects of the lives of individuals and seeks to discover some of the solutions to these personal problems. It elevates the private life of man over the political life, and views government as one of the possible vehicles for the enrichment and fulfillment of the life of individuals rather than as the embodiment of the supremacy of the political virtues. It accordingly expects from government in the international field a different role from that played by the states of today; it demands co-operative attack by political authority upon the problems of men rather than the competitive pursuit of national interest. The rejection by the sense of international community of traditional political organization and behavior is one of its principal distinguishing characteristics.

The Identity of Individual Interest. The idea of the international community is founded upon the basic identity of interest among all individuals. Building upon the sociological and anthropological truth of the essential similarity of all people and the fact that cultural and societal differences between men are learned rather than innate, the international-community sense assumes that all men share basically the same needs and desires. From this assumption that all men want basically the same things for themselves, the next conclusion is that the primary business of men of good will everywhere is to get on with the most immediate and efficient program of meeting as many as possible of these individual demands. Whatever in the way of governmental policy anywhere serves to improve the lot of individuals is deemed desirable; whatever serves any other purpose is held to be of secondary importance. This means that the sharers of the sense of international community reject most of the nationalist apparatus of modern international politics on the ground that it creates a false disharmony of interest between individuals of different national groups.

Of course the identity of individual interest of which so much is made in this argument refers to the basic humanity of individuals. Nationalism may be founded upon false premises; ideologies may be oversimplifications of what may be at best only half-truths; cultural differences may be learned and therefore synthetic. All these divisive forces of modern world life, however, are real and powerful in their effect upon human emotions, and to seek to offset them by attempts at scientific refutation is a waste of time. The only way in which an individual who denies his identity of interest with all other men can be brought to change his mind is for him to be placed in situations of direct contact with representatives of alien cultures. Once brought face to face with the obvious fact that these strangers must cope with the same sort of problems as he does, the psychological underpinnings of his faith in his own uniqueness are weakened. This is why the augmentation of direct individual contacts upon an international basis is of such importance to the creation of an international-community sense. Once enough individuals had gained the sophistication in outlook that made it possible for them to grasp the important fact of the essential sameness of humans everywhere, the concept of an international community became a potent force in world affairs.

Loss of Confidence in State Mechanism. As a result of the effect of technology, many men everywhere have developed doubts about the ultimate validity of political values. They wonder whether the demands that international politics make upon individuals return rewards that are worth what they cost and whether the fate of men is to remain forever divided into mutually competitive groups. For many the answer to these questions is in the negative; they argue that men possess the physical resources to meet the demands of modern life provided a co-operative program undertaken in a spirit of good will be initiated upon a world-wide basis. Consequently they no longer have any confidence that the international political system, founded upon the sovereignty of the state and operating upon the principles of power and of expediency, can ever produce any lasting improvement in human happiness.

Theirs, however, is not simply a theory of philosophic anarchy hoping for a day of brotherhood that will make political organization unnecessary. The advocates of the international community seek to keep their policy practical and realistic. They have no rigid formula for action except in terms of the eventual recognition of the equal right of all individuals to a reasonably adequate satisfaction of their basic needs. Therefore, although distrusting the nation-state and the system of world politics as presently constituted and motivated, they do not necessarily call for its outright rejection. Some see a system of world government as the only possible solution, but most content themselves with urging joint socio-economic policy at an international level upon the governments of the present-day world.

For many people, the doubt about the personal rewards derived from state-centered international politics has not yet matured into a recognition and an acceptance of the international community. They are disillusioned about the future of men under the nation-state system, but are unable to make the transfer of allegiance to a broader basis of identification. Nationalism, cultural isolationism, and the pressures of ideologies furnish too great an emotional obstacle for them to overcome. Lacking confidence in the value systems of current world politics and unable to accept the activist implications of the international community, they tend to take refuge in an attempted withdrawal from political currents and use an effete cynicism as a shield against the necessity of making any meaningful choices among political alternatives.

A Program of Action. A distinguishing mark of a person who shares the international community sense is his dedication to a program of action in its behalf. Of course individuals vary in the extent of their commitment in this regard as well as in the kind and extent of specific actions they undertake, but so many are the problems to be solved and so compelling is felt to be the need for their solution that purposeful activity on behalf of the goals of the community is a constant characteristic of one who feels himself a part of it.

In the next section of this chapter we shall examine the organizations that reflect this community sense and the action men undertake in its behalf. For the moment let us point out only that this action takes places at two levels. In the first place, it consists in the operations carried out by individuals in their private capacities. Most often this is done through one or another of the hundreds of private international organizations. Most of these organizations, being highly specialized, accomplish comparatively little except in the area of their particular interest; many of them seem quite remote from the subject of world peace. Yet in the aggregate their impact is great.

Mention must also be made of the vast number of individuals who, without benefit of organizational support and completely upon their own, carry on the work of the international community within the scope of their own private lives. The total effect of thousands of such persons carrying on their programs of agitation, education, and action over a period of years cannot help but make a real impression upon the consciousness of governments everywhere.

The action program in behalf of the international community operates also through the state. Governments today are potentially capable of working great improvement in the lives of individuals through co-operative international effort; all that is lacking is the will to do so on the part of contemporary leadership. Consequently, individuals interested in the advancement of the international community have banded into pressure groups in order to stimulate governmental action in that direction.

The steps taken by governments in this field include the creation and operation of special-purpose international organizations, the furthering of the social and economic work of the United Nations, and the initiation of unilateral policies of relief and rehabilitation of individuals in other states (outstanding examples are the Point IV program of the United States and the Colombo plan of the British Commonwealth). It cannot be denied, however, that governments often have mixed motives in their operations in this field; some of them have a direct national interest in the development of a real international community sense and co-operate much more willingly than do others whose policy is founded upon a perpetuation of the national differences that divide mankind. In almost every instance, the effective implementation of any such governmental policy necessitates the unremitting application of pressure by individuals and groups who subscribe to the policy themselves to the point of becoming political activists in its support.

Private International Organizations

Organization and Structure. A private international organization is composed of private persons who band together upon an international basis either for the direct accomplishment of an end they have in common or else to bring pressure upon their respective governments to initiate policy in harmony with their objectives. There are over 700 such organizations in existence at the present time, with a bewildering variety of stated purposes. They belong to either the federative type, being composed of a number of suborganizations set up upon a national basis, or else to the consolidated type, which is truly international with no organizational apparatus intervening between the individual member and the leadership of the entire group. The most important of them have certain structural features in common. They all have a central headquarters under the direction of a chief executive officer who normally serves as spokesman for the organization, together with some form of regularly scheduled conference of the entire membership or their representatives, at which general policy is made for the organization.

Purposes. 1. Economic. Perhaps the largest category of private international organizations is furnished by those whose objectives are the economic betterment of the individual members. At least three major subclassifications can be discerned. Manufacturing and trade organizations include perhaps the most influential single private international organization, the Inter-national Chamber of Commerce. Other typical examples are the International Carriage and Van Union, the International Fiscal Association, the International Federation of Newspaper Publishers and Editors, and the International Union of Architects. Labor organizations include the three most powerful international labor groups: the International Confederation of Free Trade Unions, the World Federation of Trade Unions, and the International Federation of Christian Trade Unions. Agricultural organizations include the International Federation of Agricultural Producers and various regional bodies.

2. Political. Private international organizations with a political orientation are of two different types: they are composed either of governmental officials from various states with common problems who consult together for the more efficient accomplishment of their mission, or else of private citizens whose major function is the dissemination of information and the bringing of pressure upon their respective home govrnments. The first type, composed of similarly situated government officials of various states, includes the most important of all of this category, the Inter-Parliamentary Union, whose membership is made up of legislators from many states. Other examples are the International City Managers' Association, the International Federation of Unions of Employees in Public and Civil Services, the International Institute of Administrative Sciences, the International Institute of Public Finance, and the International Institute of Public Law. Pressure and propaganda organizations include the World Federation of United Nations Associations, the International Federation for Housing and Town-Planning, the International League for the Rights of Man, and the International Union of Socialist Youth. Almost all private international organizations have a pressure-propaganda aspect as part of their program, but those given above are some for which it is the principal function.

3. Religious. Religious organizations upon an international basis are numerous, representing most of the organized faiths of the Western world. The Salvation Army, the World Jewish Congress, the Young Christian Workers, *Pax Romana* (a Roman Catholic organization for intellectual and cultural affairs), the Commission of the Churches on International Affairs, the Catholic International Union for Social Service, and the Friends' World Committee are only a few of a long list. The universal appeal of a religious faith tends to make it a convenient vehicle for organized private action upon an international basis.

4. Social. Almost as numerous as the international organizations with an economic orientation are those whose purposes may be classified generally as social betterment. Their purposes range from the suppression of the slave trade to the fostering of temperance, including the improvement of social work, welfare activities (care for cripples, dependent children, and the insane), and the improvement of health and sanitation. Representative organizations are the International Committee of the Red Cross, the International Conference of Social Work, the International Council of Women, the International Society for the Welfare of Cripples, the International Temperance Union, and those two familiar ones, the World's Alliance of Young Men's Christian Associations and the World's Young Women's Christian Association.

5. Technical and Scholarly. Technical and specialized organizations exist in most of the fields of advanced learning. The International Statistical Institute, the International Society of Criminology, the International Political Science Association, the International Law Association, and many other similar organizations exist. In all of them the purpose is the exchange of information and experiences upon an organized basis for the improvement of the technical competence of all concerned.

There remain still many other private international organizations that do not fit into any of these five categories, but the listing does at least suggest something of the scope of human activity that is affected by these bodies.

Consultation with the United Nations. Following a practice originally formalized by the League of Nations, Article 71 of the Charter of the United Nations provides for the establishment of consultative relationships between private (non-governmental) organizations and the Economic and Social Council for the purposes of mutually considering problems of common interest. The Council has prepared and keeps on file a register of such organizations which maintain a consultative relationship.

They are divided into three categories: category 'A' includes 'organizations which are closely linked with the economic or social life of the areas which they represent'; category 'B' includes 'organizations which have special competence but are concerned specifically with only a few of the fields of activity covered by the Council'; a third category includes organizations that maintain less formal relations with the Council but are available upon an *ad hoc* basis for consultation when such action is indicated. At the end of 1953, there were nine organizations in category 'A,' 92 in category 'B,' and 115 international groups were on the register for *ad hoc* consultations. The following nine organizations formed category 'A':

International Chamber of Commerce
International Confederation of Free Trade Unions

International Co-operative Alliance
International Federation of Agricultural Producers
International Federation of Christian Trade Unions
International Organization of Employers
Inter-Parliamentary Union
World Federation of Trade Unions
World Federation of United Nations Associations

PUBLIC INTERNATIONAL UNIONS

Public international unions are international organizations whose orientation and purposes are clearly toward the individual and the ends he pursues, just as in the case of the private organizations discussed above. They can be distinguished from the latter since they have as members not individuals but sovereign states. Since they are governmental, they operate upon a more formal basis than do the private groups and as a result both gain and lose in effectiveness. Their internal organization, their membership, and their functions vary so greatly that beyond certain general statements it is impossible to classify them in any meaningful fashion. All have some kind of central bureau with permanent administrators, and provision is always made for periodic conferences; beyond that, each one organizes itself largely in terms of the international instrument (a treaty or convention) which created it.

The public international organizations of specialized purposes can be divided into two groups. The first consists of those more important ones with (to quote the Charter of the United Nations) 'wide international responsibilities' which have been brought into relationship with the United Nations and are known as the 'specialized agencies.' The second includes all the remainder—several hundreds of varying size and degree of formalization—which are either geographically or functionally so specialized as not to merit relationship with the United Nations. For our purposes it will perhaps be preferable to consider the second group first.

INDEPENDENT PUBLIC INTERNATIONAL UNIONS

1. Transportation and Communication, and Economics. Since the organization and structure of these bodies differ so widely, the only possible way to summarize their operations is in terms of the functions to which they address themselves. Among the many independent public international organizations that exist, the following general types can be found.

(1) The first group is formed by those that concern themselves with problems of transportation and communication. Among them are such international riparian administrative bodies as the European Danube Commission, railway bodies such as the International Union of Railway Freight Transportation, and various regional bodies that deal with telecommunications.

(2) A second classification is that of organizations that have as their primary purpose the improvement of some aspect(s) of economic life. The Inter-American Coffee Board deals with the orderly marketing of coffee, the International Tin Committee with tin, and the now defunct Sugar Union with sugar. Agricultural organizations likewise exist, but most of their functions have been merged with the Food and Agriculture Organization, one of the specialized agencies of the United Nations.

Perhaps the most impressive example of how far states will go in creating unions to deal with economic matters is furnished by the European Coal and Steel Community, the formal institution executing the Schuman Plan for the pooling of the coal and steel industry of the six western European states of France, West Germany, Italy, Belgium, Luxembourg, and the Netherlands. This group has transcended the traditional basis of national sovereignty and has created a new instrument of government.

2. *Social, Cultural, and Scientific.* Many international unions deal with social questions similar to those dealt with by the private organizations considered in the preceding section. Although many of these unions have been absorbed by various of the commissions and specialized agencies of the United Nations, a number of them still retain their autonomy and operate with reduced scope in limited areas. Other international unions deal with cultural and scientific purposes. Such basic data as weights and measures and a standard map of the world are in the care of the International Bureau of Weights and Measures and the Central Bureau of the International Map of the World. The International Hydrographic Bureau co-ordinates and makes available to everyone the work of the various national states in the areas of hydrography and navigation.

AGENCIES AFFILIATED WITH THE UNITED NATIONS

The United Nations system includes two types of organizations that deal with questions within the particular interest of the international community: first, the commissions, committees, and 'special bodies' that are an integral part of the United Nations itself; second, the 'specialized agencies' that exist as independent international organizations but are 'in relationship' with the parent body. The Economic and Social Council of the United Nations is charged with directing the activities of the first type and of 'co-ordinating' the work of the second.

Commissions and Other United Nations Agencies. The membership of the first type of agency consists of members of the United Nations appointed to the respective bodies by action of the General Assembly. Most of these bodies have names and functions that are self-explanatory.

The first type is the functional commission. These are created to deal with a particular subject, presumably of general interest to all members. A listing of the objects with which these commissions deal illustrate the scope of

United Nations activity in economic and social affairs. Commissions exist on the following topics: economics and employment, transportation and communication, statistical questions, human rights, social questions, the status of women, narcotic drugs, fiscal questions, and population questions. Each of these bodies deals with its problem by making recommendations to the Economic and Social Council and to the General Assembly.

A second type, economic in scope and geographic in organization, is the regional commission. Three of these exist at present: the Economic Commission for Europe (ECE), the Economic Commission for Asia and the Far East (ECAFE), and the Economic Commission for Latin America (ECLA). Membership is drawn from the states in each region and other nations with particular interest. Their action is principally co-ordinating and expediting.

Procedural matters are the principal concern of standing committees. Two typical examples are the Committee on Negotiations with Inter-Governmental Agencies (public international unions) and the Committee for Consultation with Non-Governmental Organizations (private international organizations).

Less important are the two remaining types, the *ad hoc* committees and the special bodies. The first group are temporary bodies to deal with non-recurrent problems for limited times; examples include the Commission on Genocide and the United Nations Appeal for Children. The second type consists of semi-permanent administrative agencies that exercise supervisory or co-ordinating functions over particular problems. Two of the best known of these are the Permanent Central Opium Board, which supervises the international narcotics trade, and the United Nations International Children's Emergency Fund (UNICEF).

The Specialized Agencies. The specialized agencies of the United Nations are separate international organizations, each created by a multilateral international agreement. Each maintains its own membership, its own budget and administrative staff, and its own area of operations. As a result of a special agreement between each of them and the United Nations, a close working relationship involving co-ordination, consultation, and mutual assistance exists between the parent organization and all the specialized agencies and between the specialized agencies themselves. In the summary listing that follows, data relative to headquarters, functions, budget, and membership are as of the end of 1954.

1. The International Labor Organization (ILO) was established in 1919 and came into relationship with the United Nations in 1946. Seventy-nine states constitute the membership; headquarters are maintained in Geneva, Switzerland, with branch offices throughout the world. It operates upon an annual budget (in 1954) of 6,311,000 U.S. dollars Its purposes can be summarized as the improvement of the condition of labor throughout the world and the removal of grave disparities among the labor forces of various states.

Its success has been considered and it is recognized as one of the most powerful of these bodies.

2. The Food and Agriculture Organization of the United Nations (FAO) officially came into being in 1945 and was brought into relationship with the United Nations the following year. Seventy-one states formed the membership in 1954; headquarters are maintained at Rome. Its annual budget is just over six million dollars. Its general purpose is the improvement of the standard of living of individuals everywhere by obtaining more efficient production and distribution of food and agricultural products. Although handicapped by the refusal of the Communist bloc to accept membership (they theorize that food is a political weapon and should be dealt with accordingly), it has had some success in its mission.

3. The United Nations Educational, Scientific, and Cultural Organization (UNESCO) was created late in 1946 and entered into its United Nations relationship several weeks later in the same year. Seventy-two states are members (the USSR, the Ukraine, and Byelorussia joined during 1954) and over 60 national commissions now exist to execute the work within the member states. Headquarters are in Paris. The annual budget is over nine million dollars.

The preamble to the UNESCO constitution contains the famous statement that 'since wars begin in the minds of men, it is in the minds of men that the defenses of peace must be constructed.' The organization seeks to attain this end through active promotion of the international exchange of education, scientific, and cultural information. Its work has been provocative of controversy in many states, including the United States; however, its approach is felt by many to be potentially valuable in the development of the international-community sense.

4. The International Civil Aviation Organization (ICAO) began its existence in 1947 and almost immediately entered into a relationship with the United Nations. Sixty-three states maintain membership; headquarters of the organization are in Montreal. Branch offices are maintained in Paris, Lima, Cairo, and Melbourne. The annual budget is just over three million Canadian dollars. The scope of the organization's concern includes the whole of civil aviation, with emphasis on the rapid and orderly extension of civil-aviation facilities throughout the world.

5. The International Bank for Reconstruction and Development (BANK) came into being late in 1945 and entered into relationship with the United Nations two years later. Fifty-seven countries maintain membership; several other applications are pending. Headquarters are located in Washington, with a European office in Paris. The Bank is capitalized at approximately ten billion dollars, of which 20 per cent is available for the making of loans; its administrative budget runs in the neighborhood of five million dollars. The purpose of the Bank is indicated in its name; it exists as a lending and

guaranteeing agency to provide financing for governments to undertake projects of reconstruction or development.

6. The International Monetary Fund (FUND) has the same dates of creation and of adherence to the United Nations as does the Bank, its sister organization. The same 57 states that form the membership of the Bank also constitute the membership of the Fund. Its headquarters are in Washington, in the same building that houses the Bank. The Fund provides approximately eight billion dollars to be used in stabilizing the currency of the membership, in the progressive elimination of exchange limitations and restrictions of all kinds, and in the liberation of world trade.

7. The World Health Organization (WHO), which was preceded by several temporary bodies after the war, officially went into operation in 1948 and almost immediately established its relationship with the United Nations. The WHO has one of the largest memberships of all the specialized agencies: 81 states, plus three associate members. Headquarters are in Geneva and nine regional offices are maintained. Its budget is somewhat more extensive than some of the others—nine million dollars. Its objective is 'the attainment by all people of the highest possible level of health.'

The following is a brief list of the categories of its operations: control of communicable diseases, maternal and child health, environmental sanitation, mental health, social and occupational health, nutrition, public-health education, nursing, co-ordination of research, epidemiological services, health statistics, biological standardization, antibiotics, and narcotics. It co-operates actively with national governments, with private organizations, and with other international bodies, and carries on much work of its own, including an extensive program of publication.

8. The original Postal Union (UPU) was created in 1874; in 1948 its constitution was amended to incorporate an agreement bringing it into relationship with the United Nations. The UPU is the closest approximation to a truly universal international organization. Its membership totals 93, which includes all of the civilized and semi-civilized states of the world. Its headquarters are in Berne, Switzerland. The budget in 1954 was one and a half million Swiss francs. The objective of the organization is the execution of the Berne Treaty of 1874, which lays down the principal that the signatories of the treaty form 'a single postal territory for the reciprocal exchange of correspondence.' The organization has the major functions of administering the treaty, of handling complaints, and of creating new regulations to cope with the changing conditions of postal exchange.

9. The International Refugee Organization (IRO) was created officially in 1948 and came into relationship with the United Nations at the same time; it terminated its operations and ended its existence in January 1952. Eighteen states constituted its membership at the end of its existence. Headquarters were in Geneva. Its budget was quite high because of the type of

operation it was engaged in: during the 19 months from July 1950 through January 1952, its total expenditure was nearly 400 million dollars. Its purpose was implied in its name: caring for, resettling or repatriating, and transporting the hundreds of thousands of refugees made homeless as a result of World War II. Its scale of operation was global, extending wherever significant bodies of refugees were gathered: Germany, Italy, Trieste, Korea, the Philippines, China, and several other critical spots. The reduction of the refugee problem to manageable proportions and the resistance of the Communist states to its work caused its dissolution.

10. The International Telecommunications Union (ITU) grew out of earlier international agreements upon telegraphy and radio telegraphy prior to World War II. The ITU was actually created in 1934 but was reorganized in terms of a new convention in 1947. The new ITU formally entered into existence in 1949 and the agreement with the United Nations came into force at the same time. Ninety countries and territories have joined; headquarters are in Geneva. The budget is in the neighborhood of six million Swiss francs. The organization aims at the more efficient and effective use of the devices of international telecommunication. It assigns radio frequencies to members, attempts to maintain rates for telecommunication services at as low a rate as possible, and makes studies and formulates recommendations to all members on telecommunication subjects.

11. The World Meteorological Organization (WMO) grew out of the International Meteorological Organization that was founded in 1878. The WMO was formally established in 1951. The membership is made up of 58 states and 24 territories, a total of 82. Headquarters are in Geneva; regional offices are maintained in six areas of the world. The annual budget for 1954 was $363,000. Its purposes include co-ordinating and supervising the gahering and exchange of weather information and the application of the science of meteorology to all forms of human activity.

There remain two specialized agencies that have not yet come into formal existence, although draft conventions establishing them have been drawn up. These are the Inter-Govermental Maritime Consultative Organization IMCO) and the International Trade Organization (ITO). Each awaits the day when enough states ratify the respective conventions for it to go into operation.

The purposes of IMCO are clear from its name. ITO was provided for in 1948 at a meeting in Havana, where a Charter was drawn. The reduction of tariffs upon a world-wide scale, clearly implied by the Havana Charter, has aroused much resistance in many states and ratifications have been slow. In the meantime, an Interim Commission for ITO has been occupied mainly in securing the implementation of the General Agreement for Tariffs and Trade (GATT), which was entered into in 1947 and provides for bilateral negotiations between the signatories in the direction of tariff reductions.

SIGNIFICANCE OF THE INSTITUTIONS

What do all these institutions, organizations, and agencies mean with regard to the status of the international community? They represent a great accumulation of organized effort by individuals, groups, and governments upon the common social and economic problems of men. The large number of members of the various specialized agencies of the United Nations indicates accurately how widespread throughout the world is public interest in what we have termed the international community. The majority of the states of the world (excluding only the Soviet bloc and certain states racked by war or revolution) have demonstrated the insistence of their peoples that concrete action be taken in the direction of solving some of the continuing problems of individual life in a world grown more complex and insecure. The international community is not any longer the mere dream of amiable but impractical philosophers; it has grown to the level where it is a force powerful enough to bring about broad and binding action by governments.

WORLD POLITICS AND THE INTERNATIONAL COMMUNITY

THE STRUGGLE BETWEEN STATE AND COMMUNITY

In considering the implications for world politics of the existence of the international community and its progressive realization, we must first recognize the constant conflict that is inherent in the relations of the nation-state with the international community. To the extent that an individual adheres to the international community his nationalist identification is weakened. It is because this dichotomy is so clear in contemporary world affairs that the advance and the development of the international community is fought so bitterly by chauvinists in every state. There are some governments in the world whose national interest leads them to foster the growth of internationa' institutions of a community nature, but they are and promise to be for a long time in the minority.

Advantages of the State. In the struggle for individual loyalty that is going on between the state and the international community, it is self-evident that the state enjoys certain advantages. There are at least three reasons which help explain this situation.

In the first place, the state is universal in its appeal and comes before individuals at every turn in their lives. The international community, on the other hand, presents itself to most people only in terms of a single interest or a small group of them. Merely in terms of the number of appeals aimed at individuals, the state makes contact with its citizens many more times and upon many more issues than does the community. A case can, of course be made for the universality of the international community, but the great majority of men, if they are aware of the community at all, think of it in terms only of the one or two ways in which it impinges upon them directly.

A second appeal of the state is emotional. The state earns much of the loyalty of its citizens by using the symbols of nationalism and the formulas of ideology as tools. For most individuals the international community is defended upon rational grounds involving a logical and dispassionate judgment of the relative merits of the two systems. In a conflict for loyalty between emotional and rational appeals, the former enjoys most of the advantages. There are individuals whose attachment to the concept of the community is as emotional as is the sense of nationalist dedication of most other people, but thus far they constitute only a relative handful. So long as governments can evoke mass emotional reactions to the manipulation of nationalist stimuli, the rate of growth of the international community will continue to be slow.

In the third place, the state can command the obedience of its citizens in a way at present barred to the community: the reliance upon coercion. The state may compel agreement, or at least the absence of open dissent; the only adherents the community has are those who become so through voluntary action. Governments in many states have undertaken deliberate policies with the object of obstructing the growth of community institutions upon an international level and of destroying the sense of international community. The policy of the Iron Curtain states in this regard is particularly in point; the campaign against UNESCO by local governments and pressure groups in certain parts of the United States is another example.

Reasons for the Growth of the Community Sense. Why has the community sense continued to attract more and more supporters at the very same time that the intensity of international conflict has increased?

We have seen that increasing individual contact has broadened the comprehension of the outside world by individuals, and that co-operative action has been forced from states as a result. Perhaps the greatest single factor in the growth of the international-community sense, however has been the widespread revulsion of individuals against the perpetuation of a system that has brought two catastrophic wars in a generation and constantly threatens to produce a third.

From millions of men comes a plea for some new approach to international life, one that will free them from the awful uncertainty and insecurity that are the lot of everyone today. Men have placed themselves at the service of their states for generations; now, with the technology of mass destruction having become an exact science (or, as some students view it, a fine art), many of them are becoming unwilling to go on. In this attitude there is no element of either cowardice or disloyalty; the way of competition, crisis, and conflict, they seem to say, has brought only ruin and stalemate. Mankind is instead of seeking positive attack upon international problems incorporating agreement and good faith.

Since governments today require mass support from populations in order to achieve even minimal ends in world politics, statesmen have been obliged to pay grudging respect to this mass attitude. Even the Soviet leadership, whatever its ultimate intentions, has found it necessary constantly to reassure its own people that peace is its only objective. Popular rejection of traditional foreign-policy patterns as no longer being worth the trouble of dying for has not yet reached the state of anything like a mass movement, but it is significant enough to affect the thinking of political leaders and has materially influenced the conduct of world affairs.

10

Routes to World Order

$\mathbf{A}$LMOST from the maturing of the nation-state system into its present form, men have found the perpetual tensions and recurrent crises of international politics to be almost intolerable and have sought to escape from them. Schemes for organizing the states of the world in some more stable fashion have always been abundant, differing from one another in many details but all alike in attempting to restrain sovereign states from following their seemingly inescapable bent periodically to go to war upon one another.

As wars have increased in severity as a result of man's increased mastery of technology and its application to the task of killing his fellows, the urgency of the search for a device to free the world from this danger has increased. During the twentieth century, there have simultaneously taken place the most destructive wars of history and the most ambitious attempts to provide machinery to stabilize world relationships. The 'race between education and catastrophe' in which many people feel our age is engaged is growing in intensity.

With such grave issues at stake, the problems of world order move from the realm of philosophical speculation into the area of practical necessity. In Chapter 9 we discussed several of the institutions of the international community and saw that they are all aimed at the satisfaction of certain private interests of individuals. In this chapter we shall consider the actual and proposed methods of controlling the political relations of states.

Although the logic of interestate relations makes much the same demands upon governments as always and the same criteria of political success are applied to the pursuit of national interest by each state, a sensitive observer can detect a contrapuntal theme in the current international scene. Many men express their dismay at the prospect of an unending series of increasingly desructive wars. Up to the present, this implicit cleavage between governments and their people has not had major effect upon world politics.

By and large, however, the growth of private resistance to the familiar nationalist stimuli has served to introduce a perceptible restraint into the calculations of statesmen, and the course of international affairs today reveals that different value systems are gaining some acceptance. It is clear that the populations of certain states formerly extremely active in world affairs have decided that many of their traditional objectives are no longer worth the effort, and they are instead casting about for some new method of achieving their fundamental goals. Such formerly nationalistic states as France and Italy, for example, have led the way toward European unification, a movement that draws its strength from a broadly based popular movement throughout Western Europe.

With this widespread rejection of the traditional basis for world politics being an unmistakable fact, it is no wonder that the interest of statesmen and scholars alike centers as never before about the search for world order. During the past thirty-five years, two major international organizations embodying this desire have been created. The first succumbed to the nationalistic pressures of dictatorship during the 1930's and the second has not yet justified the hopes of its founders. Yet the demand for peace is voiced so clearly and so emphatically by millions of individuals that statesmen do not dare let lapse their attempts to discover a permanent basis for international stability and paece.

The common objective of all the many proposals for world order, whether actually institutionalized or yet merely blueprinted, is the elimination of the fundamental irresponsibility of states in their relations with one another. Independently of the semantic tyranny exercised by the word 'sovereignty,' what makes much of international politics unbearable for many people is that fact that states are ultimately accountable only to themselves. So long as no machinery exists to enforce the demand that they live in peace with each other, states need fear no automatic sanctions if they break out into open war. Accordingly the world exists in perpetual danger that one or more states will take the risk of destroying public order by initiating a war without concern either for other states or for the international community. A central authority to prescribe modes of conduct for international life and with power to enforce them seems to millions the only way in which individuals can be assured of the minimal peace and stability they so ardently crave.

The Methods of International Organization. There are two general approaches to the central problem of the creation of such an agency. One method retains the nation-state as the basic unit of political organization and attempts to set up machinery within which states may work co-operatively for a more rational world order. The other point of view assumes that as long as the nation-state exists, it is futile to think of peace; the dynamics of state life are such that the state institution will make inevitable the continuance of the disorder and crisis that have been the lot of man. It therefore rejects the nation-state and substitutes for it some variety of supra-national government into which the former states would fit as component parts.

The distinction between the two methods of attack is more apparent than real, however. Many of the proponents of world government accept international organization on the order of the United Nations as the first step in the direction in which they desire to move, while the defenders of the idea of state-based international organization tend to agree (although sometimes reluctantly) that its evolution will be toward the transfer of real sovereignty to the central agency. The two methods represent two stations along the same road, one somewhat farther along than the other. They differ from one another principally in the directness of their immediate attack upon national sovereignty.

THE LEAGUE OF NATIONS

As we have pointed out, international organization attempts to bring peace and order to world politics by engrafting upon the nation-state system a set of formalized institutions. This organizational framework is designed to serve two purposes.

First, it is intended to provide a framework within which world public opinion can be brought to bear upon issues, and a decision expressed that emanates from the consciences of individuals from all over the world. This 'world forum' is designed to make available a channel through which the will of the people—as apart from their official representatives and political leaders—can be expressed.

In the second place, the machinery of international organization is so constructed as to permit states that wish to co-operate for peaceful purposes to do so more easily and efficiently. Much of the perpetual crisis of international politics is due to the lack of an adequate institutional structure, forcing states to improvise techniques at a time when speedy action is vital to ward off disaster. The creation of machinery to be ready when needed enables states to concentrate directly upon the issue in hand.

The first serious attempt to create a general international organization that would serve these two purposes was made at the close of the First World War. This was the League of Nations, whose brief history was clouded by controversy, and even today judgment is far from unanimous in regard to its effectiveness or lack of it.

BACKGROUND AND HISTORY

Although popularly associated in the American mind with the name of President Woodrow Wilson, the League of Nations was the culmination of a series of movements within the principal Allied states during the war. Organizations, including both private persons and government officials, had campaigned for a permanent international body to enforce peace. During 1916 and 1917, as the prospects for an Allied victory became more encouraging, the tempo of preparations for the League intensified. In Great Britain, in France, and in the United States, government committees and influential private individuals were contributing their ideas to an evolving project which was to culminate in the Covenant of the League. By the time of the Armistice in 1918, President Wilson was the best-known advocate of the idea, but he was only the leader of an international movement of great size. It was Wilson himself who insisted that the Covenant be an integral part of the peace settlements in 1919; his victory was demonstrated by the fact that the Covenant became Part I of the Treaty of Versailles and all the other documents that made up the 'Peace of Paris,' which brought the war to an end.

The Period of Effectiveness. The history of the League is best told in phases. The first stage was the immediate postwar period, from 1919 to 1925. This era was marked by great controversy between the two principal members of the organization, France and Great Britain. The end of the war had released them from the common interest that had held them together, and their diverging policies found a convenient battle ground in the League. France viewed the organization as an instrument for the perpetuation of its supremacy over Germany, thus reflecting a continuing French concern with security; Britain, interested in securing a restoration of the balance of power and the limitation of the French hegemony in Europe, attempted to use the League for this purpose. Their constant quarrel in the League and over the prostrate body of Germany marked the early years of the organization's history. This period reached its culmination in the French occupation of the Ruhr in 1924.

The following year the international scene shifted its coloration quickly with the arrival of the 'era of Locarno.' Reconciliation replaced the hatreds of the war era, the pact of Locarno (1925) seemed to settle the troublesome issue of the German frontier in the west, and statesmen in Britain, France, and Germany sought to create a new atmosphere of cordiality and co-operation. Germany's entry into the League was a symbol of the liquidation of the old epoch and the entry into the new. From 1925 to 1930, the League was the world's political center of gravity. The world's leading statesmen congregated at Geneva, and decisions made there determined the course of world politics. World public opinion was phrased and articulated in the Assembly; great-power co-operation was a reality in the Council. It seemed as if President Wilson's dream was coming true and that the world had discovered the formula which would make peace in the world a permanent reality.

The Period of Decline. After 1930, however, the disruptive forces in world affairs took command and demolished this structure of co-operation. Two factors of almost equal importance contributed to the decline of the League in the 1930's: the first was the world-wide economic depression that began in 1929, and the second was the rise of fanatic nationalism. The will to co-operate disappeared and with it went any prospects for the League. Events underscoring this changed circumstance followed each other rapidly. In 1931 Japan committed aggression in Manchuria and withdrew from the League when opposition was voiced. In 1933 Hitler's Germany withdrew because France refused to grant arms equality. In 1935 Mussolini led his Fascist government of Italy out of the organization in a squabble over Italy's naked aggression in Ethiopia. About the same time public confidence in the League was further weakened by the failure of the democracies to resist Fascist aid to Franco in the Spanish Civil War. Even the admission into membership of the USSR in 1934 failed to galvanize the organization into action despite the fervent and apparently sincere efforts of the Soviet representative, Maxim Litvinov.

By 1935 the League was completely ineffective. The dictators had proved that no consequences would follow from outright defiance of the organization which had been supposed to be the embodiment of man's will to peace. The external machinery remained in existence after this date, the members wringing their hands over the all-too-obvious approach of World War II but being unwilling or unable to take the necessary action which alone could have staved off the coming disaster. Being located in neutral Switzerland, the League organization was able to retain a tenuous existence throughout the war; it voted itself out of existence in order to be absorbed into the United Nations after the fighting ended.

ORGANIZATION AND FUNCTIONS

Membership. At its peak membership, in 1935, the League had sixty members. Sixty-two states joined at one time or another, but two had withdrawn. During the preceding ten years four states had been admitted: Germany, the USSR, Mexico, and Turkey. Germany and Japan withdrew officially in 1935, Italy shortly thereafter, and the USSR was expelled in 1940. Of the twelve states generally recognized as sovereign which never assumed membership the United States was the most important. Thus it can be seen that the overwhelming majority of the sovereign political units of world politics between World Wars I and II at one time or another thought the League to be sufficiently important to merit membership.

Organization. The major organs of the League were the Council and the Assembly. The Assembly was the larger body, in which all members were entitled to representation and to one vote. It met regularly at least once a year and in special sessions. The Assembly was thought of as an advisory agency whose principal functions were the discussion of issues and the forming and articulating of world public opinion. Its area of competence was the entire scope of the Covenant.

The Council of the League was a smaller body. The great powers were given permanent membership in it; a number of other states were elected by the Assembly to non-permanent seats. The number of non-permanent seats was steadily increased from the original four (this gave the great powers a permanent majority) to a high of eleven at the end. The Council was thought of as the executive arm of the League, with the principal responsibility for the preservation or restoration of peace.

Certain other components of the League system enjoyed an importance of their own. The Secretariat of the League included experts in a great variety of technical fields whose duties were advisory and administrative. The chief permanent officer of the League was the Secretary-General, the administrative head of the Secretariat. This body of experts became something entirely new in world affairs: an international civil service whose responsibility was to the organization (and to the mass of humanity which it represented) instead of being confined to the peoples of a single state. The Secretariat set extremely high standards of loyalty and competence for any later group of similar nature to equal. Also parts of the pattern were the Permanent Court of International Justice (the World Court) and the International Labor Organization. These latter two were always included in the 'League system' but, as we have seen, each was actually a separate international organization in its own right.

Functions. The League was expected to function in two different ways in the achievement of its single primary objective: the preservation of world peace and the elimination of war. The first function involved taking action against short-term threats to the peace which might arise within the present structure of the nation-state system. This was thought to be the primary task of the Council, since it was more than anything else a problem of enforcement. Included in these short-run functions were three broad areas of action, in each of which the League was charged with a definite mission and in each of which some action was taken during the few years of the organization's life.

The first was the responsibility placed upon the League for the pacific settlement of disputes. As we saw in Chapter 8, many devices exist for this purpose and the League was empowered to employ them all. The record of accomplishment which it made, particularly before 1930, was not inconsiderable; several troublesome issues were removed from controversy by League intervention.

The second function, accomplished with much less success, was the creation of techniques of collective security. Several attempts were made to prescribe specific measures by which this elusive concept could become a reality within the League structure, including the Treaty of Mutual Assistance (1923), the Geneva Protocol (1924), and the General Act of 1928. None of these attained any success, although the General Act cleared the League machinery and was thrown open to accession by any state. By 1935 only about twenty states had joined, and these were insufficient both in number and in power to make a real collective security system. The most elaborate collective security measure of the interwar period was drawn up and signed outside the League; this was the Kellogg-Briand Pact (1928), which affirmed the 'renunciation of war as an instrument of national policy.'

The third area of short-run action was the reduction and limitation of armaments. The history of the League efforts at 'disarmament' is a long, confusing, and depressing tale into which there is no need to go at this time. It is sufficient to say that the governments of the member states, particularly the great powers, never became convinced that their national interest would permit any substantial over-all reduction in military preparedness, however willing any of them might be to have their opponents disarm.

The short-range functions of the League were coupled with several of longer purview. These are commonly termed the 'non-political' areas of action of the League, and it is true that they included most of the effort made in the interwar period looking to the satisfaction of the private demands of individuals. Yet this economic, social, and psychological program of the League had a distinct political connotation. Its target was the amelioration of the conditions of human existence which produce social problems that are themselves breeding grounds for war. As we have seen in earlier chapters and shall see later in this one, the same idea energizes the work of the Economic and Social Council of the United Nations. No more hopeful method of ultimately eliminating war from human society exists than that of co-operative programs to provide the rewards which societies otherwise seek to take by force.

This idea was only imperfectly understood by the drafters of the Covenant, and the League's organization for economic and social activity was incomplete and, to a considerable extent, extemporized. Commissions, committees, and other special bodies were created for particular purposes, and much of the effort of the Secretariat was spent in collecting and analyzing data in this area. Three principal organizations were established within the League structure to deal with particular areas: the Economic and Financial Organization, the Communications and Transit Organization, and the Health Organization. All of the autopsies which various authors have performed upon the defunct League of Nations agree that this area of League activity was the most successful, even though it was of insufficient scope to make any impression upon the political and security problems that crippled the organization. Its success in the League system and its hope for the future made its greater expansion and formalization in the United Nations system an inevitability.

REASONS FOR THE FAILURE OF THE LEAGUE

Membership and Motivation. Although the League included most of the states of the world at one time or another, the few absentees served to contribute materially to its collapse. The United States, Soviet Russia, and Germany were not original members. Germany was taken in in 1926; the Soviet Union joined in 1934, but by that time, the League was weakened by the withdrawal of Germany and Japan. The United States never accepted membership. Thus the League was always handicapped by an obvious lack of agreement among the very powers whose active co-operation was necessary to its success. Even among the great powers whose membership was uninterrupted there was a constant confusion of motivation. Great Britain repeatedly attempted to employ the League as an instrument of the balance of power. France concentrated upon Germany and sought to use the League to guarantee French security. Germany, on the other, attempted through the League to escape from the onus placed upon it by the Treaty of Versailles; the German people eventually chose the Nazi way of attaining this end.

There was also a constant operational difficulty inherent within the structure of the organization. The smaller states were then (as now) very vehement in their formulation of the ideal of international organization and wished through the League to gain protection against the depredations of any of the great powers. They soon became impatient at the pretensions of the major states to control of the League. They seized control of the Assembly, and amended the structure of the Council to give them a majority in that body. In this situation it was scarcely to be expected that the large states would give their enthusiastic and wholehearted support to an organization in which they were constantly faced by a hostile majority. Consequently, when crisis arrived and the League needed the armed support that only the great powers were in a position to offer, there was little or nothing forthcoming.

The Influence of Sovereignty. The Members of the League were quite clear and specific that they had not given up their sovereign independence when they entered upon their membership. Membership was voluntary and the right of withdrawal was guaranteed. This meant in practice that effective action by the organization was contingent upon an identity of interest among the members. If any individual state chose to defy the League (as several did) it had nothing to fear from the organization itself; only the members as individuals could move against the aggressor. Each of them decided whether or not to do so, not upon the basis of League action, but instead in terms of its own national interest.

So long as no serious and fundamental conflicts of interest developed the League survived and, as we have seen, during the period of coincidence of interest the League prospered. However, as soon as Japan, Italy, Germany, and the USSR (in the Finnish war of 1940–1) chose each in its turn to 'go it alone,' the key members proved unwilling to take the requisite action to stop them. Based upon a principle of voluntary co-operation—and none other could have preserved national sovereignty—the League was adequate for affirmative action arising from agreement. It was not designed to deal with a crisis involving its own membership.

The Failure of Public Opinion. Behind all the organizational faults of the Leagues lies a more fundamental factor in its failure. The League largely owed its creation to a popular revulsion against power politics and its resultant wars. The pressures of the postwar period—economic crisis, social disruption, the weakness of political democracy—undermined the commitment of millions of people to the ideal of a warless world epitomized by the League. Instead, various forms of intransigeant nationalism came to serve as the dominant force in world public opinion. This enabled political leaders, who for a while had been forced by public pressure to co-operate with each other almost against their will, again to calculate policy upon the familiar basis of the free-wheeling concept of unrestrained national interest. When peoples throughout the world once again believed that there existed objectives of foreign policy which were worth going to war over, the new approach to international relations symbolized by the League was no longer suitable.

This generalization is not fully applicable to the people and the government of many states (including perhaps the majority of the members of the League); the states that did return to their old ways, however, were the ones that possessed the power to plunge the world again into war. The experience of the League indicates that successful international organization requires a world public opinion that affirmatively supports it and demands of its leadership that the machinery be made to work effectively. The most scientifically constructed mechanism remains a mere framework without the active allegiance of the people.

LESSONS FOR THE FUTURE

The League collapsed ignominiously in the cauldron of World War II, and in the minds of most of mankind it represents one of man's complete failures. That it was a failure is undeniable; after all, if an organization designed to preserve the peace is wiped out by a global war involving its members, we can scarcely assert that the organization was a success. Its brief period of existence did contain promise of eventual good, however, and provided several lessons for future generations. It afforded many people proof that the basic idea of international organization had vitality and validity. This point was made in three distinct ways.

New Techniques. In the first place, the League experience demonstrated beyond doubt that an international organization is a far more effective instrument for implementing a 'will to peace' and co-operation than any other known basis for international relations. During the brief period of reconciliation that followed the pact of Locarno, when the major states discovered a community of interest upon which to ground a common policy, the success of the League was remarkable. New techniques of international relations which proved their inherent worth in a co-operative situation at this time included permanent conference diplomacy, the formulation of an articulate world public opinion, institutionalized procedures, and a permanent civil service of experts. The fact that this period was so brief served to emphasize the point that these procedures and the League itself could not direct the course of world affairs; being merely tools and machinery, they were given content and direction by the hands that used them.

Non-political Work. In the aftermath of the demise of the organization it was discovered that the non-political activity could have been and should have been expanded. The international co-operative attack upon the personal problems of men—the program of the international community—proved during the League era to be extremely productive. Once the barrier of national interest was crossed and attention focused upon the intimate concerns of individuals, it was discovered that joint action was both easy and profitable. The sporadic and unco-ordinated efforts of the League in this area provided in the aggregate a sizable area of agreement among all the membership and served as a base for an expanded program after World War II under United Nations auspices.

Operational Techniques. The League also provided the opportunity for many states and their leaders to learn the techniques of international organization. It is no simple matter to conduct even routine business in an organization composed of fifty-odd sovereign states of differing languages and cultures, and the consideration of questions of great importance often bogged down in the maze of operational difficulties. A great number of new procedures had to be first extemporized, then improved upon, and finally perfected and stabilized. The twenty-year history of the League provided a vast fund of experience which proved invaluable in the establishment and operation of the United Nations. The League also furnished the inspiration and example of an international civil service in the Secretariat. This group of technically trained experts whose primary loyalty was to the organization provided the international point of view in contrast to the more narrow nationalist orientation brought to the organization by the representatives of states. This idea was transferred bodily to the United Nations.

THE UNITED NATIONS

As World War II was drawing to a close, there was no doubt in the minds of the leaders of the principal Allied nations that some new venture in international co-operation was going to be undertaken to replace the League of Nations. The heritage of the League itself was, as has been pointed out, not inconsiderable; furthermore, such good results had been attained during the war by permanent political consultation at a high level that the perpetuation of this practice was felt to be indispensable to a permanent peace. The wartime United Nations Organization—the fighting alliance—served as the organizational base upon which was erected the postwar United Nations. It is an eloquent tribute to the force of the idea of international organization that even the failure and discrediting of the League did not dampen popular ardor for a renewal of the system.

Creation. The United Nations formally came into existence on 24 October

1945. The Charter itself had been completed and signed several months earlier at San Francisco. Representatives of fifty governments approved the document at that time.

This action was a culmination of years of work by many people which made possible the calling of the United Nations Conference on International Organization (UNCIO), at which the final form of the Charter was determined. The preparatory steps were innumerable, both within the various member states of the military alliance and at the international level. The progress toward the realization of the idea of the United Nations was perhaps epitomized by the several great international conferences during the war, at each one of which some new point was announced which brought the emerging organization one step nearer completion.

The initial moment at which it could definitely be said that a commitment in favor of a postwar international organization had been made was the Moscow Conference of foreign ministers, in the autumn of 1943. Here the United States, Great Britain, the Soviet Union, and China agreed to the principle of the establishment of a general international organization 'at the earliest practicable date.' This was almost immediately reinforced by the statement that was issued following the Teheran Conference of Roosevelt, Churchill, and Stalin, in which the 'Big Three' promised that they personally would initiate action to such purpose. In July 1944, the Bretton Woods Conference for postwar economic and financial stability drew up agreements establishing the World Bank and the World Monetary Fund. That autumn there convened the most important preliminary step prior to UNCIO itself, the Dumbarton Oaks Conference. Here China, Great Britain, the USSR, and the United States drew up a draft proposal for the structure of the organization which served as the basis for action at San Francisco. At the Yalta Conference, in February 1945, Roosevelt, Churchill, and Stalin agreed upon a voting formula in the Security Council (the famous 'veto') and formally called UNCIO to convene in San Francisco on 25 April 1945.

The San Francisco Conference operated primarily upon the basis of the Dumbarton Oaks proposals. This document was subject to several fundamental amendments and considerable elaboration. The greatest departure from the original draft was in the significant expansion the conference made in the economic and social activities of the organization, including the Trusteeship Council and the specifying of the functions of the Economic and Social Council. It was clear that the familiar quarrel between the great powers and the small states was going to be renewed in the new organization; at San Francisco many attempts were made to weaken the privileged role that the major states had taken upon themselves. Most of these were unsuccessful and the final form of the Charter was in general conformity to the ideas of the 'Big Four,' who had carried the bulk of the load of the war.

THE STRUCTURE OF THE UNITED NATIONS

In its structure, the United Nations is really the League of Nations with many imperfections corrected and many gaps filled in. According to the Charter itself, the United Nations has six 'principal organs,' each of which is assigned a definite role and bears a specific relation to all the others.

The General Assembly. The General Assembly is, like the Assembly of the League which preceded it, the one organ in which all members are represented. Each state has one vote and up to five representatives. Its primary function, within the original intent of the Charter, is to serve as the sounding board for world public opinion and to supervise the economic and social work of the organization. It is not given any power to take action upon substantive matters as is the Security Council; it operates by means of recommendations and advice to national states and to the Security Council. In one sense, its role is more sharply circumscribed than was that of the League Assembly. It is debarred from considering any question already before the Security Council as long as the latter chooses to keep the matter on its agenda. This was admittedly an attempt on the part of the large states holding permanent seats on the Security Council to prevent the Assembly (in which the small states would clearly be dominant) from forcing the hand of the great powers.

As matters have worked out, however, the General Assembly has not been kept in such a subordinate role. The hamstringing of the Security Council by the great-power dispute between the East and the West has made the General Assembly the center of the United Nations system. What makes this peculiarly significant is the voting formula in the Assembly, which includes a clear break in the historic rule of unanimity. On 'important' questions a two-thirds majority of all those present and voting is sufficient, while on all others a simple majority is adequate. In this way a real rupture was made in the principle of 'sovereign equality' upon which the Charter claims the organization is based. A state that votes 'no' on a question may be outvoted and thus be bound against its will.

The Security Council. The Security Council is charged with 'primary responsibility' for the maintenance of international peace and security and was originally thought of as the only organ of the United Nations which would be powerful enough to take affirmative action in this direction. It consists of eleven members and is in continuous session. Five states hold permanent membership on the Council: Great Britain, France, the USSR, the United States, and China; the remaining six are elected by the General Assembly for two-year terms. The Security Council has authority over all international disputes which may be referred to it, and it may take action in any 'threat to the peace, breach of the peace, or act of aggression.' It is empowered to impose a variety of methods of pacific settlement upon disputing states; in the event of defiance by an aggressor it may impose punitive sanctions, including the employment of such armed forces as the members are pledged to provide. The Council also has authority to initiate action looking toward the reduction and limitation of armaments.

The 'veto' exists only in the Security Council. It appears as part of the Charter provision which stipulates voting procedure in that body. Decisions in the Security Council on procedural matters require affirmative votes of seven members; decisions on 'all other matters' require affirmative votes of seven members 'including the concurring votes of the permanent members.' This process is complicated by the method of deciding whether a question is or is not procedural. This question has been held to be non-procedural in itself, thus permitting a permanent member the right to veto the question of whether or not the veto is to be applicable. The veto is thus actually a provision requiring great-power unanimity upon matters of substance. No other provision of the Charter has been more widely discussed.

The Economic and Social Council. The Economic and Social Council can best be thought of as a standing committee of the General Assembly which is primarily responsible for the execution of the parent body's mission in this field. It consists of eighteen states elected by the General Assembly for three years. It supervises most of the geographic and functional commissions of the United Nations. It functions through consultation, co-ordination, and recommendation. It has a general liaison with the specialized agencies, discussed in Chapter 9.

The Trusteeship Council. The Trusteeship Council has a general grant of power over non-self-governing territories and especially over the United Nations 'trusteeships' scattered throughout the world. These trusteeships are of three types: those taken over from the League mandate system, territories taken from the Axis powers as a result of World War II, and other non-self-governing territories voluntarily placed under the system. The role of the Trusteeship Council in exercising its responsibility is detailed in Chapter 11. Membership on the Trusteeship Council is granted to three categories of states: members administering trust territories, permanent members of the Security Council who do not administer trust territories, and sufficient other states elected by the General Assembly to make a balance between trustee states and non-trustee states.

The International Court of Justice. The fifth of the 'principal organs' of the United Nations is the International Court of Justice. This body, the direct descendant of the Permannt Court of International Justice, is an integral part of the United Nations and its Statute is included as part of the Charter. The organization and functions of the Court are discussed in Chapter 8.

The Secretariat. The Secretariat is named after the similar group which provided continuity for the League. The Secretary-General is the head of the Secretariat and is the chief administrator for the entire organization. He is empowered to take certain initiatory action in bringing before the Security Council matters that might threaten international peace and security. He is assisted by a staff drawn from all the members of the United Nations, whose function is to provide technical, administrative, and clerical assistance to the remainder of the organization.

IMPROVEMENTS ON THE LEAGUE

Membership. As the statesmen of the world, spurred on by public opinion, approached the creation of the United Nations, they were determined to correct some of the more glaring shortcomings of the League of Nations. A first improvement over the League was a more inclusive membership. Thanks to wartime unity, there were no significant absentees from the organization. All of the states which, at the end of the war, possessed any appreciable amount of power were included among the original members; only the defeated Axis and certain minor states were excluded.

The United States and the Soviet Union, the two dominant states, had been the prime movers in the drafting of the Charter, and an implicit understanding was reached that as each of the defeated former enemies could qualify, it would also be accepted into membership. Universality of membership was the goal at which the framers were aiming.

The Security Council and the Veto. The struggle between Council and Assembly, between large states and small, was minimized. As we have seen, the Security Council was given a monopoly of authority over crises and all disputes that menaced the peace. Since the Charter provides clearly for United Nations military action to punish aggression, and since the major powers would obviously be required to furnish the bulk of any such armed forces, the 'veto' was written into the Chapter. It is true that the veto has served for Americans as the principle symbol of the frustration to which the United Nations has subjected them, and much opposition has been voiced to the whole idea.

Two comments on the veto might be made at this point. In the first place, under the League rule of complete unanimity before any action could be taken, every state had a veto. The number is now reduced to five; this is at least a step in the right direction. In the second place, without the veto there would have been no United Nations at all. The record of UNCIO shows clearly that the point was sufficiently important to the USSR (and to the United States as well) that no agreement was possible and no organization would have been created had not the privileged position of the great powers been recognized in this way.

The Security Council was thus safely in the hands of the permanent members, who bore primary responsibility for enforcing the peace. On the other hand, the new 'forum'—the General Assembly—was given the power to reach conclusions and to make recommendations by far less than unanimity, and there is no veto in the General Assembly. This, it was hoped, would make the larger body even more responsive to currents of world opinion than its predecessor had been.

Other Improvements. Many other technical improvements over the League can be found in the Charter. One is the creation of the Economic and Social Council, with the special mission of co-ordinating all the non-political activity of the United Nations. Another is the inclusion of the International Court of Justice within the organization, thus making all United Nations members *ipso facto* adherents to the Statute of the Court.

THE PLACE OF THE UNITED NATIONS IN WORLD POLITICS TODAY

Where does the United Nations stand today? Feelings run high when an answer to this question is attempted, and no general summary is possible that would satisfy everyone. One proposition, however, is virtually self-evident. The United Nations has once again demonstrated that international organization, in and of itself, is no panacea for the ills of the world. The present organization remains merely a framework within which states may co-operate more effectively. If the will to do so is not present, the framework is useless because it is unused.

The cold war has paralyzed much of the activity of the United Nations but the fault, if fault there be, rests with the foreign policies of the states themselves. So long as the essential quality of the nation-state system is preserved (Article 2, paragraph 1 of the Charter says: 'The Organization is based on the principle of the sovereign equality of all its Members') the determining factor of international politics will continue to be the sovereign will of the nation-state.

Popular Support. In attempting to strike a balance upon the role of the United Nations in world politics today, a valid starting point is the question of popular support. Despite its inability to revolutionize international relations and the occasional frustrations which result, the United Nations has taken a remarkable grip upon the hopes and the outlook of the great masses of people all over the world. This is particularly true among the smaller states, many of which are recently removed from colonial or dependent status. The result of the trust that so many people place in the United Nations has been the creation of a tremendous moral force rooted in mass opinion, which statesmen must perforce recognize. Even the Soviet Union is actually very much aware of the prestige that accrues to the United Nations and is vehement in its public professions of support, regardless of what its record of action may indicate.

Though the voices of those who have lost faith (or who never really had any) may be shrill, much of mankind sees in the United Nations the symbol of what it wants the world of the future to be. This is of profound significance today. At a time when so much stress is being placed upon the dramatic devices of power politics and when international relations are conducted in an atmosphere of constant tension, there is a perceptible resistance by millions of people to the divisive pull of hysterical nationalism and a tendency to look toward the goal of a world without war. It would be stupid to assert flatly that the verdict of man today is in favor of co-operation and that war is obsolete. But it would be equally fatuous to pretend that a global will to peace does not exist or to presume that the impact of world opinion upon international politics is of no effect and that the historic ponderables—interest, policy, and power—have remained unmodified. In Chapter 9 we examined the institutions of the international community and saw how they are geared into the United Nations machinery. Power politics of the future can be expected to recognize the United Nations and its impact upon world opinion.

Successes of the United Nations. What has the organization done to merit this mass support? Perhaps its greatest victory is that, like the Abbe Siéyès in the French Revolution, it has survived. Its continued existence proves that it fills a real need. All during the period of relative international stalemate that followed the end of the war in 1945, the organizational machinery has kept working and in the process the members have gained a great deal of facility in its operation. The improvement in the climate of world affairs, noted by many observers following the 'summit' conference at Geneva in July 1955, raised hopes that the long-sought policy reconciliation between the two major adversaries in world politics was now a possibility. If it were to come about, the United Nations would become a truly effective instrument for world co-operation.

It will be remembered that the League passed through a similar period of futility only to emerge after Locarno as the most powerful force in world politics, once the policy differences between its principal members were reconciled. Procedures in the United Nations have already become standardized, the Secretariat has been assembled and trained, the outlines of the continuing tasks of the organization have been clearly delineated, and much preparatory technical and administrative data on them are already assembled. The survival of the United Nations through darkest days of cold war augurs well for its future.

But the organization also has a short but significant record of successes. As part of its duty to keep the peace, it has intervened in several international quarrels. Three of these we analyzed in Chapter 8: the Indonesian dispute, the Greek dispute, and the issue of Palestine. Other controversies in which United Nations intervention was prompt and in which such action made major contributions toward the eventual pacific settlement include the Soviet-Iranian quarrel in 1946, the Kashmir dispute between India and

Pakistan, which began in 1948, the Berlin issue in 1948, which we discussed in Chapter 7, and roughly a dozen of lesser significance.

Many people have voiced the criticism that in these disputes the United Nations has been unable to produce definitive solutions and has therefore failed in its mission, but such attacks betray ignorance of the theory and functions of the organization. It was never intended that the United Nations would either solve or eliminate all interstate conflicts; only a world government would have the power to do that, and it is clear that the United Nations is not a world government. The single object of the organization is to insure that such disputes as may arise will be settled without endangering world peace. In these limited terms its success in the disputes mentioned has been beyond question.

Also to the credit of the organization should be placed a number of less visible entries. These are the international quarrels that have not gone to the point of endangering international peace and security because the disputants realized that any such action would bring the United Nations into the picture. We have no way of knowing how many such there are, but that the intense controversy of the postwar world has produced many we can be sure.

In many ways this effect of the United Nations is its greatest success. If it can, by its existence alone, serve to deflect the course of international conflict into peaceful channels, no greater level of attainment can be asked of it.

The Korean Intervention. Of course, the most courageous step taken in the name of the United Nations up to the present time was the intervention into the Korean war. Although the confusion of motives among the membership was apparent at the time the action was taken, there is no escaping the central fact that for the first time in history the members of an international organization supported an abstract principle with arms and men.

It is true that the action was taken in the absence of the Soviet Union and that the full co-operation assumed by the organization was not present; following the USSR's return to the Security Council further action there proved to be impossible. The 'Uniting for Peace' resolutions of 1950, however, provided that if the Security Council was unable to reach a decision on a security question because of a veto or for any other reason, the General Assembly was authorized to assume jurisdiction over the question. Accordingly, further steps in the prosecution of the war and, ofter the truce of July 1953, the preparation for the post-hostilities political conference were undertaken by the General Assembly.

Despite the intrusion of narrow formulations of national interest into a question of collective security, the Korean issue carries one clear moral. The great majority of the population of the world, speaking through their representatives, registered their decision that aggression by violence should not go unresisted regardless of the cost and the danger. As we have seen it, it was a lack of this willingness to hazard the unpredictable in the pursuit of an ideal which really brought about the decay and collapse of the League.

It is obvious today that many of the states that intervened in Korea did so simply in the service of their national interest and remained unconcerned about whether or not a principle was involved. Indeed, President Truman asserted that this was so in the case of the United States. It is nevertheless clear that many states have greatly broadened their idea of national interest to comprehend the idea that everyone's best interest is served by peaceful change. It will be easier to do the same thing another time, but the likelihood of having to do it again is reduced, The more the members of the United Nations are willing to fight to keep the peace, the less danger there is of their having to do so.

Failures of the United Nations. The United Nations has failed to live up to the expectations of many of its supporters. One major failure may be fairly charged to the organization, as well as several lesser ones that derive from it.

The central inadequacy demonstrated by the United Nations since its inception has been its inability to cope with the cold war. The near-total refusal made by the United States and the USSR to any proposals involving cooperative action within the organization's scope has paralyzed action in the direction of collective security and world peace, and has seriously inhibited programs in all other fields.

Americans particularly are inclined to contend that the lack of success of the United Nations in dealing with Soviet obstructionism is a proof that the organization is a failure; we point to the success of the Soviet in applying the veto to proposals aimed at halting communism and many of us claim that the inability of the United Nations to serve as an instrument of American policy vitiates the usefulness of the entire organization.

Regardless of the merit of the American case, it is clear that no international organization of which the Soviet Union (or, for that matter, any major power) is a member can be turned into an instrument against it. The framers of the Charter were realists; they realized that unless great-power co-operation for peace was a reality, there was no use creating any organization to embody such an idea. Therefore, it is a real criticism of the United Nations to point out that it has been unable to end the cold war with a victory for the United States, but it is not a just one. The organization was not built for any such purpose and to expect it to do so is unwarranted.

Just as the problem of the solution of the cold war must be returned to the states involved, so may most of the other shortcomings of the United Nations. The 'spirit' of the organization has not come up to the hopes of its framers. States still tend to consider the United Nations just another vehicle of policy, to be used when appropriate, to be defied when necessary, and to be ignored when other techniques are more expedient. The success of the United Nations idea necessitates that it be the center around which all other areas of international life range themselves. It has not been such a center; many of the most important problems of the postwar era have been worked out without ever being brought before either the Security Council or the General Assembly.

Some states continue to make their policy choices upon grounds of unilaterally determined national interest. Some states have been more interested than others in the support of the ideal; generally these have been the smaller states who stand to gain more if the United Nations should become a real instrument of government.

A further indication of the low esteem which many 'practical' statesmen place upon the organization is its limited budget. A frequently applied comparison is enlightening: the budget of the United Nations, for all purposes, is smaller than the appropriation made by the city of New York for cleaning its streets. This niggardliness has been most blighting in its effect upon the economic and social program of the organization. Projects involving the rehabilitation and development of the underdeveloped peoples of the world (to take just one example) require large amounts of funds. No member states have been willing to make investments in the future of world peace and security in a sufficiently generous manner to accomplish really significant results.

The Abolition of the Veto. Suggestions abound for improvements in United Nations procedure. The most common proposal deals with the abolition of the veto. This idea, most prevalent in the United States, springs from the fact that the Soviet Union has made vigorous use of it on the Security Council. Unanimity among the permanent members being lacking, action becomes impossible. Of course, the United States and the other permanent members of the Security Council have also employed the veto, but all except France have avoided the necessity of being the only one in the negative. France unilaterally cast a negative vote on one occasion. In any case, the Soviet policy has had the effect of limiting the jurisdiction of the Security Council to those questions which the USSR has felt involved no danger to itself.

Schemes to abolish the veto invoke the principle of majority rule and envisage the happy state of the organization when the USSR would no longer be able to prevent action by the majority—particularly when that majority is led by the United States. Such arguments tend to overlook both legal technicalities and the realities of world politics. Charter amendment is possible, but no amendment is effective unless it is approved by all permanent members of the Security Council. In other words, the Soviet Union has a veto on the question of the abolition of the veto. The USSR would approve such an amendment only if and when it felt it no longer needed the protection of the veto. This could come about only when it had a solid majority of the membership of the United Nations on its side. In such a pass it would be doubtful if the United States itself would be so eager for a veto-less United Nations. Indeed, it was fear of such a development that prompted United States insistence upon the veto in the first place.

The Expulsion of the USSR. Some more extreme suggestions are occasionally heard urging Soviet expulsion from the organization. This again offers both legal and practical difficulties. A state may be expelled from the organization only for failing to fulfill its obligations under the Charter, and it would require a most strained interpretation of that document to make out a case against the USSR that would stand up. Certainly the majority of the membership today does not feel that Soviet policy warrants so drastic a step.

Even if it were feasible to force the Soviet Union to withdraw, such action would convert the United Nations into an American-dominated alliance aimed at the USSR. This would be satisfactory to a particular version of American national interest and would be gratifying to a vociferous segment of American public opinion, but its impact upon the world role of the United States would be unfortunate. Such an action would scarcely be reassuring to the states and populations who look to the United Nations as pointing the way to peace and would seriously compromise American claims to world leadership. Many non-communist states would be most uneasy as members of the United Nations if the Soviet Union were not also a member.

One effect of these more radical proposals for 'reform' has been to deprive the United States of much of its grounds for claiming moral leadership in the organization. The principal gainer has been India, whose government has discovered that emphatic and consistent support of the peaceful implications of the United Nations system not only serves Indian national interest but has proved to be very good world politics as well.

Summary. Within the inherent limitations of an organization of sovereign states the United Nations has justified its existence and the more realistic hopes of its framers and early supporters. It has proved to be powerless either to halt the cold war or to force a decision in it, but in theory and in operation it was not intended to deal with such a far-reaching controversy between two of its key members. When the 'agreement to disagree' of the two great camps has not been operative, the United Nations has proved to be an effective instrument for settling disputes. Its attack upon the long-range causes of war, epitomized in the Economic and Social Council, has not been under way long enough to provide sufficient information upon which to base a reasoned verdict, but there are some grounds for cautious optimism. Although there has been some disillusionment, the bulk of mankind still looks to the United Nations to provide leadership in the search for a new basis for world politics and a liberation from the stress of constant tension.

World Government

Two major subgroups can be distinguished within the general classification of proposals for world government. They are in agreement that the sovereign nation-state must be scrapped as the basic unit of world society, but they differ from one another in their prescription for arriving at a new order. One school of thought argues that such a single-headed world government can be established only by conquest and the attainment of hegemony over the whole world by a single state; the other contends rather that by democratic action and a system of federation man can establish a peaceful world order under law.

The Hegemony School

Basic Point of View. The believers in hegemony approach the problem of world organization equipped with a keen sense of history and a pessimistic opinion of the capabilities of the human species for rational action. Historically, they argue that during those periods when mankind enjoyed the closest approximation to universal peace, the world was ruled by a single strong power. Sometimes the single state was a universal empire, as was Rome; sometimes the relationship of ruler and ruled was just as real although less formal, as in the case of the *Pax Brittanica* of the nineteenth century.

They point to the diminution in the number of great powers today as proof of their thesis that another period of such peace and order is in the offing, lacking only the final great struggle for supremacy and the emergence of a single ruling state to bring it into existence. They reject the claims to independent policy by the minor members of the two great present-day alliances as well as denying that any state can remain neutral in such a struggle.

They feel that man is incapable of exercising the systematic self-denial necessary to create the rule of law in the world, asserting instead that he will abide by the moral code only when driven to it by superior force. Thus they contend that by preaching the doctrine of conquest they are seeking only the best interest of individual men; by establishing peace based upon subjugation they are attempting to save man from himself.

As might be expected, the idea of world government through hegemony is most popular with the states that consider themselves eminently qualified for the task of world rule. This has made the idea quite acceptable with one after another of the great powers of recent times. Hitler, Mussolini, and the Black Dragon Society in Japan all predicted a future in which all mankind would live in happy unity under their benign rule. Today on both sides of the Iron Curtain are found advocates of the idea, who, it is needless to say, are quite sincere in their feeling that peace is possible only under the world domination of one state. Their only major disagreement is which state they would select as the ruler.

Soviet Hegemony. The Soviet dream of world organization envisages a world freed from the 'blight' of capitalism and therefore united into one socialist brotherhood. The form of government adopted everywhere would be that of the 'people's democracy,' a political system with which the Western world has already gained a certain familiarity. The leaders of these governments would be in turn co-ordinated by a central directorate of the Communist party, dominated, of course, from Moscow. No opposition would exist anywhere to the accomplishment of Russian objectives. War would be unknown, since it is a capitalist invention; poverty, disease, and ignorance would be abolished; happiness and plenty would be the lot of man.

With this idyllic picture one hesitates to quarrel, yet it appears that the attainment of such bliss would be possible only at the end of a long series of revolutions and wars of conquest. Whether the peoples of the world, who are interested in peace now, would subscribe to this program with much enthusiasm is a proposition that is at best debatable.

American Hegemony. American proponents of the idea present much the same plan but from the point of view of the United States. Contending that this is 'the American century,' and anachronistically contemplating the 'civilizing mission' of the United States, they call for a great effort by our people to save the human race from the clutches of communist propaganda and the consequences of its own slothfulness and decay. Instead of the world-wide exportation of Soviet ideology, American thinkers conceive of a world made happy by universal acceptance of American economic and scientific organization, social values, cultural apparatus, political system, and military leadership. Once given the benefits of these enlightening forces, the rest of humanity would be free of the causes of their troubles and the sources of international tension.

Objections to the Doctrine of Hegemony. These visions are extremely flattering to the hypertense nationalism of the state proposing them, but it is difficult to take them seriously. One would hardly expect the peoples ruled by the dominating power cheerfully to accept their permanent role of inferiors. Accompanying any proposal for hegemony is always an elaborate defense justifying the particular state's claim to rule upon a variety of grounds, including superiority of culture, intelligence, virility, or virtue. To the 'lesser' peoples whose destiny it is to be ruled by the all-powerful state, accepting any such argument necessitates their agreement with an unfavorable verdict upon their own culture and capacity for self-rule. Understandably, most societies are reluctant on this score.

Under the present conditions of world politics, the attempt to realize world power would involve the state concerned in a desperate struggle with all the peoples whose liberty it was seeking to extinguish. Its claims that it was acting in good faith and with a primary interest in the welfare of individuals everywhere would be greeted by derision and resistance.

Critics of the 'peace through hegemony' school also point out how fatally easy it is for a powerful state to rationalize a policy of aggrandizement and aggression under the lofty pretensions of bringing order and civilization to the world. It is historically true that the universal empires of the past were brought into existence by armed conquest, but these structures were generally built upon populations who did not have the highly developed sense of nationalism which characterizes contemporary political life.

Finally, it is at least questionable whether a world hegemony by force, assuming it could be attained, would prove possible to maintain. So concerned would the ruling power be to put down any threats to its dominion that it would be obliged to use the most repressive measures of control of its subject populations. This would indeed be a far cry from the new dawn of peace, freedom, and security made so much of by propogandists for the idea.

THE FEDERATION SCHOOL

At the opposite pole from the theory of hegemony is the proposal to form a supra-national world government by the free act of peoples and their governments. This theory has a long history, but it has gained the most adherents and the greatest momentum in the period since World War II. Concern with the probable consequences of any future war and with what they feel to be the blindness of contemporary political leadership has bought many people in the Western world to the conclusion that the nation-state is obsolete. They argue that technology and social organization have progressed to the point where national states and their programs of action are increasingly dangerous to modern man as well as being inefficient in the solution of his problems.

Although varying in degree, all proposals put forth by people who share this belief involve a transfer of sufficient increments of national sovereignty to a new international agency to create a real world government with power to enforce its commands. This idea carries several steps farther the concept of international organization, which, as we have seen, is based upon the voluntary co-operation of sovereign states. World government of this type necessitates a loss of independence in international affairs by states who are members, and it can therefore come about only when public sentiment has progressed to the point of being willing to make the emotional sacrifice attendant upon any such transfer of loyalty.

The Essentials of Federalism. The various proposals have certain features in common. They all visualize a world government organized upon a democratic basis, with real executive and legislative authority. The government would be empowered to make law within certain prescribed grants of competence and would have power to enforce its decisions upon individuals and states. Among the subjects upon which law could be made would be the whole question of interstate relations and the disputes arising therefrom. War would be flatly prohibited, the conduct of interstate intercourse subject to fixed rules, and violators liable to swift punishment. Generally the federal government would also be granted auxiliary powers necessary to the performance of its primary mission.

Minimal Federation. This far all proposals for federation are in substantial agreement. As more details are filled in by the various groups, however, major divergencies appear and at least two distinct points of view are apparent. One, here termed the minimal, looks upon world government almost as a necessary evil, and projects its proposals upon the basis of granting the new authority only the minimum power adequate to the performance of its function of keeping the peace: most commonly this includes the maintenance of armed forces and the financial powers necessary to sustain them. This approach accepts cultural diversity as the normal lot of man and indeed sees much positive good in the nation-state as the embodiment of political community. The grouping of men into units to which they owe primary allegiance is preserved; states are urged to preserve maximum autonomy over local affairs. The major purpose of the organization is the negative one of preventing the state system from destroying itself by war. This is the general attitude of such groups as the United World Federalists in the United States.

Another form of minimal federalism accepts the preservation of the maximum of state autonomy as desirable and makes the prevention of war the major objective of any world government, but recognizes in addition that it would be advantageous for the central authority to act also in certain affirmative ways to the mutual benefit of all members. Included in this area of added power would be such economic functions as a world currency, world free trade, and world control over the distribution of raw materials; such social powers as the provision of a single world bill of rights and the elevation of educational standards; such cultural operations as the removal or lowering of linguistic barriers.

The individuals who advocate that such authority be delegated to a world government are acutely sensitive to the example of the United States in the eighteenth century. The Constitution of the United States was drafted essentially to serve the negative purpose of taking power away from the states because they were misusing it. The United States is bound together into a single nation today, however, because the Constitution also contained affirmative provisions which have served as the vehicle for effective action in the common interest. The national government of the United States performs functions which the states could not individually or severally undertake.

The federalists today do not shrink from the prospect that a world government of limited power might ultimately become the political center of gravity of the world; they argue merely that such a development will come about only when the people of the world demand it. In the meantime the new authority would have power to cope with immediate threats to world peace and would add to its effective role only as circumstances dictated and public opinion permitted. Whether purely negative or somewhat more positive in orientation, the first group of federalists is distinguished by its desire to retain the practical maximum of state autonomy and cultural diversity.

Maximal Federation. The other approach to world government may be termed maximalism or cosmopolitanism. A sizable group of dedicated, scholarly people in the United States and Europe, adopting as their own the classic Stoic concept of the brotherhood of man and the commonwealth of the rational, seeks to destroy all boundaries that divide men into hostile groups, be they economic, political, or cultural. In their view any temporizing with the present state system is self-defeating, and they urge vigorously the rapid transition of society into a single world community under a single government. They amass considerable evidence to prove that the factors dividing men are insignificant compared to their common humanity. They contend that no insurmountable obstacles exist to the accomplishment of their proposals in the relatively near future.

This group attacks the problems of world government with a very simple formula. Technology and modern development of transportation and communication, they say, have destroyed the validity of the nation-state and of national boundaries as marking the natural divisions of social groups. Instead, it is technologically possible to govern the entire world from a single seat of power. They therefore propose that men abandon the wasteful and dangerous institution of the nation-state and proceed directly to the creation of such a single world government. Nation-states would ultimately disappear, although they might for a time be retained for convenience in administration. With the abolition of interstate barriers, the whole paraphernalia of international relations, including the institution of war, would become obsolete. Man would be happier, freer, and more secure.

The proponents of this idea, recognizing that existing state governments would oppose it, propose to take direct action upon a mass base of popular demand, ignoring all existing political arrangements. The periodic manifestos that call for a 'world constitutional convention' are part of the techniques necessary for the creation of such a mass movement.

Criticisms of Cosmopolitanism. One cannot help but admire the grandeur of the vision of the plan of world cosmopolitanism and the weight of sound historical, anthropological, and psychological evidence that is adduced in its favor. Scientific studies demonstrate that men are basically alike and that cultural differences and nationalist hatreds are learned rather than instinctive. This approach is not the vapid dream of impractical idealists. It is backed by some of the most reputable scientific arguments man can muster. Yet to condemn national states and nationalist sentiments as irrational does not eliminate them from existence. Men are obstinately wedded to their prejudices; it will require more than mere exhortation to persuade them to abandon the ways of their fathers and to strike out in a drastically different direction.

The major hostile criticism of the cosmopolitan approach is aimed at its insistence that immediate far-reaching action is necessary. It is at least possible to conceive of man's becoming a citizen of the world by the gradual process of progressively broadening his horizons. One might suspect that such a pattern of growth might result in a more tenacious adherence to his new-found loyalty than would a sudden act of will. Deathbed conversions often result in backsliding when the patient unexpectedly recovers.

APPROACHES TO THE ACHIEVEMENT OF FEDERATION

Immediate Action. Mention of the tactics used by the advocates of cosmopolitanism to obtain mass support introduces another aspect of the whole issue of federalism. The method by which some such plan might gain adoption has engaged much of the attention of the supporters of the idea. Initially the movement gathered momentum as a result of mass revulsion against, and fear of, another war and its consequences.

Immediately after World War II in the United States and in Europe, organizations interested in world government sought to capitalize on this popular fear by telling people of the horrors of atomic war that would come unless they proceeded forthwith to form a federal world government. This technique produced near-sensational results for a time as the alternatives of world law or atomization were expounded. As time wore on, however, and atomic war came to be a more remote and less frightening prospect, the strength of the appeal of fear ebbed and the movement lost much support. Today the only group that seriously argues in favor of the immediate abolition of national sovereignty is the cosmopolitans, and we have seen that much of the urgency of their proposals is a tactical device to stimulate mass interest.

Other Methods. It is apparent to most advocates of world government today that progress toward the goal they desire must come through the further development of institutions that already exist or at least through the acceleration of tendencies already apparent. This means that there are actually two broad routes by which world government might be attained. One capitalizes upon the experience of the United Nations and proposes conferring upon it grants of real legislative and executive power. The other looks instead to the already strong trend toward the creation of supra-national governmental units upon a regional basis.

The first position places greater emphasis upon universality of membership and argues that the transfer of power will take place as people everywhere feel the need for it. The second contends rather that the establishment of the principle of supra-national government is the critical point. Once the techniques have been mastered and the validity of the idea established, more states will join and finally all will be members. Both positoins have considerable merit.

The United Nations Approach. It is an established fact that the United Nations, even with its limited and fiduciary powers, is able to meet and solve many problems of international life. The organization, particularly the General Assembly, has already undertaken projects of a distinctly legislative nature which tend to affect individuals in their daily lives—an omen of federalism in the making. Such broad ventures as the Universal Declaration of Human Rights and such willingness to pierce the barrier of national sovereignty as was demonstrated in the question of the Indian minority in the Union of South Africa indicate that much thinking is going on within the United Nations tending inevitably toward its evolution into a true agency of world government.

The major stumbling blocks in the path of this development are, of course, the embattled antagonists of the cold war. Not yet is either of them willing seriously to contemplate the United Nations as an instrument of government in its own right, but instead they continue to utilize its machinery as an additional tool in the struggle each is carrying on against the other. So long as this controversy dominates world politics, the United Nations cannot make significant progress in the direction of federation.

The Regional Approach. Regional federation among states who share common problems that can best be solved by the creation of common agencies is a trend that has impressed many observers with its promise since World War II. Recognizing the inability of most nation-states adequately to defend themselves against the new giants, and also aware of the many problem areas with which individual states are incompetent to deal, more and more people have begun to think in terms of regional groupings upon a federal basis.

This has reached the point of institutionalism only in western Europe, where the European Coal and Steel Community (the Schuman Plan) became an actuality in 1952. This body assumed sovereign control over the steel industry in six western European states. During the same year, an agreement calling for a European army involving the same six states was signed, and planning for additional agencies, both functional and general, was speeded up.

The pace of the movement slowed during 1953 and 1954 as the cold war relaxed and domestic political controversies affected France, Italy, and West Germany, but its advance was inexorable. An indication of the direction in which events were moving was provided by the signature of a draft treaty for a European Political Community by the six Schuman Plan states in March 1953.

Although most advanced in this part of the world, the idea is being seriously discussed in other great regions, most noticeably in south and southeast Asia, the Middle East, and Australasia. Regional federation provides a way by which many technical problems inherent in the idea of a super-sovereignty can be solved and practical experience gained in making the machinery work upon a limited geographic basis.

Since the various regions of the world tend toward a cultural homogeneity within themselves, the transfer of sovereignty to a central authority involves less emotional stress among the people than it would if a global agency with which individuals were totally unfamiliar were involved. Another advantage of the regional basis of organization as compared with a single world-wide agency arises from the lesser complexity of the problems the former would be called upon to solve. Thus it would be easier for a regional agency to build up popular confidence in the idea of a federal form by the accumulation of a record of success.

The Lessons of Europe. The lesson of the European experiment in unification is of widespread application. Despite the urgency and obvious appropriateness of some such procedure, nationalist and traditionalist forces have made it impossible to transfer any sovereignty to a multi-purpose regional government for Europe. So long as the effort to reorganize the region was expended in this direction (as, for example, through the Council of Europe), no real progress could be made. The creation of a series of 'functional' bodies, however, each charged with the performance of a single specified mission, in such order as circumstances demand and permit, seems now to be the method of putting the idea of unification into practice without calling into question the issue of ultimate popular loyalty.

The theory seems to be that as these specialized bodies multiply, some co-ordinating agency will have to be created to oversee all of them. This will be (in fact if not in name) a federalized United States of Europe.

Advocates of world government would do well to ponder the European experience. A major change in the organization of society, such as the creation of a single federal world authority, cannot come into being until the people who are to be governed are ready for it. Political institutions are the reflection of a culture; to try to impose upon a people a form of government for which they are not ready is as futile and dangerous as to try to keep them happy and obedient under a form they have outgrown.

The primary preconditions for effective world government would seem, on the basis of experience in Europe and elsewhere, to be two: a cultural readiness among the people of the world for some new method of attack upon the problems of political organization, and a positive awareness that in the federal principle they have an effective means to fill their needs. It is because of this that the 'functional' approach is felt by many people to be the most fruitful way to proceed in bringing about world government.

By advancing piecemeal, by establishing single-purpose agencies to deal with particular problems, the point can be made that another and better way exists to deal with political issues than the nation-state system. Ultimately, as more and more individual needs are met by collective action taken by some form of super-sovereignty, populations will have become so habituated to world government that the actual erection of the structure and the transfer of full sovereignty to it will be purely a formality and the recognition of an already existing situation.

PROBLEMS OF ORGANIZATION

Representation. Innumerable technical points intrude into the discussions of the details of the proposed forms of world government. Whether the world legislature should be unicameral or bicameral, with one house representing the states and the other the people as in the United States; whether the executive should be single (a 'President of the World') or plural; the method of selection of the executive, by world popular election or by means of some indirect technique; whether or not there should be a world judiciary to which cases could be appealed from national courts; the location of the world capital: all these are hotly debated. Of much more basic character is the dispute over the proposed basis of representation. Since individuals as well as states would be represented in any such organization, the question of the basis upon which such representation would be apportioned is naturally of critical importance.

To citizens of the Western democracies the normal and familiar basis of representation in a legislative body is simple numbers, but the application of such a formula to a world organization offers certain practical difficulties. The apportionment of representatives among the various states upon the basis of population would result in such states as China, India, the Soviet Union, Indonesia, and Pakistan having many more delegates than Great Britain, France, or Italy (to say nothing of such small states as Belgium and Denmark). Such an outcome cannot help but dampen the ardor of the most sincere advocate of world government in the United States or Europe.

Attempts have been made to discover a formula that would retain the democratic principle of numbers but would also provide a means whereby the Western democracies would not be submerged beneath such a tidal wave of representatives from the Orient. Literacy, wealth, and 'civilization' have been advanced as suggested criteria to modify the crude impact of sheer numbers in the legislative organ of any proposed world governmnt. A recent proposal entails the grouping of all states into three broad categories and the assignment of a fixed number of seats to all states within any category. For example, China, India, the USSR, and the United States, as 'large' states, might each be assigned twenty seats; Great Britain, France, Indonesia, and Pakistan would all be 'medium' seats with ten seats apiece; 'small' states, such as Belgium, Canada, and Burma, would be content with five places.

The whole discussion reveals a problem inherent in the nature of the movement for world government. The idea grows out of Western political experience, where a common culture provides a rational base for representation by population. When applied to the entire world, the very proponents of the idea discover that they (and the culture they represent) would be in a hopeless minority compared to the masses who do not understand representative institutions. Hence the somewhat unedifying attempt by Western apologists for world government to eat their cake and have it too by merging the democratic ideal of majority rule with some other criterion in order to keep any world organization safely under the control of their philosophy.

Democracy. This problem has an even deeper root. Unless the point of view of the proponents of world hegemony is accepted, any world government must be constructed upon a democratic basis. The fundamental concepts common to all proposals for federation are integral parts of the democratic idea: limited government, separation of powers, popular election of officials, universal suffrage, and natural rights. Although these notions are self-evident to us in the Western world, the great majority of men throughout the remainder of the world are ignorant of the forms of democracy and do not understand the dynamics of their operation. Democracy as a working principle depends upon a moral consensus among the people who are to be governed. Unless this basic agreement exists, democratic forms are perverted and the system becomes a sham. The communist 'people's democracy' illustrates such a prostitution of popular government.

Until the underlying democratic concept that everyone abides by majority decisions in good faith is understood and accepted by people everywhere, the establishment of a structure of world government would be useless and dangerous. Thus the advocates of world government are faced with a fundamental question: can the world be organized on the basis they propose in time to stave off the catastrophe of another war which might mean the end of our civilization?

If the race to save the world is to be won, it will be only as a result of the extension of the democratic idea and the perfecting of the machinery of federalism. Given the instability of international politics and the ever-present possibility of a resort to war, it is easy to become pessimistic and resigned to disaster. As we have seen in previous chapters, however many of the corrosive tendencies of international relations today are to some extent self-neutralizing and the dangers of total explosion are not as great as has sometimes been feared. It may very well be that man has a little more time in which to develop new political forms and techniques than some people have been willing to grant him. There is little doubt that the broad trend of history is toward some form of organization transcending the nation-state. The only question is whether social development will progress rapidly enough to effect the change in sufficient time.

The optimum basis of political organization is determined at any point in history by a variety of factors. The two most important of these are the maximum area it is technologically feasible to govern from a single seat of power and the maximum area within which the people feel themselves united into a single nation. Today the development of transportation and communication has made it possible to govern efficiently with the whole world as a constituency. All that is lacking is the extension of the concept of the nation into something broader that will encompass the whole of humankind.

IV

Contemporary Problems

11

Problem Areas: Political

THIS section of the book is devoted to an examination of some of the more basic international problems of the contemporary world. Many possible ways exist for us to consider these; we have adopted the device of dividing them into the three broad categories of political, economic, and psychological. In this chapter we shall consider the political problems, in Chapter 12 the economic, and in Chapter 13 the psychological. Of course, no such listing can be exclusive or exhaustive. The affairs of men and of states do not arrange themselves neatly into closed classifications. We shall discover much overlapping among the chapters as well as within any particular one, but some differentiation in emphasis will be preserved as we examine these persistent and troublesome issues.

By the 'political' problem area we mean particularly those crisis points in today's world which bear directly upon the institution of the nation-state, its present and future prospects, and the relations of states in their corporate capacities to each other. These constitute some of the more 'traditional' and familiar aspects of international politics, which are based upon the legal personality of the state. In this area is found the greatest popular awareness of international relations; the political contacts of states grip the imaginations of men in more compelling fashion than does any other level of relations.

The following list of problems does not pretend to be all-inclusive, nor does it even contain all the issues that are of primary importance today. Each of them, however, is of great significance in its own right and together they give a not inaccurate picture of the type of political issues that the world faces today.

THE BIPOLAR WORLD AND ITS BREAKUP

Unquestionably the most dramatic and compelling single feature of world politics since the end of World War II has been the existence of the 'bipolar' world. Every aspect of world relations has been affected and often dominated by the fact that the two giants, the United States and the Soviet Union, have

assumed positions of mutual hostility in general policy and upon almost
every specific issue as it has arisen. Nor have they been content to conduct
their cold war with one another in isolation; they have insisted upon attempting to enlist all of the other states of the world under one banner or the other
and upon investing any question of international relations with a peculiar
relevance derived from its being involved in the Russo-American conflict.

It would have been too much to expect all the smaller states of the world
to accept this situation with equanimity and good cheer. The less powerful
members of the world community have often felt that the bipolar world has
left them too little room in which to seek the advancement of their own interests and has presented them too bluntly and too often with the prospect
of a total war in the stakes of which they have had only a minor interest. As
a result there have been numerous counter-forces at work, seeking to reduce
the grip of the great powers and to break up the overly narrow bipolar world.
Of late this tendency has grown stronger and more apparent. If the bipolar
world is indeed disintegrating, the consequent realignments are bound to be
accompanied by a whole series of new stresses and strains, as severe (although of a different sort) as those produced since 1945 by the cold war.

The Causes of Bipolarity

Perhaps at no time since the Moslems menaced the Christian world in the
fifteenth century has so much of the future of mankind been bound up in
the relations of any two power blocs. The bipolar world is so important a
factor in the lives of all of us today that we should make every effort to
understand how and why the world arrived at such a state. The causes of bipolarity must be comprehended before any decision can be arrived at for
coping with it.

Concentration of Power. The most important single cause of the bifurcated
nature of contemporary world affairs is the reshuffling of the power pattern of
the world which grew out of World War II. Although the processes of national decline and advance originated long before that conflict (indeed, we
know already that they are continuous), they reached a climax and in some
cases completion during and after the war. At the end of the fighting all but
the most biased observers were aware that the end of an era had arrived.
Some of the great powers of the first part of the century had disappeared
entirely, others had been drastically weakened, while still others had gone
into a temporary eclipse. Certain new ones, formerly only minor participants
in world affairs, were occupying or were moving toward the center of the
stage.

Italy and France represented the former great powers reduced to secondary status; Britain's hurts were serious; Germany and Japan were temporarily impotent; meanwhile, the United States and the Soviet Union domi-

nated world affairs by virtue of superior power. India and China, the future giants, were as yet unable to mobilize their great potential.

In the postwar world only the United States and the USSR have been able to exercise any meaningful freedom of choice in determining their foreign policies. Had events worked out so as to permit them to co-operate actively, the course of world affairs since 1945 would have been very different. Conflict and competition have been the nature of their relationship, however, and everyone everywhere has felt the impact of the clash. The first factor tending toward the present bipolarity is, therefore, that only two mutually hostile states have been able to carry on foreign affairs with any real freedom since the war.

Ideological Policy. We must now look in more detail at these two antagonists in order to see how their power relationships have led to the present bipolar stalemate. Both the United States and the Soviet Union are, in comparison with most of the other participants in world affairs, relatively young and inexperienced. This youth and lack of background are most apparent in the relative inability of both governments to understand the limits upon and the responsibility accompanying great political power.

Thrust suddenly into positions of world leadership without sufficient maturity to provide a basis for action, both have been so far unable to rationalize fully the often conflicting demands of time and place. Both governments have given indications of an uncertainty regarding the demands of true national interest as well as much hesitancy and reluctance to seize upon the most expedient means of advancing that interest. Without the poise and confidence obtainable only from years of dealing with the slippery and elusive realities of world politics, the leaders of both states have been obliged to fall back upon the promptings of ideologies and the stimuli of mass emotions as a guide to conduct.

The leadership of the Soviet is beyond doubt guilty of taking the first great steps in this direction and of precipitating mass ideological struggle in the postwar world. American reaction to Soviet ideological assault, although somewhat delayed in its appearance, ultimately developed as much force as had the Russian attack. Thus Russo-American relations have proceeded in recent years upon a primarily ideological and emotional basis. This arose in the first instance out of a lack of ability to devise a realistic course of action and has kept going ever since largely on its own momentum.

At various points in earlier chapters we have delineated some of the characteristics of an ideologically oriented policy. It is sufficient at this point only to remind ourselves that an ideological battle in international politics is marked by two principal characteristics: the constant expansion of policy by both parties, and the extreme difficulty of compromise. Both arise from the fact that ideologies are viewed by their adherents as summaries of absolute moral truth. The cold war has demonstrated these symptoms. Neither the USSR nor the United States has been willing either to compromise its ideological faith or to accept a definitive limitation upon its objectives.

The Elimination of Power Vacuums. Thus we come to the third in the sequence of causes of the bipolar world. The two great powers have confronted each other with a fixed policy but each has proved to be unable to make any major impression upon the other by its own efforts. As a result each has sought to gain allies for itself and to deny them to its adversary in the hope of gaining a decisive advantage. The outcome of this race for support has been the attempted elimination of 'power vacuums' all over the world: those areas into which the power of one or the other of the great states has not yet flowed.

These power vacuums were of two types: states in which the domestic government was so weak and unstable as to make it impossible for any clear foreign-policy commitments to be made, or else states in which strong government existed but where a policy decision had been taken in favor of neutrality in the great-power conflict. Iran is an example of the first type, India of the second.

To both great powers it is unthinkable that a power vacuum should exist anywhere in the world while a titanic struggle is going on whose prize is the victory of good over evil. Both have sought unceasingly to eliminate all such areas, each using all possible combinations of persuasion, pressure, and open coercion to advance its case. A dual motive has always been present in the struggle for control of any power vacuum: the desire to gain an ally is mixed with the need to deny one to the enemy. In any case, by the early part of 1950 it appeared as if the bipolarity of the world was complete. All the power vacuums either had been obliterated or seemed well on their way to extinction and the world appeared finally to be divided between the two armed camps.

BIPOLARITY IN PRACTICE

The Loss of Flexibility. In practice bipolarity left international politics in a curiously truncated state. In the first place, all freedom of maneuver was lost. The bulk of the states of the world were tied tightly to the leader of the group they had joined (or into which they had been forced). The two giants had likewise surrendered their freedom. Each had pressed its policy to the outermost possible limits, to the point where it met the expanding policy of the other. Neither could any longer make a move without provoking an immediate retaliation by the other; in practice, therefore, each confined itself to countering any threats raised by the other. Nor was any greater freedom possible in the relations of the major states with their minor allies. The only reason for the existence of the great blocs was great-power hostility and all intra-group moves were for the single purpose of making the alliances tighter and more unified in purpose and organization.

The Inexpediency of Force. The bipolar world was one in which the resolution of differences by means of the classic mechanisms of diplomacy and compromise was no longer possible. What was peculiarly frustrating to statesmen was that the other historic device for solving international problems—force—was equally futile. The use of violence on any basis short of total war was virtually impossible since neither bloc was willing to submit to mere demonstrations or threats.

Total war was, in its turn, such a frightful prospect and the outcome so uncertain that neither party seriously considered it as a means of resolving any of the major issues. Neither side possessed a sufficiently great advantage over the other to hold out the prospect of the relatively quick victory that alone would make the effort worth while; the only certain outcome of great-power total war was widespread devastation and staggering casualties among participants and neutrals alike. There was a good deal of loose talk on both sides of the Iron Curtain about the 'preventive war': the sudden attack upon the enemy in order to forestall his later aggression. This never emerged from the area of unofficial and reckless speculation, however; neither government has ever given any indication of considering it seriously as a policy.

The Prevalence of Stalemate. With freedom of maneuver gone and in view of the extreme unfeasibility of a settlement by force, the bipolar world presented a picture of unrelieved rigidity and stalemate. Mutual frustration and bafflement have been the lot of both groups. Bickering and disagreement were the normal atmosphere of such contacts as the two camps have had with each other; crisis situations—such as the Berlin blockade—did not reach clean and total resolution but were temporized upon almost any basis that would serve to minimize tension. The only open military struggle between the groups, the Korean war and the Indochina war, were no more able to produce any clear-cut decision. Disputes dragged in interminably simply because no viable basis for compromise could be found in a bipolar situation and any absolute answer was equally impossible to discover.

All new issues of world politics came to be channeled into the peculiar structure of the bipolar world and by that fact tended to become insoluble. The movement and change that we have seen to be inherent and integral aspects of 'normal' world politics were largely destroyed by the operation of the principle of bipolarity. In this way the contemporary political scene has to a large degree not corresponded with the general picture of international relations presented in earlier chapters.

THE POSSIBLE BREAKUP OF THE BIPOLAR WORLD

Pressures on the Bipolar World. The dynamics of world politics are stronger in the long run than the policies of any two states, no matter how powerful the latter might be. The imposition of the bipolar structure upon the world was a result of the shifting patterns of power relationships in the world after 1945. We have seen that the factors of power resist being frozen into a static mold; the bipolar world was from the beginning subject to pressures tending toward its eventual breakup. Most important of these is the fact that the absolute and relative superiority in power enjoyed by the two major states toward the rest of the world has been steadily diminishing from its postwar high. Other power centers have sprung up and other problems than the exclusive one of Russo-American relations have demanded and are receiving attention from peoples and governments.

Neither great state is able to dominate and control the members of its own alliance with the same degree of confidence as formerly; consequently, intragroup relations have become a matter of new and great urgency for both the USSR and the United States. New power blocs are in the process of formation and are making inroads upon the membership of the old ones. Powerwise, it is becoming much more difficult to keep the world locked up in a bipolar cage.

Reasons for the Decline of Bipolarity. Some of the more immediate reasons for the decline of bipolarity and the breakup of the two-power world ought to be briefly indicated. Perhaps the most convincing, from the point of view of the smaller states, is the intolerability of perpetual stalemate. The domestic and international problems of the lesser powers have continued to evolve and have reached the point where serious attempts at their solution must be made. No longer will the issues of hunger, disease, economic and cultural underdevelopment, and national self-expression remain in the background while the only concern of statesmen everywhere continues to be the relationship of two global powers. Since the Russo-American problem continues unsolved and threatens to remain so indefinitely, from every quarter of the globe have come demands that governments take direct and productive action to deal with issues that have been left unconsidered.

Stalemate may be undesirable as far as the bipolar powers themselves are concerned, but they have proved to be unable to discover a formula for its dissolution. The lesser powers of Asia, of Europe, of Africa, and of the Western Hemisphere have begun to make clear that for their part they are unwilling to submit permanently to the rigidity of a bipolar world that produces no solutions but only multiplies tensions. According to this point of view the great powers may, if they wish, continue to keep their policies locked in a hopeless and endless struggle; however, they can no longer put off the rest of the world on the same basis. The smaller states aver that they are seeking some other destiny than perpetual tension forever unresolved.

Another factor entering the picture at this point is the decreasing danger of war. During the early days of the cold war, while the lines of alliance were forming and hardening, there was a real and justified fear of war and its attendant human and material damage. As each side in the great-power struggle claimed to be the only force for peace, it utilized this fear of destruction as an effective device to stimulate otherwise reluctant states to join it in alliance. The smaller states were much disturbed lest the inexperience and militant ideology of each major government unleash the catastrophe that many of them had so much historic reason to dread. This was only one of the factors that led these states to join one or another alliance, but there is no doubt that it played a major part in the thinking of many, notably the states of western Europe. In any case, for most of the participants other than the leaders, the desire to avoid war if possible and to be in a strong position if war should come was a great factor in the creation of the rigid blocs that characterize the bipolar world.

Today, however, much of the earlier fear of war has receded. Rightly or wrongly, the leaders of many states in both camps are unconvinced that the disaster of total war is imminent or even probable. In that case the alliance of which they form a part is no longer a protection but an encumbrance. The loss of the right of independent action and the indefinite postponement of their own national objectives have become too great a price to pay for protection against a danger that grows steadily more remote.

We in the Western world are aware of this attitude among the allies of the United States: Great Britain, France, and other democracies no longer yield their own position on issues to the persuasive force of an American plea for unity against the common enemy. Evidence often shows that the Soviet Union is finding its allies similarly intractable, particularly the government of China and some of the minor states in eastern Europe. Czechoslovakia and East Germany both indicated by open popular resistance during early 1953 that oppression by Russia was more of a real problem to them than any threat from the West; China likewise followed an independent course at the Geneva Conference in 1954. It is unnecessary to evaluate the validity of the position of these states as regards the lessened danger of war; it is sufficient to point out that the attitude exists and that it is having a perceptible influence on the development of bipolar politics.

Another aspect of the same frame of mind is a spread belief in the possibility of neutrality, either in the cold war or in an all-out one. Several years ago, while the great powers possessed ample ability to enforce their will upon their lesser allies, it seemed to many people as if the American and Russian governments were less hostile toward each other than both were toward any state that sought to stay aloof from the conflict. This period has passed. The shifting distribution of power has given many states the ability to conduct policies of independent action, equally free of dictation from both camps, that would have been unthinkable a few years ago.

India's stubborn refusal to become embroiled in the cold war was the first step toward the appearance of real neutralism; its example has been followed by several others. As a result, the thinking of many statesmen today is drastically different from what it was at the height of bipolarity. They recognize the extent to which the great powers are committed in their struggle against each other. The United States and the USSR are no longer able to apply coercive pressure upon their allies to the same degree. Policy makers in some smaller states also are speculating upon the possibility of avoiding involvement in any total war that might develop out of the Russo-American controversy and are tending to arrange their policies in this direction.

Most observers feel that they are tragically mistaken in this latter hope; any great-power war today would spread rapidly until it engulfed the world, regardless of what other governments sought to do about it. It cannot be denied, however, that in seeking neutrality the governments of the small states are responding to a deep-rooted and broadly based popular demand, and that the operation of the political process in recent years has given them reason to hope for success.

Symptoms of the Breakup. We have already referred to the most pervasive symptom of the dissolution of the bipolar world: the increasing independence of policy and action on the part of smaller states in all parts of the world. India set the pattern; other Asiatic states such as Indonesia and Burma have followed suit. In the Middle East, Iran and Egypt have for the most part severed their connections with the Western bloc and are seeking to pilot a course that is independently determined, though far from pro-communist. In Europe, Britain and France have both repeatedly refused to conform their entire policies to the American version of joint action.

In the Soviet world, Yugoslavia's break with the Kremlin in 1948 came about primarily because of Marshal Tito's refusal to govern all his actions by the dictates of Moscow. Following the death of Stalin in March 1953, signs multiplied that the USSR was finding China ever more determined to follow a policy formed in terms of Chinese interests rather than Russian.

Two spectacular breaks in the two alliances occurred during June 1953. In Korea, at the very moment when a truce seemed imminent, Dr. Rhee, the president of the Republic of Korea, took independent action in freeing the non-communist prisoners of war, whose fate had been the object of many weary months of negotiation; although this action threatened to upset prospects for peace the United States was forced to acquiesce and ultimately appeased Rhee with a favorable agreement. During the same month, rebellion against domestic communist and Russian domination flared in East Germany, forcing the Soviet to declare martial law and to employ naked violence to suppress the revolt. Although Soviet control was restored, major concessions to the Germans were necessary before peace returned. The uprising destroyed the illusion of solidarity among the 'people's republics' behind the Iron Curtain much as South Korea's rebellion showed up the cracks in the structure of the Western world. The world community no longer consists only of two armed camps confronting each other; it also includes a number of states not part of the two groups (or seeking to break away) which are attempting—with uneven success—to insulate themselves from the more pernicious effects of bipolarity.

A more subtle symptom of the breakup of the bipolar world is the change in the outlook of the people of many states. No longer do they view world affairs only through eyes directed by the commands of the great powers; instead, they are once again reverting to the familiar diversity so typical of world politics when it is carried on upon a more traditional basis. Some of these newer attitudes may be considered as retrogressions; one cannot but rgeret the revival of parochial nationalism in states such as France and West Germany, where once it had been thought to be extinct. In like manner the newly freed states of Asia have demonstrated their independence by a reckless employment of the same nationalistic techniques.

In other states, the gradual decline in the paralyzing numbness of bipolarity has released more forward-looking forces in many people. The increase in the movement for supra-national government in Europe is a direct outgrowth of this new attitude. To be effective bipolarity requires a bipolar mental attitude; when people cease to think of world politics as involving nothing but the choice between the Soviet Union and the United States, the psychological base of the bipolar structure is undermined.

Possible Effects of the Breakup

The Period of Transition. If the bipolar world is indeed in the process of dissolution, the next few years are destined to be a period of major reorganization and readjustment. The calculations appropriate to a two-power world will have to be either scrapped or drastically revised. Diplomacy will again be in a position to play its historic part as a harmonizing and adjusting procedure.

This transformation from a rigid and narrow frame for world politics to a fluid and flexible one will not be easy. The great powers—and many of the smaller ones as well—have made so many firm policy commitments based upon the perpetuation of bipolarity that to change them will produce stresses and upheavals of major proportions. In many ways the bipolar world, for all its perpetual crisis, offers a certain illusory stability and predictability which may seem preferable to the series of crisis situations bound to accompany such a period of readjustment.

This era of change is likely to prove particularly taxing for Americans. Our entry into world affairs as a full participant, delayed by at least one generation, was finally made in 1945; it was accompanied by high hopes of a bright future and a warming sense of rectitude that at last we had recognized the folly of isolation and were firmly upon the right path. When the dreams of peace and security faded in the postwar period and we were brought up against the stern realities of great-power conflict, we passed through a period of emotional stress and finally succeeded in adjusting ourselves to a world which we felt to be fundamentally hostile. Today we seem to have a vested psychic interest in the continuation of the bipolar world. Russian-American controversy is a phenomenon which, if not pleasant, has at least the virtue of familiarity; for us to be deprived of it by the operations of a multi-power political process would leave many of us almost defenseless psychologically. We would be faced with the necessity of learning an entirely new set of criteria by which to judge world affairs.

Americans, grown increasingly cynical as their many sincere offers for peace and co-operation have been rebuffed, today display a marked emotional tendency to shrink from the prospect of a resolution of the cold war. We have begun to learn to live with an unfriendly Russia; for many of us the strains of mastering the technique of living with a friendly one would constitute too great a price to pay for a release from the contemporary stress. Public opinion therefore discounts in advance any new hope for improvement in the cold war. Russian 'peace' feelers are immediately rejected by press and public alike, thus handicapping American diplomats who must explore them.

In this way, we do our best to retain a situation that is at least bearable, rather than venture into a hopeful but dangerous and unpredictable unknown. Yet the change is bound to come; it may indeed be already upon us. No matter how great the strain, Americans must prepare themselves for a new era in which Russian-American conflict will not be the only significant political relationship in the world.

The New Power Blocs. One probable effect of the breakup of bipolarity is the further development of new power centers. The process is already advanced to the point where there is little likelihood that it will be arrested. The most important single power group that is today relatively free from dictation by either great power is of course India and its associates in the Arab-Asian bloc. We have already made reference to the manner in which India has mobilized some of the states of south and southeast Asia to form a powerful group in the United Nations and in the Asiatic region as well. A significant tribute to India's strategic role was the fact that Indian forces were employed to police the prisoner exchange that followed the Korean truce of July 1953. At that time India was the world's outstanding neutral.

But other areas also are growing in power significance. In the Middle East the Arab states, although beset by nationalist and dynastic rivalries, are struggling to discover a formula for joint action that will liberate them forever from 'Western imperialism' and yet preserve them from Soviet expansionism. In Europe, the movement for European consolidation has been moving forward at a jerky but fairly rapid pace. True, it has been under the active sponsorship of the United States and is often viewed as part of American cold-war strategy; nevertheless there is little doubt in the minds of many Europeans that they are preparing for the day when a truly independent

Europe will become free of control by either Moscow or Washington. It is also obvious that the government of the Union of South Africa is also seeking immunization from the cold war by establishing itself as an independent power center. Finally, the case of China must be considered. Whether it is to be communist or democratic, one thing about the future of China is certain: it is going some day to attain great-power status and it will, in the long run, be nobody's satellite. No matter how one may view the present status and role of China, its future is clearly that of an independent power center.

The Mediation of the Cold War. Another possible outgrowth of the end of bipolarity is an increasing attempt on the part of the independent power centers to mediate the cold war. This has also already become apparent; India's neutral position in the United Nations has enabled it to move affirmatively upon several occasions in the direction of an intervention between the disputing powers. Its most active policy in this regard was its persistent search for a formula of settlement of the prisoner-of-war issue in Korea. Britain and France, although they have not yet gone to the extreme of intervening actively and directly between the United States and the Soviet bloc, have nevertheless restrained American action when they feared it might go too far. Several times since the end of the fighting in Korea Winston Churchill urged a renewal of top-level conversations between the USSR, the United Kingdom, and the United States in the hopes of bringing about a major relaxation of tension. This became a reality in the negotiation over the Austrian peace treaty in May 1955.

Since all the new and growing power centers of the world are marked by a real or incipient impatience toward both great powers for (as they see it) constantly threatening the world with war, it is only natural to expect them to redouble their efforts at pacification as their capacity to exert significant power continues to increase. As long as one of the overriding concerns of the new power centers continues to be peace, they will continue their attempts not only to prevent hot war from growing out of cold but also to bring about a material improvement in the climate of world affairs by restoring Russo-American relations to the level of at least mutual tolerance and co-existence. Whether they will be successful or not and, if they succeed, when the world may expect some relaxation in tension, is not yet clear.

The Strengthening of the United Nations. As the bipolar world loses its definite character and new power blocs appear to rival the formerly dominant states, a real possibility exists that one outcome will be the strengthening of the United Nations. All students know that the greatest obstacle to the success of the world organization has been Soviet-American conflict; it is also clear that most of the other states of the world have real hopes that the United Nations has a better prospect of success in store for it if the grip of bipolarity could be loosed. None of the other potential great powers has any inherent vested interest in aggrandizement; all need peace and co-operation in order fully to realize their potential, and most of them recognize this fact. If the two great states should lose their capacity jointly to control the United Nations machinery and instead be obliged to share the directing power with other peace-minded states, the opportunity for a real expansion in the world role of the organization would be at hand. If that day should arrive, world-wide co-operation upon a hitherto undreamed-of scale could become a reality.

This expansion of the scope of the United Nations would take place throughout the organization but most definitely in two particular areas. In the first place, the peace-enforcing activities of the Security Council would be far more effective. In Chapter 10 we examined the 'veto' and discovered that in itself it is only a symptom and not a cause of the paralysis that grips the United Nations. If the USSR could be brought to understand that its real national interest can best be served by co-operative action within the organization instead of a reckless disregard for it, the veto would cease to be a serious consideration. If both the great powers should become persuaded that the future of mankind is of more importance than the outcome of any particular power controversy and that both would prosper most in a peaceful world, they would be more willing to co-operate in the enforcement of peace. The Security Council would then become what it was originally intended to be: the collective voice of the world insisting that all international conflicts be settled peacefully.

The other great expansion of United Nations activity would be in the area of economic and social activity. Permanent peace is possible only when the social, economic, and psychological factors that cause war are eliminated. Nothing is more absolutely a step in the right direction than the United Nations program in this area. Yet bipolarity and its attendant tensions have served to restrict real activity of this sort to almost nothing. Once the normal flexibility of world politics is restored, the voice of the international community will be hearkened to more frequently, and man may once again turn to the business of making this planet a better place for all to live.

Possible Dangers. It may be remarked that the foregoing is an over-optimistic picture of the future. This may well be a just criticism. The period of readjustment necessitated by the dissolution of bipolarity will be accompanied by much indecision and wavering on the part of all states as they seek a viable policy in a new situation. Periods of readjustment are always full of tension and potential danger as new and unexpected situations demand action. Statesmen, operating without any clearly defined lines of policy, might be tempted to take drastic or thoughtless action that would never even be considered under a more settled system. In a complex and changing set of relationships the outcome of any crisis is more uncertain than when the pattern of politics is more stable.

No one can be certain that the world will pass safely through the transition period that will follow the final breakup of the bipolar world. If it does not, if war and crisis eventuate before the final re-establishment of peace, it may well turn out that the bipolar structure of the world was the only means open to men to preserve the peace in the middle of the twentieth century. Recognizing, however, the will to peace on the part of most men everywhere and the brighter prospects that accompany the possibility of a world of divided power, the chances of passing safely through the readjustment period are good enough for most of us to feel that the risks are well justified.

New Bases of Political Organization

Another problem area of great importance to contemporary man is the search for a new basis of political organization. Governments and private individuals in all parts of the world are becoming dissatisfied with the presently constituted nation-state as the primary political unit. Many of them are seeking to discover some new and different method of organizing political power and of achieving their political purposes more effectively. Almost all possible avenues are being considered, and many of them have been explored to some extent by particular governments. The over-all impact upon world politics of this concern with the future of the nation-state cannot help but be great; it promises to become more and more significant as time goes on.

The Inadequacy of the State

Perhaps it would be premature to speak of the 'end' of the nation-state as being imminent or in sight. It is undeniable, however, that policy makers in most governments today are seriously handicapped by the limitations of the state form of organization and are searching for some new basis upon which to organize. We have stressed in the first part of this chapter that since 1945 only the United States and the Soviet Union have possessed sufficient power to carry on a relatively self-determined foreign policy. What were the factors that inhibited all other states and made them succumb to the pressures of bipolarity? What is wrong with the nation-state today?

Over-concentration of Power. As in so many cases dealing with world politics, the answer to the question must be phrased first in terms of power. The two giants of world affairs today represent the greatest concentrations of political and military power, actual and potential, that have existed since the modern state system was born. Never before in modern times has so much of the effective force of state authority been concentrated in so few hands.

No citizen or official of one of the smaller states of the world can contemplate this disparity without becoming disturbed. To face the future calmly in a condition of being doomed to permanent inferiority has already proved to be impossible for many minor states and is becoming more difficult for all of them. The old type of national state, with an area of less than half a million square miles and a population ranging from five to seventy million, is nearly obsolete compared to continental giants such as the USSR and the United States. The political technology of the modern day has made it possible to mobilize the potential power of millions of square miles and hundreds of millions of people under a single government, and anything less cannot ever rival the massive leaders of today. The instruments of modern power are mass-produced and mass-employed, and sheer lack of size has made the old states of Europe and the newer small states of Asia and the rest of the world unable to compete upon any basis of equality. The problems of the technology of the mass are insoluble for the small state.

If this were all, it would be serious enough for the great majority of men who live in the smaller states of the world. But our discussion of bipolarity has already revealed another characteristic of concentrated power in the modern world: its proclivity to concentrate further. Not only do the smaller states realize their permanent status of power inferiority but they are concerned lest the already truncated independence they enjoy will be further absorbed into one or the other of the great-power concentrations. The old (pre-1939) type of 'great power' is not only incapable today of very much freedom in its policy, but it is unsure of even being able to guarantee its continued existence. France, for example, knows that its independence could be snuffed out in an instant by either great power; so do all the little states of the Middle East and southeast Asia. If independence today is such an illusory thing, dependent upon the whim of the major powers, it is no wonder that so many people are willing to exchange sovereignty for some new organizational form that promises more real security.

Problems Transcending the Nation-State. In another way the state form of organization fails today in most parts of the world to measure up to the demands placed upon it. In many important areas the problems that governments are called upon to deal with transcend national boundaries in their scope; they demand action broader than any state could take unilaterally. Included in this category are the pressing social, psychological, and economic tensions that are so apparent in every part of the world.

The devastation of World War II created problems of economic reconstruction and recovery in Europe that far exceeded the capacity of any single state to handle; the development of industrialization and the elevation of the standard of living of the people are tasks beyond the ability of any of the states of Asia or Africa. Yet these are only a few of the problems which men insist that governments solve. Because of the limited physical and human base upon which most nation-states are organized, they are helpless to take meaningful steps toward the relief of these pressures.

Even in the political field, the problems presented by the postwar world overlap state boundaries, and governments are at a loss how to proceed. The political technique of subversion and the policy problem of devising means to cope with Soviet-sponsored and Soviet-directed Communist parties have demonstrated again the inability of the nation-state to deal with political and security questions that are global in their extent.

NEW FORMS OF POLITICAL ORGANIZATION

The search for new forms of political organization that will offset the most serious shortcomings of the state form has taken several directions. In every case something more fundamental is being sought than the traditional association of states in which each participant guards its sovereignty jealously and procedure is based solely upon consultation and prior agreement. In each of the types of organization discussed below, some rearrangement of sovereignty is involved. It should also be kept in mind that this listing is primarily a catalogue of trends. Some have gone a considerable distance toward realization, while others are still in the stage of discussion or planning. Each of them, however, has been suggested by responsible statesmen as a possible way out of the crisis in which the nation-state finds itself, and each therefore holds promise for the future.

International Organization. The first new structure that should be mentioned in this connection is general international organization on the order of the United Nations. We have discussed the United Nations in some detail in Chapter 10, and at this point we need only to stress again the manner in which it represents an attempt to surpass the state form. The organization is all-inclusive in its membership, is permanent, and enjoys a broad range of action. We have already seen how the United Nations has jurisdiction in the political sphere through the operation of the Security Council and, in certain cases, the General Assembly; indeed, the very existence of the Security Council offers proof of the fact that many statesmen feel that individual states can no longer be permitted to handle their disputes themselves. In addition, the United Nations is designed to provide organization for solving the non-political questions that are global or at least supra-national in their effect. The Economic and Social Council, the Trusteeship Council, the commissions, and the specialized agencies all have as their reason for existence the need for co-ordinated solutions to problems common to individuals in many states.

General international organization is the most ambitious step yet taken by states in the direction of a new basis for political organization. Yet the United Nations is perhaps too ambitious a venture for the present stage of world politics. The states of the world are not prepared to make workable an organization in which membership is universal and with a projected scope of authority far beyond what any international body has yet enjoyed. There are still too many political conflicts among the major states, and too much of a tendency to attempt unilateral action, for the peace-enforcing machinery to be effective. There are also too many technical questions unsolved and too much intrusion of political considerations for the economic and social work to be truly significant.

And yet, the nations of the world seem to agree that the United Nations is necessary and must be preserved. Even the divisive pressures of bipolarity proved incapable of destroying it, and the process of learning its capabilities and its limitations goes on constantly. Its obvious direction of development is toward a real agency of international government and the solution of questions of war or peace on a collective basis, as well as matters of the health, security, and prosperity of men. When this will happen, or even whether it happens is beyond the capacity of anyone to tell. There is no doubt, however, that events are moving in this direction.

World Government. It is likewise unnecessary to discuss world government in detail again. We have seen that the basic motivation of the world government movement has been its conviction that the nation-state system cannot, by its very nature, preserve the peace. Factors of both technology and human psychology figure largely in this process of reasoning. The destructiveness of war and the explosive potentialities of the state system are stressed as reasons why men must transfer their primary loyalty from the state to some more broadly based body.

We have also seen how world government has remained to a great extent in the realm of discussion; the decision to merge national sovereignties into one great whole has involved so many considerations of practical politics and of conflicting emotions that most governments have been extremely wary of such a far-reaching step. The all-at-once creation of a world government by the deliberate act of will of the states of the world is such a remote possibility at the present level of world understanding as not to deserve serious consideration.

The very extent of the movement, however, and the quality of the leadership it has attracted are proof that the need for some such action is urgent. Some way must be found, the defenders of the idea seem to say, to breach the limitations upon political action imposed by the existence of state sovereignty. The most important service yet performed by the demand for world government has been the focusing of popular attention upon the inadequacies of the present system. By a constant advocacy of extreme methods of approach, the movement has made the less radical but nonetheless far-reaching measures of other types much more palatable to governments and peoples alike. Although they reject universal federalism or cosmopolitanism, many people have found regional or functional federation to be much less difficult to accept.

Regionalism. In considering supra-national organization on a less-than-universal basis it is once again appropriate here to inquire into only one or two aspects of the question. Federation, either regional or functional, is most advanced in Europe, where the Schuman plan, the project for a European army, and the 1953 proposal for the political federation of six Western states has made the idea of a limited super-sovereignty a commonplace in the past few years. It is only natural that the citizens of western Europe should be among the leaders in devising and seeking to implement schemes of supra-national organization. In Europe, people are keenly aware of the decline in the power and prestige of once great states, and are at every turn reminded of the obsolescence of the traditional state form. Nor do their problems any longer permit of effective unilateral action. Furthermore, having passed through all the various phases of nationalist emotion, they no longer have the same degree of frantic attachment to the symbolism of the nation-state.

No one can yet foresee the outcome of the European experiment in regional and functional federalism; at this point in history, however, one may be certain that the movement offers much hope and opportunity for real accomplishment and that it has already progressed too far to be lightly shrugged off. Nationalist revivals may slow it down or halt its progress temporarily; the rivalry and ambitions of political leaders may obscure it; nevertheless, to millions of Europeans its attractions are so great that it must be given a complete and fair trial before they will agree to its abandonment.

In other parts of the world the cause of limited supra-national government is in a situation not much better than that of universal world government. The areas in which regional organization would appear to be appropriate include southeast Asia, the Middle East, Latin America. Natural functional groupings include the sugar-growing states of the world, the cotton-producing areas, and similar economic or social groupings. But throughout the remainder of the world there is not the willingness to dispense with rigid sovereign independence that one finds in Europe, because these peoples have not experienced the same events or suffered the same disillusionments as have the Europeans. Independence is still too new and too precious to be lightly given up to a super-sovereignty. As a result, outside Europe most states are content today to seek organizational forms that preserve the complete identity of the nation-state.

Special-Purpose Groupings. Of the new forms of political organization the most numerous category is made up of the special-purpose organizations that preserve the essential characteristic of the state—national sovereignty. Generally these are created to serve a single purpose and are of limited jurisdiction and scope. In theory they are no different from any alliance between sovereignties; they are negotiated and take effect exactly in the same way as does any of the traditional forms of international agreement.

Despite their external resemblances to the ordinary and familiar type of international instrument, however (which we earlier discovered to rest upon a temporary identity of interest and therefore to be inherently unstable and liable to dissolution), closer examination of these new special purpose groupings reveals a fundamental difference in theory and in effect. In the first place, these groupings provide for much more intimate relationships than normally exists between sovereignties. They are also obviously designed to lead toward ever more close co-operation and hence are difficult to withdraw from once they are entered into. When a state becomes involved in one of these bodies, its domestic and foreign policies become so intertwined with those of the remainder of the membership that breaking off the relationship, although legally permissible, becomes practically impossible. In practice, therefore, these special bodies serve to limit and weaken sovereignty by depriving a state of its former complete freedom of action in the area covered by the agreement.

The foregoing points can perhaps be made more clear by reference to a few of these bodies. Perhaps the best known to Americans are the North Atlantic Treaty Organization (NATO) and the Organization of American states (OAS). In Europe, among others are found the Organization for European Economic Co-operation (OEEC) and the European Payments Union (EPU). Each of these bodies serves as the vehicle for closer co-operation on a more permanent basis than would be expected from a treaty relationship between sovereignties.

NATO. The NATO, an organization of fifteen European and North American states was created in 1949 to provide for mutual defense and joint action in case of attack. Other alliances of the past have had similar objectives; what makes NATO unique is the degree of planning, close co-ordination, and tight integration that goes on within the framework. No aspect of sovereignty is so central to statehood as control over one's own armed forces, yet there exists a permanent NATO armed force pledged to the collective defense of western Europe rather than to the mere protection of the homelands of the various members. There are a common headquarters and common strategic and tactical plans; for operational purposes the armed force is deemed to be a single entity. Officers of one state give orders to the troops of another; the industrial establishments of all members produce the materials of defense on a basis of specialization and division of labor. With so much of the defense of Europe being entrusted to an international body and with so much consequent effect upon the international body and internal policies of all its members, NATO (or something like it) has already become a permanent part of the conduct of political affairs in Europe; it has transcended the status of a mere alliance.

OEEC. The OEEC has in the same way served to merge the economies of the western European states. Set up originally to carry out the European end of the Marshall Plan of 1947 by creating ways for the European states to co-operate in their own economic recovery, it proved in practice to be an effective instrument. Its basic idea is the unity of the economy of Europe, and by promotion of intra-European trade and by channeling the flow of commodities into the states where they would be of the greatest value to recovery, it facilitated the most efficient utilization of the resources of the continent. At the present time the work of the OEEC has progressed so far that the members find their economies closely integrated. Economic isolation for any of the OEEC countries, even if it were politically expedient, would be impossible without paying a tremendous cost in loss of production and a decline in the standard of living. When, after 1950, the purely economic aspect of American aid gave way to the concern with rearmament, the OEEC again was of great assistance in making possible the maximum effort by the various European states; it has thus served as a valuable adjunct to NATO.

These two examples illustrate what these special-purpose groups do. They start on a basis of complete national sovereignty, it is true; but in their concern with getting the job done that they were set up to accomplish, they take such action as seems to be necessary and expedient without concern for the effect upon political philosophy and international law. As techniques mature and ramifications develop, the drift toward a more unified organization speeds up. The tendency in most of these special-purpose groups is toward federation or consolidation.

In this way NATO led to the European Defense Community and Western European Union, and OEEC led to the Schuman Plan. Although these two are perhaps the most striking examples, the likelihood of such an evolution is present in all of these organizations. The special-purpose grouping, which in practice goes beyond the formal treaty arrangement, is one of the dynamic aspects of the search for a new basis of political organization.

The Merging of Small States. A more specialized form of the flight from the nation-state is epitomized by the several instances when small states have merged their identities with those of other states, either joining a larger one or assisting in the creation of an entirely new state. This is not yet a major trend but it is interesting and potentially important. It indicates a realization on the part of small states (often not yet fully independent or only recently so) that no matter how great the joys of sovereignty may be, they are scarcely worth the price of tension and insecurity which they exact. By choosing membership in a larger political community, the small states sacrifice complete self-determination but gain in return the greater protection and more solid economic foundation that flow from membership in the broader organization.

In 1948 the people of Newfoundland, offered a choice between self-government looking toward independence and membership in the Dominion of Canada, by popular vote chose the latter. Independence was less attractive than membership in a going concern. In the same way, federations are being planned for the British possessions in the Caribbean, and in 1953 an East African federation was created. More difficult to accomplish but perhaps more significant in the long run is the proposed political merger of the six Schuman Plan states of Europe. Beginning with the customs union of the three low countries (Belgium, the Netherlands, and Luxembourg—known as 'Benelux') and spreading in many directions, by 1955 the movement had gained enough momentum so that even skeptical and hardened politicians were taking it seriously. This proposal does not contemplate a federation of limited scope; what it has in mind is the creation of a new political entity known simply as 'Europe.' Other such proposals are occasionally heard. The likelihood of their early adoption is not great, but they serve once again to underscore the need felt by peoples and governments for a base of political organization more efficient and rational than the nation-state.

Conclusions. The final conclusion on this subject would seem to be inescapable. It is beyond question that the present period of history is a transitional one. The modern state emerged in the sixteenth century and by 1800 had surrounded itself with a complex of emotional attachments. Four centuries ago the state had a rational base as well: it represented the maximum area that could be efficiently governed from one seat. Today the technologies of peace and of war have made the old-style nation-state obsolete and impractical. Much larger areas—perhaps the entire world—can be governed as easily from one center as Louis XIV ruled France from Versailles, while states of the old type can no longer govern themselves.

We are in an age of giants, and the smaller states of the world are seeking to adjust themselves to the changed situation. They have attempted various techniques, as we have seen; all of them, however, eventually confront the immutable truth that the old state form upon which their organization is based cannot survive. The time will come, and soon, when this realization will become general and what is now only a tendency will become a powerful force. The whole framework of world politics will be altered to accommodate a society composed of fewer, although larger, members; even after this change takes place, however, the matter of rationalizing the relationships within the new community of large states will remain to be dealt with. Many obstacles of all sorts—legal, political, psychological, and emotional—remain to be overcome before new and acceptable forms of organization are discovered. But that they will be found and put into operation is either a certainty or, at least, one of the major probabilities of the future.

THE END OF IMPERIALISM

IMPERIALISM IN THE STATE SYSTEM

One of the dominant characteristics of the nation-state system at its height was the tendency toward the creation of great colonial empires. Once Europe became no longer a fertile field for imperial expansion because of its division into national states, the search for overseas empires was on. All the major states felt that their preferred status required the possession and exploitation of massive colonial possessions; many of the great international conflicts of recent history have hinged upon the possession of some colonial territory. Germany, Italy, and Japan—the late-comers upon the international scene— were driven to demanding and taking empires for themselves almost as soon as they had attained political maturity in the nineteenth century, even though most of the desirable territories of the world had already been appropriated and most of the other colonial powers had satiated themselves. Even the United States, after a long quarrel with itself and its historical tradition, eventually succumbed; the end of the war with Spain in 1898 found the United States in possession of a far-flung (if not particularly large) empire in the Pacific and in the Caribbean. It can be fairly said that the pursuit and control of colonies was until recently a normal accompaniment of international politics.

Reasons for Imperialism, Valid and Invalid. Imperialism as a phenomenon has been analyzed often and there seems to be fairly general agreement that the empire-building urge was in most cases the result of a combination of motivations. Certain basic factors appear in nearly every instance of a policy of imperialism and should be mentioned.

Security considerations have always been present and have often been paramount. States have sought colonies in order to secure advanced bases, strategic locations on communications routes, access to critical raw materials of strategic value, or sources of manpower. Britain's empire was constructed for the most part with an eye to the value of the colony to a naval power; this explains the chains of British-controlled islands that extend across all of the oceans of the world. France, on the other hand, made manpower an object of its colonialism: she exploited her African and Asiatic colonies to balance Germany's preponderance of population.

Economic reasons have also shaped many imperialist programs. Marxist and Soviet theory makes this the entire explanation, purporting to discover an 'imperialist stage of capitalism,' when capitalist states are directed toward imperialism as a desperate last resort to stave off the imminent collapse of their system. This argument, like so much communist theory, ignores both human psychology and recorded history and need not be taken seriously. Nevertheless, the search for raw materials and for controlled markets has frequently led states to adopt particular imperialist tactics, and economic motivations help explain much of imperialism.

Finally, the search for prestige has exerted much influence upon the imperialist drive. Possession of a colonial empire has been thought to make a state 'great' and to add several cubits to its stature. Imperial Germany demanded 'a place in the sun'—a colonial empire of its own—as a badge of its entry into the ranks of the great powers. It is useless to point out, as many astute students have done, that most colonial empires were losing enterprises economically (the Dutch and Belgian were conspicuous exceptions) and instead of adding power they were usually sources of weakness because of the extensive dispersal of armed force they required and the constant danger of rebellion by the subject peoples. The rewards in prestige have usually been considered to be adequate by political leaders and peoples alike.

Of course states and peoples were adept at concealing the real reasons for imperialism behind a wall of rationalizations. The usual form taken by this self-deception was that of stressing the 'civilizing' role of the imperialist power and asserting that in taking on the colony the state was only performing a duty of the highest importance. Britain cheerfully assumed the 'white man's burden' of freeing Asiatics and Africans from the bondage of slavery, savagery, and ignorance; France was proud of its *mission civilatrice;* the Filipinos were the 'little brown brothers' of the Americans. The significance of missionary activity cannot be underestimated in this connection. The salvation of souls from perdition and their conversion to truth were deemed ample reason for annexation of territory and the destruction of native self-rule. There was no shortage of reasons to explain imperialism, whether one sought active motivations or moral justifications.

Characteristics of Imperialism. Of course, every imperial power was unique in the way it approached the problem of governing its empire. Some were, in general, influences for good upon the people of the colonies; others harmed their colonies more than they helped them. Some earned the bitter enmity of their subject peoples; others instead secured and retained a high degree of loyalty. Yet certain fundamental similarities can be discovered in the way any imperialist power ruled its subject territorities.

In the first place, imperialism normally demanded that a colony be ruled in the interest of the mother country instead of in the interest of the residents of the territory. Empires were for the purpose of the aggrandizement of the homeland, and the lot of the colonial peoples was determined by what was good for the colonizer. Economic, cultural, political, and military policies were dictated by this general motivation.

In the second place, economic exploitation was the rule rather than the exception. Whatever economic resources the territory offered were viewed as enriching the mother country, and little attempt was made to balance expenditures so as to equalize matters. Extractive wealth—mineral and agricultural—was usually exploited by a system of absentee landlordism, by the export of raw materials for processing elsewhere, and by the maintenance of a system of subsistence agriculture for the bulk of the native population. This pattern was followed regardless of the commodity involved; it was the same whether it was petroleum in the East Indies, diamonds in Africa, sugar in the Philippines, tin in Malaya, or rice in Burma.

A third characteristic of classical imperialism was the withholding of self-government from colonies and the granting of it only under extreme duress. Exceptions could be found—the policy of the United States in the Philippines is one—but self-government was generally regarded as a weakening of the imperial bond, and was resisted.

A final common feature was forced acculturation. For a variety of reasons, some practical and others ideological, most imperialist powers felt impelled to import their own cultures into their colonies and, if need be, to destroy any competing native social order and value system. Language, law, education, and religion alike were forcibly molded into the image of the master people, and native organizational forms were either discouraged or forbidden. In Africa native tribal customs were frowned upon by Britain, France, Portugal, and Germany; in Asia, elaborate civilizations, much older than those of their Western rulers, were crushed or driven underground. Perhaps no other aspect of imperialism proved to be more infuriating to the subject peoples when they gained national self-consciousness. Western claims to cultural superiority, tied in as they were with a complex of racial issues, ultimately created a heritage of bitterness which has made the adjustment of non-Western cultures to the remainder of the world most difficult.

THE DECLINE OF OLD-STYLE IMPERIALISM

The great colonial empires of the past are gone, all postwar attempts of imperialist powers to retain colonial territories seeking independence having failed; in the truncated remnants of the old empires that remain, colonial policies are being undertaken that represent drastic revisions of earlier programs. Old-style imperialism has entered into its final fatal decline. What were the causes of this basic reversal of direction in the acquisition and rule of colonies?

The Decline of the Imperial Powers. One basic reason for the end of imperialism is the decline of the old imperial powers. The imperial giants of the pre-1914 world were Great Britain, France, the Netherlands, Belgium, and the United States; the first three were the leaders both in the extent of territory ruled and in the wealth of their empires. We are all familiar with the fate that befell the states of Europe. The power decline suffered by all the European powers made them incapable to rule and exploit these territories in anything like the manner of an earlier day. The states of Europe were so much occupied in maintaining their existence and independent status in a world growing steadily more unpropitious for them that they had progressively less and less power to spare for their empires.

No colonial power ever dominated its empire by military strength alone, however. The technique of control used was compounded of a willingness to use unrestrained violence upon occasion and a bland assumption of superiority and the right to rule. This refusal even to consider any equity of treatment between homeland and colony usually left the native population baffled and unable to find any aperture in the wall of pride and prestige which the imperialist group built around themselves. Such native opposition as appeared was crushed ruthlessly.

This fragile structure which supported imperialist rule in Asia, Africa, and other parts of the world crashed beyond repair during World War II. The Japanese, an Asiatic and non-white people, proved not only to Asiatics but to the entire world that white claims to superior power and ability were false. The defeats inflicted upon the Allies in the Pacific in 1942 marked the end of an imperialist era. That the Japanese were finally defeated was immaterial; the damage to the colonial psychology was irreparable. With their prestige destroyed, the only way the old colonial states could retain their empires was by power alone, and this they could no longer do. They were unable to withstand the disruptive pressures that had been building up throughout the entire colonial world.

Native Mastery of Western Technology. One of these disruptive forces went almost unsuspected until it broke with near-cataclysmic force. This was the fact that the native populations of the colonies, for many years deprived of most opportunities for self-advancement, had nevertheless profited greatly from their long and close association with Western technology. Despite their normally subordinate role in comparison with that of the imperial elite, they learned many valuable lessons from their contact with Western learning and technology. Ironically enough, it was the very insistence of the colonial powers on the forced assimilation of Western culture that speeded up this process and made its eventual completion certain. Being forced to learn Western languages, natives found themselves able to profit from the wealth of scientific and humanistic data accumulated in the libraries and laboratories of the West. Once armed with this information and made wiser by the insights it produced, the native populations of many colonial empires found themselves able to turn the resources of Western technology against their masters.

Of course, the understanding of Western techniques and the capacity to employ them in the pursuit of nationalist objectives was confined to only a tiny portion of the native population of each territory, but this was the key group. Technicians in production and distribution were able to administer and build up the indigenous economy; specialists in political leadership were able to create formidable political groups by the employment of modern techniques of organization and mass communication.

It is somewhat disconcerting to Western observers today to see the extent to which the former colonial peoples, intent on learning Western methodology in order to gain self-determination, have copied the worst of the West as well as the best. Economic exploitation is as unfair when carried on by a native group as when it is the practice of foreigners; corrupt political practices are as great a prostitution of democracy when done by former subjects as when done by imperialists. But in any case, the lesson is clear: the former colonial territories are thinking in terms of the future. They are still 'backward,' it is true, but they are now on the move toward the mastery and the manipulation of Western technology. That in itself would spell the end of old-style imperialism even if there were no other factors involved.

The Rise of Nationalism. When all is said and done, however, the force that destroyed the base upon which imperialism rested is nationalism. Imperialist techniques were effective only upon a non-political or apathetic population. As soon as the bulk of the people of any given area came to share the mass emotion of nationalism, major revisions in the relationships between ruler and ruled became inevitable. Nationalism is a mass movement; no elite, however constituted, can for long hold out against a population that is aware of its unity and is agreed in general terms upon its objectives. Once the peoples of the colonial areas went on the march, there was no longer any hope of saving the old system.

It has been since 1945 that the effect of colonial nationalism has been the most conspicuous. Colonial revolutions, violent and non-violent, have taken place in many subject territories in Asia and Africa. These have been generally successful in gaining complete or virtual independence when they have been backed by an aroused populace. In other colonies, colonial powers have attempted to meet the demands of rising nationalism in order to stave off impending revolt. New policies have been inaugurated which reverse earlier tactics and are aimed generally at granting more political autonomy and native self-determination.

But although the effect of native nationalism has been most obvious since the end of the war, it is actually much older. From the beginning, the arrival of European imperialists, with all their paraphernalia of racial superiority, was a cause of resentment and hostility in native populations. In central and south Africa, where the natives were organized on a tribal basis and live in a late Stone Age stage of development, the amount of opposition was negligible. In North Africa and the Middle East, social organization was somewhat more elaborate but the nomadic way of life of many of the people made it more difficult to develop a true mass resistance. In south and southeast Asia, where a large population with a complex culture was present in most of the colonized areas, opposition was at its greatest. India's objections to its subordinate status dated from the appearance of British rule; the French had a constant struggle with native groups in Indo-China; the Dutch faced similar problems in the Indies. The opposition to imperial pretensions on the part of subject peoples is not a purely postwar condition.

Since 1945, however, native nationalism has grown stronger and has succeeded where formerly it had failed. In addition to the factors noted earlier, some additional reasons might be mentioned.

In the aftermath of World War II there appeared (as there had after World War I) a great wave of sympathy for all peoples struggling to be free.

After a great victory over a foul tyranny it seemed to millions of people only just and fair that any group seeking independence should be granted it. This attitude was not confined to states without colonies of their own; sizable proportions of the population of each of the imperialist states were supporters of all movements for colonial independence, even those directed against their own governments.

Secondly, the effects of the war upon Asiatic imperialism were far-reaching. Not only did the Japanese victory over the white states serve to provide an example which others in Asia sought to emulate, but native nationalism received an opportunity to express itself during the struggle. Resistance movements of different sorts existed in all the territories overrun by the Japanese, and these formed the nucleus of political organizations for independence and self-government at the end of the fighting. During the confused period that began with the surrender of the Japanese troops, these irregular native groups (led in most states by Western-trained agitators, communist and otherwise) took over control of the governmental apparatus. By the time the Europeans arrived to resume control, the native governments were busy ruling their territories and were in no mood again to surrender control of their political futures to alien hands. This situation occurred in Indonesia, in Burma, in Indo-China, in Malaya, and to some extent in the Philippines. The experience of independence and self-government provide the spark to native nationalism and all attempts to extinguish it were successfully resisted.

A third factor helping to explain the rise in colonial national spirit has been the improved communication within each area and between it and the rest of the world. This has meant that any successful revolt served as an example to all the others, and has intensified the movement everywhere. The colonial areas are no longer isolated; they are in contact with the United Nations and with groups of sympathizers everywhere, and each encourages the others. The force of nationalism occasionally results in excesses; the strength of the emotion frequently obscures the vision and good judgment of the leaders of these groups, as in Iran and Burma. Such states are repeatedly led astray by their frenzied national self-identification and xenophobia.

The Future of Imperialism

Imperialism as we have employed the term in this section has no future; the day when great states could rule subject areas in blithe unconcern for anything except the interest of the mother country has long since passed. It is self-evident, however, that there are yet millions of people in the world who are not prepared for self-government; to grant freedom immediately to all men everywhere would scarcely be doing them a kindness. When we realize this fact we see that for a long time to come many such areas must remain under the sponsorship and administration of some foreign country. What we shall examine in this section is the future of colonial policy: the probable course of development in methods of leadership and guidance employed by states that have control over these subject areas.

The Trusteeship Council and Article 73. The United Nations followed the example of the League of Nations and made national control over dependent and non-self-governing territories one of its matters of concern. In the United Nations system there are two areas of competence over colonial matters. In the first place, the Charter created a Trusteeship Council, which was to have jurisdiction over all trust territories for the ultimate disposition of which the organization has responsibility. According to the Charter, there are three types of trust territories: the surviving League of Nations mandates (largely German and Turkish territories stripped from the losers in World War I), territories detached from enemy states as a result of World War II (the colonial empires of Italy and Japan), and any territories voluntarily placed under the system by states responsible for their administration. Over these areas the United Nations through the Trusteeship Council has clear jurisdiction, and the state whose flag flies over them is merely a trustee.

The responsibility of the ruling state is clear; under the terms of the Charter it must govern the area with the primary purpose of promoting the 'political, economical, social, and educational advancement' of the people and their 'progressive development towards self-government or independence.' In other words, trust territories are not areas for economic exploitation or security planning; the rights of the inhabitants of the area are deemed to be pre-eminent. Generally speaking, the Trusteeship Council has been successful in seeing to it that these obligations are carried out by the trustee powers. No greater reversal of traditional imperialist objectives could be imagined.

The trusteeship system is of very limited application. The Charter also contains a statement of general colonial policy which is much broader in its scope and which foretells even more graphically that the trusteeship arrangement the future of colonial policy. Article 73 of the Charter consists of a 'Declaration Regarding Non-Self-Governing Territories.' All members of the United Nations who 'have or assume responsibilities for the administration of territories whose peoples have not yet attained a full measure of self-government' now admit the principle that 'the interests of the inhabitants of these territories are paramount' and agree to make this the guiding notion of their administration. Several specific obligations are accepted by each colonial state, including principally the insuring of the advancement of the people, the development of self government (although, be it noted, not necessarily 'independence'), and the transmission regularly to the Secretary-General of information about the manner and the extent to which each of them is honoring its pledge.

No coercive method is prescribed to enforce this declaration except that of publicity and public opinion. Yet the implications of this declaration are of enormous scope. At the time of its signature all the colonial powers of the world were in the United Nations, and the acceptance of this declaration meant that all the non-self-governing areas of the world would thenceforth be ruled in the primary interest of their inhabitants. That there have been defections from this lofty ideal is undeniable, but that it exists in the first place is powerful evidence that the day of old-fashioned colonialism has passed. Public opinion today emphatically insists that all men receive the practical maximum of self-government, and colonial powers are now seriously limited in the use to which they can put their colonial possessions. The stresses of the cold war and the requirements of rearmament and defense have occasioned many departures from this generalization, but even the colonial powers realize that indefinitely to put off the demands and the right of subject peoples is no longer possible.

New Colonial Policies. In accordance with the different attitude toward the administration of subject areas, new colonial policies are rapidly being developed and carried into practice by all the major states with dependencies. In general they all aim at the implementation of Article 73, although the speed and the specific details obviously vary in each case, depending upon local conditions and the particular situation of the ruling power.

Great Britain, with the most extensive empire in the world, has undertaken a many-sided program of fostering the development of its dependent peoples and speeding the transition toward self-government. Learning its lesson from the loss of India and Burma, it has instituted fundamental reforms in virtually all its possessions. Since 1945 it has initiated projects of federation that will grant political autonomy for its Caribbean possessions and for its East African territories. In those areas—such as the Gold Coast—where native development has proceeded far enough, it has established native legislatures and administrations. In the more backward areas it has deliberately sought to encourage the redevelopment of native culture with a judicious admixture of Western technology; while sponsoring the growing self-discovery of the natives it also assists in the introduction of modern techniques of public health, communications, and government. After making allowance for the unevenness of any democratically determined policy of this sort, Britain's record in the execution of the obligations it assumed under Article 73 compares favorably with that of any other state, and it seems sincerely interested in moving its dependent peoples toward genuine self-government as rapidly as their development permits.

France has had a more stormy time in its colonial adventure since 1945 than Britain. It has had to contend with a long and expensive colonial war in Indo-China (and eventually lost at least half the territory) and with riots and outbreaks in North Africa. Its internal political instability has also deprived it of the continuity in policy which is necessary for an orderly transition from an old era to a new. Nevertheless, partly from a genuine concern for the rights of subject peoples and partly as a result of its inability to compe subservience, France has also undertaken in some degree to carry out the new colonial policy. In its Central African colonies, a new paternalism has to some extent replaced the more distant rule of another day. A much greater degree of official concern now exists for the welfare of the natives in such matters as health, education, and economic status. There is a notable difference between the French and the British policies, however. The French view the development of the natives toward self-government as possible only through a continually closer approximation of France itself; the progress of the people is to take place through a greater assimilation of French culture. Native ways are not discouraged, but the emphasis is upon France and all things French. Because the French had so much farther to go, their immediate progress has not been so obvious as Britain's.

The Netherlands lost much of its empire with the successful revolt of Indonesia. It has attempted, in that portion left to it, to prevent further defections by following a more enlightened program. Belgium, with most of its empire concentrated in one great area in Central Africa, the Congo, has not had major native movements to contend with and has sought to prevent them by revising its policy in the general direction of native improvement; the great profit accruing to the home government from the colony make sufficient funds available for the purpose. Some observers speak of the Congo as the 'garden colony' of Africa today. Spain and Portugal have not made any great change in their colonial administrations; Portugal's record is the better of the two. As a result colonial problems are building up which these states will be called upon to deal with in the future.

Finally, the United States is also moving with great rapidity toward self-government for its dependent possessions. Philippine independence was a promise before World War II; it has been a reality since 1946. Puerto Rico has acquired the status of a 'commonwealth' with complete autonomy, and in 1953 President Eisenhower offered it complete independence. The minor island possessions are likewise the object of programs of modernization and improvement, with emphasis on the daily lives of the inhabitants.

THE ROLE OF THE NEW STATES

Any discussion of imperialism and colonial policy today must include a brief consideration of the role of the states newly escaped from dependent status. Approximately a dozen such states have became full-fledged members of the international society since the end of the war. In general their behavior has demonstrated certain common characteristics derived largely from their recently acquired independence, and although all will undoubtedly become more and more aware of the responsibilities attendant upon sovereign status, at the present time they tend to produce problems of a unique sort.

Policy Characteristics. Certain ingredients appear in the policies of all these new states. Perhaps the most pervasive is anti-colonialism. Acutely conscious of their own independence and the struggle most of them passed through in order to achieve it, they assume the role of liberators of all peoples remaining under alien rule anywhere. This necessitates the active or passive support of all independence movements in colonial areas and constant agitation before world public opinion in favor of these groups. It also makes necessary a hostility toward all colonial powers, particularly their own former rulers. This opposition is not confined to colonial questions but often extends into other policy areas as well. In the United Nations the new states arc constantly urging an extension of the trusteeship system and exert great pressure on the colonial powers in the direction of greater implementation of Article 73.

A second common characteristic is neutralism, actual or attempted. We have already discussed the tendency of many states to feel that the cold war is no concern of theirs and to seek to insulate themselves from it. This is particularly true of most of the new states. They seek not only to avoid involvement in the quarrel but to conduct relations with both sides with studied impartiality. This impedes the attempts of the United States to organize the entire free world (of which these states form a part) against the Soviet threat; they have, however, been equally immune to the blandishments of the Russian bloc.

They also display a third common approach to policy: self-assertiveness. They uniformly resist any proposal from any quarter that smacks of coercion in any form; they insist upon the most literal respect for their complete independence. Their recent non-self-governing status is fresh in their minds and they are intensely aware of the symbolism of sovereignty. As a result they are often accused of being unco-operative and belligerent.

Paradoxically enough, another point upon which they generally agree is strong support of the United Nations. Although almost bumptious in their independence, they sincerely work within the United Nations apparatus and play a large part in its deliberations. The reason for this contradiction lies in their insecurity. Most of the new states are small and all have major problems of internal organization to solve before their own regimes can enjoy real security. The maximum development of their own resources depends upon a world in which peace and security are available for everyone. Distrusting the bipolar blocs as being potentially a cause for war, they place their faith and their trust in the United Nations instead. Only in collective guarantees of security can the safety of small states be found.

The Future of New States. Excessively nationalistic and intent on playing a major role in world affairs, the new states at the present time constitute something of a special problem for all the other states. The direction of their future development depends to a considerable extent upon the course followed by their nationalism. If it follows the example of Europe, for an indefinite time in the future the new states will continue to be xenophobic and unco-operative, and they will recede from this extreme position only by learning as the result of war and devastation that sovereign independence is not the greatest of all joys. If, on the other hand, the new states are able to profit by the example of others and can absorb the lessons of the interdependence of peoples and the ultimate futility of unilateral nationalism without passing through the disillusionments themselves, their concern with peace and security may well make them leaders in the drive to create a worldwide system of guarantees.

The question will be answered in terms of the attitude and policy of other states during the present period of transition. This is of primary importance to the United States, since we are vitally interested in such an era of peace and stability. If American policy is patient and forbearing, if we do not indulge the temptation to employ our superior strength to coerce these smaller states, if instead we take account of their foibles and make allowances for their inexperience and the powerful emotions to which they are subject, the opportunity for winning them over to a co-operative attitude is great.

The case of India is particularly pertinent. India, as the United States has already learned to its discomfiture, simply will not submit to coercion, even in its own interest. Instead, the Indian government has demonstrated a great eagerness to learn from the West and to work as an equal partner for common security. Only upon this basis can the new states be won for the forces of freedom, and it would not seem over-idealistic to claim that their adherence would be worth the trouble it requires.

12

Problem Areas: Economic

W E turn now to a consideration of some of the more fundamental economic factors in contemporary international affairs. Although we have stressed that economic determinism is not a key to the explanation of all the crisis issues of today, we cannot dismiss economic questions lightly. Perhaps the most frequent type of international contact is economic, and the interest of individuals in this aspect of interstate relations is always high.

In the following discussion of economic questions, the influence of national policy and the political relationships of states will become quite apparent. Political factors condition and modify economic judgments to an often surprising extent. During the past hundred years, states have come to employ national economic power as a weapon of policy. In the process, they have materially diminished the area of economic freedom open to individuals.

The trend toward increased collectivism (the growing centralization of economic control in the hands of government) which is discernible in every quarter of the world has been intensified by two very different social forces that have come to coincide in their direction. In the first place, in response to popular demands, governments have increasingly intervened into the economic order to extend more and more guarantees and protections to individuals. While gaining greater economic security, men have had to forego a great amount of economic freedom. Second, the requirements of international life have forced governments to exert more and more control over their domestic economies. Either to apply pressure on other states or to protect themselves from foreign coercion, increasing state control over economic life has been a step taken by virtually all governments. The conduct of foreign affairs today requires considerable political direction of economic life and very few states have been in a position to avoid it.

ECONOMIC NATIONALISM

The first and perhaps the most basic problem to be considered is economic nationalism. This phrase has many possible meanings, but its general import is clear. It refers to the national attitude (and the resulting policy) which assumes that the function of the national economic system is to strengthen the international hand of the state. It is thus a denial of the economic theory upon which the societies and governments of the Western world are founded.

Classical Economics. According to 'classical' economics, in the normal economic order the motivation for all economic activity is private profit. The theory therefore calls for the maximum economic freedom for individuals; the 'free market' is one in which prices are determined by the interplay of supply and demand, without governmental interference. In free societies, the primary focus of attention has continued to be the profit of individuals, even though extensive governmental intervention was permitted. In return for certain forms of protection, individuals have given up some liminal freedoms which proved to be of little worth in practice.

This individualist concern with economic life had its international implications. Classical international-trade theory is a completely developed body of doctrine. It argues generally that the profit of all is best served by the creation of a world-wide free market. In other words, goods and services should flow across boundaries without any governmental impediment; free trade and a high velocity of exchange of goods and services are characteristics of a healthy economic order.

Mercantilism. Classical economics is largely a product of the eighteenth century and the rise of industrialism. Before that time the prevailing economic theory of international life was mercantilism. This doctrine, thought by all to be dead and buried during the nineteenth century, has staged a recovery and now inspires much of what we call 'economic nationalism' in this chapter.

Mercantilism differed from classical economics in that the basic economic unit was thought to be the state, rather than the individual. The purpose of economic life was not to return private profit, but to strengthen and to enrich the state. This conferred upon the government the right to direct and control the economic life of all individuals to give the maximum benefit to the state. It was empowered to use any weapons that proved practical and effective: coercion, proscription, persuasion, subsidy, and any others appropriate.

Underlying all government policy in a mercantilist regime was the idea that the state must prepare itself for the ultimate test of its power of self-preservation: war. As a result, governments sought two general economic objectives: the attainment of the highest possible degree of self-sufficiency, and the accumulation of great stores of visible wealth with which to finance a war—gold, silver, and precious stones.

Common policies of mercantilist states included the control of exports and imports so as to maintain a 'favorable' balance of trade (an excess of exports over imports—the object being to have treasure flow into the state), the stimulation by subsidy of politically desirable forms of economic activity, the discouragement of other less valuable forms of economic life, the passage of 'sumptuary' laws to control the pattern of consumption, and, perhaps best known, the acquisition of colonies. The overseas empires served as markets for domestic production, as sources of raw materials, and as reservoirs of manpower. In general, therefore, mercantilism can be summarized as a rejection of the claims of the individual to economic freedom and an assertion of the superior rights and demands of the state, the 'people,' the 'community,' or some other collective abstraction.

Economic Nationalism. Neo-mercantilism, or economic nationalism, rejects the antiquated economic concepts of historic mercantilism but accepts its political assumptions and much of its technique. No longer are governments so unsophisticated as to believe that the only forms of wealth are precious metals and stones, and the simple faith in the 'favorable balance of trade' has been replaced by an understanding of the mechanism of international payments. But governments today adhere to the political rule that each state can trust no one but itself and must constantly be prepared for a forced isolation.

The economic destiny of the state is all-important; it must be always ready for the necessity of conducting war, and in this process it is free to employ all the economic instruments of coercion it has available. Individual economic objectives are subordinated; private purposes that serve public goals are encouraged while others are discouraged or prohibited. Modern 'macro-economics,' with its emphasis on the concepts of the 'economy' and the 'gross national product' and its proclivity to calculate the roles of individuals as integers in a greater whole, provides a convenient theoretical rationale for this process.

THE CAUSES OF ECONOMIC NATIONALISM

It must be admitted that economic internationalism, despite its theoretical defensibility, never gained anything like universal acceptance. Even during the period of its greatest effectiveness, internationalism was rivaled by a variety of programs of government intervention. The most frequently used device was the protective tariff, although other aspects of mercantilist practice also appeared. Nevertheless, during most of the nineteenth century and up to World War I, commodities, services, and persons moved with remarkable freedom in international channels. What were the factors that led states from that condition to the present one in which extensive government control of economic life is a normal feature of international politics?

Economic Results of Two Wars. Two wars, in which immeasurable amounts of wealth were wasted and great productive facilities were destroyed, undermined the economic foundations of many states, particularly in Europe. Part of the productive plant of the major European states was wiped out and the remainder rendered obsolescent; the financial structure of most of them was also weakened by the liquidation of income sources and the exhaustion of credit. The mechanics of international trade operated in such a way as to threaten to drain the impoverished countries of their already depleted reserves.

Faced with this situation, after 1919 many European governments and several in other parts of the world undertook restrictive policies. They sought to insulate their economies from the effect of the international business cycle so as to get on with the central problem of domestic recovery with maximum speed and efficiency. Import and export controls, restrictions upon international movement of money and credit, limitations on immigration and emigration, and many other techniques familiar today appeared for the first time in the wake of Versailles.

Many of the officials responsible for these policies recognized the economic fallacies inherent in all of them, and they rationalized their decisions by terming them emergency measures of temporary duration. Of course, we know that the trend, thus begun regretfully and hesitantly, has continued without interruption; no state has been able to dispense completely with some such pattern of controls. Indeed, the arrival of a second world war at a time when the world had not yet recovered economically from the first served to intensify the problem and to make more acceptable the idea that the economic life of individuals, particularly in its international aspects, is an appropriate area for government control in the political interest of the state.

The Effect of Nationalism. The ultimate causes of economic nationalism, however, do not lie in the economic crises precipitated by war. The economic problems of the world are not confined within national boundaries but, in nearly every case, transcend them. The issues are common to nearly all states, and the situations following World War I were such as not to be susceptible to real solution on any unilateral basis. Yet all states attacked these problems on their own. No serious attempt at a co-operative approach to joint action was ever made between 1919 and 1939; the most ambitious undertaking, the World Economic Conference of 1933, was a failure because of the refusal of the United States to participate. The Roosevelt administration, interested in the maximum freedom of domestic action, was unwilling to have its attention diverted or its resources dissipated on any international projects; the United States was following the lead of other states toward systematic economic nationalism.

Actually, the rise of economic nationalism is best explained as a part of the rise of nationalism in general. International co-operation in the economic realm necessitates a popular recognition that all men are in the same condition and that prosperity for one group necessitates prosperity for all. But economic tension, instead of deepening the awareness of the common plight of mankind, had just the opposite effect. In the chaos of postwar Europe after 1919, individuals were beset by a lack of both economic and social stability. The result, as we have seen, was a great wave of nationalist revival as men turned to the state for support when other loyalties proved useless and unrewarding.

Nationalist particularism demanded that governments serve the economic needs of their own peoples first and entirely, and that relief be rapid and direct. It was especially insisted that the citizens of the state be freed from the competition—always characterized as 'unfair'—represented by other states. In this way the cycle was set in motion. Economic pressures stimulated nationalism, which in turn dictated policies that served to deepen the economic imbalance.

The twentieth century has witnessed the reversal of a historic trend. For three hundred years previously, men had been engaged in a 'flight from the state': a social movement that emphasized the atomistic structure of society and made the individual the focus of all social concern. The movement reached its climax in the concepts of the limited state, political democracy, and economic individualism, each developed at its fullest between 1815 and 1914. After World War I a counter tendency asserted itself; all over the world men turned again to the state and found in political values a significance which only a few years earlier they had been denying. As a result, totalitarian government, authoritarianism, and collectivism came to replace the institutional forms of another day.

In this process economic nationalism fits naturally. Individual economic welfare is not completely discredited; it is merely given a subordinate place in the scale. The first obligation of men is to strengthen their state and to assist it in every way to gain its objectives.

The Trend toward Retaliation. Once begun, economic nationalism proved to be highly contagious. Systematic control of its international economic relationships gave a state a great advantage in dealing with other states whose citizens were free to follow their own bent. It seemed to many observers that the totalitarian governments (the first to employ these techniques extensively) had stumbled upon the real answer to the economic dilemma of the postwar world. Other governments followed their lead, but sought to make their policies just a little more extensive and rigorous than the original. This merely invited retaliation; meanwhile other states were caught up in the process.

One by one, as their more or less free economies proved unable to deal effectively with a world grown increasingly controlled, the states of the world succumbed to the pressures of economic nationalism. Today no state of any consequence feels that it can trust its economic health to the mercies of the free market; each instead keeps itself in a position to take the greatest advantage possible of any lapse in the vigilance of its fellows.

The fear of retaliation is perhaps the most serious impediment to the successful exploitation of the international-community sense which we have seen to exist. Many governments are interested in making moves toward a more rational framework of economic policy, but they fear to do so because of the danger of exposing themselves to the rapacity of others. Consequently, each new step toward internationalism can be undertaken only after a tortuous course of preliminary negotiation among all parties involved and the exchange of guarantees that each will not take advantage of the other.

THE EFFECTS OF ECONOMIC NATIONALISM

Control over Economic Life. Economic nationalism is characterized by extensive government control over individual economic activity, domestic and foreign. The areas of control in which detailed regulation is common may be indicated briefly.

Regulation of production and consumption is usual. The production of commodities deemed essential to national security—such as military equipment—is encouraged or, if necessary, forced. Some states limit, by licenses and other devices, the amount of a particular item that may be produced; the Soviet Union uses this device on most consumer goods. The manufacture of other goods is prohibited outright because of the desire to preserve stockpiles of raw materials, or some other security reason. For every control over production there is a corresponding one over consumption; goods that cannot be produced are never consumed.

There are always stringent controls over international trade. Imports and exports alike fall within the scope of government action; licenses and permits become a feature of international exchange. Some commodities cannot be traded at all; no American may sell a 'strategic' commodity to anyone behind the Iron Curtain. The extent and type of control over any commodity are determined by either of two criteria. In the first place, the commodity may have peculiar significance in itself. Uranium ore may not be exported from the United States because of its strategic significance, while the import of textiles into the United States is limited by high tariffs because of competition with domestic production. The second criterion arises from the political orientation of the foreign state involved. If its attitude is friendly, economic intimacy is often encouraged; if it is hostile, controls may be applied as a means of exerting pressure. One need only contrast American policy toward Great Britain since 1945 with our economic relations with the Soviet bloc to discover many examples of this principle at work.

A special form of trade control is exchange regulation. If foreign currencies cannot be used to finance international exchange of goods freely, trade of necessity is reduced to a barter basis in a bilateral relationship. This form of economic activity is always less extensive than the freer variety and is very much easier for governments to control and manipulate.

A final form of economic regulation has to do with the limitations upon the international movement of persons. Although arising generally out of a complex of political-psychological causes, ample economic justification is always advanced for such policies. Emigration is restricted by states that fear to lose members of their working force; Great Britain has faced this problem since 1945. Immigration may be encouraged for the same reason (France has had a policy of selective recruitment of labor since 1945), but many states today are highly selective about the occupational specialties of the immigrants they admit. Even the United States—the traditional refuge of the oppressed— follows some selectivity in admitting aliens. Immigration may be kept low for the purpose of maintaining a high domestic wage level, as favored by much of organized labor in the United States; it may, on the other hand, be deliberately stimulated to depress wage rates by creating a labor surplus. Tourist travel may be made difficult for the people of a state while the government is inviting tourists from other lands; many European states, especially Great Britain and France, have taken this step since 1945. In these and many other ways the increased mobility arising from improved transportation is controlled and made to serve a political purpose.

Increased Political Rigidity. Striking as it does deeply into the private lives of individuals, economic nationalism serves to deepen the gulf separating national groups today. It stands directly athwart the movement toward interpersonal community relationships that we commented on in Chapter 9. Particularism as represented by the trend toward economic unilateralism contributes largely to the political rigidity of the world today.

The cause of political separatism is particularly well served by the notion of self-sufficiency as a desirable national objective. The old mercantilist dogma is implicit in every nationalist economic policy: the state must be willing and able to fight a war without allies in which it would be forced to depend entirely upon its own economic resources. Objections to the economic validity of particular policies are refuted by the simple argument that 'the security of the state must be guaranteed.' Thus each state pursues security through self-sufficiency.

As world boundaries are presently drawn, no state can achieve this goal. Even the United States and the USSR, each of continental expanse and both endowed more richly than any other political units, can never free themselves of dependence upon foreign sources of supply of key commodities. Nevertheless, governments persist in making the attempt. Stockpiling and the discovery of synthetic substitutes are suggested as methods of escaping the necessity of foreign supply, or else expansive policies are undertaken to gain control of such sources. As a necessary reciprocal policy, each state seeks to impede the progress of at least its principal rivals toward any kind of self-sufficiency.

Thus, to the normally competitive character of international politics has been added a new and particularly resentment-provoking dimension: economic warfare. A state that enjoys an economic advantage over another and capitalizes upon it incites bitterness and retaliatory policies by the affected government. In such a climate, any disposition to compromise and co-operation has a difficult time surviving. Economic nationalism and its implementation help maintain the tense quality of most international relationships today.

Increased Costs to Individuals. Individual citizens bear the cost of the restrictive practices of economic nationalism. The cost of commodities purchased by the consumer is higher as a result of protective tariffs and other import controls. With the government enjoying first claim upon the output of the economy, increased costs are passed on. Critical raw materials are kept out of private production; plant renovation and new construction are dedicated to government-sponsored production; competition for labor diverts manpower from civilian employment. The total effect of economic nationalism upon individuals may be briefly stated: it furthers either an absolute reduction in the standard of living or at least its stabilization below its optimum level.

In return for this burden, the citizen receives as return the knowledge that his government is taking steps to insure itself against destructive pressure from abroad and to build up its strength against a possible war. No one but the individual himself can decide whether these rewards are sufficient; if his decision is that the costs of economic nationalism are balanced by the return, no one else is in a position to question it. He is paying an economic price for a political reward, and policies to this end will continue to be accepted and demanded as long as people feel that this is a fair exchange. Change is possible, as we noted in Chapter 9, when political values are felt to be less important than personal ones.

The Drift Toward Totalitarianism. Economic nationalism serves to strengthen the trend toward totalitarianism that has already placed democracy and the free society on the defensive in many parts of the world. Once government sets about regulating the daily economic activities of its citizens, no matter how genuine is its devotion to the cause of individual freedom, dangerous precedents are created.

The people become accustomed to the presence of government in areas of life where formerly it was a stranger. Even though the original expansion of function was begun as the result of a crisis situation, and even though most steps are felt at first to be 'emergency' and 'temporary,' we know from experience that governments do not easily retreat from advanced areas of control. What was originally a means tends in practice to become an end in itself, particularly when it has been given the sanction of usage over a period of years. Economic nationalism is an enemy of the limited concept of government.

A second effect of such programs is more subtle, affecting the government officials themselves. With new authority over the lives of individuals and no necessity for justification of action other than the demands of national security, an opportunity is created for the appearance of a type of bureaucrat otherwise uncommon in democracies. This is the man to whom political power is its own justification; he owes his ultimate loyalty not to the people whose servant he ostensibly is, but to some generalized abstraction: the state, the party, or the prevailing ideology. Nazi Germany and the Soviet Union are among the totalitarian states of the modern age staffed principally with this sort of personnel.

No state with a strong democratic tradition has so far completely succumbed to this type of leadership, but it is obvious that there are individual office-holders of this description in all democracies practicing economic nationalism. To main the purity of democratic ideals in the face of the demands of economic nationalism demands a degree of popular and official self-discipline which is difficult to reach in a time of crisis.

THE REVIVAL OF INTERNATIONAL TRADE

Under the principles of economic nationalism, trade between states languishes everywhere in the world. Generally speaking, current practice permits only such kind and amount of trade as directly serves the political purposes of the various governments or, at best, such trade as does not interfere with concepts of national interest that are constantly expanding. Under the impact of political considerations, trade is being forced into unnatural channels and goes forward only by generous subsidy and open coercion.

The states of eastern Europe, for example, had developed over the years a naturally complementary relationship with those in the western half of the continent, exchanging their raw materials (coal and timber) and food products for the manufactured goods and specialized services of Britain, the Low Countries, France, and Germany. The political division of Europe after 1945 brought this trade to a virtual standstill. The Iron Curtain has forced the Soviet satellites to direct their trade eastward toward Moscow. No matter how ideologically satisfying this might be, the economic facts remain that the Soviet has no deep economic need for the products of eastern Europe (except those of industrialized Czechoslovakia and East Germany) nor can the USSR provide in exchange the finished goods eastern Europe requires. The result has been a strained and mutually frustrating relationship.

In like manner, although with less of a stultifying effect, the producing states of the West have suffered from the loss of their markets to the East. The only way the European democracies can pay for the imports of food and raw materials they require is by exports; denied their normal markets in eastern Europe, they must find other outlets. This has been a difficult task during a period when their own economies have been passing through an era of rehabilitation and transition.

While it is yet visionary to conceive of a trading area which would include the whole world and in which commodities and credit would move freely, most students agree that international trade practices must be freed to some extent before there can be any lasting improvement in the economic health of the world. Modern industrialization makes use of so many resources from all parts of the world and seeks markets in so many widely separated places that the most efficient utilization of our production techniques requires a more liberal trade policy on the part of all governments.

THE AMERICAN TRADE PROBLEM

The trade problem facing the United States and the policy adopted for dealing with it are central to the over-all issue of the revival of international trade. The end of World War II found the United States with the greatest concentration of productive capacity ever gathered within one state. While all the other industrial states had suffered losses in plant and reduction in capacity as a result of the war, American production had expanded greatly. From one point of view the economic situation confronting the United States bordered upon the ideal: the world was in great need of many commodities that only the United States could supply, and the industrial plant of the United States was equipped to satisfy this pent-up demand. A happy future of trade and profit seemed inevitable.

The course of history since 1945, however, has brought about bafflement and confusion instead of the economic Eden some had forecast. The problem of international trade has been a constant source of irritation to Americans and foreigners alike and, under a variety of disguises, has formed a part of nearly every foreign-policy venture undertaken by the United States since the war.

Continuing Elements of the Problem. Certain elements of the American trade problem are relatively permanent, arising from the political and economic structure of the world. These factors must form the basis of any policy.

The first of these is the great productive capacity of the United States. Goods of all kinds are pouring out of the American industrial plant, and under a capitalist economy they must find markets. Although the principal market for American production is domestic, the 6 to 10 per cent that is represented by exports is an important element in American prosperity. It may indeed on occasion prove to be the margin between depression and stability; in certain industries, the percentage of exports goes much higher. Certainly it is in the American interest to export the commodities for which there is a foreign demand. The fact that an exportable surplus is always being produced makes our trade problem a continuing one.

A second element, also apparently destined to be of long life, is the great foreign demand for American products. Readers of newspapers are familiar with the global 'dollar gap' which affects many states. The reason there is a shortage of dollars in the world arises from the wide demand for American goods which can be purchased only by dollar balances. Among the most desired commodities are industrial machinery, agricultural products, consumer goods, and energy sources (coal and petroleum). These are necessary to maintain and to raise the standard of living of peoples everywhere, as well as to create new industrial plants in underdeveloped areas.

A third factor complicating the problem is the political significance of United States exports. American policy assumes that the success of the USSR in expanding its sphere has depended largely upon economic maladjustments in many parts of the world. Although unable really to fulfill its promises, the Soviet Union has convinced millions of people that its policy favors drastic economic reform. American goods have therefore come to be a major weapon in the struggle against Soviet power and communist ideology. United States policy assumes that a people whose demands are being satisfied under a free capitalist society would not be in a mood to listen to Soviet promises of a better world 'after the revolution.' It has become politically necessary as well as economically desirable to maintain a high level of exports.

Impediments to Trade. Thus far in our discussion the American trade situation appears completely favorable. The goods are available for export in great quantity, the demand for them is universal, and the national interest would be served by a high level of trade. Why, then, is trade a constant frustration and a political problem? Three further factors resolve this paradox; all are specialized impediments to what otherwise would be a normal and satisfactory relationship.

The first is the inadequate purchasing power of the free world. Very few areas of the free world—and they are small and relatively unimportant—are able to purchase American goods in any significant amount. The other states either lack the dollars completely or, possessing credit balances, simply cannot afford to spend them.

In Europe, the major cause of this situation is the aftermath of the war; the loss of capital, the devastation, and the costs of domestic rehabilitation have seriously limited the ability of the European states to make purchases in the high-priced American market. American inflation after 1946 only aggravated this situation. In the rest of the world—the 'underdeveloped areas' —the great concentration of wealth and the low popular standard of living make these states poor markets. For the most part, their cultures are not geared to any major consumption of American products without there first taking place a social revolution. The free world, developed and underdeveloped, wants and needs the production of the United States, but lacks the means to pay for it.

A second impediment to trade is the political prohibition of trade with the Soviet bloc. Although it was never a principal market area for American commodities, the removal of this large segment of the world's population from the consuming area (the Chinese people were called by one author '400 million customers') again has served to reduce the potential purchasers of American goods.

A third limiting factor is United States domestic policy on international trade, particularly on the issue of tariffs. All trade is actually a process in which goods and services are exchanged; money and credit are mediums to facilitate this exchange. If goods are to move at all in international channels, trade must be a two-way process. Yet American policy toward tariffs, despite significant modifications attained through the operation of the Reciprocal Trade Agreements Act (1934 and later renewals), remains wedded to the principle of protection. American tariff regulations are stringent enough to keep most foreign-produced goods from reaching the American market in quantities large enough to build up credit balances.

The only satisfactory way for other states to obtain the dollars with which to finance extensive purchasing of American goods is for them to sell equivalent amounts of their own production in the American or some other dollar market. Yet either because of the inability to match American production costs or because of the price differential imposed by United States tariffs, relatively few foreign commodities find their way into the hands of American consumers. Foreign states are unable to earn more than a small fraction of their dollar requirements by selling in the American market.

UNITED STATES TRADE POLICY

There has been no unanimity in American government circles on the method to be used in coping with these problems. The situation has been attacked piecemeal by policy moves essentially short-run in their outlook; at the same time, various branches of the government have pursued mutually contradictory policies. Congress seemingly remains unconvinced of the necessity of any reasoned trade policy; since 1945 each renewal of the Reciprocal Trade Agreements Act has been accompanied by bitter controversy and progressively greater limitations upon the powers of the President to take action for lower tariffs and freer trade. The announced policy of the government, enunciated by the executive branch after the war and reiterated frequently since (most recently by President Eisenhower early in 1955), is to participate in all international movements for the relaxation of barriers to trade. The Senate of the United States, however, has made clear its opposition to American participation in the International Trade Organization, and the implementation of the General Agreements on Tariffs and Trade of 1947 has gone forward without very much enthusiasm from the legislative branch.

Despite the divided counsels within the American government, however, two general policy techniques have been developed since 1947 to increase the volume of trade. One, the creation of purchasing power abroad, is designed to deal with the more or less short-run difficulties inherent in the postwar world; the second, an attempt at a general reduction of trade barriers, looks toward a permanent enlargement of the world trading areas.

The Creation of Purchasing Power. In a number of different ways the United States government has systematically sought to eliminate or at least to reduce the effect of the lack of purchasing power abroad by the artificial creation of dollar balances. It has been generally recognized that this can be done only for a limited time, but the policy goal has been the stimulation of foreign economies so that they would be able to continue on their own momentum after the deliberate policy of American assistance was terminated. At least four different ways were used to inject dollars into other states.

The first—and, dollar-wise, the largest—was that of outright dollar grants to foreign governments. The principal agencies through which this program was handled were, of course, the Economic Co-operation Administration (ECA) and its successors, the Mutual Security Administration (MSA) and the Foreign Operations Administration (FOA). The former was confined in its effect to the sixteen 'Marshall plan' nations that held membership in the Organization for European Economic Co-operation (OEEC); the MSA took over not only the European-grant program in 1951 but also a congeries of other programs in Latin America, the Middle East, and the Far East; the FOA gathered together all United States operational aid programs in 1953. Dollar grants were direct gifts and the American government retained sufficient control over the expenditure of the funds to see that they were expended primarily for purposes of economic reconstruction and development. This phase of the program was substantially terminated by 1955.

A second method, comparable in size to the first, was tied up with the program of rearmament of the United States and its allies which was begun after 1950. The rearmament policy contributed to purchasing power abroad in several different ways: (1) the United States subsidized the rearmament of its allies directly with cash grants; (2) American construction of military installations on foreign territory and the permanent maintenance of American garrisons there directed a steady stream of dollars into the domestic economy of each host country; (3) American 'off-shore procurement' of military supplies purchased abroad represented also a considerable transfer of dollars.

A third technique is represented by the Point IV program of technical assistance and co-operation. Less impressive in dollar total than the two previous ones, it has had as its aim the stimulation of the dollar-earning capacity of the underdeveloped areas. By the gradual introduction of Western technology into new areas it is hoped that they would become significant producers of many types of goods and would therefore be better able to purchase commodities in the American market.

The fourth program involved less direct government participation. It was the deliberate stimulation of American travel abroad, particularly by tourists. Tourist expenditures abroad are difficult to determine, but estimates of the 1955 total run over three billion dollars. This again represents a not inconsiderable transfer of American funds into foreign hands.

The Reduction of Tariff Barriers. The United States emerged from the war officially committed to the advancement of world trade through the reduction of trade barriers and the substitution of multilateralism for bilateralism in international economics. Its principal associates in the United Nations echoed this pledge; even the USSR was on record to this effect. The vexing conditions of the postwar world, however, have served to condition and to reduce the meaning of this general policy. Economic nationalism is at its height in most current discussion of tariff reduction. Despite this difficulty, however, the United States has participated in two general international programs for the reduction of tariffs.

The first line of action taken by the United States was the drafting of the Charter proposed for the International Trade Organization, designed to be one of the specialized agencies of the United Nations. The organization has never come into existence, since an insufficient number of ratifications has been given. The United States must bear a large measure of the responsibility for this inaction; the Congress has been sensitive to the various group pressures interested in the maintenance of a high level of tariff protection for American industries. This reluctance to enter into a definite commitment was in strange contrast to the leading role of the United States in the framing of the ITO Charter in 1947.

The second major effort in the direction of the liberation of trade practices is the General Agreement on Tariffs and Trade (GATT), entered into at Geneva in 1947 as the culmination of over one hundred sets of bilateral negotiations on tariff reduction among the twenty-three participating states. This multilateral attempt to enact a single great tariff reduction was again made upon the invitation of the United States. Material reductions were made in tariffs as a result of the original signing of GATT. Two later conferences were held for the same purpose: one at Annecy, France, in 1949, and the largest of all at Torquay, England, in 1950 and 1951. The outcome of these extensive negotiations was a disappointment to those who had hoped for major modification in the trade policies of the participants.

All states were willing to make token concessions and were eager to take advantage of any reduction in the barriers of other states. When the discussion proceeded to economic fundamentals, however, none of the states represented was willing to abandon to any real extent the pattern of trade controls under which it was presently operating. Most of them argued that their own economic situations were such that they should be permitted exemptions from the general rules of free trade; they also displayed a tendency to prefer ironclad bilateral barter agreements under strict control to agreements looking to the resumption of free multilateral trade with complete currency convertibility. In other words, almost all the states felt that the protection of their own economies was of more importance than the restoration of normal trade patterns. The fact that their economic troubles could never be solved without international action seems to have escaped all but a few of the negotiators.

From this general charge the United States cannot be exempted. Although the difficulties of selling goods abroad without making purchases in return became apparent to us long ago, the protectionists are once again making their appeals. We are warned about the dangers of flooding the American market with cheap foreign merchandise; the impoverishment of large sectors of American industry is held to be imminent. Even national security is pressed into the service of protection, as in the case of the American watch industry that urges its subsidy by tariff on grounds of keeping critical skills employed. 'Peril point' legislation, automatically increasing tariffs the moment any foreign commodity shows signs of competing successfully in the American market, makes American claims of an interest in multilateralism and freer trade sound somewhat hollow.

The American trade problem is not insoluble. To attack it successfully, however, the United States will have to abandon a policy appropriate for a debtor nation and adopt a program based on its role as the world's greatest creditor. For a time a slogan expressing this idea gained currency on both sides of the Atlantic: 'Trade, not aid' was supposed to be the recipe for curing the imbalance in economic relations. So far, however, the American people have been unable to muster enough understanding and vision to make such a wholesale readjustment of policy. International economic relations continue to annoy and irritate Americans; they will continue to do so until a long-range policy with clear objectives is devised.

THE FREE WORLD TRADE PROBLEM

The simplest way to analyze the trade situation facing most of the non-communist states of the world is to think of it as the reciprocal of that facing the United States. Here in the United States we have the greatest supply of the world's most wanted goods and are eager to sell them; we also have the bulk of the dollars which alone can pay for these commodities. On the other hand, the remainder of the world needs the goods but lacks enough dollars to purchase them. Being unable to obtain raw materials and capital equipment, the free world is further inhibited from earning sufficient dollars to make its purchases by producing and selling its wares in the United States. To the limited extent that it can penetrate the American market, it is handicapped by American tariff policy. These are the basic elements in the trade problem as it concerns the free world outside the United States.

Impediments to Trade. To some extent the obstacles to trade by the states of the non-communist world are the reverse of those that apply in the case of the United States.

In the first place, the bulk of the free world suffers from a relative inability to produce. This condition has several causes. First in time was the war, which ruined productive facilities, dispersed skilled labor forces, impaired transportation and distribution networks, and materially affected all sectors of their economies. This was particularly true in Europe, but applied to some extent in other parts of the world. Just as recovery seemed to be at hand, the Korean war and the consequent rearmament of the free world again served to divert the effort. Rearmament makes the industrial wheels of a state turn, but it scarcely produces an exportable surplus of goods to move in international trade. Even Britain, which has made a major effort to direct its production into export channels, has found that its attempts have not eliminated its trade deficit.

Second in importance among the impediments to trade are trade barriers. Trading by most free world states is handicapped by the numerous devices that stand in the way of the orderly movement of goods across international frontiers, even among fellow members of the Western alliance. In dealing with the United States and in trading with each other, quotas, import and export restrictions, exchange control, subsidies, barter agreements, and the rest of the familiar techniques serve to impede the flow of trade. Each state is able to rationalize its retention of these practices in terms of its own peculiar problems, but such rationalizations, however convincing they may be, do not move goods in trade.

A final specialized impediment is currency control and the whole issue of convertibility of currencies. Although a fantastically complicated problem, we may outline it briefly. What we call 'multilateralism,' the free movement of goods from state to state in the classic fashion, requires the accumulation of credit balances by any one state in the currency of other states, and their free convertibility into any national medium of exchange. Britain, for example, might amass a credit balance in French francs which it might wish to use to pay off a debt incurred in Mexican pesos. This would require that francs be converted into pesos or either into pounds sterling according to the needs of the transaction. For trade to flow smoothly, it is necessary that each currency of the world be freely convertible into all others in order to meet the changing requirements of credit.

In the postwar era the financial situation of many of the producing states, particularly in Europe, grew perilous. As a means of protecting the value of their own money, many states limited or prohibited the exchange of their own currency for that of other states. This was especially true when governments feared the necessity of giving up their own limited dollar credits in exchange for their own money. Any state holding balances in sterling, for example, could not under currency control obtain dollars in exchange; it was obliged to spend its stock of pounds in Britain or in some other state whose monetary system was intermeshed with that of Britain.

The reasons for exchange control of all sorts have considerable validity in light of the circumstances in which many states found themselves; we could hardly expect states to suffer bankruptcy in the name of multilateralism. What is unfortunately also true, however, is that currency control inhibits international trade.

Trade Policy in the Free World. The actual policies followed by most of the free world outside the United States have been suggested in the foregoing analysis. Multilateralism, however desirable in theory, has been felt by most governments to be practically unattainable in their present condition. Instead, the predominant trade technique has been barter agreements and state trading upon a bilateral basis. The OEEC and its offshoot, the European Payments Union (EPU), have been regarded as a step toward multilateralism by the states of western Europe. In the face of dire need they have joined a common trading pool and goods have moved within western Europe with a freedom unique in modern experience.

Observers have, however, detected the beginning of a new and portentous trend: the tendency among Europeans to view the European trading area as an accomplished fact and then to plan trade relations between the new Europe and the remainder of the world on the old basis of bilateralism. This is at best a doubtful step toward multilateralism; it is questionable if a united Europe that carries on bilateralism with the rest of the world serves in any effective way to advance the cause of revived international trade on a worldwide basis.

A final word must be said about American trade relations with the free world. Rightly or wrongly, most of the lesser states feel their economic situation to be such as to merit special consideration in trade policy from the United States. They no longer desire cash grants; instead they ask for the opportunity to trade in American markets upon a basis of free competition. They demand that the United States open itself up in the name of multilateralism, while they (the other states) continue to enjoy the protections and advantages that bilateralism brings.

The operations of the free economy in the United States are resented, particularly its tendency toward inflation. Inflation makes the competitive position of other states unfavorable and reduces the value of their carefully husbanded dollar balances. Their attitude is understandable. Nevertheless, the United States has refused to make the concessions demanded; we have neither abandoned our official policy of multilateralism nor significantly lowered our tariffs. American trade policy leaves much to be desired, but so do the policies of virtually all our partners in the alliance of the free world.

EAST-WEST TRADE

The problem of trade between East and West, between the Soviet world and the non-communist states, is much more of a political question than an economic one. There is no economic justification for the interruption of trade between the two worlds and the constant efforts to eliminate it entirely. The strained economic relations are a function of the bipolarity that governs so much of contemporary world politics. The decision to cut off the trade was made for the most part by the United States in the hope that this would bring effective economic pressure to bear upon the Soviet Union.

It is admitted that all parties are the losers in this process, but the aim of American policy is to make the USSR suffer the more; ultimately the Soviet may be obliged to come to political terms with the West in order to gain re-admission to the circle of trading nations. Indications are multiplying that this goal is not illusory; the ouster of Malenkov from leadership in the Soviet Union in 1955 was admittedly due to economic crisis, particularly in agriculture. It may well be that Moscow will make some of the desired political concessions as the price for the resumption of East-West trade.

Strains on the Western Alliance. One aspect of the whole problem of East-West trade merits special attention. It is relatively easy for the United States to dispense with trade relations with the states behind the Iron Curtain; they were never a principal market for American industry and the economic costs which the policy entails are relatively minor compared to the possible political rewards it might win. For the principal allies of the United States, however, and for many of the minor ones as well, to do without East-West trade involves a real sacrifice. Not only was eastern Europe for many years a natural market for western European industry; it assumes a special importance for European states since they feel they are being unjustly excluded from the American-controlled world market.

Consequently, the American policy of flatly forbidding its allies to trade with the Soviet world has proved to be a source of discontent and outright defiance. Britain, France, Italy, the Benelux countries, all have looked longingly at the great market and the source of raw materials that lie behind the Iron Curtain. The leadership of the Soviet Union has not overlooked this attitude; it has repeatedly offered trade concessions to the European states in the hope of splitting the solid front of the Western alliance and isolating the United States. So great had this divisive pressure become that, beginning in 1953, the United States officially relaxed the ban and announced its willingness to have its European allies trade with the East in non-strategic goods.

Another state in which the problem is growing acute is Japan. Japan and China have a complementary economic relationship; for the preservation of its industrial health and its standard of living, Japan must trade on the mainland of Asia. For political reasons the United States has attempted to force the Japanese to trade only with nationalist China (Formosa) and to boycott the communist regime on the mainland. This is economic idiocy; no possible way exists to carry it out except the indefinite subsidization of Japan from the United States treasury. The United States may well face in the near future the unhappy alternatives of permitting Japan to trade with communist China or having Japanese resentment bring about the rupture of the American alliance. This problem—how to keep our allies from trading with the Soviet world without destroying the Western bloc—has thus far defied solution by American policy makers.

Conclusions on East-West Trade. Economic stability in the world is unlikely without the resumption of East-West trade. No normal relationships are possible anywhere as long as the world remains divided into two hostile trading areas. What the interruption of East-West trade actually means, however, is that economic stability in the world cannot come about until a major political reconciliation takes place between the two great antagonists, or at any rate until the bipolar world breaks up and the Russo-American controversy no longer represents a constant threat of world destruction.

The economic rift between the communist and the non-communist worlds is only an extreme symptom of the supremacy of political considerations over all others in today's nationalistic world. Since economic problems grow out of political and psychological conditions, it is in political and psychological terms that their solutions must be found. It is useless to search for purely economic answers. The escape from the economic crisis of our time can be found only by means of the same set of instruments that precipitated it in the first place: the national state, the concept of national interest, and the techniques of national policy.

UNDERDEVELOPED AREAS AND PEOPLES

The third economic problem area is represented by the underdeveloped areas and peoples of the world and the prospects and opportunities (and dangers as well) arising from the probability of their early opening and development. The underdeveloped areas—which in this chapter are thought to include south and southeast Asia, the Middle East, much of Latin America, and most of Africa—have been sometimes romantically termed 'the last great frontier.' In this enormous area live millions of people in substandard conditions of squalor, disease, or savagery. Many of the territories they inhabit, however, have great potential wealth, but nowhere is it being adequately used for the good of the inhabitants. If modern technology and civilization represent the blessings that we of the Western world contend they do, a great opportunity exists to extend modern techniques of all sorts to the underdeveloped areas. In the plans of the United States, Great Britain, and the United Nations to take the initiative in opening these areas to Western economic and cultural influence, there lies a possibility of adding a significant new factor to the economic structure of the world.

Economic Status of the Underdeveloped Areas. The most marked characteristic of the underdeveloped areas is an almost shocking waste. Human and natural resources are employed in a recklessly inefficient manner. Labor is low in cost and is used at an extremely low level of productivity. Because labor is inefficient, the exploitation of resources—mainly agricultural and mineral—cannot be carried on at any rewarding level. Neither does any industrial plant worthy of the name exist anywhere in the area. These factors combine to produce populations that are poverty-stricken (although each contains a tiny group of wealthy aristocrats), uneducated, disease-ridden, and apathetic.

The underdeveloped areas face an unfavorable situation in international economic relations. Their low productivity prevents them from entering the world market except by the sale of raw materials and agricultural commodities. All the industrial and manufactured products that they purchase must be financed through the sale of their exports. Since they sell low-cost commodities and purchase more expensive processed ones, they are rarely able to satisfy their national demand for the goods of modern machine production. Although almost all of these areas are politically independent (most of them attained freedom fairly recently; Latin America has the longest record), they retain the marks of a 'colonial' economy. Many of their principal sources of wealth are foreign owned, and the profits from the enterprises never stay in the territory but go to absentee proprietors. Thus the profits fail to strengthen the domestic economy or to increase the purchasing power of the people.

Three different sources can be found for the urge to develop these areas. The first comes from the states of the Western world. Many of them have reached the conclusion that both their own prosperity and world economic stability would be enhanced by the creation of modern, industrialized, technologically up-to-date economies in the underdeveloped areas. By operating their own industrial plants and raising the standard of living of their peoples, they would become more attractive markets for other producing states. Increasing production in the underdeveloped parts of the world would vastly augment the supply of goods available for consumption in the world. Greater capacity to purchase goods would broaden and deepen world demand. From the Western point of view, development of unindustrialized areas is a policy of enlightened self-interest.

The peoples of the underdeveloped areas themselves are the second source of interest. The spread of national self-consciousness has helped to awaken them to an awareness of their technological backwardness; they now demand that Western technology be brought to them. They understand the importance of the industrial base of the high Western standard of living and they look to their governments to extend some of these benefits to them.

Communist expansion is the third inspiration for development. Soviet propagandists are adept at capitalizing on the social and economic inequities of the underdeveloped areas. The Western democracies seek to undermine the Soviet appeal by proving that capitalist democracy can satisfy the legitimate demands of the people more efficiently than communism, and with less impairment of individual freedom and loss of human dignity.

THE PLANS OF DEVELOPMENT

Various schemes for the development of these areas are in operation at the present time; some are unilateral, some multilateral, some carried on through the United Nations. All of them place on the people of the area the primary responsibility for initiating and carrying through any program; the role of the outside state or agency is that of an adviser, expediter, and teacher.

Categories of Assistance. There are two broad areas into which all the various types of assistance fall. The first category aims at increasing productivity and industrialization. Generally, three things are required of an underdeveloped area in order to proceed with industrialization: capital, heavy equipment, and technically trained personnel. Various devices have been worked out to permit each underdeveloped area to gain these three necessities.

The second type of assistance is fundamental to any significant progress toward the industrialization of society. It has to do with basic improvements in the conditions of life of a people so as to equip them physically and psychologically for the more rapid tempo and the emotional strains of an industrialized existence. The preparation for industrialization requires such measures as an increase in the food supply through the improvement of agricultural techniques, the broadening of educational facilities to eliminate illiteracy and to make the people capable of fitting into industrial processes, and the initiation of public-health programs, epidemic control, preventive inoculations, and the like.

Current thinking, especially in the United States, has tended to give the second category a higher priority than the first. Unless a solid foundation is first constructed, any industrial development would be a hothouse growth without any real permanence. This emphasis upon social reform has been resisted to some degree by the leaders of the underdeveloped states themselves. Many of them would prefer to begin the program by the manufacture and distribution of salable goods so as to return a reasonably quick profit. Many of the difficulties inherent in the whole program have arisen over this issue.

Point IV. The American program of technical co-operation and assistance to the underdeveloped areas has been known as 'Point IV' ever since it was included as the fourth foreign-policy point in President Truman's inaugural address in 1949. Although hailed at the time of its formulation as a 'bold new program' and enthusiastically supported by its advocates in government and private life, it has never reached the proportions hoped for by many. In a period of war and crisis, the attraction of a program of long-range scope, calling for patient negotiation and constructive effort with little promise of early visible return, has never been great. Congress approved the program in principle, and in 1950 appropriated $34 million for its implementation.

In 1951 the Technical Co-operation Administration, which administered the program, was largely absorbed into the operation of the Mutual Security Agency. This necessarily meant that the technical assistance aspect of United States aid was subordinated to military aid and rearmament. Point IV came to be a minor adjunct to the cold-war strategy of the United States. This was a blow to many of the project's supporters, but they retained their faith and continued to press for a reaffirmation of the basic idea.

Actually, despite the budgetary and political limitations under which the program was forced to operate, it attained considerable dimensions within a few years. By mid-1955 agreements between the United States and over thirty states in the underdeveloped areas were in effect, providing for American technicians to furnish assistance in the development of national programs in agriculture, education, and health—the basic areas of social rehabilitation. Programs of industrial development were not nearly so widespread.

In the execution of the Point IV program for the exploitation of natural resources and the development of transportation and industry, the principal stumbling block has proved to be a lack of finance capital. The original American idea had been to satisfy this requirement by means of private investment. American investors, however, have been wary; they prefer government guarantees of their loans, particularly against nationalization or expropriation of the industries they help finance. Congress has not so far been willing to make such a guarantee. On the other hand, the underdeveloped states still retain a deep-seated and often unjustified fear of a renewed imperialism by Western states; they prefer outright grants from the United States government to private investment.

When this fundamental disagreement was added to the lack of accord regarding the kind of projects on which the money was to be expended, it is easy to see why large-scale financing of development enterprises has been lacking. It has had moderate success in Latin America, and two factors may be suggested to explain this: the American investor knows the Latin-American situation, and the Latin Americans themselves do not fear American imperialism as greatly as do other states in many parts of the world.

The Colombo Plan. Great Britain's major venture into the opening of underdeveloped areas is being undertaken in co-operation with the other members of the Commonwealth through the 'Colombo Plan.' This scheme for the 'Co-operative Economic Development in South and Southeast Asia' came into existence at a conference of Commonwealth foreign ministers at Colombo, Ceylon, in 1950. Its object is stated in its title; it concentrates upon Asia as the most critical area. It originally envisaged a six-year program of development at a total cost of about five billion dollars. Its geographic scope includes the British dominions in Asia, British colonies in the area, and such independent southeast Asian states as care to participate. The program was specifically designed to dovetail with Point IV, with United Nations programs of technical assistance, and with any other plans that might appear in the future.

Although full of promise and with a modest degree of accomplishment, the Colombo Plan has run into some of the same difficulties as has Point IV. The projects have proved difficult to finance. Most of the Commonwealth members are either, like Britain, already strained to the limit to finance rearmament or else are themselves short of investment capital. There has been some tendency to look to American private investors for funds. It has been hoped that a program in which the Commonwealth is officially participating will prove attractive enough to tempt American dollars. Thus far this approach has not been notably rewarding.

United Nations Programs. Since its creation, the United Nations has been active in programs of economic development in the underdeveloped areas. Most of the specialized agencies have a particular interest in these regions, and the Economic and Social Council has been charged since 1948 with overall planning and supervision of United Nations activity in this field. Several bodies were set up to carry on the work, notably the Technical Assistance Board (TAB), the Technical Assistance Committee (TAC), and the Technical Assistance Administration (TAA) within the Secretariat.

By and large, the United Nations has had the same kind of record of accomplishment and failure made by the United States and the Commonwealth: expert advice is easy to provide and is welcomed by the host governments, but financing the recommended projects has proved a near-impossibility. The most obvious possible source of capital is the International Bank of Reconstruction and Development, but the Bank is following an extremely conservative course in making loans. Most of the sizable number of development projects it has financed have been self-liquidating, and we have seen that these make little contribution in themselves to long-range development.

The United Nations sends three types of technical assistance missions to host countries: survey missions, advisory missions, and operating missions. All are composed of experts, their fields of competence depending upon the requests made by the host government in the first place. By 1955, over fifty states had concluded technical-assistance agreements with the United Nations. Many of these were fellowship programs, under the terms of which observers from underdeveloped areas travel to study techological practices in other states; there are approximately thirty genuine assistance programs of either the survey, advisory, or operating type under way. A wide range of functions is covered in their activities, extending from the establishment of systems of government statistics to campaigns against tropical and other diseases.

Other Plans. The obligations of Article 73 of the United Nations Charter have brought many other development plans into being. States responsible for non-self-governing territories have the duty of fostering not only their capacity for self-government, but also their progress toward economic and social maturity. In every case where this pledge has been taken seriously, administering authorities have set programs in motion. In the African and Western Hemisphere portions of the British empire, in the African colonies of France, in the Belgian Congo, in the American possessions, the story is substantially the same. Responsible governments are attempting to bring the advantages of Western techniques to their subject peoples while sparing them the more unpleasant accompaniments of modern industrialization. Most of the world is rapidly catching up with Western civilization.

REACTIONS TO THE PLANS

We have seen that the programs for the underdeveloped areas frequently have had rough going. The biggest single problem is financing the ambitious projects, but an important factor in the relatively small success so far attained has been the attitude of the governments and the populations of these areas themselves. This side of the problem merits consideration. Why do these states persist in what appears to us to be looking gift horses in the mouth?

Fear of a Renewed Imperialism. Underlying all the relations of the underdeveloped areas with the outside world is an ill-concealed fear that an attempt will be made to renew imperialist practices; it affects the entire foreign outlook of nearly all these states. It has been noticebly present in all the negotiations between them and the various states offering assistance. Of all the southeast Asian states invited to participate in the Colombo Plan, only Burma has accepted; both Burma and Indonesia have rejected Point IV agreements with the United States. They seem unable to persuade themselves that any motive prompts the offers of assistance other than a plot to deprive them of their political freedom and control over their own economic destinies. This helps explain why the reaction of the underdeveloped areas to the United Nations program of assistance has been much more spontaneous and co-operative.

Two reasons exist for their preference for United Nations action. In the first place, they trust the United Nations where they do not have confidence in the national states, such as Britain and the United States; second, programs under United Nations jurisdiction remain to a considerable extent under their own control through their voting power in the General Assembly. The underdeveloped areas, if their protests are to be believed, are avid for technical assistance; rather than sacrifice their independence and freedom, however, they would seem to prefer to remain backward. This may be an overstatement, but certainly the policy of many of the Asian states with regard to American assistance appears to bear out this view.

Closely connected with the fear of imperialism is the disinclination of these states to accept political commitments along with technical assistance. This has seriously impeded American execution of aid programs in south and southeast Asia. The Mutual Security Act of 1951 specified that in order to receive any American assistance (including Point IV), the recipient state would be required to enter into certain commitments. These would have had the effect of joining the state to the common effort, political and military, against the forces of communism and Soviet imperialism.

By and large, this has proved unacceptable to the sensitive nationalisms of Asia. These states, seeking to avoid involvement in the cold war and to maintain cordial relations with both sides, considered agreement with the American conditions a surrender of their political independence. In 1952 Burma rejected a MSA pact with the United States on these grounds; the cabinet of Indonesia fell over the same issue a few weeks later. Our relations with India have been needlessly complicated because of these conditions attached to our aid. Only Thailand, the Philippines, and Pakistan have been willing to join political support of the United States to programs of technical assistance. The other young states of Asia insist upon the literal maintenance of their independence of status.

Resentment of Inferiority. Although realizing their need of assistance and advice, the underdeveloped areas are nevertheless resentful of their status of tutelage and resist any overt recognition of their inferiority. This often takes the form of disparaging the very Western ideas and methods they are so anxious to learn. Since technological underdevelopment is clear for all to see, the native leadership comes to place an exaggerated importance upon cultural values and political equality. Western advisers have been obliged to act with the utmost delicacy in order not to wound sensitive feelings and thus endanger the whole program.

Resistance to Social Change. Many of the native leaders resist the social change and redistribution of economic rewards implicit in any program of modernization, industrialization, and Westernization. Particularly in the Arab world, but generally throughout the underdeveloped areas, local leadership is drawn from an aristocratic minority. Although sincerely patriotic and interested in the welfare of their peoples, these leaders have little relish for any program of development that would alter the basis of political and economic power. Any improvement in the mass standard of living would immediately set in motion social forces leading to revolutions in many other areas of life. Consequently, the leaders are anxious that the programs of dvelopment proceed slowly and that the whole enterprise be kept under their control.

In some cases assistance programs have been abandoned because of their revolutionary implications. An example is provided by Iran. In 1947, the Iranian government requested and received the advice of a private American advisory mission on projects of modernization and development. Iran's position was uniquely fortunate in that ample funds were then available from the country's vast petroleum wealth. The heart of the American proposals, however, was a social revolution involving the destruction of the old semi-feudal structure of Iranian society. This proved too much for the ruling circles in Iran; the American mission was thanked and sent home, while its proposals were laid aside. It was not until 1954, after the settlement of the Anglo-Iranian Oil Company dispute, that the first steps toward implementation of the recommendations were taken.

CONCLUSIONS

Certain conclusions appear from the consideration of the underdeveloped areas. Politically they already form part of the world society. Economically and technologically they are still backward, but they are already indicating their unwillingness to remain so. Unable to assimilate Western processes by their own efforts, they must be furnished assistance from the outside. The attempts to give such aid have had an uneven success, owing to the hesitancy and financial inability on the part of the Western states and to a variety of forms of resistance on the part of the underdeveloped states themselves.

What is needed is the formulation and successful application of a plan that will provide the technological and financial assistance that the underdeveloped areas require and at the same time will preserve their political independence and do no irreparable injury to their dignity and sense of maturity. The discovery of this plan and its application in detail will be a task of great difficulty. In view of the extent to which the world needs the development of these areas and the possible rewards that would follow its accomplishment, however, it would be impossible to think of a task more worthy of the effort.

13

Problem Areas: Psychological

M OST of the material problems of contemporary international affairs are resolvable by the technological and scientific resources that man now has at his command. We know how to make individuals healthier, better fed, and better educated. We have techniques of production and distribution that can insure an adequate supply of commodities for everyone. We have political methods that make possible the efficient organization of the entire world on the basis of a single government and could thus eliminate much of the wasteful competition that characterizes so much of interstate life. We know how to lift the ever-increasing burden of war and preparations for war from the shoulders of mankind.

Yet our brief survey of the state of world affairs has shown that man is not using his scientific information for his own betterment. Instead of a world in which all men work together toward the progressive elimination of poverty, disease, and ignorance, we find that nations are ever more avid to build up their defenses against one another, that mutual hostilities and suspicions are deeper and more bitter, and that a great proportion of the scientific knowledge of which we boast is applied to the creation of more powerful engines of destruction. At a time when individuals should be enjoying the fruits of man's progressive conquest of the physical universe, they are instead even less secure than when they were the slaves of superstition and ignorance. This is especially true in the Western world, where men are the most 'modern' in their orientation to the new technology and yet the most oppressed by individual and group fears. Where can we find the answer to the paradox that at every turn inhibits the best efforts of statesmen to discover a better way for all humanity to follow?

Man is the prisoner of his emotions. In the pursuit of the irrational and intangible ends demanded by his psyche he obstinately refuses to serve his best economic and physical interests. Examples of both the illogic and the power of the psychological factor in international politics are easy to discover. In this chapter we shall examine three of them: ideological conflict, pathological nationalism, and intercultural tension.

The impact of these forces upon world affairs is such as to cause some

366

students of international politics to feel that much of the current emphasis in the field is misplaced. The nation-state, they argue, is itself a psychological phenomenon; so are the concepts of national interest, national policy, and international conflict. If that is so, then the underlying cause of all international problems can be found in the group and individual attitudes of men. No lasting change in the nature of world affairs can be accomplished without major modifications in the psychic orientation that men bring to any consideration of international matters. Only by focusing the attack upon psychological maladjustments can we bring about any change in our climate of conflict and tension. This thought is expressed in the famous statement from the constitution of UNESCO: 'Since wars begin in the minds of men, it is in the minds of men that the defenses of peace must be built.'

It is relatively uncommon to approach international politics through an analysis of individual and group attitudes. Interstate relations have been studied as juristic, political, economic, military, or social phenomena, but attack upon them as psychological factors is still something new. The fields of social psychology, cultural anthropology, group dynamics, and related areas that concentrate upon group attitudes and behavior are just beginning to make their contribution to the comprehension of world politics. This new point of view has been of great encouragement to all who feel that the understanding and control of international politics is necessary to the future of civilization.

New insights have been developed and new hypotheses advanced, several of which have been discussed in the preceding chapters. It is not our purpose here to attempt to summarize or digest the conclusions of the social psychologists and their associates. Any such treatment by a non-specialist would run the danger of oversimplification with the consequent risk of misleading the reader. It is sufficient to keep in mind that the psychological approach to world politics keeps us aware of the pervasive influence of psychic factors and now offers the possibility of attacking problems of interstate conflict and tension at their point of origin: the minds of men. In this task we may all co-operate. Peace will come only after man decides to live in harmony and mutual understanding with his neighbors.

Ideological Conflict

Ideological conflict is not a new phenomenon in international politics. From the very beginning of the nation-state system the international political scene has furnished examples of controversies and struggles that had as their origin the existence of ideological differences. These quarrels have demonstrated the peculiar characteristics of ideological conflict: great bitterness, long duration, and great difficulty of conclusion, whether by victory or by compromise.

The contemporary world is undergoing the latest in the series of such great battles, that between the United States and the Soviet Union. In earlier chapters we have frequently referred to this aspect of world politics. At this point we shall examine it and its implications for the future in more detail.

THE NATURE OF IDEOLOGIES TODAY

By an 'ideology' we mean the more or less formalized belief system of a people: the fundamental truths which the group accepts as the basic items of its creed. Although most formal ideologies are accompanied by elaborately developed logical justifications of an almost theological character, for popular consumption they are reduced to a series of simple maxims or phrases which individuals accept as revealed truth. For example, some of the items in the American belief system are exemplified by the following familiar statements: 'all men are created equal'; 'free enterprise'; 'a government of laws and not of men'; 'millions for defense but not one cent for tribute.'

Furthermore, all ideologies have a moral orientation. The ideology is considered to be a summary of the social virtues of the group and a mark of its unique excellence. Thus, if all men are created equal, as Americans believe, there is an implicit assumption that any other group which does not share the same conviction is to that extent immoral and hence of lesser worth.

Finally, if an ideology is to be truly national, there must be agreement on its terms by the overwhelming mass of the people. Many belief systems exist in any society. These are competing constantly for the loyalties of the people, and unless one triumphs over the others and succeeds in winning the adherence of the great bulk of individuals, the ideological structure of the state is incomplete. In modern times the development of techniques of communication and propaganda has made it far easier to obtain mass agreement to the particular ideology which the ruling group in the state supports.

Major Contemporary Ideologies. Of course the ideologies with which the world has the greatest concern today are those of the United States and the Soviet Union. The bulk of the world is caught up in the struggle between these two systems, and everyone is concerned with the eventual outcome. A brief examination of the two systems is therefore appropriate.

Soviet ideology (we are referring here to the belief system of the people as distinguished from the government) consists of a somewhat incongruous mixture of elements drawn from Russian history, Marxist theory, and Russia's indigenous European-Asiatic culture. These interact to produce a mass attitude marked by several strong characteristics. Russian ideology stresses patience, fatalism, a low regard for human life and dignity, a fervent patriotism, a glorification of authority, a distrust of democracy, and a suspicion of everything foreign. In the hands of the Soviet leadership these group attitudes have become very useful weapons of foreign policy and are identified in the Russian mind with the particular social system and political objectives of the Soviet government.

American ideology is not so clear-cut or so easy to analyze. In the main it is the traditional democratic theory of the eighteenth century, emphasizing the dignity and worth of the individual, natural law and natural rights, limited government, and the maximum freedom and self-determination of individuals and peoples. This heritage (which Americans share with other peoples of the Western world) has been modified by the peculiar environmental conditions of the American experience: our frontier tradition, which exaggerated individualism; our industrial progress, which elevated material considerations from their former subordination to the spiritual; and our centuries of political isolation from Europe, which gave us a more or less unsophisticated outlook on international relations. The American ideology therefore stresses political democracy, individual freedom, and capitalist economics; it also generally assumes the inherent superiority of the American version of these concepts over all analogous but differing manifestations of them.

The mass characteristics produced (or strengthened) by the American ideology are difficult to isolate; a European list of them would be different from an Asiatic list, and any American attempt is bound to differ from either. Favorable critics claim that the American mass attitude in world politics is individualistic, democratic, peace-loving, hostile to dictatorship and tyranny in any form, and sympathetic with the downtrodden and the underdog. Hostile (or merely critical) observers admit the basic validity of these characteristics but add also that the American attitude is impatient and materialistic, and inclined to truculence and belligerency.

Other political ideologies are developing in today's world and may yet rise to challenge the dominance of the two mentioned. In Europe various national belief systems are beginning to merge into a distinct consciousness of 'Europe'; a separate European ideology may be developed which will in effect be a rival to the established creeds of the United States and the USSR. India is accompanying its national development with the systematic creation of a political ideology reflecting Indian culture and tradition as well as its maturing national interest. There are signs that communist China may be following the same route as India; indeed, it would be too much to expect that a society so alien to the Russian in every respect would be content to accept as its prevailing belief the ideology of the Russian state. To these must be added the distinct creeds of the Arab states and the developing sense of uniqueness felt by the Union of South Africa, the Argentine Republic, and certain smaller states.

It may almost be laid down as a historical generalization that a necessary step in the progress of a state toward maturity is the development of a distinct ideology. In all the states mentioned, governments and private groups have already spent much thought and considerable effort in working out in articulate form the fundamental beliefs which the people share and whose embodiment the policy of the government represents.

The Militancy of Contemporary Ideologies

Although ideologies are a familiar aspect of international affairs, the role they play today is more significant than it used to be because of their greater militancy. This is directly connected with the increasing intensity of modern nationalism, a phenomenon we shall discuss later in this chapter. It may be said that modern ideologies—and certainly this includes the creeds of the United States and the Soviet Union—are no longer content merely to assume the superiority of the political, economic, and social system they are defending; instead they create a compulsion in peoples and governments to demonstrate that superiority and to force its acceptance by lesser groups. The moral content of ideology today is so strong that peoples are no longer willing to enjoy their own privileged position as possessors of absolute truth, but instead cannot rest until other societies, still the prisoners of false doctrines, are shown the error of their ways and made to conform to the right. An almost missionary zeal permeates the official (and unofficial) custodians of the national creed in almost all states today.

In other words, a part of the ideological equipment of major states is the demand that the area of belief of the ideology be systematically expanded. This is usually backed by a specific policy designed to accomplish that goal. Governments are therefore led into making the search for ideological conformity an essential part of their foreign policies. Such a policy is a fertile breeding ground of ideological conflict.

Soviet Ideological Policy. One need not look far for examples of this tendency; many can be found on both sides of the Iron Curtain. Perhaps it is at its most extreme form in the Soviet world, where Moscow has demanded complete ideological subjugation from as many of its satellites as it could coerce into such a relationship. In the first years after 1945 all the states of eastern Europe were bluntly ordered by the Kremlin to make themselves over into small-scale models of the Soviet Union. Marshal Tito's expulsion from the Cominform derived from his refusal to conform in every detail to directives from Moscow. It was not sufficient for these states to imitate the externals of Soviet belief and practice. What the Politburo was seeking was a genuine conversion and a revamping of the psyche of the minor states so that they would be indistinguishable from Russia. Any reader of George Orwell's *1984* will recall the necessity felt by the ruling group to make individuals 'love Big Brother'; this was the problem the Soviet leaders faced in dealing with their minor associates.

American Ideological Policy. In the United States the official militancy of the American ideology has not assumed such extreme forms. Most of the allies of the United States have been states that already shared the basic beliefs of Americans. To the extent that differences have existed, the United States has not attempted to insist upon complete ideological subjection from its associates. It is true that American policy in Europe has tended to prefer the political leaders and parties that are identified with institutions most closely resembling their American counterparts; these have generally been of the moderate, anti-Socialist Right. Among these are the Conservatives in Great Britain under Winston Churchill and Anthony Eden; the conservative 'Third Force' coalition in France, whose best-known leaders are Georges Bidault and Pierre Mendès-France; the Christian Democrats in West Germany under Konrad Adenauer; and the Christian Democrats in Italy under Alcide de Gasperi and Mario Scelba. Generally we have recoiled from the Socialist parties of the moderate Left.

This same predisposition to identify and evaluate foreign political issues in terms of American values has shown up in American policy in Asia—with results much more unfortunate. Asiatics generally do not proceed ideologically upon the same basis as do Americans, and it is deceptive and misleading to attempt to analyze Asiatic problems in terms of such concepts as 'democracy,' 'capitalism,' or 'individualism.' These are ideas that are real only to a vigorous middle class, and there is no middle class of any importance in Asia. Far too often for the success of American policy, what we have thought to be the 'democratic, capitalist, and individualist' elements of Asiatic society have turned out instead to be the defenders of an outworn and dying feudal authoritarianism. The only thing these groups have had in common with American democratic ideology was an anti-communism which in practice was more opportunistic than sincere. In Chiang Kai-shek's China, in South Korea, in the Philippines, and in many other places, we have led ourselves astray in this manner.

Whereas official American policy has not gone far in insisting on ideological conformity from the allies and associates of the United States, it must be admitted that influential private and semi-public groups in American society have vigorously advocated such militancy. Many protests were raised when American financial assistance under the ECA was used to finance 'socialist experiments' in Britain or to perpetuate unstable political practices in France. These same groups also argue that Spain, West Germany, and Greece (some include Turkey also) should receive preferred treatment among all the European allies of the United States because of the vigor of their anti-communist policies and the unquestionably conservative and capitalist orientation of their governments. Chiang Kai-shek, Dr. Syngman Rhee, and Bao Dai of Viet-Nam have been among their favorite Asian leaders for the same reasons.

These groups generally represent ultra-conservative elements in American politics, whose domestic policies reflect the same preoccupation with the 'inroads of socialism' that they demonstrate in foreign affairs. Thus far they have not won the approval of the United States government for their program of ideological selectivity on the basis of imitation of American institutions, but they continue to press their case.

The Totalitarian Implications of Ideologies. Modern ideologies are militant because they tend toward the totalitarian. That is, the growth of ideological consciousness in a people is accompanied by the increasing role of the state and the augmentation of the demands made by the state upon the loyalties and services of the people. This is not uniquely a phenomenon of post-1945 politics; it was seen in one state after another in the period since World War I.

An ideology does not become militant and totalitarian until some social force is released which destroys the prevailing beliefs of the mass of the people. Whenever the faith of the mass of men within a society is shaken in the fundamental truths by which they had been ordering their lives, mass insecurity grips them and they feel themselves alone and rootless in a hostile world. For people in this condition, with their old beliefs destroyed and nothing left by which to govern their lives, a totalitarian ideology comes as a welcome relief. Here at last is a creed in which they can lose themselves and the consciousness of their own failures and frustrations; here they can once again feel complete and effective. If their personal inadequacies can no longer be borne, if family and church and society can no longer furnish the sense of belonging which they demand, at least as members of an ideological group they can find a substitute that satisfies them.

Out of every great social cataclysm has come a great mass movement. In our day these take the form of national ideologies. A few examples will illustrate the point. Italian Fascism, German Nazism, and Russian Bolshevism all grew out of societies that had suffered the twin shocks of internal decay and military disaster during World War I. The people of these states emerged resentful, defeated, and bitter. They flocked to the new ideologies that promised them the fulfillment they so lacked in their decadent societies; if in return the new ideologies demanded the surrender of their freedom of individual choice, they reckoned the exchange a favorable one. Other examples are easy to find. The Fascism of Franco Spain grew out of the collapse of the monarchy and the frustrations of the republican period; Peron's Argentinian totalitarianism capitalized on the discontent of the urban masses.

These and other totalitarian ideologies all have certain characteristics in addition to the ones mentioned above. They all demand the merging of the personality of the individual into the greater being of 'the movement,' 'the party,' or 'the state.' The individual is under the control of the duly chosen leadership in all his actions and responds to their commands without conscious thought. These dogmas all promise the believer a rosy personal future if he remains true to the faith and performs his duties diligently.

To bridge the gap between the unpalatable present and the glorious future, the ideology also provides scapegoats who are allegedly guilty of all the sins of the moment. The scapegoats are convenient outlets for the energies of the membership and also serve to intensify ideological solidarity through a common object of hatred. The particular unfortunates chosen as targets vary with the state and its circumstances, but two popular groups are an unpopular minority in the population or imprecisely identified enemies whose machinations are of foreign origin. Thus the Nazis vented their spleen on Jews and communists; the Italian Fascists on Socialists and communists (and democrats as well); the Soviet on 'Western imperialists' and their 'spies'; the *Peronistas* on 'Yankee imperialists.' This ideological intensification serves to support the policy of the government through the techniques of propaganda.

Generally, totalitarian ideologies demand an expanding policy that both glorifies the state and satisfies the missionary drive common to such attitudes. Thus a modern totalitarian ideology represents a powerful force, compounded of the resentments and urges of a whole people, and statesmen are forced to deal gingerly with it. Many of the gravest crises of our time have come about because such ideological demands multiplied to the point where governments gave up the attempt at control and submitted to them.

Is American Ideology Totalitarian? A word must be said in this connection about the emerging American ideology. Many people of great sincerity feel that the United States has fallen into the trap of ideological totalitarianism. True, no major social change in the United States has produced mass rootlessness and insecurity; it is argued, however, that the rude shocks suffered by the American people in the postwar era have transformed their outlook and made them as rigorous and uncompromising on ideological issues as our authoritarian adversaries. These critics point to the development of the preoccupation with 'loyalty,' and its identification with official policy, as a serious symptom of an incipient totalitarianism. They are concerned about 'super-patriotism'—the idea that no individual has any scope of private freedom and rights which can withstand interference by governmental activity in behalf of public security—and feel that if this idea is widely accepted the freedom with which the American tradition is identified will be in serious danger.

This is a somewhat overdrawn picture. There are individuals and groups in the United States who represent the totalitarian school of thought, it is true; they have grown stronger since World War II as the frustrations of the postwar era have accumulated. It must be admitted also that it is dangerously-easy to identify loyalty and patriotism with a servile conformity to whatever policy enjoys popular favor at the moment. There has also been an unmistakable tendency to find scapegoats both for our own failures and for the blows to our self-confidence dealt by an inscrutable Providence. The bankruptcy of American policy toward China, for example, is in actuality due to a combination of an unrealistic and fatuous series of moves by the United States since 1945 and the release of forces in Asia over which we had no control. But to admit that would be too great a blow to the American ego; many of us there-fore prefer to believe that the whole catastrophe was brought about by a handful of communist spies in the Department of State. In doing so we relieve ourselves of any personal responsibility for the failure of our policy and satisfy our frustrations by persecuting those who symbolize that failure.

These are disturbing symptoms to one who retains faith in the good sense of the American people and the ultimate practicability of democracy. Never-theless, a totalitarian American ideology remains a possible future danger rather than a present reality. The ultimate destiny of the democratic process will depend to a great extent on the ability of the American people to with-stand the pressures leading them toward such an extremist ideology.

IDEOLOGICAL CONFLICT IN INTERNATIONAL POLITICS

In a very real sense ideological conflict represents the clash of masses of people rather than of governments, and it tends to take place in an atmos-phere of profound popular emotional involvement. To the extent that ideolog-ical issues are involved in interstate disputes, they aggravate the severity of any disagreement and serve to intensify and perpetuate the struggle. Resolu-tion of the conflict becomes extremely difficult unless the ideological quarrel is either settled, ignored, or allowed to die away naturally. Much of the rigidity of the present political structure of the world is caused by the extent to which mass emotions are involved on both sides of every dispute, and the best efforts of statesmen to reduce the tension are often frustrated by the very stubbornness of the ideological orientation which in one way or another they helped to create. Let us now analyze some of the characteristics of ideo-logical conflict and some examples of its occurrence in the world today.

CHARACTERISTICS OF IDEOLOGICAL CONFLICT

Moralistic Orientation. Ideological conflict is a struggle of differing moral codes. All ideologies are summations of the principles of moral right and wrong by which a society governs its conduct, and in any ideological clash there is bound to be disagreement on certain of these principles. When moral issues are involved, the defenders of each ideological position inescapably tend to identify themselves with truth, virtue, and right; their opponents be-come the antithesis of each of these. Ideological adversaries view their op-ponents as being guilty of far more than mere error; their offense is greater because of the moral issue involved. Any group, internal or foreign, which disagrees with the prevailing creed is by that fact sinful and evil; the opponent is an enemy of everything that the group stands for.

This makes ideological warfare between states a peculiarly bitter relation-ship, since each participant considers its enemy to be the embodiment of evil and as endangering the fundamental principles of society. In such an atmosphere it becomes very difficult for any issue of the dispute to be considered on its merits, since each is viewed in the peculiar light thrown by the intense ideological struggle. For example, the examination of any of the long series of 'peace offensives' undertaken by the Soviet Union since the breakup of the wartime alliance and the initiation of the cold war as a familiar aspect of American life never produces any grounds for encouragement. Any tentative Soviet proposal is analyzed with little seriousness and small hope of success because of the American ideological assumption that 'you can't trust the Russians.' The fact that 'trust' has little to do with the establishment of any working relationship between two great powers is simply ignored because of our ideological predispositions. The Soviets have reacted in the same way. Convinced of the basic malevolence of American intentions, they are adamant in rejecting any American proposals that do not contain the ironclad guarantees they demand against what they feel to be inevitable duplicity.

The longer an ideological struggle continues, the more convinced each nation becomes that the controversy is indeed a moral one and that the particular position it is maintaining is the only one in harmony with the eternal principles of right and justice. Thus specific policy problems are fitted into the moral framework, and the whole of foreign policy becomes the attempt to achieve the realization of a set of moral truths.

Persistence. On moral issues there is no ground for satisfactory compromise; as a result, ideological quarrels are persistent and difficult to dispose of in any final way. In a dispute between good and evil, all moral codes teach that the eventual triumph of the good is inevitable. It is therefore unnecessary, in addition to being immoral in itself, to seek to compromise with evil as a way of ending a dispute. As a result, an ideological quarrel between states drags on and on, since neither side can find any moral justification for ending it short of total victory. Indeed, no basis short of complete triumph can usually be found that would be acceptable to all parties.

The cold war provides a good example of this tendency. From the American point of view, the danger that must be avoided at all costs in Russo-American relations is 'appeasement,' by which is meant any American concession that might represent some partial agreement with the Soviet ideological position. 'Appeasement' as a concept grew out of the pre-1939 period when the diplomats of western Europe sought to satiate Hitler by allowing him to make one territorial seizure after another. The failure of this policy made a deep impression on the American consciousness, and its rejection is a basic tenet in the American ideological position today. In order to avoid the temptations of appeasement, American attitudes stress the ideological depravity of the Soviet and ruthlessly dismiss any possibility of a compromise between the USSR and the United States as 'wishful thinking'.

Therefore, on any agreement with the Soviet Union American policy places prerequisites that would have the effect of gaining the essential ideological points for which the United States is contending; by and large they add up to a confession by the Soviet that everything it has done since 1945 has been morally wrong. Of course no Soviet diplomat will agree to any such moral judgment on the conduct of his own state; indeed, Soviet ideology demands as much from the United States in return. And so the ideological controversy goes on, and neither side is able to devise a formula of escape.

Inconclusiveness. What adds to the perplexing character of ideological conflicts is its very inconclusiveness. It is almost impossible to win an ideological battle in any ordinary sense. Since moral issues are so deeply involved, the only way in which one party can gain any meaningful victory is for its opponent to admit that it was in the wrong. Furthermore, to be truly satisfying, this admission must not be the result of coercion or an unwilling concession, but must represent a sincere change of heart and a genuine sense of repentance. It is difficult to imagine any set of circumstances that would induce a people to renounce their ideology and to accept instead the creed of another state; particularly is this true in a period when the people concerned have been busy defending their own system and reinforcing their loyalties against what they have felt to be hostile onslaughts. To expect a people enthusiastically to endorse a judgment of moral turpitude against themselves is to expect a great deal, yet this is what each party to an ideological conflict is seeking.

It is also useless to press ideological issues by military means or other form of physical coercion. If successful, such tactics may bring military victory or other tangible reward, but the ideological goal remains tantalizingly beyond reach. If it is true that 'a woman convinced against her will, is of the same opinion still,' the same principle is equally true of nations. Defeat in World War II did nothing to alter the fundamental beliefs of the German or Japanese people; the Allies recognized this when they undertook the reconstruction of the society and the re-education of the people of these states. A military defeat induces the defeated people to reflect upon the causes of their setback and to resolve to do better next time; it seldom, if ever, causes them to feel that they were sinful, immoral, or wrong in the policies they undertook to support by the war. Unless they have such an attitude, the ideological objectives of the war cannot ever be attained, and such a reaction is so rare and infrequent as not to be worth counting on as a serious policy matter.

Ideological War. Many people are concerned lest the intensity of the mass emotions provoked by ideological controversy might lead the great states into taking irrevocable steps and thus plunge the world into a final great war of annihilation. There is no doubt that ideological war—that is, war fought only for ideological objectives—would be the most frightful kind of struggle imaginable. If such a war involved (as it certainly would) the two great political blocs of the world, one of two outcomes would be inevitable: the utter extermination of one of the camps, or the mutual exhaustion of both of them. In either case the destruction and loss of life might mean the collapse of modern civilization. Any ideological war today would be fought with a bitterness and a tenacity that would permit of no other result because of the fundamental character of the emotional issues involved.

Of all the possible bases for armed conflict between the Soviet and the Western blocs, however, ideological differences would appear to be one of the least likely. The leaders in both great camps realize the danger of any such ideological conflict and they are always careful not to permit themselves to be pushed too far. War in modern world politics is a desperate gamble at best; realistic leadership reserves the use of war for situations offering substantial gain and sufficient promise of success to justify extreme measures. Ideological issues do not qualify on either ground.

The gain to be derived from any ideological war is insubstantial at best and probably would prove illusory, and the prospects of victory are so clouded under the present distribution of power as to make any adventure of this kind foolhardy. War is always possible in international politics, and ideological war is always a danger; if global war comes to this generation, however, it will in all probability arise out of a clash of interests in concrete situations rather than through antipathies grounded in ideological issues.

The Falsity of Ideological Issues. A final characteristic of ideological conflict must be mentioned. The issues of such a quarrel are always unreal and actually serve to complicate international affairs unnecessarily. Ideological issues are false, and ideological conflict is pointless and futile (although apparently inescapable) because of one simple fact: international politics does not consist of a quarrel between absolute good and absolute evil. It consists, instead, of human statesmen pursuing realistic objectives in the material world. World politics is by its very nature relative, not absolute. An ideological policy that phrases an issue in absolute moral terms and pursues it by absolute means in search of absolute victory is a policy that can never attain success in the real world. It serves only to confuse and complicate a situation that by its very nature is already sufficiently complex.

Thus a government that devotes any considerable portion of its policy and power to the pursuit of ideological goals is to that extent diluting and weakening its concentration on what should be its primary business, the prosecution of its national interest. Whether the Soviet Union is good or evil, moral or immoral, is in the strictest sense immaterial to the United States; what should concern our government entirely is the real threat posed to American national interest everywhere in the world by the Soviet government and Russian power. Concrete situations, realistic policies, attainable objectives: these are the business of states, rather than the self-defeating pursuit of moral absolutes and the attempt to impose moral perfection on all who differ.

RUSSIAN-AMERICAN IDEOLOGICAL CONFLICT

Some special attention must be paid to the Russian-American ideological conflict in the light of the characteristics of such disputes just discussed. There is no doubt that this is the greatest such quarrel in the modern world and perhaps the greatest of all time; certainly its potentialities for destruction far surpass any others afforded by history. An understanding of some of the features of the conflict is necessary to a comprehension of the basic forces of world affairs.

CAUSES OF RUSSIAN-AMERICAN IDEOLOGICAL CONFLICT

Why did the ideological quarrel develop? The initial cause is, of course, the ideological gulf that exists between the two states, and certainly without this fundamental cleavage the quarrel would not have grown to its present proportions. But ideological divergencies exist between many other states without the development of such bitter controversy. It is noteworthy that the ideological differences existed between the United States and the Soviet Union before 1945, long before the cold war began or was even dreamed of. It was only after the war that the dispute grew ominous. Are there any factors bearing directly upon the relationships between the two in the contemporary world which helped produce the present dispute and which keep it going? At least three such factors may be seen.

First, during and after World War II the two states were thrown into a close, almost intimate relationship with each other for which both were unprepared. Neither had any familiarity with the other; no bond of common experience or sympathy derived from long contact provided a common ground. The differences between the two cultures, the social and political organizations, and the belief systems burst upon the two peoples with great suddenness. Neither side made any great effort to understand the other; indeed, circumstances were such that any such effort would have been very difficult of accomplishment even if the will had been present.

A second factor is the fact that the ideologies of both states were inherently expansionist. Both Marxist communism and individualistic democracy implicitly assume the eventual conquest of all men by their doctrines; both look forward to the rapid expansion of their areas of acceptance. This idea was at first imperfectly understood by both states, and each saw no necessary conflict between the two theories. During the war there was much discussion in both states about the extent of ideological unity that existed, but closer examination revealed the basic dynamism of both democracy and communism. The expansion each ideology required affected all postwar relationships between the two states and contributed in large measure to the ideological controversy of today.

A third special factor is the difference in the status and outlook of the two states. The United States came out of World War II a 'have' power, with all its major internal problems solved or under control, and it therefore enjoyed social stability; the USSR emerged from the war still a revolutionary society, with the most important questions of the distribution of power and the rewards of society yet unresolved. In international outlook the same divergence of policy was to be seen. By 1945 the United States had attained all its major objectives and asked for nothing more than the organization of the world on the basis of the preservation of the *status quo*; the USSR felt that it had yet a long way to go and looked forward to a continuing series of fundamental changes to its own advantage. This difference in point of view soon found ideological expression. The Soviet Union sees in the communist revolution a highly moral device for gaining its national ends, while the United States employs the ideas of world law and international organization as ideological devices of unquestioned moral validity which also protect American interest in the *status quo*. Thus each of these factors—mutual unfamiliarity, dynamic belief systems, and status differences—plays a part in perpetuating the Russian-American ideological conflict.

Ideological Issues. No complete listing of the ideological issues between the two states is possible without making a detailed point-by-point analysis of the two creeds. In general, however, it can be said that the quarrel centers around three great points, each of which represents a whole family of specific issues.

The first of these is the world role to be played by the two states. Each ideology looks forward to the day when the world is organized entirely in harmony with its principles; each assumes that its state is destined to be the one true world leader. This leads to constant policy disagreements between them as each seeks to realize its own destiny and to impede the progress of the other. Ideologically there is no room for peaceful co-existence, let alone harmony and co-operation; each ideology assumes the necessity for victory over the other. Thus ideology makes the Soviet Union and the United States natural and eternal enemies, since both aspire to a position of leadership that can be occupied by only one.

The second great ideological issue deals with the political system each employs and with the attempts each is making to expand it. The Soviet Union expounds the virtues of the 'people's democracies' and claims that only under such a political system can the individual find true security and happiness and, at the same time, the correct balance be struck between individual freedom and collective (group) authority. The United States is dedicated to the individualistic democracy of the Western world, with its emphasis on individual freedom of choice, individual responsibility, and limited government; the 'people's democracy' is denounced as a monstrous fraud concealing naked dictatorship. Each seeks to impose its political system on the states under its control or tutelage; each seeks to deprecate and to undermine the system of the other.

The third ideological issue is, of course, that of the economic systems. This, perhaps the most widely understood and most frequently discussed of all the ideological differences between the two states, is summed up as a battle between capitalism and communism. The economic issue, striking as it does at such a basic concept as private property, is probably the most powerful of the three in its impact upon Americans. It is not so clear, however, whether the Russian people distrust the United States because it is capitalist or because of the external threat it represents to Russian policy. But certainly Americans recoil emotionally from the Soviet Union because of its communist dogma; communism constitutes a basic threat to the pattern of individual life in the United States, which is to such a great extent rooted in the institution of private property.

The list above often breaks down, of course, in practice. Nearly every specific ideological controversy between the USSR and the United States has implications that extend into all three of these areas. The listing does, however, show at least the range of the quarrel and serves to indicate the extent to which both ideologies have totalitarian implications. Each of these three points is defended or attacked on grounds predominantly moral. To Americans, Russian power, Soviet-style government, and communism are all the acme of immorality and sin, while American power, political democracy, and capitalism are highly moral and good. As one would expect, Soviet expositions of the same points take exactly the opposite tack.

The Future of the Ideological Conflict. The generalizations about the termination of ideological conflict apply with particular emphasis to the Soviet-American dispute. The controversy has been going on since the end of World War II and shows no signs of abating; indeed, the differences are deepening and appear to be permanent. Up to the present time no suggested compromise on the ideological issues has stood the slightest chance of acceptance. No one can now be certain of the future course of the struggle, but it will be very probably result eventually in one of three possible outcomes.

The first possibility is that the conflict will intensify to the point of ideological war. This was discussed above; although it can never be discounted entirely, it remains the least likely of the three.

The second is permanent continuation of the struggle until it becomes an accepted way of life; Orwell's vision of the world in *1984* assumed this outcome. In one sense this is the most likely of the three possibilities in that it would eventuate if present tendencies were merely continued without change. This would be doubly unfortunate for men everywhere, and especially in the two states involved. They would be subjected to the constant diet of tension and crisis which is the necessary accompaniment of ideological conflict; thus the psychic insecurity that plagues our age would be strengthened and made

PROBLEM AREAS: PSYCHOLOGICAL 381

permanent. The perpetuation of the ideological conflict would also nullify any attempts at the removal of the real objects of controversy between the states by the diplomatic techniques of compromise; no improvement in political relations would be possible.

The third possible outcome of the ideological struggle is its gradual relaxation until it either disappears or else diminishes to the point where it permits more or less normal relationships between the governments on policy matters. This is the happiest possible outcome, for if it took place a real improvement in the climate of world affairs would occur.

Other ideological quarrels of the past have ultimately been put aside by their participants: Britain and France, Britain and the United States, and Greece and Turkey are examples of former ideological foes who were able to discover enough in common to make closer relationships possible on a basis of identity of interest. Whether or not this will take place between the United States and the USSR as a longer period of contact brings about greater familiarity, less suspicion and fear, and more tolerance is beyond the capacity of anyone to foretell. One thing, however, is certain: political relationships will never improve until the ideological climate is more propitious to agreement and compromise than it is at the present time.

OTHER IDEOLOGICAL CONFLICTS

Although the Soviet-American ideological conflict is the greatest and most significant one in the world today, it is far from being the only one. Such quarrels can be found in many other parts of the world, differing from the massive dispute between the two giants only in specific issues. All display the same general characteristics and all threaten to be as persistent and as difficult to dispose of as their prototype, the controversy between the USSR and the United States.

The European-American Dispute. Born of the frictions arising from the very closeness of the Western alliance against the Soviet Union, the American-European ideological struggle is a relative newcomer to the family of such quarrels and is still peripheral in its impact. The bloc included in the NATO has a great deal in common with the United States, including agreement on most fundamentals of belief. Nevertheless, the tensions of the postwar world and the requirements of policy have produced considerable ideological disagreement and this threatens to become worse if the bipolar world dissolves.

Europeans condemn American immaturity, materialism, impatience, and preoccupation with physical power. They also find much fault with American culture and delight in making many invidious comparisons with themselves. Americans, on the other hand, point out European decadence, impracticality, and oversophistication as contrasting with the simpler but more wholesome American way of life. Americans criticize European inability to understand

or to employ the techniques of political democracy; Europeans point to political corruption in the United States and inconsistencies in policy (such as
the logical contradiction between American tariff policy and the foreign-aid
program of the United States), and inquire if American democracy is after
all so much more successful than the European variety. All in all, the dispute
between Europe and the United States is at the present time more of an
annoyance than a danger to orderly relationships; if it should grow in intensity, however, it could menace Western solidarity and offer a tempting
opportunity for Soviet expansionism.

   Asiatic-Western Conflict. It is perhaps inaccurate to speak of an 'Asiatic
ideology'; nevertheless, there is a sufficient degree of coincidence in the
various attitudes of the Asian states in their relations with the Western world
to create a clear ideological schism between the two groups. The states of the
West are learning today that Asiatic societies are constructed on a value
system different from Western ones. Added to the Asian philosophical position which emphasizes patience, fatalism, tolerance, and xenophobia is the
new leaven of nationalism. The interaction of the strangely combined elements makes Asian attitudes difficult for the West to comprehend. Korean
intransigeance, Burmese and Indonesian isolationism, Indian neutralism,
and Chinese expansionism are all, oddly enough, products of basically similar ideological forces.

   Furthermore, just as the West fails to understand or sympathize with Asiatic atttitudes, the new ideologies of Asia obdurately refuse to credit the
Western states with any motives other than mere expansionism and a sordid
imperialistic urge. Each party to the quarrel insists on picturing the other in
the image of a bygone day, and cannot be brought to a full understanding of
the changed circumstances. This dispute, if perpetuated, may have serious
consequences; it has already materially obstructed American efforts to mobilize the strength of the free world against Soviet expansionism.

   Asiatic-Communist Conflict. By the same token, serious ideological differences exist between the international communist movement and this same
Asiatic ideological pattern. Although Soviet policy has been more successful
than American in coping with 'the new Asia,' this success has been more
through Soviet adoption of Asiatic nationalist goals than through the inculca-
tion of ideological harmony. Actually, whenever the Soviet has attempted to
disseminate the pure Moscow ideological line it has met instant and con-
certed resistance. Nowhere in Asia is communism a true mass movement.
Even in China the communist ideology is the possession of only a small elite
group of Chinese who feel themselves uprooted from their heritage and thus
have become susceptible to the Marxist line. Despite the superficial identity
in belief which is displayed by Moscow and Peking, Mao Tse-tung himself is
the authority for the statement that the goal of the present regime in China is
to 'Sinify' Marxism so as to make it palatable to the local conditions.

Communism has failed to strike deep roots into the soil of Asia for the same reasons as has Western democracy. Individualism simply does not have any meaning for Asians; their society is geared to group life—the family, the tribe, the clan—and the individual gains significance only as a member of a larger community. Communism fails to attract Asians because of its materialism. Asiatic life is intensely religious in the sense that every Asian—Buddhist, Moslem, Confucian, or whatever—is always conscious of his intimate relationship with the eternal and of his prospects for immortality. No dogma which, like communism, rejects the supernatural and stresses the contemporary and the material can win mass adherence in Asia. Western states may take some comfort from the fact that their ideological failure in Asia is balanced by an equal ineptitude on the part of communism.

THE CULT OF NATIONALISM

We turn now to a brief examination of the more extreme forms of nationalism as they occur in the world today. Throughout our discussion of world politics the phenomenon of nationalism has been constantly in the foreground. We include an analysis of extreme nationalism in this chapter because in any form it is a function of group attitudes and can be fully understood only when considered in such terms. We have defined nationalism as the sense of unity shared by a people which makes them want to live together in a state and to see that state prosper. We shall now consider some of the ways in which extreme forms of that sense of unity influence the course of world politics today.

THE STATUS OF NATIONALISM TODAY

The emotion of nationalism is undergoing a multi-formed development, both in direction and in speed, in various parts of the world. In some areas nationalist loyalties are losing their effectiveness and are being replaced by a growing allegiance to a larger basis of organization than the state. In others, however, the decline of nationalism has not been followed by the appearance of a new loyalty and a vacuum of belief has thus been created. At the same time other parts of the world are still in the expanding stage of nationalism; the old appeals retain their potency and indeed their effectiveness may be increasing. It is in these last-named areas that there develops what we call the 'cult of nationalism.'

Areas of Declining Nationalism. Although a decline in the degree and extent of nationalist commitment by individuals has taken place in many states during the past two decades, in western Europe this condition has become so widespread as to attain the status of something like a mass movement. Individual identification with nationalist goals has sharply decreased in such states as Italy, France, the Low Countries, Scandinavia (notably Denmark and Norway), and West Germany. Many reasons have been advanced to explain this development, and several unquestionably have some pertinence.

Among these are the disillusionment brought about by two wars in one generation; the growing emotional maturity of the people, which tends to diminish importance placed upon 'political' values; the cyclical course often taken by nationalism; and the recognition of the inefficiency of the nation-state, at least on a scale as small as that found in western Europe. In any case, nationalist attitudes have decreased in potency to such an extent that proposals for lasting European union or consolidation are farther advanced in the middle of the twentieth century than they have been at any time since the days of Charlemagne. The principal new vehicle of popular loyalty is the growing idea of a European community, although there is considerable sentiment favoring the world-wide organization of political society. On the other side of the world, another state showing signs of being in the declining stage of nationalism is Japan; the same factors are at work here.

Two comments should be made about the decline of nationalism. In the first place, all the states in which it is taking place have a glorious past but have recently suffered severe reverses. Included in this classification are several of the pre-1939 great powers and some that were great at an earlier time. The world today is so organized that they can never hope to regain their former eminence. It is possible that the lessened appeal of nationalism for them derives partly from the fact that the goals the nationalist spirit usually seeks are forever beyond their reach.

In the second place, it is impossible to foretell the ultimate outcome of the decline of nationalism. While the over-all lessening in the militancy of the spirit has been going on, counter forces seeking to revive the old attitude have been at work and have achieved some success. Particularly in France and in Japan has the renaissance of nationalist emotions been marked, to the extent that some of the echoes of earlier belligerency and arrogance have been heard again recently. It may be that the cyclical theory of nationalism will be proved wrong and that these and all the other states now dismantling their nationalist apparatus will ultimately return to their former ways. On balance, however, the indications still point to the continued progress of all of them toward some new and perhaps broader basis of loyalty.

Areas of Expanding Nationalism. In opposition to the foregoing trend, however, many other peoples are still in the growing and expanding stage of nationalism. These states are of two types: the newly great large states, including the United States and the Soviet Union in one group and China and India in another, and the smaller states, including both those that have only recently become independent and those whose popular consciousness is newly formed despite a longer period of legal independence. Among the smaller states whose nationalism is most extreme are the Argentine and Brazil in the Western Hemisphere; Ireland, Poland, and Yugoslavia in Europe; Egypt and the Union of South Africa in Africa; Iran, Israel, and Turkey in southwest Asia; Indonesia, Burma, and the Philippines in southeast Asia; and Korea in the Far East.

The outlook of the peoples in all of these states, great and small alike, is distinctly colored by their fervent nationalist orientation. This affects their ideas of national interest, their choice of political objectives, the policies they pursue, and the type and extent of the settlements they will accept.

Perhaps no clearer or more impressive example can be found of the compelling force of a runaway nationalism than the conduct of the government of South Korea during the truce negotiations of June and July 1953. At a time when all the major participants in the struggle on both sides were willing to end the fighting on an inconclusive note, South Korea alone was insistent upon either continuing the war or obtaining a complete satisfaction of its nationalist demand for Korean unification. The motives that had brought most of the parties into the fighting in Korea were mixed on both sides, but this was not so as far as Dr. Rhee and his associates were concerned. Korean nationalism demanded unification and would be satisfied with nothing less. In the pursuit of that objective the South Korean government was willing to wreck prospects of a truce and even to face the possibility of fighting on alone against any combination of enemies. Extreme nationalism frequently drives a people to taking action that defies good sense, but there exists no effective means of restraining such a policy once mass attitudes are thoroughly aroused.

CHARACTERISTICS OF THE CULT OF NATIONALISM

In many of the states in which nationalist attitudes are on the rise, there exists a condition that may be termed 'pathological' nationalism or the 'cult of nationalism.' This arises when the intensity of nationalist feelings rises to the point where the normal set of social values is drastically altered and national goals and aims are elevated to a position of unchallenged superiority over all others. Not only does individual loyalty to other groupings, such as family, trade union, church, and so on, diminish sharply, but in many cases the private person is denied the right to membership in these groups if their demands conflict with those of the state. Pathological nationalism has an immediate and marked effect on the conduct of foreign affairs by the government, and often forces a policy entirely different from the one that would be if nationalist demands were kept at a more restrained level. We shall examine the impact of the cult of nationalism on the policies of specific states in a moment; first, let us distinguish a few of its characteristics.

Totalitarianism. In the first place, extremist nationalism is totalitarian: that is, it encompasses every aspect of individual behavior. Every moment of the day the individual is reminded that he is a part of the greater whole, the nation, and in all his actions he is charged with a responsibility to it. His economic life, his family life, his religious life, his recreational life, all of these are functions of his fundamental and most important level of being as a member of a national group. The individual cannot escape the nation. The criterion of 'patriotism' or 'loyalty' or 'good citizenship' is applied to everything he does, no matter how personal or intimate.

In Fascist Italy, for example, it was regarded as a mark of good citizenship to marry early and to have large families; such a course was urged upon Italians as a means of showing their patriotism. Nazi Germany went farther: such was the demand for children that unmarried German girls were feted if they produced them (especially boys). Literary and artistic creation, athletic competition (the 1936 and 1952 Olympic games furnished striking examples), scientific progress, and industrial production are only a few of the other areas of social life that are made to feel the stimulus of nationalist pressures. All human activity is considered to be political in its implication and is fitted into the requirements of the nationalist program of the moment.

Authoritarianism. The cult of nationalism is also authoritarian. The political values of nationalism intrude into all areas of the individual's life; the state becomes a supreme arbiter of all modes of human conduct. Men are no longer permitted freedom of choice in situations in which formerly the state had no legitimate interest; every choice, being fraught with political significance, become a legitimate matter of state concern and direction. In free societies, the line of employment a man follows is left to individual discretion and circumstances; a super-nationalist nation comes more and more to place men in the positions in which they will contribute most directly to the national strength. Where an individual shall live is again a matter of state control, as are such additional aspects of private behavior as emigration, membership in organized groups, religious affiliation and participation, and the structure of family life. Both Nazi Germany and Soviet Russia have forced individuals into particular jobs, decreed where they should live (even to deporting entire communities), destroyed 'unpatriotic' organizations and substituted new ones in which private membership was obligatory, and even sought to undermine the family institution as a dangerous rival of the state for the loyalty of the people.

Authoritarianism and totalitarianism are really two aspects of the same phenomenon: the popular rejection of individual freedom in return for the great psychic security obtained from membership and participation in the greater entity of the nation. A rough but reasonably accurate guide to the degree to which any particular nationalism has reached the proportions of a cult is the determination of the extent to which they have transferred the control over the many intimate details of private life to the nation and to its external manifestation, the state.

Emotionalism. The new nationalism, representing as it does a great emotional commitment on the part of the people, is extremely sensitive and unstable. Nationalist outbursts with profound policy consequences are likely to occur at any time in a people whose sense of political identification with their government and with each other is deep and immediate. A sense of 'national honor' is keen and the people are ever alert to discover any slight on it by any other group, to resent it keenly, and to demand that their government obtain immediate satisfaction. The cult of nationalism tends to classify all other peoples and governments either as close friends or as bitter enemies. National tradition and history as well as the particular policy objectives the government is seeking become invested with a sacred significance, and resistance or opposition by any other state produces a reaction of outrage.

The contemporary world abounds with examples of such hypertense nationalist emotions; we need go no farther than American attitudes toward the Soviet Union to find many. Nothing irritates American public opinion more than for the USSR to question the purity or the magnanimity of the motives of the United States. To many of us this Russian refusal to accept our assurances of good intentions is proof of the essential decadence and depravity of the Soviet Union and the permanent impossibility of ever doing business with it on any friendly basis.

Impatience. A final characteristic of the cult of nationalism has a special pertinence in a crisis situation involving international conflict. Being so charged with emotionalism, highly nationalist people tend to be extremely impatient. Nothing is more frustrating to an individual than to undergo a strong emotional experience preparatory to action, and then to have that action indefinitely postponed. In such a situation there is a tendency toward an explosion of some sort simply as a way of relief from a tension that has grown unbearable. This is always a danger when a nationalist conflict is under way. If the statesmen who are conducting policy do not feel that the struggle is worth a war, they are seeking to discover some viable compromise, but the conflicting nationalisms that have been intensified by the mounting tension of the crisis are often insistent on action. Thus the task of the statesman is a dual one: he must settle the conflict on the one hand and at the same time attempt to manipulate the inflamed attitudes of his people so as to forestall their making impossible demands upon him.

EXTREME NATIONALISM IN THE GREAT POWERS

In the great powers today there is a clear tendency toward the type of nationalism we have been discussing. In the United States and in the Soviet Union, in China and in India, nationalist attitudes all point in the same direction, although to different extents. The most advanced forms are found, of course, in the Soviet Union and in China; the United States and India have not yet reached the same pitch. In the USSR a frankly totalitarian and authoritarian nationalist creed subordinates all individual life to the constant demands of the state. Nazi Germany is the only modern rival to the USSR in the degree and extent of control exercised over the individual in the name of the international mission of the state. In China, the undeveloped nature of the Chinese economy and society has made the task of creating a belligerent Chinese nationalism more difficult for the communist rulers, but their objectives are clear, and much progress has already been made.

In the United States, the traditions of individual freedom have stood in the way of any rapid movement toward anything like Nazi or Soviet nationalism. Nevertheless, the concept of 'national duty' generally accepted by Americans today is much broader than it was twenty years ago; the responsibilities of nationalism bear much more heavily now. The demand for conformity, the discouragement of dissent, and the rise of anti-intellectualism are only three indices of the extent of the growth of American nationalism. Indian nationalism is still formative; however, the struggle for independence from Britain gave the mass of the population the beginnings of a real nationalist spirit. Events since independence have served to confirm and strengthen this tendency.

Characteristics. Large-state nationalism has a few characteristics that mark it off from the small-power variety. Most noticeable is a drive toward leadership. Of the four states mentioned above, two—the United States and the USSR—are accepted as great powers, while China and India aspire to that status. The respective nationalisms demand that this position of eminence be recognized by everyone and that the state move steadily into a greater world responsibility. American nationalism dreams of a world organized according to an American plan in which happiness would be universal under our leadership; the USSR frankly admits its goal of a communist world. India has not yet raised its sights higher than Asian leadership and acceptance as an equal at the council tables of the world.

The problem has been most frustrating for China. Being a revolutionary government, and a communist one as well, the new regime has been treated as a pariah by the United States and many of its allies. Diplomatic recognition and admission into the United Nations are sought frantically by the Chinese communists as being formal evidence of their arrival at international respectability and world leadership. The longer these are denied the more insistent Chinese nationalism becomes in demanding them.

A second nationalist characteristic is expansionism. Nationalism demands that great states export and impose their ideology upon their lesser neighbors. This is sometimes called 'cultural imperialism'—a deliberate policy of forcing a major power's cultural standards on such states that are unable to resist successfully. It is usually a matter of great gratification when a small state adopts some particular cultural practice of a large one; Americans are generally quite pleased that Coca-Cola has become popular in Europe.

A third characteristic might be called dominance. A large state that is highly nationalistic is convinced of the innate superiority and rectitude of its institutions and its policy. Therefore, in any international situation touched upon by the nationalist credo, it is impossible for such a state to adopt any attitude but that of attempted dictation. Free discussion between equals is impossible because in terms of the nationalist attitudes the participants are not at all equal; one state is right and the other wrong. Thus a powerful nationalist state seeks to impose its will on all others and often is willing to go to considerable lengths of coercion in order to satisfy its insistence upon the recognition of its superior position.

THE CULT OF NATIONALISM IN THE SMALL STATES

We named earlier some of the smaller powers of the world whose policy indicates that they are in the grip of virulent nationalism. We found them to be located in nearly every part of the world: the Western Hemisphere, Europe, Africa, southwest Asia, southeast Asia, and the Far East. Each of these states faces unique circumstances and is in a different stage of national development. As a result, each has demonstrated its nationalist orientation in a fashion peculiar to itself. Nevertheless, it is possible to distinguish in their behavior certain common characteristics which we might list as marking off small-state nationalism.

Defensive Orientation. In the first place, small-state nationalism is different in that it is primarily defensive. The nationalist attitudes of the great powers are affirmative and positive in direction; these peoples look forward to ever-increasing power, glory, and importance. On the other hand, the fundamental nationalist point of view of the people of a minor power is negative; nationalist emotions are directed against something or somebody. This attitude grows out of the recent political history of most of these states. All of them have emerged from a subservience to a more powerful state, either as a direct colony or as an economic or political vassal. This release from what is felt to be bondage was accomplished by the outburst of a nationalist movement for independence, and thus the birth of group self-consciousness occurred in terms of a reaction against external forces.

This attitude has carried over into the period of national independence and serves effectively to govern the general conduct of national policy. Argentine and Brazil are escaping from economic domination by the United States and Europe; Egypt, the Union of South Africa, and Burma from political adolescence under British tutelage; Poland, Yugoslavia, and Turkey from centuries of being footballs of great-power politics; Indonesia, Korea, and the Philippines from colonial status; Ireland from centuries of alien rule by Britain. In each state the primary object of nationalist revulsion is the particular circumstances of its former status. All of them are determined never to slip back into the condition from which they are emerging, and all the resources of nationalist persuasion are devoted to keeping the people alert to the danger of doing so.

Introversion and Xenophobia. The consciousness of their bitter past and the stimulation of nationalist sentiments has turned nearly all the peoples of the small states inward in their search for social values. In every state mentioned the cultural history of the people has been repeatedly searched to discover ancient traditions and virtues which are applicable to their present status of independence. The rejection of everything alien, even if it is good, is demanded by the more extreme advocates of a purely indigenous nationalism. This lends it a strangely withdrawn character.

Whereas large states are seeking to extend the scope of their nationalist creed, the small states reverse the direction and attempt to confine their doctrine to the minimum group of people who share the common tradition. In the Moslem world—including Iran, Egypt, Indonesia, and Pakistan—extremist nationalism is allied with Moslem fanaticism, and the most vociferous spokesmen for the destruction of foreign influence and the retreat into obscurantist primitivism are religious leaders. In Israel, the same tendency can be seen: the strictly Orthodox Hebrew leaders are insistent upon the minimum contact with the outside world. In the Western Hemisphere, each of the various Latin American states is seeking out its Spanish (or Portuguese) heritage. Ireland's insistence on the deliberate re-creation of its Gaelic culture is another example of this introversion.

Belligerent Independence. We have already remarked on the belligerent independence of smaller states whose nationalism is aroused. This reaction is not a surprising one, for it is derived from history and the course of world politics. With independence—political, economic, or cultural—being such a new thing, the people in any such state are insistent that everyone recognize it fully. Any government official who espouses a policy that might be interpretated as subordinating his government to the whims of a great state runs immediate and serious danger of being summarily repudiated by his people.

The government of Indonesia learned this to its sorrow. In 1952 a cabinet fell from power because it had negotiated a mutual-security agreement with the United States; the population felt the agreement made Indonesia a vassal of the United States and made overly great concessions to American policy. Mohammed Mossadegh, the Iranian premier who manipulated public opinion so shrewdly until he fell victim to an army coup in August 1953, found himself the prisoner of the nationalism he had helped to create during the long negotiations with Britain over the expropriation of the Anglo-Iranian Oil Company.

Repeatedly, small-state nationalism has been so intent on avoiding positions of inferiority and on the full measure of equality of status that policies clearly in the national interest have been rejected. Nothing has made the lesser powers of the world more difficult for the great states to deal with. The United States has been most directly affected because the American policy of creating a vast alliance of the entire free world has brought it face to face with small-state nationalism in every portion of the globe. In each case such small states have proved fractious and difficult to convince of the necessity for common action.

Unfortunately, in too many instances American nationalism has been in its turn aroused by the obduracy of the smaller states. As a result the American government has attempted to employ direct coercion to attain its ends; resistance and then nationalist quarrels of no small dimensions developed. The seriously confused status of United States relations with India and Indonesia is an example of what happens when American urgency collides with small-state suspicion. This problem only serves to redouble the intricacy of the task of creating unity in the free world without in any way reducing the necessity for it.

THE ACCOMMODATION OF CULTURES

The final psychological problem to be considered in this chapter is perhaps the most fundamental to the cause of the future development of mankind and underlies the two previously discussed. It is the pattern of emotional reactions produced in people of all states when they are brought into sudden and intimate contact with cultures other than their own. In one sense it is obvious that the creation of a world political system that will bring peace and security instead of perpetuating crisis must depend on first bringing into existence a widely based sense of a common destiny among men everywhere. Chapter 9 was devoted to a consideration of the extent to which an international-community sense has developed.

Yet in terms of the immediate and future course of world affairs, it is only too apparent that the day when men all feel themselves part of a single family is yet far off. Political harmony among states must wait upon the construction of a shared system of values which men in all parts of the world accept and act upon. Most of these values are what sociologists call 'cultural,' and the present disharmony, which is reflected in nationalist disagreements and international political conflict, is rooted essentially in cultural tensions. The accommodation of cultures is certainly as important as any other single problem in international relations, and may perhaps be the most critical.

INTERCULTURAL CONTACT AND TENSION

The Role of Technology. Intercultural contacts between peoples have been greatly accelerated in this century by the impact of technology. Societies formerly were permitted to isolate themselves and to develop their own value systems and institutions in terms of their own evolution. In the past fifty years rapid transportation and communication have brought even the most remote parts of the world into contact with the main streams of civilization. Many of these contacts have been sudden and forcible; one example among many is the dramatic 'opening' of Japan to the outside world by Commodore Perry of the United States in 1854. Today, with political organization on a

world-wide scale a reality in the United Nations and with all the great powers
and many lesser ones carrying foreign policies which project their interest
and their power into the out-of-the-way places of the world, the comfortable
cultural isolation which most societies enjoyed not too many years ago is a
thing of the past.

Intercultural Tension. Close and frequent intercultural contacts between
widely differing groups inevitably produce many possible points of friction.
Once international relations break through the barrier of formal interstate
contact and become a matter of 'peoples speaking to peoples'—and technology makes this increasingly the case—the possibilities for misunderstanding, lack of sympathy, disagreement, and conflict multiply as the many cultural differences are discovered and seized upon. Since these cultural forms
penetrate deeply into the organization of a society and touch on fundamental
areas of human action where emotions run high, intercultural tension tends
to move quickly to a high pitch of intensity. Antipathies of this sort also often
seize on a minor cultural symbol as the object of national resentment. Many
Frenchmen accept Hollywood as a symbol of everything objectionable in the
United States, while many Americans feel that the stereotype of French
social relations involving hand-kissing, heel-clicking, and bowing epitomizes
the decadence of France.

Areas of Intercultural Tension. Any of the myriad social relations that go
to make up a culture may serve as an area of intercultural tension; there is
no way to predict in advance which particular social custom will produce
such tension. Nevertheless, certain broad areas are common sources. The
first area is that of moral codes. Standards of good and evil differ and disagreement in these terms is likely to be fundamental and acrimonious. Perhaps a projection of the moral issue is the conflict that arises over different
systems of personal and family life, particularly codes of sexual behavior.
Also in this category is the issue of religious belief and organization, particularly involving evangelical, missionary faiths. An interesting subject for
speculation is the extent to which the American attitude toward Asia has
been affected by the fact that for many years that continent was thought of
principally in terms of a field for religious missionary activity. Accustomed
to thinking of Asians as pagans who had not been shown the true religion,
Americans today sometimes find it difficult to take these people seriously in
political terms.

Another area of intercultural tension is intellectual life. This arises today
largely because of the Western assumption that Oriental societies have no
intellectual tradition worthy of consideration. Stemming from unquestioned
Western superiority in technology and science, this attitude has been extended into the humanistic fields. Asiatic resentment at being considered the
intellectual inferiors of the West is natural. A final area of tension is that of
political, economic, and social organization. These institutional structures

are always an outgrowth of the particular cultural tradition and value system of a people, and quarrels about the superiority of one over another can never be decided in any rational way.

Political Results. Probably the most immediate political effect of an intercultural disagreement is the immediate stimulation of the nationalist attitudes of the peoples involved. Faced with a strange and often disquieting lack of understanding from another people, each group turns for reassurance to its own creed and draws strength from the reaffirmation of its principles. The more we Americans come into contact with alien forms of government, for example, the more convinced many of us become that the particular system we have is the best for all people everywhere if only they had the wit to adopt it. The Briton who journeys abroad and punctuates his trip with repeated rejections of everything foreign is a stock character. Thus intercultural disharmony serves to deepen and strengthen the other divisive factors at work in international politics.

The effects of this division on the actual policies of governments have already been noted: an increasing rigidity in the relations of the states involved and the consequent difficulty of settling disputes as they arise. It is this fact which has led some observers to suggest that the best course for the United States to follow in its relations with the USSR is to have as little to do with it as possible. In that way intercultural contacts would be minimized, fewer points of nationalist conflict would arise, and the possibility of amicably adjusting the conflicts of interest that do come up would be greatly strengthened. This is a position supported by considerable logic and historical evidence—American relations with imperial Russia were at their best during the nineteenth century, when intercultural contacts were virtually nonexistent—but it would require, as would any proposal for cultural isolation, our rejection of an expanding technology.

THE PROBLEM AS IT AFFECTS THE UNITED STATES

The problem of intercultural tension and of the need of intercultural understanding is particularly pressing as it affects the United States. This is true for a double reason. In the first place American policy has as its ultimate goal the creation of a world community of tightly knit relationships governed by world law. We have seen that such a society is possible only on the basis of a high degree of cultural integration or accommodation. Secondly, the problems of intercultural adjustment have been more perplexing for Americans than for any other people of the Western world since 1945. For no one else has it been so important to develop techniques for intercultural adjustment, and for no other people has the task been so difficult.

The Nature of American Culture. Of the many things that can be said about the broad subject of American culture, only a few are especially pertinent to the present discussion. Perhaps the most significant aspect of the

American cultural pattern is that it is highly indigenous. Although originally an offshoot of the main stem of the Western tradition, American environmental factors speedily altered the direction and speed of development until a distinctly American way of life appeared. This phenomenon was noted by Edmund Burke as early as the eighteenth century; the westward migration during the nineteenth century only intensified particularist tendencies. Even the great influx of immigration during this period failed to leave any major imprint on the American scene; the 'melting pot' effect rapidly assimilated widely variegated ethnic elements into a common American culture.

The throughout its entire formative period the American consciousness was generally turned inward in search of the peculiar manifestations of the American genius. Thus cultural contacts with other groups were, with certain notable exceptions, kept at a minimum; the average American was so preoccupied with his personal problems and the conquest of his environment that he was scarcely aware of the existence of other ways of life. Such intercultural attitudes as existed were generally stereotypes founded on history and tradition rather than impressions gained from direct personal contact. Perhaps the strongest of these was a persistent Anglophobia arising from the revolutionary experience of the eighteenth century and kept alive by grammar-school history and Fourth of July orations.

The effect of this cultural isolation was strengthened by a combination of circumstances, including the force of geographic separation, the course of European political development, and the Industrial Revolution. These enabled the United States to remain relatively aloof from the main streams of international political life. Isolation was more than a reasoned national policy throughout the entire nineteenth century; it was a fundamental cultural attitude. Americans came to feel that their non-involvement in the periodic crises of world affairs was due either to the excellence with which political and cultural matters were handled by the leaders of this country or to some form of moral pre-eminence that entitled them to receive favors from Providence. It became a mark of America's superior virtue and intelligence that the United States was able to play a lone hand in such international ventures as it undertook up to 1900; American ability to overlook or ignore the entirely fortuitous quality of this state of affairs was unlimited.

Indeed, American culture as it matured in the nineteenth century came to display most of the marks of a typical provincial society. Some of these were an exaggerated attachment to familiar places and social processes, a distrust of alien influence in any area of life, an inability or a refusal to learn new procedures from others or even to admit that there were any worth learning, a flaunting of the aspects of the culture of which we were the most proud (technological advance, industrial production, and a high standard of living are only three examples) as being conclusive proof of the merits of

American culture, and—most subtly—the transformation of admitted weak points into concealed sources of strength.

This tendency to make virtues of one's own shortcomings is common in all provincial societies but is particularly marked in the United States. Thus American diplomatic failures (often the result of an unrealistic American public opinion) are excused on the ground that diplomacy is a dirty and tricky business, ill suited to the frank, open-hearted, honest, and uncomplicated American character. The relatively low standards of taste in the United States are explained away by semi-learned conclusions that literary and artistic creativity are marks of a decadent society; in a truly virile and healthy one, it is claimed, individual interest is centered more on building and creating material things of enduring value.

American Intercultural Contacts. The twentieth century, and particularly the period since 1945, has brought American culture, developed in relative isolation from other cultural streams and armed with a provincial distrust of all outsiders, into headlong and continuous contact with the rest of the world. The comfortable isolation of the nineteenth century disappeared in the wake of the Spanish-American War; the reluctance of the American people to admit this fact was finally dissipated after 1945, two wars and a depression later. Through all the vicissitudes of the past three decades, one trend has been constant: each year has seen more and more intercultural contacts being made between the American people and the outside world they thought they had foresworn.

Generally speaking these contacts have been unhappy for Americans. Not only did they discover that their cherished institutions and values were not the only ones in the world, but they also found out that peoples of other cultures displayed no great eagerness to imitate American behavior in order to share in the lofty order of excellence of the United States. Instead, peoples of alien societies have shown an unseemly stubborness in clinging to their own cultural standards, and some have had the temerity to imply that their ways are preferable to ours. The realization that the rest of the world is not eagerly awaiting the opportunity to become just like the United States but that instead each group intends to follow its own line of cultural development has been a source of dismay and—in some cases—lasting shock to many Americans.

As a matter of fact, when we Americans realized in 1945 that the nineteenth century was forever gone, we made a sincere effort to grasp the implications of membership in the world society. The good intentions of the United States were real and, we thought, should have been obvious to all. We wished everyone well; the greatest boon that we knew to confer on them was the opportunity, by diligent application and hard work, to take for themselves the salient features of American culture. In that enterprise we stood ready to aid them with a genuine generosity unique in international politics.

When our offers were rebuffed—sometimes completely, as by the USSR; sometimes partly, as by various European states who take our dollars and our military support but reject our cultural standards—American reaction was natural: a nationalist revival set in.

Large segments of American public opinion now bemoan the loss of our isolation as if it were our virtue and bitterly oppose any further steps in the direction of economic or cultural relations with the outside world. The foreign-aid program of the United States is now almost entirely a military one; this is a reflection of a new 'realism' in policy which no longer has any patience with the foibles of eccentric cultures. The attitude of the American government seems to be one that demands political and military support in return for any aid our nation extends, and no nonsense about intercultural accommodation. Indeed, the period of the cold war has actually been one of retrogression in American intercultural outlook; as a people we no longer expect to be loved or admired but instead many of us are reconciled to envy and bitterness from all with whom we associate.

The Need for Intercultural Understanding. This new cynicism is as unrealistic as was the earlier optimism. It was folly for Americans to expect all (or any) peoples of different cultural traditions eagerly to quit their historic patterns of behavior and undertake a slavish imitation of the United States. It is just as fatal in the long run, however, to assume a permanent lack of understanding between the rest of the world and ourselves. Technology is not arrested simply because many Americans have had their feelings hurt; it goes on every day about its task of knitting the world more closely together. Our contacts are going to grow more numerous and ever more intimate, and the world is with us to stay. We simply cannot endure cultural isolationism any more than we could survive political isolationism. The attainment of any part of the grand design of American foreign policy requires that the United States take the lead in the development of a genuine intercultural accommodation. A world of law and order in which orderly processes replace violence and fear can come about only after significant progress has been made toward the creation of a body of shared values among peoples in all states.

The foregoing discussion, in concentrating on the United States, may have given the impression that the failure to move more rapidly toward this goal is primarily the responsibility of Americans. This is not at all true. Cultural provincialism is not an American monopoly; other societies have as much smugness as we have and as great a tendency to cling to their own procedures. There is a great deal in American culture which is worthy of imitation by others, and their failure to do so makes them the greater losers.

The problem is really a multilateral one; intercultural understanding will not come about through the absorption of all other systems into the most powerful single one. It can occur only as the result of a long process of many-sided intergroup contacts, in the course of which each culture borrows from the other. Each one acquires for itself such particular features as take root naturally and serve a desirable purpose, but maintains tolerance, sympathy, and understanding for such cultural differences as persist despite this intimate relationship. It is not the existence of cultural divergencies that is the cause of international and intergroup tension, but rather the emotional reaction of peoples to the differences.

Nevertheless, the primary responsibility for intercultural harmony must rest for a considerable time on the people of the United States. Not only is it in our real national interest that such understanding develop as rapidly as may be possible, but taking the lead in the process is one of the responsibilities of the power that is ours. Unless we move in this direction, the United States will follow one of three courses: an unprofitable and ultimately futile isolationism, an uninformed and inept attempt to cope with a world whose dynamics we do not understand, or an attempt to establish an American-created world authoritarianism under rigid control from the United States. None of these policies provides any assurance of success, but all are pregnant with danger. Any of them would lead us to a path of cultural development which might involve the steady and permanent surrender of the freedom that is such an integral part of our way of life. It is one of the paradoxes of history that the United States must, in order to save the freedom that is peculiarly its own, discover effective techniques to give it away to all other peoples who will accept it.

V

The Future

14

The Future

Iᴛ has become commonplace to point out that mankind is at a crossroads in history and that future generations will suffer the consequences—for good or ill—of the critical decisions that our age is making and will continue to make. This platitude is like so many others, however, as true as it is banal. Perhaps contemporary society is no more at a watershed of history than were many previous generations, and our role may not be original with us; other ages have been faced with equally grave responsibilities. Nevertheless, whether ours is a uniquely perplexed destiny or merely one shared by our ancestors, the choices that have fallen to us are both difficult and important. What we decide now will affect the world for decades to come.

It therefore seems appropriate at this concluding point in our inquiry to take a look at the future. Our vision is, of course, limited; we shall not be able accurately to predict details of the course of events during the next phase of the history of international relations. At the very least, however, we may take an over-all view of the range of possibilities of the future, examine the good and bad portents, and review some of the unsolved problems with which we may expect to grapple in the years to come. In this way we may be able to gain some insight into the dimensions of the task facing mankind and perhaps gather a few clues how to proceed.

PROSPECTS AND PROBABILITIES

THE PROSPECTS

The Alternatives. Using what logic we can apply to a situation and a system which we have learned to be fundamentally illogical, we may postulate initially that the future of the world political system either will be marked by change or by stability. If change occurs it will be either destructive or constructive; furthermore, the pace of either type of change may be rapid, or it may be more gradual and evolutionary. In this way, we arrive at five possible alternative routes which the future of world politics and the state system might take, depending on both the direction and the speed it assumes: (1) complete and sudden destruction; (2) gradual deterioration, marked by progressively greater inability to solve problems and meet challenges; (3) a continuation of the present system with no great change—the middle course; (4) gradual improvement, marked by progressively more effective solution of problems; (5) rapid and radical transformation into a different and much better system.

RELATIVE PROBABILITIES

Destruction and Transformation. Which of these alternative developments is most likely to occur? Admitting that all five are theoretically and perhaps practically possible, can we pick out certain of them as being more likely to take place than others? It is perhaps safest to start by relegating both extremes—the first and the last in the list above—to the category of the least possible. Rapid destruction of society or its equally rapid transformation is possible in any period of history, and instances of the occurrence of each can be found. In any situation, however, sudden and extreme institutional and social change is usually the least probable outcome; man seems to prefer other, less drastic solutions to his problems. Certainly it must be admitted that today we possess the technical knowledge either to wipe out civilization and perhaps humanity or to reorganize society on a basis of abundance for all. Human will, rather than the limits on human intellect, holds us back from accepting either of these courses. While recognizing as always that judgments about the future behavior of men are inevitably subjective, we may nonetheless conclude at this point that it is relatively unlikely that either total catastrophe or total renaissance will mark the future of international politics.

Deterioration or Evolution. More probable than sudden explosion or sudden reform is the prospect of gradual modification of the state system in response to external pressures. This evolution may result in a multiplying frustration as the system proves more and more incapable of satisfying the demands placed upon it, or it may culminate in a gradual overhaul and revision of the structure of international society and the successful resolution of issues that presently defy attack. In other words, the system may prove itself unable to adapt to circumstances and eventually break down, or it may develop new capabilities to meet new problems.

The Trend to Frustration. We have pointed out several factors in international life the cumulative effect of which is to speed the trend to deterioration. Among these we considered the following: the rigidity of the world political structure, marked by bipolarity and the inability to compromise meaningfully; the intensity of nationalism and nationalist conflict, which leads to the rejection of all solutions to problems except absolute ones; the present failure to control the trend toward bigger and more deadly weapons and techniques of destruction; and the fact that so many basic problems of human life overreach state boundaries and hence do not permit of easy solution in a state-centered world. These are only a few of the conditions that combine to create a slowly growing impression that the fundamental problems of international life are, and will continue to be, insoluble. If this attitude should become the prevailing one in the minds of men, the resultant atmosphere of frustration and defeat would inescapably spell the ultimate failure and collapse of international relations. We cannot foretell what would replace the present system, but that it would be vastly different and of no guaranteed greater effectiveness we may be sure. The deterioration and collapse of the present framework of world affairs must be admitted to be a genuine possibility. It would require only the projection and intensification of trends already present to become a reality.

Constructive Evolution. On the other hand, possibilities of constructive evolution in international affairs are also present in the contemporary scene, and forces are at work which give us at least as much reason to hope for final success as to fear final defeat. There are grounds enough for a restrained optimism, or at least enough to discourage an unrelieved pessimism. These hopeful portents have also been considered earlier, and reference to a few of them might offset the impact of the bleak prospects of defeat. In the main, they reflect attempts to escape from the more oppressive consequences of the inability of the state system to meet the demands placed upon it. They combine to furnish real evidence that the controlling trend of the future of world politics might be a reasonably happy one, or at least that the negative omens can be balanced by positive ones.

We have already discussed the evolving sense of international community, which is the first of the favorable factors. It would be unrealistic in the extreme to claim that this particular attitude is dominant in world affairs today or that it will become so relatively soon, and no such contention is made here. It would be equally inaccurate, however, to deny that the international-community sense exists and that it is exerting a perceptible influence on the course of events. There is also some basis for feeling that this sentiment is on the increase and that it will be even more influential in the future as something of a counterweight to the divisive and potentially upsetting force of nationalism. It takes its expression most frequently in the form of supranational consensus and an emerging world public opinion.

A second favorable sign in world politics is the growing caution of statesmen. Although the conditions that produce breakdown and war are ever present, it is clear that policy makers in all major states are less willing today to run the risk of being responsible for total disaster. The net effect of this self-imposed restraint is to head off many of the dangers of the day and to give the world more time. Caution on the part of national leaders provides time for the nations to work out alternatives, time to allow heated passions to cool, time to develop bases for understanding—more time, perhaps, than some pessimistic observers have been willing to grant mankind. If statesmen continue to recoil from the possibility of putting civilization to the final awful test, the prospects for progress and the discovery of adequate techniques of operation on an international level will be brighter.

A final ground for hope grows out of the first two: the growing trend toward the creation of new international and supra-national agencies to deal with new problems. It seems obvious that new situations call for new approaches, and that part of the failure of contemporary international society to resolve the crises of our age is due to the inadequacy of available techniques. Only by the development of new institutional procedures can constructive evolution in international politics become a reality. There are no grounds at present for being certain that any of the newer institutions we have today will necessarily provide the answers man is seeking; perhaps they will all ultimately fall short. Only by creating such new agencies, however, experimenting with them, discarding the failures, and improving those that offer promise of success can any progress be made. In the trend epitomized by the creation of such bodies as the United Nations and the European Coal and Steel Community one can find considerable reason to feel that evolution of international society toward greater efficiency is a real possibility.

The Middle Ground. We have examined briefly the four different types of change that may occur in the pattern of international politics in the years ahead: explosion, deterioration, evolution, and transformation. There remains a fifth future possibility: that no significant change either for good or for ill will be forthcoming and that the pattern of interstate relations will continue very much as it has been in the past and is today. Many compelling reasons lead one to believe that this is most likely to be the actual course followed by the world.

Perhaps the greatest single factor that would tend to keep international society in the same paths as it is now is an undeniable human trait: the desire to cling to and to retain social patterns and institutions that are familiar and sanctified by usage. The shortcomings of the present state system are not difficult to discover and we have made much of them in this volume; the system is not without its real advantages, however. Not the least of these is its familiarity. Modern civilized man is at home in the state and feels in harmony with his environment when he is accomplishing the traditional purposes of national interest in the time-honored way.

Among the other reasons for the probable survival of the present system are the monopoly of power exercised by the state form over individuals and the compelling emotional attachment felt by most of us for the traditions and goals of nationalism.

If one accepts as a working hypothesis the idea that international relations will continue in the future much as in the past, this does not rule out of the picture the possibility of change, even of substantial change. The forces of deterioration and evolution considered above are real and powerful, and even if they do not become dominant they will materially affect the day-by-day course of international politics.

Indeed, it is not difficult to envisage the nation-state system of the future functioning according to the same principles as energize it today, but at the same time being affected by (and affecting) the twin forces of deterioration and evolution. Perhaps the international scene of the next generation or two will be the final battleground between these historic trends; out of such a struggle would come the decision on the ultimate direction in which civilization will move. More likely the struggle between stagnation and change will take place within the state system and, as in the present era, the tide of battle will ebb and flow. For a time progress might be in the ascendant and impose its will upon the system; then reaction would set in and frustration would again become the order of the day, to be later replaced by a new era of progress as the cycle begins again.

In many ways this alternative seems the most probable of all; one is always on scientifically sounder ground in predicting limited social change and the perpetuation of institutions than in forecasting upheavals and revolutions. Nevertheless, in good conscience we cannot rule out the possibility that one or the other of the extreme roads mentioned earlier may be the one chosen. International explosion is always possible; less likely, but also conceivable, is a sudden voluntary transformation of the system. The first is so terrifying to contemplate, however, and the second so difficult of achievement, that either radical outcome is relatively unlikely. Somewhere between the steady and uninterrupted deterioration into complete frustration and the continued smooth evolution toward a new and better system lies the more probable future course of world politics.

ISSUES OF THE FUTURE

No tabulation of the pressing issues with which international society will have to deal in the future can be much more than a reflection of the interests and prejudices of its compiler. We have already learned that international problems grow out of specific historical contexts and that accident and chance play a significant part in the determination of the crises of any particular age. None of us can be certain of the next twist of fate that will present us with another perplexing decision. The most we can do it to attain the best-possible understanding of the present in order to be better prepared for the eventualities of the future. It would therefore be unwise to make a list of current issues and to imply that their solution would insure a smooth and satisfying future. Nevertheless, it is possible to enumerate some of the problems of the present day which promise to continue unsolved into the immediate future and perhaps into the long-range future as well.

In the three preceding chapters we examined a number of specific problem areas of current international politics. Here we shall phrase the issues in somewhat different terms. The political, economic, and psychological problems we considered earlier are examples of questions that grow out of particular conditions of time, place, and participants. They are, in other words, truly contemporary. The smaller number we shall briefly analyze in this section are inherent in the present structure of world affairs and are to a great extent independent of time or place. They give evidence of being at least semi-permanent; it is probable that they will continue to plague later generations despite possible major changes in their geographic, psychological, or material bases. Because of their fundamental and enduring character, we may assume that their future importance will be at least as great as their present significance.

In this chapter we shall consider five such basic issues. They are not listed in any order of importance; rather, since they are so interconnected, it would be logical to consider them as being of equal pertinence. The five chosen for consideration here are the issue of war; the issue of communism; the issue of Asia; the issue of atomic energy; and the issue of international organization.

THE ISSUE OF WAR

None of us needs to be reminded of the impact that the prospect of war has had on our lives; in an age when anxiety is endemic this fear of a new war may well be the most powerful of our insecurities. Much of the climate of international politics today is the result of a near-hysterical search by governments for some insulation against their being engulfed in another holocaust which might return men to the Dark Ages. It seems clear that little respite will be granted us in the future from this continuing danger and that we shall have to wrestle with the problem of war for long years to come. What can we say at the present time to throw this issue into some sort of perspective?

We have come upon the institution of war at every turn of our analysis of international affairs. We have examined its place as the only final determinant of international disagreements, we have considered different techniques and philosophies of warfare, we have studied its incidence and its prospects in the contemporary world. We have concluded that war is a 'normal' aspect of international affairs and that to abolish the institution would necessitate a complete reconstitution of international society. If man is unwilling or unable to undertake such a thoroughgoing renovation of the methodology of international affairs, he must perforce prepare himself to live permanently with the knowledge that an outbreak of mass hostilities is always possible and, futhermore, that such a conflict would involve the new dimensions of destruction brought into being by an ever-expanding technology. Under these conditions, it would appear that a reconsideration of some of the implications of war would be of some help.

What Can Be Won by War? Perhaps the first concern should be to remind ourselves of what can be won by means of war. We need to keep in mind that war as an instrument of policy in the nation-state system is subject to serious limitations. Certain objectives, for example, are forever beyond its reach. It cannot convince a defeated enemy of its moral blindness and inherent unworthiness; it cannot win friendship, nor can it extirpate hatred. If war must be lived with, it should be confined to such purposes as it can efficiently accomplish. This is particularly true when we consider total war. This type of struggle, with its objectives of absolute destruction, is feasible only when such goals are truly dictated by national interest. To unleash such engines of mass destruction as the hydrogen bomb in pursuit of an unattainable objective or a frivolous one would be to justify the most extravagant prophecies of the doom of civilization. Only by being aware of what can be gained by war—and, equally important, what cannot be gained by it—can we maintain our existence under the present system.

Will We Pay the Price for Peace? Very few, if any, humans can honestly say that they prefer war as a method of existence to peace. Almost all of us as individuals would prefer to live out our lives in relative harmony with our neighbors, settling such disputes as may arise by non-violent means. It is usually as political beings, as citizens of a state and members of a nation, that we become belligerent. If war is such an undesirable condition among states, it must follow that peace is preferable. What is not so clear is whether we shall be willing to pay the price for peace.

Peace can be maintained, even in the nation-state system, if the will to do so is present. The avoidance of war requires that at least three principles be active in the foreign policy of every state. These 'rules of peace' might be phrased as follows: (1) never get into a situation where war is inevitable; (2) use all alternative methods of settling disputes; (3) accept less than total victory in any situation. If states were to embody these ideas in their relations with one another, the maintenance of peace on a reasonable basis of stability would be a much easier task than it is at present. We must admit that it would be difficult to persuade the people of any powerful state to accept these ideas and the foreign policy they necessitate; to gain adherence by all major states would be a truly formidable task. Some such concept, however, would seem to be the real price for peace, and in no other way can the worst effects of the institution of war be escaped.

Can War Be Limited? Another question arises out of the experience of the past few years, when a number of small wars have been settled inconclusively without being permitted to spread into major conflagrations. Can war be limited? The war that frightens us is total war, and if some technique could be developed for confining small conflicts, much of the horror and uncertainty of contemporary world politics would be lessened. Of course, the answer to the question—as we asked it—is an affirmative one; we have already seen that statesmen can limit hostilities as regards participants and locale. What we are really asking, however, is whether we shall be willing to limit war. Will we agree to suffer occasional tactical defeats in special situations in order to gain our strategic goal of peace?

If we agree that war can and should be limited so long as it cannot certainly be eliminated, major policy revisions must be undertaken by all states in order to realize that goal. We must recognize the inexpediency of objectives that can be attained only by major war and plan to employ only such forms of national power as can be successfully committed without risking total hostilities. We must reorganize our thinking so as to recognize the grounds for possible compromise and the practical steps necessary to realize such agreements. These, too, are bitter pills for tender nationalisms to swallow, but the alternative is clear: if the world is unwilling to limit war, it must face the consequences that will follow total war.

These, then, are some of the implications of the problem of war in the future. Since war is a thoroughly normal phenomenon in the nation-state system, it is essential to discover a basis for survival within the system. We should consider the possibilities for confining and limiting war as regards purposes, goals, and techniques. If the questions we have asked can be satisfactorily answered, perhaps the whole problem could be reduced to manageable proportions. If they cannot, future generations may face the crises of total war in a vastly accentuated degree.

THE ISSUE OF COMMUNISM

The second problem with which the world of the future will almost certainly have to deal is that of communism. This sinister ideology, which in forty years has grown from miniscule beginnings to the most formidable threat to freedom in the world today, presents men of good will everywhere with hard choices and difficult courses of action. Its significance shows no signs of abating, and ultimately some definite policy will have to be adopted toward it. It does not appear as if the present generation of leaders has yet discovered a formula that tells us how to deal with communism, and the resolution of the problem in any final way belongs to the future. It is possible at this time, however, to review certain facets of the problem of communism without pretending to offer a final diagnosis or suggesting any precise course of action.

What Is the Communist Problem? Fundamentally, communism is an ideology. As such, however, it existed for more than a century without becoming a major political force. It is only since the belief system became clothed with political power that it has developed into an international factor of the first order of importance. To seek to attack communist ideas without reference to their political manifestations is pointless. The communist problem does not center around the truth or falsity of Marxist dialectic and the doctrine of the decline of capitalism; it gains its significance from the fact that organized political bodies professing these doctrines make up a large part of the world political scene. These states constitute a pressing problem that calls for decision and action.

Viewed in these terms, the communist problem has three forms. Initially, it is an organized plan of political expansion centering in the Soviet Union and executed on the traditional stage of international politics (although involving several novel techniques). Secondly, it is a program of domestic subversion and revolution in which the crucial struggles take place within all non-communist states. Third, it is the current form of the historically familiar trend to totalitarianism and authoritarianism, which has assumed different guises in different periods but always seeks to extinguish human liberty and to destroy the concept of the innate dignity of man. In all three forms, communism presents a continuing challenge to states that seek to establish an international order of peace and stability based on individual self-realization. On all three levels the free societies of the world are combating the threat.

Why Has Communism Grown? How can we explain the growth of communism from its humble beginning to its present awesome dimensions? As late as 1945, there was only one communist state in the world; why, then, has the ideology become such a grave danger to freedom in such a short time? There are three possible reasons, each explaining a part of communist success.

In the first place, it has capitalized on political weakness. It has become a foregone conclusion that whenever a 'soft spot' develops in the postwar world communist influence and Soviet power will seek to exploit such weakness. Any state unsure of its policy or its power can expect to be made an early object of communist pressure.

Second, it has exploited human misery and social maladjustment. It has played on the unquestioned injustices of the world and capitalized on the widespread desire for a more equitable distribution of the rewards of modern society. The communist movement has been alert to seize upon any delay on the part of the free world to deal effectively with international problems created by internal tension. It has been able to twist sincere social protest into mass revolution.

Finally, communism owes much of its success to the contemporary decline in the vigor of democratic belief and practice. Totalitarianism and authoritarianism have always stood ready to ensnare man whenever he has lost his faith in his own capacity for government. Today, when so many societies are shaken by doubt and dissension, communism has had very fertile soil in which to grow. In summary, then, we see that the growth of communism in recent years is due not to any major change in the doctrine itself but rather to the opportunities presented it by the failure of the free world to meet its challenges.

What Can We Do About Communism? Communism is a many-sided phenomenon and must be fought on all fronts where it seeks to advance. Some possible avenues of counter-action immediately suggest themselves on the basis of the foregoing analysis of the problem. Military force can be used to resist the plan of communist expansion. In many situations armed might is the only appropriate technique for dealing with the threat, but we must remain aware of the inherent limits on its utility. Second, we must undermine the communist appeal to the discontented by providing answers to vital social questions and at the same time preserving human freedom. Third, we must revitalize the concept of individual dignity and freedom by making democracy again a force that can capture the imagination and zeal of men everywhere. When the problem is put in these general terms, the path of the free world might seem deceptively simple. Working out these principles in practice, however, will be a task that will challenge the greatest ingenuity of the political leadership of the future.

THE ISSUE OF ASIA

The Western world has been slow to realize that Asia is in the grip of a deep-seated revolution the effects of which can make major alterations in the pattern of world politics. Keenly nationalistic, driven by an obsessive anti-colonialism and a nagging insistence on equality in status, the states of Asia are forcing themselves upon the attention of the Western world. Great and small states alike are more significant in world affairs than they were a generation ago. The West has yet to discover a basis for dealing effectively with this new feature of world affairs; many different approaches have been attempted, but none has had any real success. The world can attain real stability only after these new participants in world politics have found their place in the pattern; as a result, the issue of Asia has become one of the critical problems of the future of world politics.

Will Asia Become Communist? To many Americans the principal ground for concern about the 'new' Asia is that it is tending toward communism. Several Asian states—most notably China—have come under communist rule, and other states are in danger of slipping into the same orbit. Yet we must not forget that communism did not make the Asian revolution; it has merely capitalized on it. Whether or not Asia becomes completely communist will in the last analysis depend not on what the communists do but rather on the policy of the West. Asians are demanding internal and international freedom today; communism promises these and thus gains Asian loyalty. We in the West know the falsity of such communist gestures, but so far we have been unable to make either our rebuttals or our alternative proposals adequately palatable to Asians, whose fear of a renewed imperialism is almost pathological. To save Asia from communism will require that we reformulate our appeals to Orientals—to take account of what they themselves want rather than what we should prefer that they have—and to back the appeals with action that is meaningful in Asian terms. Only in that way can the communist threat to Asia be stopped and perhaps turned back.

Can Asia Be Stabilized? Even if the communist danger to Asia be warded off, there remains a host of other problems. The most generalized of these is that of a chronic instability, international and domestic, which afflicts almost the entire continent. So long as internal political convulsions and violent international controversies rack Asia, the world cannot know real peace. Although any capsule solution to as huge and many-sided a problem as stability in Asia cannot help but be oversimplified, one general remark seems in point. Asia's troubles stem generally from political immaturity: a driving energy is linked to a lack of experienced political leadership. Perhaps the West can make its greatest contribution to Asian stability by expediting the continent's orderly transition into maturity by giving assistance when it is asked for, exercising patience and tact, and always avoiding the appearance of seeking to impose intellectual or cultural domination. It may be that this will prove insufficient; perhaps Asia must suffer all the 'growing pains' which any adolescent passes through while becoming an adult. This would be unfortunate, but the West cannot count on stability in Asia until maturity comes to its young states.

THE ISSUE OF ATOMIC ENERGY

Much has been made of the importance of technology in contemporary world affairs. For most of us the problem is phrased most poignantly in terms of the issue of atomic energy. In this powerful force man has discovered a potentially revolutionary source of energy that could transform society, yet he is gripped by fear that this power will instead be used to destroy him. Many observers feel that the final verdict on man's future on the earth will be rendered in terms of his ability to control the destructive implications of atomic energy and to release its potentiality for good. Certainly none would deny that the next era of world history will be materially affected by the decisions arrived at concerning atomic power.

Can We Control the Bomb? Most urgent of the necessities facing the world in dealing with atomic energy is that of controlling its use as a weapon. If we cannot control it and if we are destined to be blown up by it, the hopeful potential of atomic power will turn out to be a hollow mockery. Devising a system for eliminating atomic weapons (for 'control' really means elimination) has so far proved impossible for statesmen, and the world has instead launched on an atomic-armaments race. No one is satisfied with this development, yet no acceptable alternative has yet been presented.

The attempts at control have failed up to now because of one major consideration: the large states have continued to feel that they would gain more from unilateral exploitation of atomic weapons than from any proposed control system that was mutually acceptable. For real control to come about, all the major powers must first agree that freedom from the danger of atomization is worth more than any possible advantage to be gained from using the bomb. We pointed out above that war can be avoided in the nation-state system only by a deliberate program of voluntary self-restraint. So long as this attitude is not present and formalized, no control system can be really effective. When and if the attitude does become general, the establishment of a control system will no longer be difficult. In this case, as in so many others, the final decision will be rendered not in the councils of statesmen but by the crystallization of public opinion around a particular point of view. Only the future can tell whether such opinion will form in time.

How Significant Are Atomic Weapons? In recent months a new dilemma has forced itself upon the attention of Americans. Conditioned since Hiroshima to the idea that atomic weapons are the decision-forcing tools of modern warfare, we have tended to place most, if not all, of our policy eggs in the atomic basket. This idea became verbalized during 1954 and 1955 as the theory of 'massive retaliation.' The realization has slowly dawned, however, that Soviet possession of equally devastating weapons serves to neutralize whatever advantage we once might have had in atomic power. Mutual destruction is now possible. This fact produces the disconcerting awareness that the true measure of military strength today is not really a nation's atomic capacity but rather its ability to wage 'conventional' war. Despite the formidable power represented by the bomb, the consequences of retaliation are so frightening that there is a strong possibility that atomic techniques will never again be used in war on a mass scale. This throws us back to pre-atomic days in our calculations; the limited war discussed earlier as the only type man could afford will have to be waged with conventional weapons supplemented by 'tactical' atomic weapons, such as artillery. Thus the military aspect of atomic energy may well prove ultimately to be a monumental waste of time and resources; its principal result may be lingering resentments on the part of states who felt they were bullied and threatened by the states that possessed atomic weapons. This latter development is already partly realized.

Can We Realize the Atomic Potential? The other side of the coin of atomic energy is, of course, its peaceful exploitation. If controls on its destructive power should be erected on an international basis, it would seem that they might constitute a framework for co-operation in making the advantages of atomic power available to the maximum number of people. Such, at least, was the import of President Eisenhower's atomic proposals to the United Nations in 1953; the first concrete steps toward the creation of a peaceful 'atomic pool' were taken during the summer of 1954. The problem of harnessing this great force for human good is a technical one which we already know how to attack; political considerations alone stand in the way. Here, too, we may remind ourselves that public opinion alone can decide whether we and our posterity are to enjoy the maximum advantages of this greatest of technological advances. In atomic power we have a tool of great possible value in attacking many of man's most deep-rooted problems. Only the mass of mankind can decide how soon and in what way the program will be initiated.

THE ISSUE OF INTERNATIONAL ORGANIZATION

One of the few relative certainties in the future of international politics is that there will be some form of international organization as long as the nation-state system holds together. We have ample evidence that the need for some such agency is so strongly felt and generally shared that no one can conceive of doing without it. The issue of international organization, therefore, is not really one of whether or not there shall be any, but is rather one of direction, form, and degree. It is a question of whether the international organization of the future will continue to be an adjunct process, coexisting with other methods of conducting international affairs, or whether it shall grow in importance until it eventually comes to occupy the keystone position in international society.

We have already considered these various alternatives. The problem is restated here so that at the end of our introduction to the study of international politics we may be reminded of one fundamental fact that bears upon the whole subject: institutions are vehicles of human action. If we choose to follow a course that demands the elaboration and perfecting of the mechanisms of international organization, there can be no doubt that immediate improvement in the present procedures will take place. If, on the other hand, we do not demand such extensive action requiring major institutional change, we may count upon a perpetuation of the present limited role of international organization.

The resolution of the issue of international organization, therefore, rests ultimately upon basic decisions yet to be made by man. If, for example, the decision of humanity is against war and the system that makes it possible, international organization may grow into a real instrument for world government. If we decide, however, that these goals would require more of a sacrifice than we are prepared to make, international organization will remain of minor importance. No one can now predict which way humanity will decide.

Bibliography

THE NATION-STATE

Bosanquet, Bernard, *The Philosophical Theory of the State*, 4th ed., New York, Macmillan, 1930.
Browne, Waldo (ed.), *Leviathan in Crisis: An International Symposium on the State*, New York, Viking, 1946.
Burns, C. Delisle, *Political Ideals*, London, Oxford University Press, 1932.
Carr, Edward H., *Nationalism and After*, New York, Macmillan, 1945.
Cassirer, Ernst, *The Myth of the State*, New Haven, Yale University Press, 1946.
Cobban, Alfred, *National Self-determination*, Chicago, University of Chicago Press, 1947.
Coker, Francis M., *Organismic Theories of the State*, New York, Columbia University Press, 1910.
Hawtrey, R. G., *Economic Aspects of Sovereignty*, New York, Longmans Green, 1930.
Krabbe, Hugo, *The Modern Idea of the State*, New York, D. Appleton, 1927.
Laski, Harold, *The Problem of Sovereignty*, New Haven, Yale University Press, 1917.
McIver, Robert, *The Modern State*, New York, Oxford University Press, 1926.
——, *The Web of Government*, New York, Macmillan, 1947.
Maritain, Jacques, *Man and the State*, Chicago, University of Chicago Press, 1951.
Oppenheimer, Franz, *The State*, Indianapolis, Bobbs-Merrill, 1914.
Soltau, Roger H., *An Introduction to Politics*, London, Longmans Green, 1951.
Ward, Paul W., *Sovereignty*, London, Routledge, 1928.
Willoughby, Westel W., *Fundamental Concepts of Public Law*, New York, Macmillan, 1924.

NATIONAL POLICY

Bailey, Thomas A., *The Man in the Street*, New York, Macmillan, 1948.
Barrett, Edward W., *Truth Is Our Weapon*, New York, Funk and Wagnalls, 1953.
Beard, Charles A., *The Idea of National Interest*, New York, Macmillan, 1934.
Bernays, Edward L., *Propaganda*, New York, Liveright, 1928.
Dahl, Robert A., *Congress and Foreign Policy*, New York, Harcourt Brace, 1950.
Einzig, Paul, *Economic Warfare*, London, Macmillan, 1940.
Elliott, William Y., et al., *United States Foreign Policy, Its Organization and Control*, New York, Columbia University Press, 1952.
Gibson, Hugh, *The Road to Foreign Policy*, Garden City, Doubleday, 1944.
Gordon, David, and Dangerfield, Royden, *The Hidden Weapon*, New York, Harper, 1947.
Kennan, George F., *American Diplomacy, 1900–1950*, Chicago, University of Chicago Press, 1951.
——, *Realities of American Foreign Policy*, Princeton, Princeton University Press, 1954.
Lasswell, Harold, *World Politics Faces Economics*, New York, McGraw-Hill, 1945.
Leites, Nathan, *The Operational Code of the Politburo*, New York, McGraw-Hill, 1951.

Linebarger, Paul M. A., *Psychological Warfare*, Washington, Infantry Journal, 1948.
London, Kurt, *How Foreign Policy Is Made*, New York, Van Nostrand, 1949.
Markel, Lester, et al., *Public Opinion and Foreign Policy*, New York, Council on Foreign Relations, 1949.
Marshall, Charles B., *The Limits of Foreign Policy*, New York, Henry Holt, 1954.
McCamy, James D., *The Administration of American Foreign Affairs*, New York, Knopf, 1945.
Morgenthau, Hans J., *In Defense of the National Interest*, New York, Knopf, 1951.
Nicolson, Harold, *Diplomacy*, 2nd ed., New York, Harcourt Brace, 1950.
Selznick, Philip, *The Organizational Weapon*, New York, McGraw-Hill, 1951.
Summers, Robert E. (ed. and compiler), *America's Weapons of Psychological Warfare*, New York, H. W. Wilson, 1951.

NATIONAL POWER

Baldwin, Hanson, *The Price of Power*, New York, Harper, 1948.
Barker, Ernest, *National Character and the Factors of Its Formation*, London, Methuen, 1927.
Cressey, George B., *The Basis of Soviet Strength*, New York, Whittlesey, 1945.
Earle, Edward M., *Makers of Modern Strategy*, Princeton, Princeton University Press, 1944.
Emeny, Brooks, *The Strategy of Raw Materials*, New York, Macmillan, 1934.
Gross, Feliks, *Foreign Policy Analysis*, New York, Philosophical Library, 1954.
Kulischer, Eugene, *Europe on the Move*, New York, Columbia University Press, 1948.
Mackinder, Halford J., *Democratic Ideals and Reality*, New York, Henry Holt, 1942.
Merriam, Charles E., *Political Power: Its Composition and Incidence*, New York, Whittlesey, 1934.
Notestein, Frank W., et al., *The Future Population of Europe and the Soviet Union*, Geneva, League of Nations, 1944.
Ogburn, William F. (ed.), *Technology and International Relations*, Chicago, University of Chicago Press, 1949.
Russell, Bertrand, *Power: A New Social Analysis*, New York, Norton, 1938.
Sprout, Harold, and Sprout, Margaret (eds.), *Foundations of National Power*, 2nd ed., New York, Van Nostrand, 1952.
Spykman, Nicholas J., *America's Strategy in World Politics*, New York, Harcourt Brace, 1942.
Staley, Eugene, *Raw Materials in Peace and War*, New York, Council on Foreign Relations, 1937.
Strausz-Hupé, Robert, *The Balance of Tomorrow*, New York, Putnam, 1945.
——, *Geopolitics*, New York, Putnam, 1942.
Weigert, Hans W., et al., *New Compass of the World*, New York, Macmillan, 1949.

DYNAMICS OF INTERNATIONAL POLITICS

Angell, Sir Norman, *The Great Illusion*, New York and London, Putnam, 1913.
Aron, Raymond, *The Century of Total War*, New York, Doubleday, 1954.
Burnham, James, *The Struggle for the World*, New York, John Day, 1947.
Carr, Edward H., *The Twenty Years' Crisis, 1919–1939*, London, Macmillan, 1940.
Dallin, David, *The Big Three*, New Haven, Yale University Press, 1945.
Dickinson, C. Lowes, *The International Anarchy*, New York, Century, 1926.
Fay, Sidney B., *The Origins of the World War*, 2nd ed., New York, Macmillan, 1935.
Fox, William T. R., *The Super-Powers*, New York, Harcourt Brace, 1944.
Friedrich, Carl J., *Foreign Policy in the Making*, New York, Norton, 1938.
Haines, C. Grove, and Hoffman, R. J. S., *The Origins and Background of the Second World War*, New York, Oxford University Press, 1947.
Holborn, Hajo, *The Political Collapse of Europe*, New York, Knopf, 1951.
Keeton, George, *National Sovereignty and International Order*, London, Peace Book Company, 1939.

Kennan, George F., *Realities of American Foreign Policy*, Princeton, Princeton University Press, 1954.
Kieffer, John E., *Realities of World Power*, New York, McKay, 1952.
Leites, Nathan, *The Operation Code of the Politburo*, New York, McGraw-Hill, 1951.
Mende, Tibor, *World Power in the Balance*, New York, Noonday Press, 1953.
Nicolson, Harold, *The Congress of Vienna: A Study in Allied Unity, 1812–1822*, New York, Harcourt Brace, 1946.
Niebuhr, Reinhold, *Christianity and Power Politics*, New York, Scribners, 1940.
Schuman, Frederick L., *Europe on the Eve: The Crisis of Diplomacy, 1933–1939*, New York, Knopf, 1939.
Schwarzenburger, Georg, *Power Politics*, New York, Praeger, 1952.

INTERNATIONAL CONFLICT

Bernard, L. L., *War and Its Causes*, New York, Henry Holt, 1946.
Brinton, Crane, *The United States and Great Britain*, Cambridge, Harvard University Press, 1945.
Brodie, Bernard, *The Absolute Weapon*, New York, Harcourt Brace, 1946.
Bush, Vannevar, *Modern Arms and Free Men*, New York, Simon and Schuster, 1949.
Carr, Edward H., *German-Soviet Relations Between the Two World Wars*, Baltimore, Johns Hopkins University Press, 1951.
Churchill, Sir Winston, *The Second World War*, 6 vols., Boston, Houghton Mifflin, 1948–53.
Dean, Vera M., *The United States and Russia*, Cambridge, Harvard University Press, 1947.
Dulles, John Foster, *War or Peace?*, New York, Macmillan, 1950.
Dunn, Frederick S., *War and the Minds of Men*, New York, Council on Foreign Relations, 1950.
Eagleton, Clyde, *Analysis of the Problem of War*, New York, Ronald, 1937.
Kahin, George McT., *Nationalism and Revolution in Indonesia*, Ithaca, Cornell University Press, 1952.
Langer, William L., *The Diplomacy of Imperialism*, New York, Knopf, 1935.
Lippmann, Walter, *The Cold War*, New York, Harper, 1947.
Moon, Parker T., *Imperialism and World Politics*, New York, Macmillan, 1926.
Shotwell, James T., *War as an Instrument of National Policy*, New York, Harcourt Brace, 1929.
Vagts, Alfred, *A History of Militarism*, New York, Norton, 1937.
Wolfers, Arnold, *Britain and France Between Two Wars*, New York, Harcourt Brace, 1940.
Wright, Quincy, *A Study of War*, 2 vols., Chicago, University of Chicago Press, 1942.

ESCAPE FROM CONFLICT: INFORMAL TECHNIQUES

Birdsall, Paul, *Versailles, Twenty Years After*, New York, Reynal and Hitchcock, 1941.
Blackett, P. M. S., *War, Fear, and the Bomb*, New York, McGraw-Hill, 1948.
Boggs, S. Whittemore, *International Boundaries*, New York, Columbia University Press, 1940.
Burnham, James, *Containment or Liberation?*, New York, John Day, 1953.
Dean, Vera M., *The Four Cornerstones of Peace*, New York, McGraw-Hill, 1946.
Dennett, Raymond, and Johnson, Joseph (eds.), *Negotiating with the Russians*, Boston, World Peace Foundation, 1951.
Kennan, George F., *American Diplomacy, 1900–1950*, Chicago, University of Chicago Press, 1951.
Machiavelli, Niccolo, *The Prince*, New York, Modern Library, 1940.
Maclaurin, John, *The United Nations and Power Politics*, New York, Harper, 1951.
Morgenthau, Henry, Jr., *Germany Is Our Problem*, New York, Harper, 1945.
Nicolson, Harold, *Diplomacy*, 2nd ed., New York, Harcourt Brace, 1950.

Opie, Redvers, et al., *The Search for Peace Settlements*, Washington, Brookings Institution, 1952.
Plischke, Elmer, *The Conduct of American Diplomacy*, New York, Van Nostrand, 1950.
Röpke, Wilhelm, *The Solution to the German Problem*, New York, Putnam, 1946.
Satow, Sir Ernest, *A Guide to Diplomatic Practice*, 2nd ed., New York, Longmans Green, 1922.
Warburg, James P., *How To Co-exist Without Playing the Kremlin's Game*, Boston, Beacon Press, 1952.
Ward, Barbara, *Policy for the West*, New York, Norton, 1951.

ESCAPE FROM CONFLICT: FORMAL TECHNIQUES

Brierly, J. L., *The Law of Nations*, 4th ed., Oxford, Clarendon Press, 1949.
——, *The Outlook for International Law*, Oxford, Clarendon Press, 1944.
Carlston, Kenneth, *The Process of International Arbitration*, New York, Columbia University Press, 1946.
Chase, E. P., *The United Nations in Action*, New York, McGraw-Hill, 1950.
Dickinson, Edwin B., *Law and Peace*, Philadelphia, University of Pennsylvania Press, 1951.
Evatt, Herbert V., *The United Nations*, Cambridge, Harvard University Press, 1948.
Haviland, H. Field, *The Political Role of the General Assembly*, New York, Carnegie Endowment, 1951.
Hudson, Manley O., *International Tribunals*, Washington, Brookings Institution, 1944.
——, *The Permanent Court of International Justice*, rev. ed., New York, Macmillan, 1943.
Jessup, Philip C., *A Modern Law of Nations*, New York, Macmillan, 1948.
Lauterpacht, Hersch, *The Function of Law in the International Community*, Oxford, Clarendon Press, 1933.
Lissitzyn, Oliver, *The International Court of Justice*, New York, Carnegie Endowment, 1951.
Maclaurin, John, *The United Nations and Power Politics*, New York, Harper, 1951.
Nussbaum, Arthur, *A Concise History of the Law of Nations*, rev. ed., New York, Macmillan, 1954.
Oppenheim, L. F., *International Law*, 2 vols., ed. H. Lauterpacht; vol. I, 7th ed., 1948; vol. II, 6th ed., 1944; New York, Longmans Green.
Ralston, J. H., *International Arbitration from Athens to Locarno*, Stanford, Stanford University Press, 1929.
——, *Law and Procedure of International Tribunals*, Stanford, Stanford University Press, 1926.

THE INTERNATIONAL COMMUNITY

Brown, Philip W., *International Society*, New York, Macmillan, 1923.
Chase, Stuart, *Roads to Agreement*, New York, Harper, 1951.
Corbett, Percy, *Law and Society in the Relations of States*, New York, Harcourt Brace, 1951.
DeHuszar, George B. (ed.), *Persistent International Issues*, New York, Harper, 1947.
Douglas, William O., *Strange Lands and Friendly Peoples*, New York, Harper, 1951.
Elliott, William Y., et al., *International Control in the Non-ferrous Metals*, New York, Macmillan, 1937.
Feller, Abraham, *The United Nations and World Community*, Boston, Little Brown, 1952.
Finer, Herman, *The United Nations Economic and Social Council*, Boston, World Peace Foundation, 1946.
Holcombe, Arthur, *Human Rights in the Modern World*, New York, New York University Press, 1948.
Huxley, Julian, *UNESCO*, Washington, Public Affairs Press, 1947.

McMurry, Ruth, and Lee, Muna, *The Cultural Approach: Another Way in International Relations,* Chapel Hill, University of North Carolina Press, 1947.
Mitrany, David, *A Working Peace System,* London, Royal Institute of International Affairs, 1944.
Northrop, F. S. C., *The Meeting of East and West,* New York, Macmillan, 1946.
Reinsch, Paul A., *Public International Unions,* Boston, Ginn, 1911.
White, Llewellyn, and Leigh, Robert D., *Peoples Speaking to Peoples,* Chicago, University of Chicago Press, 1946.
White, Lyman C., *International Non-governmental Organizations.* New Brunswick, Rutgers University Press, 1951.
Wright, Quincy (ed.), *The World Community,* Chicago, University of Chicago Press, 1948.

ROUTES TO WORLD ORDER

Borgese, Guiseppe, *Foundations of the World Republic,* Chicago, University of Chicago Press, 1953.
Brinton, Crane, *From Many, One,* Cambridge, Harvard University Press, 1948.
Corbett, Percy, *Post-war Worlds,* Los Angeles, Institute of Pacific Relations, 1942.
Cousins, Norman, *Who Speaks for Man?,* New York, Macmillan, 1953.
Evatt, Herbert V., *The United Nations,* Cambridge, Harvard University Press, 1948.
Ewing, Alfred C., *The Individual, the State, and World Government,* New York, Macmillan, 1947.
Hawtrey, R. G., *Western European Union,* London, Royal Institute of International Affairs, 1949.
Hemleben, S. J., *Plans for World Peace Through Six Centuries,* Chicago, University of Chicago Press, 1943.
Hutchins, Robert A., et al., *Preliminary Draft of a World Constitution,* Chicago, University of Chicago Press, 1947.
Kelsen, Hans, *The Law of the United Nations,* New York, Praeger, 1952.
Levi, Werner, *Fundamentals of World Organization,* Minneapolis, University of Minnesota Press, 1950.
Lie, Trygvie, *In the Cause of Peace,* New York, Macmillan, 1954.
Mangone, Gerard, *The Idea and Practice of World Government,* New York, Columbia University Press, 1951.
Meyer, Cord, Jr., *Peace or Anarchy?,* Boston, Little Brown, 1947.
Parmelee, E. A., *Geo-economic Regionalism and World Federation,* New York, Exposition Press, 1950.
Ross, Alf, *The Constitution of the United Nations,* New York, Rinehart, 1951.
Schuman, Frederick L., *The Commonwealth of Man,* New York, Knopf, 1952.
Summers, R. E. (ed. and compiler), *The United States and International Organizations,* New York, H. W. Wilson, 1952.
Walters, Frank P., *A History of the League of Nations,* London, Oxford University Press, 1952.
Woodward, F. L., et al., *Foundations for World Order,* Denver, University of Denver Press, 1950.

PROBLEM AREAS: POLITICAL

Aron, Raymond, *The Century of Total War,* New York, Doubleday, 1954.
Bailey, Thomas A., *America Faces Russia,* Ithaca, Cornell University Press, 1950.
Ball, W. MacMahon, *Nationalism and Communism in East Asia,* New York, Institute of Pacific Relations, 1952.
Blanshard, Paul, *Democracy and Empire in the Caribbean,* New York, Macmillan, 1947.
Boyd, Andrew, and Boyd, Frances, *Western Union,* Washington, Public Affairs Press, 1949.
Chamberlin, William H., *America's Second Crusade,* Chicago, Regnery, 1950.

Clark, Grover, *A Place in the Sun,* New York, Macmillan, 1936.
Cooke, Hedley V., *Challenge and Response in the Middle East,* New York, Harper, 1952.
Crankshaw, Edward, *Russia and the Russians,* New York, Viking, 1948.
Dean, Vera M., *The United States and Russia,* Cambridge, Harvard University Press, 1946.
Deutscher, Isaac, *Russia: What Next?,* New York, Oxford University Press, 1953.
Holborn, Hajo, *The Political Collapse of Europe,* New York, Knopf, 1951.
Karunakaran, K. P., *India in World Affairs, 1947–1950,* New York, Oxford University Press, 1950.
Langer, William L., *The Diplomacy of Imperialism,* New York, Knopf, 1951.
Linton, Ralph (ed.), *Most of the World,* New York, Columbia University Press, 1949.
Loewenstein, Karl, *Political Reconstruction,* New York, Macmillan, 1946.
McGuire, Paul, *There's Freedom for the Brave,* New York, Morrow, 1949.
Reynaud, Paul, *Unite or Perish,* New York, Simon and Schuster, 1951.
Roosevelt, Eleanor, *India and the Awakening East,* New York, Harper, 1953.
Schapiro, J. Salwyn, *The World in Crisis,* New York, McGraw-Hill, 1950.
White, Theodore H., *Fire in the Ashes,* New York, Sloane, 1953.

PROBLEM AREAS: ECONOMIC

Bingham, Jonathan, *Shirt-sleeve Diplomacy: Point 4 in Action,* New York, John Day, 1954.
Brown, William A., Jr., *The United States and the Restoration of World Trade,* Washington, Brookings Institution, 1950.
Buchanan, Norman, and Lutz, Friedrich, *Rebuilding the World Economy,* New York, Twentieth Century Fund, 1947.
Condliffe, J. B., *The Commerce of Nations,* New York, Norton, 1950.
Cortney, Philip, *The Economic Munich,* New York, Philosophical Library, 1949.
Einzig, Paul, *Economic Warfare,* London, Macmillan, 1940.
Ezekiel, Mordecai (ed.), *Toward World Prosperity,* New York, Harper, 1947.
Feis, Herbert, *The Changing Pattern of International Economic Affairs,* New York, Harper, 1940.
Feis, Herbert, *Seen from E.A.: Three International Episodes,* New York, Knopf, 1946.
Gordon, Margaret, *Barriers to World Trade,* New York, Macmillan, 1942.
Harris, Seymour (ed.), *Foreign Economic Policy for the United States,* Cambridge, Harvard University Press, 1948.
Heilperin, Michael, *The Trade of Nations,* New York, Knopf, 1947.
Hirschmann, Albert O., *National Power and the Structure of Foreign Trade,* Berkeley, University of California Press, 1945.
Javits, Benjamin A., *Peace by Investment,* New York, Funk and Wagnalls, 1950.
Lasswell, Harold, *World Politics Faces Economics,* New York, McGraw-Hill, 1945.
Meade, James E., *Problems of Economic Union,* Chicago, University of Chicago Press, 1953.
Mikesell, Raymond F., *United States Economic Policy and International Relations,* New York, McGraw-Hill, 1952.
Randall, Clarence, *Foreign Economic Policy for the United States,* Chicago, University of Chicago Press, 1955.
Staley, Eugene, *The Future of Underdeveloped Countries,* New York, Harper, 1954.
Vogt, William, *Road to Survival,* New York, Sloane, 1948.
Ward, Barbara, *Policy for the West,* New York, Norton, 1951.
Wilcox, Clair, *A Charter for World Trade,* New York, Macmillan, 1949.

PROBLEM AREAS: PSYCHOLOGICAL

Barghoorn, Frederick, *The Soviet Image of the United States,* New York, Harcourt Brace, 1950.

Buchanan, William, and Cantril, Hadley, *How Nations See Each Other*, Urbana, University of Illinois Press, 1953.
Cantril, Hadley, *Tensions That Cause Wars*, Urbana, University of Illinois Press, 1949.
Dunn, Frederick S., *War and the Minds of Men*, New York, Council on Foreign Relations, 1950.
Fromm, Erich, *Escape from Freedom*, New York, Rinehart, 1941.
Gelber, Lionel, *Reprieve from War*, New York, Macmillan, 1950.
Hayes, Carlton J., *The Historical Evolution of Modern Nationalism*, New York, R. R. Smith, 1931.
Hoffer, Eric, *The True Believer*, New York, Harper, 1951.
Hunter, Edward, *Brainwashing in Red China*, New York, Vanguard, 1951.
Inkeles, Alex, *Public Opinion in Soviet Russia*, Cambridge, Harvard University Press, 1950.
Klineberg, Otto, *Tensions Affecting International Understanding*, Social Science Research Council, New York, 1950.
Kohn, Hans, *Prophets and Peoples*, New York, Macmillan, 1946.
Lasswell, Harold, *World Politics and Personal Insecurity*, New York, McGraw-Hill, 1935.
Northrop, F. S. C., *Ideological Differences and World Order*, New Haven, Yale University Press, 1949.
———, *The Taming of the Nations*, New York, Macmillan, 1952.
Snyder, Harold, *When Peoples Speak to Peoples*, New York, American Council on Education, 1953.
Toynbee, Arnold, *The World and the West*, New York, Oxford University Press, 1953.

THE FUTURE:

Barr, Stringfellow, *Citizens of the World*, New York, Doubleday, 1953.
Bevan, Aneurin, *In Place of Fear*, New York, Simon and Schuster, 1952.
Becker, Carl, *How New Will the Better World Be?*, New York, Knopf, 1944.
Cousins, Norman, *Modern Man is Obsolete*, New York, Viking, 1946.
Davis, Elmer, *Two Minutes Till Midnight*, Indianapolis, Bobbs-Merrill, 1955.
Dean, Vera M., *Foreign Policy Without Fear*, New York, McGraw-Hill, 1953.
Dulles, John Foster, *War or Peace?*, New York, Macmillan, 1950.
Fosdick, Dorothy, *Common Sense and World Affairs*, New York, Harcourt Brace, 1955.
Halle, Louis J., *Civilization and Foreign Policy*, New York, Harper, 1955.
Jessup, Philip C., *A Modern Law of Nations*, New York, Macmillan, 1948.
Morgenthau, Hans J., *Scientific Man versus Power Politics*, Chicago, University of Chicago Press, 1946.
Schuman, Frederick L., *The Commonwealth of Man*, New York, Knopf, 1952.
Slessor, J. C., *Strategy for the West*, New York, Morrow, 1954.
Somerville, John, *The Philosophy of Peace*, New York, Gaer Associates, 1948.
White, Theodore H., *Fire in the Ashes*, New York, Sloane, 1953.
Whyte, L. L., *Everyman Looks Forward*, New York, Henry Holt, 1948.

Index

Area and Population of Members of the United Nations

Name of Country	Total Area[1] (Square Kilometres)	Estimated Population[1] Date	Estimated Population[1] Total	Date of U.N. Membership
Afghanistan[2]	650,000[3]	1951	12,000,000[3]	19 Nov. 46
Argentina	2,808,492	July 1951	17,644,000	24 Oct. 45
Australia	7,703,867	July 1951	8,431,391	1 Nov. 45
Belgium	30,507	July 1951	8,678,386	27 Dec. 45
Bolivia	1,098,581	July 1951	3,054,037	14 Nov. 45
Brazil	8,516,037	July 1951	53,377,000	24 Oct. 45
Burma[2]	677,544	July 1951	18,674,416	19 Apr. 48
Byelorussian SSR	207,600	Jan. 1939	5,567,976	24 Oct. 45
Canada	9,960,170	July 1951	14,009,000	9 Nov. 45
Chile	741,767	July 1951	5,911,758	24 Oct. 45
China	9,736,288	July 1951	463,500,000[4]	24 Oct. 45
Colombia	1,138,355	May 1951	11,266,075	5 Nov. 45
Costa Rica	51,011	July 1951	825,070	2 Nov. 45
Cuba	114,524	July 1951	5,469,444	24 Oct. 45
Czechoslovakia	127,827	Mar. 1950	12,339,674	24 Oct. 45
Denmark	2,219,935	July 1951	4,358,200	24 Oct. 45
Dominican Republic	49,543	July 1951	2,166,791	24 Oct. 45
Ecuador	275,000	Nov. 1950	3,203,000	21 Dec. 45
Egypt	1,000,000[5]	July 1951	20,729,000	24 Oct. 45
El Salvador	34,126	July 1951	1,919,597	24 Oct. 45
Ethiopia	1,060,000	1951	15,000,000[3]	13 Nov. 45
France	550,986	July 1951	42,239,000	24 Oct. 45
Greece	132,562	Apr. 1951	7,600,000	25 Oct. 45
Guatemala	108,889	July 1951	2,886,567	21 Nov. 45
Haiti	27,750	Aug. 1950	3,111,889	24 Oct. 45
Honduras	115,205	June 1950	1,505,465	17 Dec. 45
Iceland[2]	103,000	July 1951	145,000	19 Nov. 46
India	3,288,241[6]	Mar. 1951	356,829,485[6]	30 Oct. 45
Indonesia[2]	1,491,564	1951	76,500,000[3]	28 Sept. 50
Iran	1,630,000	1951	19,139,563	24 Oct. 45
Iraq	435,415	July 1950	5,100,000	21 Dec. 45
Israel[2]	21,000	July 1951	1,516,000	11 May 49
Lebanon	10,400	July 1951	1,285,000	24 Oct. 45

Name of Country	Total Area[1] (Square Kilometres)	Estimated Population[1] Date	Total	Date of U.N. Membership
Liberia	111,370	1949	1,648,000[3]	2 Nov. 45
Luxembourg	2,586	July 1951	300,000	24 Oct. 45
Mexico	1,969,367	July 1951	26,332,100	7 Nov. 45
Netherlands	32,388[7]	July 1951	10,264,311	10 Dec. 45
New Zealand	268,666	July 1951	1,947,000	24 Oct. 45
Nicaragua	148,000	July 1951	1,088,008	24 Oct. 45
Norway	324,222	July 1951	3,294,000	27 Nov. 45
Pakistan[2]	947,663	Feb. 1951	75,842,000	30 Sept. 47
Panama	74,010	July 1951	817,200	13 Nov. 45
Paraguay	406,752	July 1951	1,425,000	24 Oct. 45
Peru	1,249,049	July 1951	8,558,000	31 Oct. 45
Philippines	299,404	July 1951	20,245,800	24 Oct. 45
Poland	311,730	Dec. 1950	24,976,926	24 Oct. 45
Saudi Arabia	1,546,000[3]	1951	6,000,000[3]	24 Oct. 45
Sweden[2]	440,122	July 1951	7,073,069	19 Nov. 46
Syria	181,337	July 1951	3,290,912	24 Oct. 45
Thailand[2]	511,937	July 1951	18,836,000	16 Dec. 46
Turkey	767,119	Oct. 1950	20,934,670	24 Oct. 45
Ukrainian SSR	576,600	Jan. 1939	30,960,221	24 Oct. 45
Union of South Africa	1,224,206	July 1951	12,683,000	7 Nov. 45
USSR	22,270,600[8]	1946	193,000,000[8]	24 Oct. 45
United Kingdom	244,002	July 1951	50,558,000	24 Oct. 45
United States	7,827,680	July 1951	154,353,000	24 Oct. 45
Uruguay	186,926	Dec. 1949	2,365,000	18 Dec. 45
Venezuela	912,050	July 1951	5,071,120[9]	15 Nov. 45
Yemen[2]	195,000	1951	4,500,000[3]	30 Sept. 47
Yugoslavia	256,880	July 1951	16,339,548	24 Oct. 45

[1] Information concerning area and population taken from United Nations *Demographic Yearbook 1952.*
[2] Not an original Member of the United Nations.
[3] Approximate figure. Specific data not available.
[4] Taiwan (Formosa) in July 1951 had an estimated population of 7,712,000—area: 35,961 square kilometres (includes islands of Taiwan and the Pescadores).
[5] Inhabited and cultivated area: 34,824 sq. km.
[6] Including Hyderabad (area 212,807 sq. km., population 18.7 millions) and excluding Kashmir-Jammu (area 213,040 sq. km. and population about 4.4 millions). The political status of these areas is not yet determined. The population of the tribal areas of Assam (about 560,000) is also excluded.
[7] Excluding inland waters.
[8] Including Byelorussian SSR and Ukrainian SSR. Estimate issued in 1946.
[9] Excluding tribal Indians estimated at 105,120 in 1950.